TEACH ME YOUR WORD

A Bible Study Course
from
Genesis to Revelation

Catherine Appleby

Sister Catherine Appleby studied at University College, Cork and at Bristol University. After obtaining first class Honours in Philosophy and English Literature she worked with secondary school pupils for some years. However, since completing her MA in Theology in 1978 she has worked exclusively with adults in Christian Scripture group work and in giving talks on Biblical themes. She was born in Weston-Super-Mare and now lives in Gloucestershire where she assists in many scripture study activities.

TEACH ME YOUR WORD

A Bible Study Course
from
Genesis to Revelation

by

Catherine Appleby MA., Dip. Theology

Illustrated by M.T. Hosmalin

Smith – Much Wenlock – Shropshire

First published 1994

British Library Cataloguing in Publication Data

Appleby, Catherine
Teach Me Your Word
I. Title II. Hosmalin, M. T.
220.6

ISBN 1 872665 21 7

Published and produced in England
by RJL Smith & Associates Much Wenlock Shropshire ©1994

Dedicated

to

Mary

Contents

Contents (contd)

New Testament (contd)

List of Illustrations

Abbreviations

GNB Good News Bible (1976 - American Bible Society)

JB Jerusalem Bible (1966 - Darton Longman & Todd)

NEB New English Bible (1970 - Oxford University Press)

NIV New International Version (1979 - Hodder & Stoughton)

NJB New Jerusalem Bible (1985 - Darton Longman & Todd)

NRSV New Revised Standard Version (1989 - Collins)

REB Revised English Bible (1989 - Oxford University Press)

RSV Revised Standard Version (1952 - Nelsons)

INTRODUCTION

Teach Me Your Word is a chapter by chapter guide to the entire Bible. Questions on the text, supplemented by a few brief explanatory notes encourage prayer, private or group reflection and prayerful reading. The course is based on the Revised Standard Version and includes those parts of the Apocrypha which are accepted by Roman Catholics and Orthodox as Deutero-Canonical.

Teach Me Your Word will prove a useful aid for:

- the 'ordinary' church-goer, who is often puzzled by parts of the Bible, especially in the Old Testament; who isn't nourished by dry, critical works but who needs some explanation of modern Biblical scholarship and, above all,longs to be fed at the table of the Word of God.
- Bible Study groups, which need material to assist reflection, research and discussion.
- Anglicans and Catholics who have struggled in the past twenty years with new service books that use the Bible in a new way. This course highlights the use of scripture in the liturgy.
- all Christians who want to refresh and deepen their understanding of Jesus' Scriptures - the Old Testament; and the story of our salvation - the Good News.

With so many Bible study courses available one may ask why another one? The answer is that nearly all daily Bible reading material is from the more fundamentalist, evangelical school. There is little from Catholic or Anglican sources for popular study or discussion of the whole Bible, including the Apocrypha; and much of Catholic popular material is geared not to a steady reading of the Bible, but merely to the readings from scripture selected for Sunday Masses. Thus many church going Catholics, while exposed to quantities of scripture in the course of the Church's year, are unfamiliar with the Bible as an indispensable source for their personal devotion, prayer and theology.

Acknowledgements

This Bible Course represents many years of reading, pondering, praying and studying the Bible. I would like to thank all those who have encouraged me over the years, especially Mary, who suggested the book in the first place, and my sister Gabrielle, who typed the whole manuscript, and R.J.L. Smith & Associates for producing and publishing this book.

CMDA
March 1994

OLD
TESTAMENT

UNTIL DAY BREAK JACOB WRESTLED.
... YOUR NAME ... SHALL BE ISRAEL ...
... JACOB CALLED THE PLACE
"THE FACE OF GOD
BECAUSE THERE HE MET GOD FACE TO FACE + SURVIVED.
GENESIS. XXXII:24.31.

AN INTRODUCTION
TO
THE BOOK OF GENESIS

Most people have some familiarity with this book, the first in the Bible. At least they have heard of Adam and Eve, the talking serpent, the 'apple' - perhaps too of Noah's ark and the Tower of Babel. Some phrases like the spare rib, adam's apple, the olive branch, have become part of the language, but it is not an easy book to understand. How are we to take it? Is it meant to be understood literally? How do we explain its strange discrepancies? Do we really believe that the first eleven chapters teach us history in our sense of the word? Are we all actually descended from Adam and Eve? How could Cain have lived in a city? Was the whole world really destroyed in the time of the Flood?

If we read Chapters 1-11 as a magnificent parable, composed during the Babylonian exile, but drawing on very ancient materials, and containing snatches of folk tales, genealogies, Babylonian myths, all combining to tell profound theological truths in story form, we shall be much nearer beginning to understand these chapters. Scholars have noted several underlying sources: Jahwistic (J) which uses the divine name of Jahweh throughout; Elohistic (E) which designates God by the noun Elohim; a later source not found much in Genesis, but used in the later books of the Pentateuch, known as Deuteronomic (D); and a Priestly source (P) containing documents largely, though not entirely, consisting of law and genealogies. The whole book teaches primary truths about God and man and creation: the fall of man, the effects of sin, and God's design of redemption.

Chapters 12-50 present three great sagas - the epic of Abraham, the man of faith; the epic of Jacob, a story of conflict and the triumph of God's grace; the epic of Joseph - a story of destiny and of God's Providence.

To profit from a personal study of the book, it is best to let each story make its own impact: read it as a parable, a meaningful commentary on the history of God's dealings with its creatures. What do we learn of God? What is the inspired writer saying?

GENESIS 1:1 - 2:4

This chapter, the first in the Bible, has caused more controversy than almost any other. It can, quite simply, be understood as a hymn in praise of Creation and of the Sabbath.

1. Read the whole chapter aloud. It is poetry. Notice the symmetry:

Day 1 - Day 4	light - sun, moon, stars.
Day 2 - Day 5	waters - fish and birds.
Day 3 - Day 6	earth and seas - cattle and man.
Day 7	fulfilment and rest.

2. Notice the emphasis on the goodness of creation. Read Psalm 104 and Romans 8.
3. Can you see any foreshadowing of the New Testament understanding of the work of God's Spirit in this chapter and in Psalm 104?
4. What is the doctrine of humanity contained in this chapter? See verses 26 to 31. Can we base our own understanding of human dignity on this section?
5. What does this chapter contribute to modern debates on ecology?

GENESIS 2:5 - 25

This is an *ALTERNATIVE* (and more primitive) account of the creation, dating probably from the time of Solomon. Its meaning is theological, not historical. (See Ezekiel 28:13-17 for another version of this myth).

1. This story is a parable. Pick out the various parts and explain the underlying meaning of each.
2. Jesus quotes verse 24 (Matt.19:5). Can a doctrine of marriage be gleaned from this chapter?

GENESIS 3

Like Chapters 1 and 2, this narrative has provoked endless discussion. The writer is drawing on ancient traditions to express in story form the meaning of the fall of man. It is not intended as a literal account of historical events, though it may reflect some ancient memories from oral traditions. However, Eve is nowhere else mentioned in the Old Testament, and Adam probably not either, as the word in Hebrew *'adam'* simply means *'man'*.

1. What was the sin of Adam and Eve? What made them conscious of nakedness? What sort of knowledge of good and evil did they acquire?
2. Pick out the verses that indicate a close intimacy with God. If you have the opportunity then read C.S.Lewis' *Perelandra* Chapter 5.
3. How are the curses against the serpent, the woman and the man to be understood?(See verses 14-19).

GENESIS 4

This chapter is a new account of sin and its effects - jealousy, homicide, vengeance; but it is also a reflection on the ambiguities of our situation, our abilities and our passions.

1. Abel is the first innocent victim, and his blood has been compared with Christ's, but notice that his death only leads to revenge and to more death, while Christ's blood cleanses us all from sin. Trace the revenge theme in the stories of Cain and of Lamech.
2. Cain is punished, but not abandoned by God. This theme recurs in the stories of Ishmael and of Esau, and in the New Testament parable of the elder son (Luke 15:25-32). Note the variety of Cain's descendants: stockbreeders, musicians, tinkers. In what sense is Cain Everyman?
3. Do you have any sympathy for Cain, or do you identify with Abel? What does this tell you about yourself?

GENESIS 5:1-6:4

This is, for us, an offputting chapter, but genealogies have an important place in the Bible, and contain much teaching if we know how to look for it. cf. Matt.1 and Luke 3. The story of the Nephilim in 6:1-4 reflects the ancient myths concerning giants. The sacred writer seems to be pointing out an ambiguity in these great ones - a demonic aspect, familiar in the personalities of such men as Hitler, Stalin, Peter the Great...

1. Notice the emphasis on 'in the likeness of God', and 'in his own likeness'. Is there any analogy between our sonship of God, and Christ's?
2. Ponder on verses 21-24. We are twice told that Enoch 'walked with God' as did Adam and Eve (3:8). This intimacy of God with humankind is often referred to in the Bible especially in the Ark theme and in the Emmanuel theme. Consider the ways in which these promises are fulfilled in Christ.
3. Consider the mysterious story in 6:1-4. On the face of it, it is a legend of the commerce of angels with human wives resulting in giant offspring. Can you find any spiritual, psychological or theological meaning in it?

GENESIS 6:5-22

The story of Noah is based on two narratives which have been interwoven. In one, the animals were paired, the flood was caused by a terrible cataclysm (7:11) and the waters prevailed for a hundred and fifty days (7:24); in the other account, seven pairs of clean animals and one pair of unclean were rescued from the Flood, which was caused by six weeks of rain (7:4), and lasted for forty days (7:17).

1. What was the source of human wickedness? Do we know why Noah found favour with God?
2. What is meant by the covenant, first referred to in 6:18? Look up the word in a Bible dictionary.

GENESIS 7

The story of the flood is continued in this chapter.

1. The ark of Noah was often used in the early Church as a symbol of baptism. Why do you think this was so? Look up 1 Peter 3:18-22.
2. Jesus refers to 'the days of Noah' (Matt. 24:37-39, Luke 17:26-27). What warning is there for us, 'this generation', in this chapter?

GENESIS 8

The story of the flood is concluded.

1. Note the well-known symbols in this chapter: the dove, the olive branch. What do they mean (a) in the original story, and (b) in modern English?
2. The theme of God's control of events is a fundamental one in the Bible. It is very clearly and neatly expressed in this chapter. Trace the sequence from 'God remembered Noah' verse 1, to the final promise and guarantee (verse 22).

GENESIS 9

This chapter concludes the story of Noah. It combines a version of the covenant with Noah with a disagreeable little story (verses 20-27) against the alcoholism of the Canaanites (represented by Ham).

1. The covenant with Noah is a covenant God has made with all humankind. Note its terms (verses 1-7). Look up Acts 15:20-21 and note the similarities. Do you think the terms of this covenant can still form a basis for international law?
2. The covenant is guaranteed by the order of nature, symbolised by the rainbow. In how many ways can the modern ecological movement take inspiration from this chapter and from Genesis 1?
3. The Bible has a few references to the degradation of drunkenness. There is another in Proverbs 23:29-35, and another in Isaiah 28:1-8. What have these three passages in common?

GENESIS 10

This chapter is of great importance to historians because it contains valuable references to ancient migrations of peoples. For details look up the commentaries.

1. What does this chapter teach us about the brotherhood of man, and our relationship to God? Cf. Acts 17:26.
2. Pick out as many place names as you can that sound familiar.
3. Could verse 9 be an inspiration to missionaries?

GENESIS 11

This chapter contains a further parable relating the origins of man's sin and divisions. It is inspired by a Babylonian ziggurat - a temple-tower.

1. Compare the story of the Tower of Babel with the story of the day of Pentecost (Acts 2:1-13). What was the basic fault of the men and women in the story of the Tower of Babel?
2. Trace the genealogy from Noah to Abraham.

GENESIS 12-25

This saga is, above all, a story of faith. Abraham is claimed as the ancestor of the Jews, through Isaac, and of the Arabs, through Ishmael. He is above all the man who knew the one God, and submitted himself to Him. There is no doubt that Abraham was a historical character, and that the main outlines of his life story are preserved for us in the Bible. However, oral traditions, while reliable on basic facts, can contain variants, where many details and even names differ. An example of this is the story told twice concerning Abraham and Sarah (Genesis 12:10-20, 20:1-18) and once concerning Isaac and Rebecca (Genesis 26:1-11).

GENESIS 12

Abraham, introduced at the close of chapter 11, now begins his journey of faith. The story contained in verses 10-20, entirely repulsive to our notions, has evident importance for the writer of Genesis as he tells it in three versions. It probably relates to a memory of a threat to the integrity of the primal ancestress, and her providential preservation.

1. Abraham's nomadic wanderings through the Holy Land are marked by sites of altars where he encountered God (cf. verses 7,8). What is the difference between Abraham's encounters with God and Cain's?
2. There are three versions of the story which is told in verses 10-20. The others are in 20:1-18 and 26:1-11. Sort out the differences, and note down the resemblances. What are we meant to learn from these odd stories?

GENESIS 13

The contrast between Abraham and Lot carries the narrative on to a climax which is reached in Genesis 19.

1. What do we learn of Lot in this chapter? Is there a lesson for us in his choice of the Jordan valley?
2. Note Abraham's growing intimacy with God (see verses 4, 14 and 18). What do we learn of guidance in this chapter?

GENESIS 14

This episode has received great attention from later Biblical writers, because of the mysterious appearance of the high priest Melchisedek, king of Salem (later Jerusalem).

1. Look up Psalm 110 and Hebrews 5:6, 7:28. What conclusions does the New Testament writer draw about a) the mystery hidden in this scene, and b) the claims of Christ to be 'a priest forever after the order of Melchisedek'?
2. Melchisedek was 'priest of God Most High', even though he was a pagan. What do you think this passage can teach us about God's attitude to non-Christian religions?

GENESIS 15

The ancient covenant-making involved walking between the divided parts of sacrificed animals. In this case God himself is party to the covenant and, symbolised by a flaming torch passes between the covenant victims.

1. Abraham's wife's barrenness seems to make meaningless God's promise to him. In verses 2-3 is described his first attempt to circumvent this difficulty. Do we sometimes doubt God's great promises and resort to limited interpretations and stopgap solutions? Find examples from your own experience.
2. St Paul has much to say about verse 6. Look up Romans 4, especially verse 3 and verses 17-25. Luther said still more. Notice that the faith of Abraham is based on trust in God's love, truth and power, not in an intellectual assent to propositions. How great is my faith in God's power to change me?

GENESIS 16

This chapter describes Abraham's second expedient. He begets an heir through Sarah's slave girl. According to the custom of the time, the child would have been adopted by Sarah as her own.

1. Ishmael is not the child of promise, but he is loved and protected by God. What does this tell us about God's use of even our sins, mistakes, contentions to bring about his designs? See what Paul makes of this in Galatians 4:21-31.
2. Hagar calls God *ELROI* - 'God of seeing'. On many occasions in the Bible this sense of God's vision of us brings peace and reassurance. Look up Psalm 139 for a meditation on this. What should my attitude be, fear or confidence?

GENESIS 17

The covenant with Abraham is now sealed by the circumcision of all the males in Abraham's household, and Abraham and Sarah are given new names.

1. God is addressed by another name - El Shaddai - God Almighty or perhaps even 'Mountain God' (JB). List the ways in which God shows himself in this chapter to be almighty.
2. From the time of Abraham, all Jewish males have been circumcised, as a sign of the covenant. What are the Christian signs of our relationship with God?
3. Abraham laughs at the thought of becoming a father so late in life. Look up John 8:56 for a Christian commentary on this incident.

GENESIS 18

This is a very ancient cultic legend from Mamre (Hebron), used by the sacred writer to express Abraham's deep intimacy with God. Notice the ambiguity about the number and nature of the divine visitors. (cf. verses 2,13,16,17).

1. This is the classic example of hospitality (cf. Hebrews 13:2); Matt. 25:35 develops it. If we really practised it, we would encounter Christ every time we opened our front door. Do we believe this? Think about its implications.
2. Abraham bargains with God, begging for the people of Sodom. God is prepared to save the whole town for the sake of ten righteous folk. Do we take seriously enough our duty as intercessors? How do we fulfil this duty?

GENESIS 19

Continuation of the same ancient story. Notice that the Sodomites are above all condemned for their inhospitality to strangers. Modern readers are disturbed by the primitive morality of verse 8.

1. This incident has left its mark on many passages in the Bible. Look up Deut.29: 22-23, Jer.50:40, Wisdom 10:6,7, Matt. 11:23-24, Luke 17:28-32; and for a more advanced moral view Jude 7, and 2 Peter 2:6-8.
2. Notice that Lot and his family were saved because Abraham had interceded for them (verse 29 - 'God remembered Abraham'). What other intercessors are mentioned in the Bible?
3. The last part of the chapter (verses 30-38) contains a disagreeable little story about the origins of two of Israel's neighbours - the Moabites and the Ammonites, rather like modern jibes about Taffy or Paddy. However, it does emphasise the kinship between Moabites and Ammonites and Israelites. David through his great-grandmother Ruth was descended from the Moabites - so was Christ. Look up Ruth 4:13-22, and Matt. 1:5.

GENESIS 20

A second version of the story first told in 12:10-28.

1. Notice that Abraham is described as a prophet (verse 7), and that he is expected to pray for Abimelech. Various kinds of prophets occur in the Bible. Look up Judges 4:4, Exodus 15:20, 1 Chronicles 17, 1 Chronicles 25:1, Habakkuk 1:1. List the different activities of these prophets.
2. What is the lesson contained in this chapter? How do you react a) to Abraham, b) to Sarah, c) to Abimelech?

GENESIS 21

The birth of Isaac, and an alternative account of the rejection of Hagar and Ishmael. Abraham's covenant with Abimelech.

1. 'Isaac' means 'laughter', and there are several references both to rejoicing and to mockery. He is the son of promise, miraculously appearing when his parents were old; and, in chapter 22, a type of Christ, but his personality is colourless in comparison with that of his father and of his sons. This theme of election and covenant is presented quite baldly in the Old Testament - God has chosen Isaac and not Ishmael; Jacob and not Esau. What do we learn from this about judging people and circumstances?
2. Collect together the references to Ishmael: 16:10-12; 17:20; 21:12-21, and note that 'God was with the lad'. What does this mean? What does this teach us about God's attitude to other races and religions? Does election mean that others are excluded from God's love, or that some are called for the performance of a role with regard to and for the sake of others?
3. Another shrine connected with Abraham is at Beersheba (verses 31-33). Here he experienced God as everlasting. Make a list of the attributes of God so far mentioned in Genesis.

GENESIS 22

The testing of Abraham, climax of the Abraham epic, and the origin of much Old Testament theology concerning the redemption of the firstborn. Isaac is seen by the fathers of the Church as a type of Christ.

1. Look up the various commentaries on this chapter within the Bible: Wisdom 10:5; Sirach 44:20, Hebrews 11:17-19; James 2:21-24. What different lessons can be drawn?
2. This severe test of Abraham's faith is recorded in a very primitive setting, with its undertones of child sacrifice. What is the UNIVERSAL lesson hidden in the story?

GENESIS 23

Abraham acquires a piece of land at Hebron. Here Sarah is buried, and in time it will be the burial place of Abraham, Isaac, Rebecca, Jacob and Leah - the patriarchs (cf. Gen.49:31).

1. Look up all the references to Sarah in Genesis: (12:10-20; 16:1-6; 18:6-15; 21:1-10). What sort of person was she?
2. Look up the New Testament references to her: Hebrews 11:11; 1 Peter 3:5-6. What aspects of her character are here emphasised?
3. Consider the three stories of the threat to the ancestress - 12:10-20 and 21:1-10 for Sarah; and 26:1-11 for Rebecca. What is the real point of these stories?

GENESIS 24:1- 25:11

These chapters introduce the adult Isaac and bring the epic of Abraham to a conclusion. They also contain the long narrative of the wooing of Rebecca in the style of Wisdom literature, wherein God speaks through circumstances and men's actions, rather than through oracles and visions.

1. Notice the servant's faith in God's guidance. List the sequence of events leading to the prayer of verse 24:27.
2. What qualities do you notice in Rebecca?
3. What traits in the character of Isaac are brought out in 24:62-66?
4. Review Abraham's life in the light of Isaiah 41:8 - 'Abraham, my friend'.

GENESIS 25:12-34

The epic of Jacob begins in this chapter - a story of conflict, and of the triumph of God's grace.

1. Reflect on the mystery of divine election in the light of this chapter; also compare with Malachi 1:2-4 and Hebrews 12:14-17.
2. At the fall of Jerusalem in the sixth century BC Edom took advantage of the situation and occupied Judah, cf. Obadiah and Ezekiel 35:5-12. This may explain the historical reason for Biblical rejection of Esau, Edom's ancestor. Note down the contrasts in this chapter between the two brothers.

GENESIS 26

Isaac, the promised son, is a shadowy figure, the victim in chapter 22, the dupe in chapter 27. Only in this chapter does he take centre stage. However, we note several qualities: his retiring, contemplative disposition (24:63), his devotion to his mother and to his wife (24:67); his affection for the son who is so different from himself (25:28). God appears to him (26:2,24), and the God he worships is described as the Fear or Kinsman of Isaac (31:42, 53).

1. Ponder on the possible meanings of the title 'Kinsman of Isaac' (JB), and what it tells us of God's intimacy with his chosen ones.
2. Note down the occasions when God reassures Abraham and Isaac in these chapters.
3. There are hints in these stories of tensions in family life. List some examples.

GENESIS 27

This chapter gives us the famous story of the deception of Isaac by Rebecca and Jacob, and the rejection of Esau. The choice of Jacob does not imply any approval of his morality, but is entirely

a question of his election by God for a particular function in history - to be the ancestor of the chosen people.

1. Notice the parts played by Isaac, Rebecca, Esau and Jacob, and reflect that none of them is consciously or deliberately following God's designs, yet, they are furthering them. Does this happen in our lives?
2. Isaac blesses each son. Note the details and the differences.
3. Look up Romans 9:10-16 for a New Testament commentary on this story.

GENESIS 28

The two brothers are once more contrasted in their destiny and in their attitude to God.

1. Esau takes a wife from the daughters of Ishmael. Look up the other references to Esau in Genesis 33:1-16; 36. What do we learn of his character and attitudes?
2. What was the significance of Jacob's dream? At what point in his career does it occur? Notice verses 20-22. Does this attitude indicate strong faith?

GENESIS 29

The story of Jacob's marriages and the births of his twelve sons reflects: a) ancient traditions concerning the ancestors of the tribes, and b) legendary origins of the later tribes' circumstances and fortunes. The 'Rachel' tribes were to be very important for much of Israel's later history, but, undeniably, several of Israel's greatest heroes (Moses, Aaron, David) belonged to 'Leah' tribes, and Judah, itself a 'Leah' tribe, was the only kingdom to survive the Assyrian conquest at the end of the eighth century BC.

1. Compare the wooing of Rachel with that of Rebecca.
2. Note down the meanings of the names given to each of Jacob's sons, and look up the location of each tribe on a Bible map.

GENESIS 30

Both narratives in this chapter - Rachel's efforts to obtain a son (mandrakes were associated with fertility), and Jacob's manoeuvres with the sheep - strike us as disagreeably primitive, but they contain important teaching about God's relationship with human kind and his use of human expedients to achieve great ends.

1. Notice God's apparent preference for Leah! Where would she appear in the genealogy of Christ in Matthew 1?
2. What do you make of the story of Jacob's flocks? Why is it in the Bible? Has it a moral?

GENESIS 31

This is a lively chapter, with the vivid character vignettes and highly amusing dialogue. The writer is a great story teller.

1. Trace God's interventions in this episode; especially verses 3, 9, 11-13, 24, 29, 42, 48-50, 53.
2. Reflect on the different titles given to God in this chapter; see verses 5, 13, 29, 42, 53.

GENESIS 32

The two brothers are once again contrasted. The scene by the ford of Jabbok reflects a very primitive account, shown in the confusion of pronouns. The author places it here at a crucial point in Jacob's life.

1. What were Jacob's feelings as he approached Seir, the country of Esau? In what ways was he given encouragement from God?
2. Compare Jacob's prayer in this chapter with his vow at 28:20-22. What progress has he made in his relations with God and in his self-understanding? What do you make of verses 13-21?
3. What is the meaning of the scene by the ford of Jabbok? Are there any parallels in our own lives?

GENESIS 33

The contrasting destinies of the two brothers are underlined again in this chapter.

1. Notice the oscillations in Jacob'a attitude between trust in God and fear of his brother. With which brother do you have the greater sympathy? What are Jacob's priorities in his family?
2. There are two indications of Jacob's spiritual progress in this chapter. What are they?

GENESIS 34

This chapter combines two traditions: a) the seduction of Dinah by Shechem, his acceptance of circumcision, and his treacherous murder by Simeon and Levi; b) a proposed matrimonial alliance between Shechemites and Israelites on condition of the circumcision of the former, and the treachery of the Israelites.

1. The origin of this disagreeable story seems to be the alleged treachery of the Simeonites. However, compare this with a different tradition in that tribe (Judith 9:2-3), where the emphasis is on the vengeance on the seducer of Dinah. What are your feelings about the story?
2. Jacob protests but does nothing. What should have been a glorious return home is marred by rape, strife, treachery and revenge. Note how Jacob's sons are now beginning to take over from their father. Why do you think this story has been recorded in the Bible?

GENESIS 35

Jacob's triumphant return to Bethel (cf. 28:20-22) is succeeded by tragic events. Note that there is an alternative account of the naming of Israel at verses 9-10.

1. Draw out the various encounters with God in this chapter.
2. Notice the pattern in this chapter: an encounter with God is followed by suffering. Can suffering ever be said to be a blessing from God?
3. Look up Hosea 12 for unfavourable traditions concerning Jacob.

GENESIS 36

This chapter is entirely devoted to Esau and the Edomites. These genealogies mean little to us, but they were very precious to ancient peoples, setting each individual within his clan or tribe, so everyone has a designated place in God's scheme.

1. There is another explanation in this chapter of the separation of Israelites and Edomites, knowing nothing of the quarrel between Jacob and Esau. What is it?
2. Look up a good map of Canaan of the time of the patriarchs. Pick out as many places as you can find which are mentioned in this chapter. What does this tell us about the historical facts that lie behind these lists?

GENESIS 37-50

The epic of Joseph has been written up as a moral tale in the fashion of the Wisdom school. In fact, in many ways Joseph is presented as the model young man envisaged in Proverbs. His inevitable rise to fortune, despite setbacks, his magnanimity in victory, and his trust in God's providence are all depicted in a 'smooth' portrait. Little of his real emotions emerge. Jacob appears in this narrative as a relatively minor character.

GENESIS 37

The Joseph epic begins in this chapter.

1. Notice the characters and behaviour of Joseph, Jacob/Israel, Reuben and Judah. With whom do you sympathise?
2. Joseph has two dreams. Compare these experiences with the visions of Abraham, Isaac and Jacob.

GENESIS 38

This chapter contains ancient material concerning the origins of the tribe of Judah. Its morality, very strange to us, is based on the levirate law (cf. Deut. 25:5-10, Ruth, and Matt. 22:23-28). Note that Onan's sin is not 'birth control', but a refusal to obey the levirate law, thus subordinating his family's interests to his personal desires.

1. Notice Judah's foreign alliances, and especially his relations with the Canaanite Tamar, an ancestor of David and of Christ. What does this tell us of the strange workings of Providence? Look up Christ's genealogy in Matt.1, and note the women mentioned.
2. With whom do your sympathies lie in this story? Why?

GENESIS 39

We are now back to Joseph. He is a key figure 1) because his adventures explain the Egyptian origins of the Hebrews, and 2) his sons Ephraim and Manasseh were to be the ancestors of two of the most powerful and populous tribes in Israel.

1. Pick out the references to God in this chapter. How do they differ from those in the Jacob epic?
2. Trace the rise and fall of Joseph's fortunes. What were the qualities that enabled him to succeed?

GENESIS 40

There is an important play on words in this chapter. In verse 13 'Pharaoh will lift up your (the chief butler's) head' means he will restore his position. In verse 19 'Pharaoh will lift up your (the chief baker's) head' means he will hang him.

1. Pharoah believes he has absolute power. Show how the writer makes it clear that God is in control of events.
2. The chief butler, typically, forgot his obligations to Joseph: verse 23. Trace the theme of man's forgetting and of God's remembering in Genesis.

GENESIS 41

The narrative continues smoothly and fairly rapidly.

1. Trace the references to God's intervention through dreams and events.
2. Notice Joseph's energy and enterprise. What qualities has he inherited from his parents and grandparents?

GENESIS 42

The story becomes more involved. There is evidence of two traditions that have been worked together to form a single narrative.

1. Notice the underlying emotions in this chapter, especially verses 4, 7, 9, 24, 28.
2. Draw out the actions and attitudes of Reuben in this chapter and in 37:21-22.

GENESIS 43

This was originally an alternative tradition that has been incorporated into the narrative by the inspired writer, hence the apparent repetition.

1. In this chapter Judah is prominent. Compare his actions with those of Reuben in chapter 42, and with his own intervention at 37:26-27.
2. Why was Joseph so moved at the sight of Benjamin?

GENESIS 44

This is the same tradition as that contained in 43, with the same interest in Judah.

1. Trace in these chapters the gradual awakening of the brothers to repentance for their crime against Joseph.
2. What do we learn new about Judah in this chapter?

GENESIS 45

The story reaches a climax. Notice the carefully controlled emotional excitement in the narrative, and the quickening of pace.

1. Compare the brothers' reaction (verse 3) with 50:15.
2. Read carefully verses 4-15. What is the theological statement in these verses?

GENESIS 46

The style changes from the smooth, Wisdom style narrative, to that of the Abraham and Jacob sagas, with their visions and genealogies.

1. What is the atmosphere of Jacob's last vision? Trace his other encounters with God from Bethel (28) to Beersheba (46).
2. What benefits would come to Israel's descendants from their sojourn in Egypt?

GENESIS 47

This chapter is composite. Verses 1-4 and 5-11 contain two versions of the same incident - Pharoah's welcome to the Israelites, with a conclusion at verse 12. Verses 13-26 should follow chapter 41 - an account of Joseph's agrarian policy. The final verses (27-31) describe Jacob's last years in Egypt.

1. Notice that Jacob blessed Pharaoh. What is the significance of this gesture?
2. What do you think of Joseph's compulsory purchase of land?

GENESIS 48

The story here is an explanation of the greater prominence and wealth of the tribe of Ephraim, though descended from a younger son. Another 'younger son' story!

1. Jacob reviews his life. What has he learned from his experiences?
2. What titles does Jacob use in describing God? See verses 3, 15, 16.

GENESIS 49

This ancient poem describes the situation of the Israelites perhaps about the time of David. It is later than the song of Deborah (Judges 5) and earlier than the Blessings of Moses (Deut.33).

1. Look up each of the tribes on the map and notice how their geographical position influences their fate. Does this necessarily mean that the whole chapter is spurious?
2. What lies behind the references to Reuben, Simeon and Levi, and Joseph?
3. In what way can verses 8-12 be described as Messianic?
4. Compare verses 29-32 with chapters 23, 25:5-11 and 35:27-29.

GENESIS 50

The Book of Genesis is brought to a close with the chosen people beginning their long sojourn in Egypt.

1. What is the underlying theme of this section, emphasised once more by Joseph in verse 20? cf.45:5, 7.
2. Compare the account of Jacob's death and burial with Joseph's.

AN INTRODUCTION TO EXODUS

'And as he was praying, the appearance of his countenance was altered, and his raiment became dazzling white. And behold, two men talked with him, Moses and Elijah, who appeared in glory and spoke of his *EXODUS* (departure), which he was to accomplish at Jerusalem.' (Luke 9:29-31).

From the earliest days of Christianity, Jesus' passion, death and resurrection have been seen as the fulfilment of the saving work of God which was inaugurated with the exodus of his chosen people from Egypt, their crossing of the Red Sea (Passover), their desert wanderings, and their entry into the Promised Land.

'I want you to know, brethren, that our fathers were all under the cloud, and all passed through the sea, and all ate the same spiritual food and all drank the same spiritual drink. For they drank from the spiritual Rock which followed them, and the Rock was Christ'. (1 Cor.10:1-4) St Paul adds: 'Now all these things happened to them in figure (1 Cor.10:11) - for our instruction'.

The Book of Exodus is therefore a seminal book, for Christians as well as for Jews, telling the story of God's choice of a people from among an oppressed band of slaves in Egypt, his revelation of his Name to Moses, his deliverance of the people and his gift to them of the Law, by which they were able to come to know his will for them. As we have the book today it draws on the ancient traditions already found in Genesis, ie. the J, E, D and P narratives. The events described probably occurred during the reign of Rameses II (compare: Exodus 1:1) about 1250 BC. The biblical record was put together in its present form during the Babylonian exile.

EXODUS 1

Time has passed since the death of Joseph and a new Pharaoh 'who knew not Joseph' is oppressing the Israelites. The narrative, while containing definite historical material, is in the form of a folk tale with Wisdom themes - clever midwives, and Pharaoh the wicked fool! It is clear from his name that Moses had in some way an Egyptian origin. The story of his birth and childhood - a typical 'lost child' fable - explains his connections with the Egyptians, and also with the Midianites, a nomadic people frequently mentioned in the Bible, perhaps from Arabia, perhaps from Sinai.

1. Look up Psalm 105:23 ff for a commentary on Exodus.
2. What use has Matthew 2 made of this chapter?
3. Note the references to God in this chapter, verses 17, 20, 21.

EXODUS 2

The early life of Moses is presented as a 'rag-to-riches' folk tale, but it clearly reflects a tradition that Moses had Egyptian and Midianite origins.

1. Notice the underlying theme of God's Providence. Draw out the occasions.
2. For a New Testament commentary on this chapter read Acts 7:23-29 and Hebrews 11:24-28.
3. Moses is clearly conscious of his Hebrew ancestry. How is this underlined? Yet compare: verse 19.

EXODUS 3

One of the most important chapters in the Old Testament, in which the sacred name of *YAHWEH* is revealed, a name so hallowed by Jews that it is never written or pronounced. The forms of Jehovah, Jahweh, are scholarly reconstructions.

1. Notice the link verse in 2:24, and then note the references to the patriarchs in chapter 3.

2. How does the Name of God attempt to describe him? How does God reveal himself in this chapter?

EXODUS 4

The narrative is a typical 'prophetic call' narrative, following a pattern of call from God, objection by prophet, reassurance from God, and response of the prophet. Compare: Jeremiah 1.

1. List Moses' objections and God's response. What opinion have you formed, thus far, of Moses' character?
2. Aaron is introduced for the first time, not as a priest, but as prophet and spokesman (7:1). Look up Genesis 20:7 and find another aspect of prophecy which is very relevant to Moses.
3. The very strange incident at verses 24-26 has been variously explained. It is probably connected with the importance of circumcision and of the *FIRST BORN*. Compare: verses 22-23. St Therese of Lisieux explained it mystically in relation to Christ, '..the bridegroom of blood'. Is there any sense in which consecration to Christ can be called a sacrifice even unto death? In what sense can Christ's 'wedding' with humanity be said to make him a bridegroom of blood?
4. Notice how quickly the story moves in this chapter,from Moses' objections, God's reassurance, to the intervention of Aaron, the journey and the gathering of the Israelite elders. Have you any experience in your own life of God's swift intervention to change things?

EXODUS 5

There are many vivid details in this chapter, showing acquaintance with Egyptian customs, but it's still a folk tale, with lively dialogue between Pharaoh, Moses and the slave drivers!

1. Reflect on the complaint of Moses at verse 22-23. Is he justified?
2. Throughout this narrative Pharaoh is he who does not *know* the Lord (verse 2). What are the characteristics of those who do not know him?
3. Contrast the attitude of the Israelites at 4:29-31 with that shown in verses 20-21. Do we ever experience these alternations of mood?

EXODUS 5:22 - 6:30

An alternative account of the call of Moses is placed here by the narrator to re-emphasise Moses' vocation at this point, and to move the story on to the great Plague Narrative which begins in the next chapter.

1. Notice God's promises: 'I will bring you out' (verse 6), and 'I will take you as my own people' (verse 7), and 'I will bring you to the land' (verse 8). How do these promises confirm those to the patriarchs, eg. Genesis 46:3-4 and go beyond them?
2. History is very important to the narrator; Moses' genealogy anchors him in the Israelite tribes. Compare: verse 26-27. Trace Moses' descent from Levi, the third son of Jacob, and Aaron's descendants. Make a table of this family and add to it as you explore further in the Bible.

EXODUS 7-11

The Plague Narrative combines several traditions very skilfully, resulting in a lively account, rich in details and in humour. The theme revolves around the revelation of God's nature to Pharaoh, to the Egyptians, and, eventually, to all mankind. But Pharaoh's heart 'is hardened'. This phrase is repeated again and again. The hardening is not the cause of the plagues, but a reaction to their removal! (Compare: 7:13,22, 8:15, etc.) Because of his attitude the signs do NOT reveal knowledge of God to Pharaoh, so the plagues are a judgement on Pharaoh and on the Egyptians. This important reflection on man's hardness of heart recurs throughout the

Bible, see, for example, Psalm 95:8, Luke 16:31, etc. We take the entire Plague Narrative (chapters 7-11) as one long section.

1. Trace the references to the hardening of Pharaoh's heart: 7:13, 22; 8:15, 19, 32; 9:7, 12, 34; 10:20, 27; 11:10. and show how all other resistance (wise men, sorcerers, magicians, officials) is overcome, but not Pharaoh's. What does this tell us about the condition of sin in man?
2. Pick out the occasions when Aaron used his rod.
3. Look up Wisdom 16-18 for an imaginative commentary on these plagues.
4. What is the theological basis of this narrative?

EXODUS 12-15

Passover, Exodus and Deliverance.

This section draws on a variety of traditions, partly narrative, partly from the liturgy of the Passover.

EXODUS 12

The instructions contained in this chapter obviously reflect a later date when the Israelites were settled in their land, rather as the account of the last supper in the New Testament depends on early liturgical formulas. Note the repeated emphasis on handing on the story to later generations.

1. Why did the Angel of Death 'pass over' the houses of the Israelites? How has this event been interpreted in the gospels?
2. Draw out the essential features of the Passover that have been taken into the liturgy of Easter. Why have the redemption of the Jews and the resurrection of Christ been linked in theology and in liturgy?

EXODUS 13

This chapter contains some liturgical material (vv 1-16), and some narrative.

1. What do we learn about God's guidance and care for us in verses 17-22?
2. Look up 1 Corinthians 10:1-2 and 1 Peter 1:17-21 for the New Testament theology of this section.

EXODUS 14

The prose account of the crossing of the sea marks the beginning of the Exodus proper, the central event in the Old Testament, confirming to his people that God performs what he promises. The theme of Exodus recurs again and again in the Psalms and in the Prophets; and in the liturgy of the Christian Church it is seen as a foreshadowing of the resurrection of Christ at Easter and of the pilgrimage of the people of God through the trials of this world to the promised land of heaven.

1. What can we learn here about God's fidelity, and about our trust in his promises?
2. Draw out the reactions of the people in this scene. Have we ever felt as they did in verse 31?
3. Read Wisdom 10:13-21 for a summing up of these events.

EXODUS 15

An ancient hymn, probably from the thirteenth century BC. God is praised as the sole Author of salvation. The oldest section is the Song of Miriam (verse 21).

1. Pick out all the attributes of God that are celebrated in this song.
2. Miriam now appears for the first time (unless she is the unnamed 'sister' of 2:4) referred to as the prophetess (Compare: Judges 4:4). Look up the other references to her in Numbers 12:1-16,

Numbers 20:1, Deuteronomy 24:9, Micah 6:4. She was clearly an outstanding figure. What impression do you form of her character?

3. Notice the turn of events at verses 22-27. The people need water, they complain, Moses cries out to God, who responds with a miracle. What does this teach us about prayer?
4. 'I am the Lord who heals you'. How is this illustrated by the springs of Elim? Reflect on this passage in the light of God's forgiveness and of the sacrament of reconciliation.

EXODUS 16-18

The Wandering in the Desert.

These traditions are now clustered into two main blocks: Exodus 16-18 (preceding Sinai) and Numbers 10 ff. (after Sinai). Doublets (Exodus 17 and Numbers 20; Exodus 16 and Numbers 11) reflect the complex history of the tradition.

EXODUS 16

The stories of the manna and of the quails reflect memories of desert wanderings.

1. This story concentrates on the manna rather than on the quails (Compare: Numbers 11). Consider God's patience with and generosity towards the grumbling Israelites. Have we ever encountered him in this way?
2. Look up Wisdom 16:20-21 for a development of the manna tradition, and then see the use to which this story has been put in the New Testament, for example, in John 6 and in 1 Cor. 10:1-13.
3. Collect the reactions of the people in this chapter. Are they true to life?

EXODUS 17

One version of the Meribah story (the other is in Numbers 20), and a battle with the Amalekites, presumably over water supplies. The Amalekites were said to be descendants of Esau (Genesis 36:12,16). They came from Mount Seir and the Negeb.

1. Compare the accounts of the Meribah incident in Numbers 20 and in Psalm 78: 17-20 and Psalm 106: 32-33. What light is shed on Moses' sin, which cost him the Promised Land?
2. What do we learn from verses 8-15 of the power of intercessory prayer?

EXODUS 18

Moses' father-in-law is variously named Jethro, Reuel and Hobab, according to the different traditions. All agree that he represents Midianite influence on Moses.

1. What do we learn in this chapter of Moses' family life? Compare 2:15-22 and 4:18-26.
2. Jethro advises Moses to organise his oversight of the people and to trust his subordinates. What does this incident tell about a) the character of Moses and b) about Church government?

EXODUS 19-24

The Covenant at Sinai.

These chapters describe the preparations for the covenant (19), the granting of the Decalogue (20), the Book of the Covenant (21-23) and the ratification of the covenant (24).

EXODUS 19

The covenant (berith) made by God with Noah (Genesis 9) and with Abraham (Genesis 15), is now made with the whole people of Israel through Moses. God appears in very striking and dramatic fashion.

1. What is the meaning of the covenant described in this chapter? See verses 3-6.

2. Notice the preparation and purification of the people. How should we prepare for encounters with God - in the liturgy, in the sacraments, in important occasions in our lives?

EXODUS 20:1-19

The Ten Commandments are inserted here into the Narrative as a concrete illustration of the covenant demands. Through the giving of the Law, mankind is given moral dignity.

1. Consider the first three commandments (verses 2-9) and 'translate' them into our own situation.
2. What are the basic laws for family, social, industrial and political relationships?
3. In what sense can the giving of the Law be said to be a liberation for the people?

EXODUS 20:22 - 23:33

The Book of the Covenant probably dates from the time of the Judges, but has been inserted here as it applies to the spirit of the Decalogue. Law and Covenant belong together. Holiness is demanded of the covenant people, because their vocation is to reflect God's holiness to the world while offering him 'acceptable worship'. God's Law or Torah is an act of grace and its demands, because they are specific, bring peace and security.

EXODUS 21

These laws concerning human rights reflect the conditions in Israel during the early days of the colonisation of Canaan.

1. Notice that at least Hebrew slaves had rights safeguarded by law. What were these rights?
2. What crimes carried the death penalty? Note the distinction between murder and manslaughter.

EXODUS 22

Various laws concerning property, and religious taboos.

1. What laws in chapters 21 and 22 governed the ownership of and responsibility for animals? Do these have an application today?
2. What rights has a burglar?
3. Draw out the principles that governed the protection of private property.
4. Notice the concern for the poor, the widow and the orphan. Give examples.

EXODUS 23

The duties and rights of persons are inalienable. The chapter also contains a calendar of the great festivals. There are similar calendars in Exodus 34, in Leviticus 23 and in Deuteronomy 16.

1. Find advice for magistrates in this chapter.
2. What were the principles governing the observance of the sabbath? Compare verses 10-12 and 20:8-11 with Deut. 5:12-15. Can we *KEEP SUNDAY SPECIAL* from the principles here given or is there more to it?

EXODUS 24

Two accounts of the ratification of the covenant are contained in this chapter. In one the covenant is consummated by a meal (vv 1-2, 9-11); in the other the people are sprinkled with blood (vv 3-8).

1. Read this chapter carefully, then look up the three gospel accounts of the Last Supper (Matt. 26:26-29, Mark 14:22-25, Luke 22:14-20) and 1 Peter 1:2,19 and Hebrews 12:18-24. What aspects of the covenant are emphasised a) by the Old Testament writer and b) by the New Testament writers?

2. Compare the parts played by Moses, Aaron, his sons, the seventy elders and the people.

EXODUS 25-31

The building of the Sanctuary.

These seven chapters concern the building of the tent of meeting and the ark of the covenant, and contain very ancient material. Our Christian custom of building and furnishing beautiful churches, providing exquisite altar linen, and vestments is derived from the Biblical notion of celebrating God's presence among his people by providing as beautiful a setting as is humanly possible, with every talent employed, every sense involved.

EXODUS 25

The ark was a rectangular chest, carried on poles, containing the Decalogue (testimony v.16). The mercy-seat (v.17) was the sign of God's presence among his people.

1. Notice the contributions made by the people. What does this symbolise? How do *we* contribute to the fitting worship of God?
2. The ark was a rectangular chest, carried on poles. It signified God's abiding presence among his people. In what ways is he present in the world today?

EXODUS 26

The tabernacle or tent of meeting belonged to the desert, but much of the description probably reflects the Temple of Solomon.

1. What four layers of curtains covered the tent? Draw a ground plan.
2. John says that the Word of God 'dwelt among us' literally 'set up his tent among us' (John 1:14). What is he implying about the presence of Christ in the world?

EXODUS 27

The altar for burnt offerings, the sacred space round the sanctuary, and the lamps are all described.

1. The altar is for the holocausts, the burnt offering. See verse 3. What is the special significance of the altar of holocaust?
2. The lamp (verses 20-21) burns before the altar, and before our altars. What does it signify?

EXODUS 28

The instructions are now given for the priestly vestments. The ephod here described was a kind of breastplate in which were kept the sacred dice, urim and thummim (v.30).

1. List the garments of the high priest (verse 4). What is the meaning of the names of the tribes on the ephod (verses 9-12, 29)?
2. Take each vestment and apply its symbolism to Christ our High Priest.

EXODUS 29

The rites for the consecration of priests.

1. Analyse the various parts of the ceremony of consecration of priests: the purification, the clothing, the anointing and the sacrifices.
2. How does the New Testament apply these ceremonies to Christ? Compare: John 19:23-24, Matt. 3:13-17, Hebrews 9.
3. Morning and evening sacrifices were offered perpetually (verse 39), when God promises to meet his people. How is he present today?

EXODUS 30

The altar of incense was different from the altar for burnt offerings. Note the poll tax (vv.11-16) and the reference to it in Matthew 17:24!

1. The altar of incense and the basin for ablution indicate the need for prayer and for purification from sin. How is their purpose described in this chapter?
2. What is the universal prayer of the Church?
3. What sacraments make use of water, oil, salt? What do these elements signify?

EXODUS 31

The craftsmen are given their instructions, and a note is inserted to emphasise the sacredness of Sabbath worship.

1. Bezalel and Aholiab were inspired by the Spirit of God with technical skill. The Spirit is the agent of creation in Genesis 1:2, and of the Incarnation in Luke 1:35. What does this teach us about the cooperation of man with God's creative activity?
2. Look up the Cloud of Unknowing 71-73 for an application of this passage to the experience of prayer.

EXODUS 32-34

This episode reveals a dissident faction in the desert who tried to set up the figure of a bull to symbolise the presence of God, instead of the ark of the covenant. The bull was not an idol, but a pedestal of the unseen Yahweh. However, the danger of idolatry (the bull symbolised strength) was very great. Notice the part played by Aaron. Clearly the faction was an important one. Moses is seen as mediator, intercessor, man of prayer, intimate with the Lord.

EXODUS 32

1. What is the real meaning of the golden calf incident? Has it a message for modern life? What are the 'golden calves' we worship and what consequences does this have?
2. What do you think of Aaron's reactions and behaviour?
3. Trace the course of Moses' intercession for the people.

EXODUS 33

This chapter contains various narratives concerned with God's presence among his people either through the intercession of Moses, or symbolised in the Tent of Meeting.

1. What kinds of presence of God are mentioned in this chapter? See verses 2, 9-11, 14, 19-23.
2. Trace the spiritual development of Moses from the beginning of Exodus.
3. What is meant by the glory of Yahweh? Compare verse 18 with 24:16-17; 40:34-35, and 1 Kings 8:10-11.

EXODUS 34

The covenant is renewed after the Golden Calf incident. God always forgives repentant sinners.

1. What does this chapter tell us about God's forgiveness and mercy?
2. What aspect of the covenant is emphasised in this chapter?
3. Read verses 29-35 and show:
   - how it is God's response to Moses' desire in 33:19, and
   - how it is a foreshadowing of the divine indwelling of the Christian.
     Compare: 2 Cor. 3:7-18.

EXODUS 35-39

This section largely repeats Chapters 25-31; there the instructions were given, here they are carried out.

EXODUS 35:1-36:7

The materials for building and furnishing the sanctuary are collected and the craftsmen appointed.

1. What types of skill were needed for the construction of the sanctuary?
2. What does this teach us about the use of talents (Compare: Matt. 25:14-20) and about our contribution to the Church?

EXODUS 36:8 37:29.

The tabernacle is built and finished.

1. In what way does the ark foreshadow the Church?
2. Read carefully 37:6-9 and then look up Isaiah 6:1-10, and Ezekiel 1:4-28. What influence did the description of the sanctuary have on the visions of the prophets?

EXODUS 38-39

The altar of burnt offering is set up, the priests vested, and all the work completed according to God's commandments to Moses, symbolising the re-making of the world and all its people in God's image (25:40; 39:43).

1. The sanctuary was paid for with atonement money. Do you think this is significant? In what way?
2. What phrase is repeated continually in this account of the building of the sanctuary? What significance does it have for us?
3. Read 39:32-43 and compare Genesis 2:2-3. What do these texts tell us about a) man's cooperation with God and b) man's place in the scheme of things?

EXODUS 40

The account is completed, and the Book of Exodus ends with the picture of God's abiding presence among his people.

1. The Book of Exodus ends with the description of the abiding presence of God. What does this tell us about divine guidance and divine indwelling?
2. Describe the ark in your own words from the information supplied in this chapter.

AN INTRODUCTION
TO
LEVITICUS

If you are in love with facts and details, if you are dependable, decisive, painstaking and systematic; concerned with order and rituals, stable and conservative, in other words, if your Myers-Briggs type is ISTJ,* you will love the Book of Leviticus! If you are in love with change; imaginative, impulsive, enthusiastic, bored with detail... you will not find it an easy book to read; but whatever your personal tastes and talents, this is, for Jews, one of the most important books in the Bible, and for Christians a basic guide to all the other Old Testament books, helping us to understand references to sacrifices, rituals, ceremonies. The principles of atonement and of purification are contained in it, and the institutions of sabbath and jubilee.

It is divided into three main sections:

- the sacrificial ritual (Chapters 1-7)
- the investiture of priests (Chapters 8-10)
- the Holiness code (Chapters 11-26) with an appendix (Chapter 27).

Though the book contains much very ancient material, it did not reach its final form until after the exile.

LEVITICUS 1-7

The rituals for sacrifice.

There were five types of sacrifice: the burnt offering or holocaust, in which the victim was entirely consumed; the cereal offering or oblation of agricultural produce; the peace offering or communion sacrifice, a sacred banquet; the sacrifice for sin; the guilt offering.

LEVITICUS 1

The burnt offering or holocaust, in which the victim was entirely consumed was an atonement for sin. It was common among the Canaanites.

1. The holocaust represented a total gift to God, since the entire victim was burnt. What would this mean to the person making the offering? See verses 3,4. Do you think that desire for healing and atonement for sin can be expressed in such gestures?
2. What examples of holocaust are there in the life of a Christian?

LEVITICUS 2

The oblation of wheat or other produce was known to the Egyptians as well as to the Canaanites. It is unlikely that it was offered in the desert, as it presupposes a settled, agricultural way of life.

1. Notice the emphasis on purity. The wheat must be fine flour, unleavened, and cf. Malachi 1:7. Why this emphasis? Do we pay enough attention to externals indicative of an inner attitude in our worship?
2. Compare verse 13 with 2 Kings 2:20 and with Matt. 5:13. What is the value of salt? Why is it used in the baptismal rite?
3. How do *we* make a holy offering to God?

* ISTJ is an abbreviation used in Myers-Briggs Personality Types: **I**ntroverted **S**ensing **T**hinking **J**udging

LEVITICUS 3

The peace offering or communion sacrifice, in which the worshipper shared by eating a portion himself, of what was offered, was the most common form of sacrifice.

1. The peace offering or communion sacrifice was a fellowship meal, in which part of the animal was consumed and offered to God (verses 3,4 etc.); the rest was eaten by the worshippers. How does this convey the idea of communion?
2. We call part of the eucharist "holy communion". What therefore does it essentially mean?

LEVITICUS 4:1 - 5:13

The sins of the covenant people, whether deliberate or accidental, had to be expiated by sacrifice.

1. These sacrifices were offered in expiation for sin. How can we sin *UNWITTINGLY* (verses 2,13,22,27)? Is there any sense in which we need healing for our unconscious and therefore unknown sins?
2. Notice that all classes of people are involved (4:3,13,22,27). Is there room in our modern world for *COLLECTIVE* reparation for sins? Why? What form could it take?

LEVITICUS 5:14 - 6:7

Guilt offerings are hardly distinguishable from sin offerings.

1. The guilt offering concerned the healing of relationships either directly with God (5:15) or with the neighbour (6:2-3). Notice the emphasis on restitution. Is this an area we often neglect nowadays? With what results?
2. How do these laws underline God's hatred of sin and its consequences, and his desire for man's healing and forgiveness?

LEVITICUS 6:8 - 7:38

A sacrifice is offered daily, and the fire is kept alight perpetually, signifying the continuity of the worship accorded to God by the covenant community. Sacrifices may be offered in thanksgiving (7:12), in fulfilment of a vow (7:16) or as a free will offering (7:16), as well as in expiation for sin. Creation is fundamentally good (Genesis 1:31) and mankind offers joyful praise, freely.

1. Note the number of times that the offering is described as "most holy". What is the essential meaning of holiness?
2. The priest is provided for by part of the offering. What does this tell us about the total dedication required of the priesthood?

LEVITICUS 8-10

The ritual for priestly investiture is described as having begun with Aaron and his sons, though it was probably of later date, but the origin of the priesthood is envisaged as having been part of the Mosaic covenant.

LEVITICUS 8

The priests were consecrated to God as indicated here but the *anointing* was of later origin. It did not belong to the priesthood until the Second Temple. It was originally a royal privilege. The priest was , ipso facto, a sacred person according to his function: the king *became* a sacred person at his anointing.

1. Trace the order of events in the investiture ceremony. What is the symbolic meaning of each?

2. What is the significance of the blood and of the chrism? On what occasions does the Church make use of chrism?

LEVITICUS 9

This chapter is possibly a continuation of Exodus 40, inserted here by a later writer.

1. Aaron and his sons assume their functions and perform the prescribed sacrifices. Then Aaron and Moses bless the people (verses 22-24). How does God reveal himself through his priests?
2. Read Hebrews 5:1-4 for a New Testament commentary on this passage. How does Jesus' sacrifice reveal God's Glory?

LEVITICUS 10

The account of the sacrificial ritual ends with some anecdotes that in their turn introduce the ancient food and other laws of chapters 11-15.

1. What was the sin of Nadab and Abihu? (See also verses 8-10). What do you understand by Aaron's reaction?
2. Why does God seem so severe?

LEVITICUS 11-26

The Holiness Code proper (17-26) is introduced by the law of purity which enshrines religious taboos of great antiquity. These reveal the beginnings of a sense of sin, of man's unworthiness before an all-Holy God, and of the sacredness of all that is connected with God.

LEVITICUS 11

The animals are not scientifically classified, but according to general observation.

1. Is there any hygienic basis for the distinction between clean and unclean animals? cf. Acts 10 for a New Testament reappraisal of these laws. Note verses 41-45 for the theological basis for this chapter. What does it teach us about purity of soul, mind and body?

LEVITICUS 12

The loss of blood, either in childbirth or in menstruation, was regarded as a loss of vitality, and even of a loss of union with God, the source of life. Rituals are the means of restoring this union.

1. This chapter has unfortunately led Christians in the past to think of childbirth as in some way unclean, because the ancient reverence for the mystery of life that lies at the heart of the rituals, was lost. How can our liturgy today express reverence for new life, and joy at a new birth?
2. The time of retirement after the birth of a girl was double that for a boy, because the mother of a new daughter might need added protection from a new pregnancy, not because she was doubly unclean! What does New Testament have to say about discrimination against females?

LEVITICUS 13-14

Leprosy covers all kinds of skin diseases.

1. What does leprosy symbolise? Read these chapters giving a spiritual meaning to the rites for cleansing.
2. Look up New Testament references to leprosy, especially Jesus' touching of lepers, eg. Mark 1:41. Why did Jesus break these taboos?

LEVITICUS 15

Everything connected with the transmission of life was sacred and mysterious.

1. Do these laws reflect a sense of shame at normal bodily functions or a sense of the sacred? How is respect for the integrity of each person expressed by Christians?
2. What is the underlying meaning of personal modesty? cf.Genesis 3:7-11.

LEVITICUS 16

This chapter contains the ancient ritual of annual atonement for all impurities. Azazel (verses 8,10,26) was the name of a demon, the scapegoat, who lived in the desert.

1. Sketch the various ceremonies of the Day of Atonement, listing popular pre-Israelite customs which have been purified and taken over.
2. What do we learn from these rites of the idea of substitution? How does this prepare the way for Christ's atoning sacrifice?
3. Could Good Friday be referred to as the Christian's Day of Atonement? What are a) the essential similarities, and b) the essential differences?

LEVITICUS 17-26

The Holiness Code in its present form probably dates from the sixth century BC, but it contains much ancient material.

LEVITICUS 17

The satyrs mentioned in verse 7 indicate goat-like creatures who were believed to haunt ruins or wildernesses. cf. Azazel (16:8).

1. What do we understand by *HOLINESS* in these chapters? Is there more than a ritual element? See verse 7.
2. Read carefully verse 11. How does this explain much of Israelite law? Does it have any significance for us Christians?

LEVITICUS 18

The laws in this chapter, while presented as part of ritual cleanliness, have moral implications also. Incest was common in Egypt and in Canaan.

1. Draw out the elements in this chapter that are part of traditional Christian morality.
2. What is the moral reason for the prohibition of incest?
3. Read carefully verse 21. Is there any modern equivalent to sacrificing children to Molech?

LEVITICUS 19

This chapter contains a collection of laws based on the Ten Commandments. It refers therefore to moral rather than to ritual regulations.

1. Draw out the principles for worship in this chapter (verses 3, 4-8, 30).
2. What does this chapter teach about a) family relationships, and b) social justice?
3. Apply these laws to our present day experience, noting especially verses 10, 12, 13, 15, 33-34.

LEVITICUS 20

The Law was given in the previous chapter. Now the penalties for its breach were imposed.

1. What were the penalties for child sacrifice, disrespect for parents, adultery, bestiality, incest and idolatry?
2. What do these laws tell us about the society in which the Israelites had to live? Do any of these conditions occur today? Can we draw strength from verse 26?

LEVITICUS 21

Rules safeguarding priests from ritual impurity. Contact with the dead produced uncleanness.

1. Priests were to avoid all pagan practices (verses 5,10), to practise continence and to be without physical blemish. What are the spiritual equivalents of these ordinances?
2. The prophets encouraged the people to avoid legalism, eg. Isaiah 56:3-5. Jesus followed in this tradition. What did he say about the distinction between ritual and moral purity? See, for example, Mark 7:1-23.

LEVITICUS 22

Purity surrounding the communion sacrifices.

1. 'I will be hallowed among the people of Israel; I am the Lord who sanctify you' (verse 32). Pick out the words or phrases in this chapter which emphasise this.
2. How is God 'hallowed', as we pray in the Lord's Prayer?
3. In what way should the spirit of this chapter be applied to our Christian worship? Compare Paul's strictures on the behaviour of the Corinthians at the Eucharist (1 Cor. 11).

LEVITICUS 23

This is the Priestly writer's calendar of festivals (cf. Exodus 23 for the Elohistic writer's list).

1. List the feasts and describe their main characteristics.
2. What are the Christian parallels to:
   a) Passover
   b) the Feast of Weeks
   c) the Day of Atonement?

LEVITICUS 24

Later regulations from the Temple in Jerusalem, rather than from the early (desert) period have been added to the Law of Holiness.

1. Notice that in the case of blasphemy here recorded, Moses makes no decision until the will of God is known. What does this teach us about judgements?
2. The community has been defiled by the man's blasphemy. Do we share any collective sense of guilt for serious crimes committed in our name? What should be done in such cases nowadays?

LEVITICUS 25

The sabbatical year and the Jubilee year (cf. Exodus 23:10-11).

1. These ordinances are based on the principle of God's absolute ownership of the land. What do they tell us about the social basis for our attitude to God, to our work, to our property, and to each other?
2. Does the Church's custom of a periodical Holy Year have any meaning in this context?

3. Have we any responsibilities to those in debt? Could the World Bank and other international financial organisations take any principles from this chapter with regard to Third World debt? In what way?

LEVITICUS 26

It was customary to conclude covenant treaties with blessings and curses. In a world where the enforcement of the law could not be confided to the police, the whole community had to be imbued with the sense of possible results to society from good or bad behaviour. The notion of an individual's "freedom of choice" to do good or to do evil without regard to the consequences for the whole community would have been quite alien.

1. Read aloud the Blessings (verses 3-13). The central theme of Leviticus is stated in verses 11-13. How do these Blessings apply to the members of the Church?
2. What does the second half of the chapter (verses 14-46) tell us about God's justice? See especially verses 40-45.

LEVITICUS 27

Persons, animals and other possessions could be vowed to God.

1. What does this chapter tell us of the seriousness of vows?
2. Should we tithe our property in favour of the Church or of the poor? Work out what that would mean if we all took the law of tithing seriously.

AN INTRODUCTION TO THE BOOK OF NUMBERS

Many people are put off by this book, and tend to refer to it disparagingly, because they open it at Chapter 1 and find seemingly endless lists of names. They turn the pages to Chapter 5 only to find more laws of the kind they had struggled through in Leviticus, and are tempted to give up. This is unfortunate, because some of the most interesting stories in the Pentateuch can be found between Chapters 11 and 27 sandwiched between lists, genealogies and laws. It's well worth the effort - and even the drier sections can be found to contain some nuggets of gold, if you look hard enough!

The story of the desert wanderings is resumed from Exodus, with a census (1-4), the offering of gifts (7), the celebration of Passover (9) forming the prelude to the departure from Sinai (10). Spies are sent to Canaan from Kadesh (11-14) but the people lose courage, reject the promised land, and are punished by thirty-eight years of wandering until they reach the plains of Moab (20-25). The Midianites are defeated, and Transjordan is settled by the tribes of Reuben and Gad (31-32). The book therefore is largely a story of failure, for the people's rejection of the land of Canaan as their promised land is punished by a long desert period, symbolic of man's rejection of God's promises, and his consequent alienation. But God never forsakes his people, and the book ends on a note of hope.

NUMBERS 1-2

Israel is presented as a sacred community organised under God's leadership for holy war. Descent from Abraham was essential. Hence the genealogies. The census seems to be connected with the redemption of the first-born.

1. List the tribes in order of size. Which is the largest? Do you think this has any significance for the later history of Israel?
2. The Levites were set apart and not numbered. Why?

NUMBERS 3-4

Having listed the tribes descended from Jacob, the writer now lists the sons of Levi, exempt from military service, because destined to take charge of the cult.

1. The Levites were set apart as "first born" belonging to the Lord. What is their equivalent in today's Church? Why did the first-born belong to God? What does redemption mean here?
2. How were the duties of the Levites divided between three families?

NUMBERS 5

These laws were additions to the Holiness Code (Lev. 11-16).

1. Trial by ordeal was common until the middle ages. Is there any sense in which it can be justified?
2. In what way can it be said that there is a real recourse to God in these ancient, semi-magical rites?

NUMBERS 6

There are several references to the nazirite vow in the Bible (Judges 13:5-7; 1 Samuel 1:11; Luke 1:15; Acts 21:22-24).

1. Abstention from wine means refusal of a life of ease (cf. Jer. 35:5-8). Is there any place for such abstention in the Christian life?

2. Hair was believed to be a sign of strength, so allowing it to grow signifies the action of the divine power in the worshipper (cf. Judges 16:17). How do we allow the Holy Spirit free rein in us?
3. Note the ancient priestly blessing, verses 22-27. What does it mean to "put God's name upon the people of Israel"?

NUMBERS 7

The wagons were used to transport the Tent of meeting through the desert. Each tribal leader contributed to the offerings to be made for the dedication of the altar. This section is part of the great Priestly Narrative from Exodus 40ff., into which has been inserted the legal material of Leviticus.

1. Notice the repetition of words like "anointed", "consecrated", "offered". On what occasions is similar ritual used in the Christian church?
2. Read carefully verse 89, and notice the words used to convey a great sense of climax. What was the experience of Moses? How does God communicate with us in our liturgy?

NUMBERS 8

The consecration of the Levites is described.

1. What did the lamps symbolise?
2. The separation of the Levites is restated. cf. Hebrews 12:18-24 for a New Testament theology of the first-born.
3. What features in this chapter have been brought into the ordination of priests and of ministers in the Church?

NUMBERS 9

The ritual for Passover, supplementing Exodus 12.

1. Note the clause allowing the Passover to be celebrated a month later for those who have contracted ritual impurity, and cf. 2 Chronicles 30:15-20 for a further development away from legalism to a greater trust in God. Is legalism still a danger in the Church?
2. Read verses 15-23 carefully. What do they tell us about guidance? How do we follow the guidance of the Holy Spirit?

NUMBERS 10

Much of this chapter relates to the "holy war".

1. Make a plan of the battle formation described in this chapter.
2. What was the significance of the trumpets? cf. 9:15-23 and show how God used human instruments to guide his people.
3. Moses asked Hobab to lead them and "serve as eyes for" them. Hobab was son to Reuel a Midianite, therefore a foreigner (cf. Exodus 18). Are there occasions when we need help from apparent outsiders in the spiritual life?

NUMBERS 11-14

Chapters 11-12 contain some lively stories, on the theme of God's patience with the people's grumbling. This "murmuring" theme is hinted at in Exodus, but is much more strongly emphasised in Numbers. There seem to have been two traditions concerning the desert wanderings. The first, that it was a "honeymoon" period during which God formed his people as a bridegroom loves a young bride, has a few traces in Exodus 16, and is found in Hosea 2:16, Jeremiah 2:2, and lingers on in Mark 1:12-13. The second strand sees it as a time of testing of

Israel, of disobedience and rebellion against God. It is found in Numbers 11,17,21, in Ezekiel 20, Psalm 106 and Nehemiah 9:16-37.

NUMBERS 11

Stories of events during the desert wanderings are linked to ancient place-names (vv3, 35).

1. Moses complains to God freely, echoing the mood of the people. What is God's response? What can we learn from this about prayer?
2. How are the elders called? What likeness is there between this scene (verses 16-30) and Acts 2:1-11? What are the differences?
3. Compare verses 26-30 with Mark 9:38-40. What lessons can be drawn from both incidents?

NUMBERS 12

This chapter is largely devoted to Miriam (cf. Exodus 15:20), and her relations with her two brothers, Moses and Aaron.

1. Consider the attitudes and behaviour of each of the three. What do we learn of Moses' character?
2. What hints are there in the Bible that Miriam was a forceful person in her own right? Compare this scene with Exodus 15:20 and with Micah 6:4.

NUMBERS 13

Two traditions are combined: The Priestly Narrative (13:1-16, 21, 25-26, 32-33; 14:1-3, 5-10, 26-38); the ancient Yahwistic saga (the rest of chapters 13-14), which emphasises the part played by Caleb.

1. Compare this list (verses 4-15) with the list in Numbers 1.
2. How far did the spies go in their exploration of Canaan? Why was their report so discouraging? Compare their arguments with those of Caleb. Do we sometimes miss opportunities through timidity and lack of faith in God's promises?

NUMBERS 14

1. What arguments did Caleb and Joshua use to persuade the people? Are these a development on 13:30?
2. Trace the course of Moses' pleading with God.
3. God forgives the people but he warns them that they must suffer the consequences of their sin. How do verses 39-45 show that they still had much to learn in their relationship with Yahweh, their God?

NUMBERS 15-19

Another section of law, containing the account (16) of the rebellion of Korah, Dathan and Abiram, emphasising the divine origin of Aaron's authority in the community. Note that while chapters 11-14 concentrate on the leadership of Moses this section reflects a tradition from Aaronite circles.

NUMBERS 15

Various laws concerning sacrifice and sin offerings.

1. What do verses 1-21 teach us about offerings that are pleasing to God?
2. Why was there no forgiveness for the one who sins "with a high hand" (verse 30 - defiantly - NIV)? Compare this with the teaching on Pharaoh's "hardening of the heart" (Exodus 7-10) and with Jesus' teaching (Mark 3:28-30).
3. Why was sabbath breaking so severely dealt with?

NUMBERS 16

Two parallel narratives are fused: a) the political revolt of the Reubenites, Dathan and Abiram–verse 1-2, 12-15, 25-34; b) the religious claim of the Korathites against the Aaronites –verses 1-11, 16-24, 27, 35.

1. What was the ground of complaint in each case? See verses 12-13, verse 3. How far were these complaints justified?
2. What lay behind these complaints to explain in some fashion so drastic a punishment? See verses 11,30.
3. Notice the title given to God by Moses and Aaron (verse 22). What does it mean in this context?

NUMBERS 17

The story of the rebellion is concluded with a narrative emphasising the importance of Aaron. NB. The numbering varies in different Bibles. We follow RSV.

1. Look up all we know so far of Aaron: Exodus 7:1-7; Exodus 28-29, Exodus 32:21-25; Lev. 8-9; Lev. 10:1-3; Numbers 12. How do we come to know more of him and to see him in a new light in this chapter?
2. Read Wisdom 18:20-25 for further commentary on these scenes.

NUMBERS 18

The function of the priesthood was seen as above all to offer sacrifices in expiation for ritual sins. The priests were to be supported by the tithes of the people and by designated portions of sacrificial offerings.

1. Notice verses 1-8 for the priest's office. How does it foreshadow the work of Christ? cf. Hebrews 5:1-10, 7:25, 9:14.
2. Notice God's provision for the priests and levites. They were to have no inheritance in the land, but God himself will be their portion, and will give them all they need. Make a list of all that is to go to the priests and levites from the offerings.
3. Read 1 Samuel 2:12-17 for an abuse of these regulations.

NUMBERS 19

An ancient, semi-magical ritual is taken over into the doctrine of the atonement cf. Lev. 16.

1. Draw out the details of the cleansing of the water. Is this cleansing from impurities entirely external, or does it have an underlying meaning?
2. What was done with the ashes of the heifer? What was the meaning of this rite?
3. Compare this water of cleansing with 'holy water' in our churches today.

NUMBERS 20-25

This section contains narratives from different sources of the wilderness tradition. The main theme is the steady advance of God's people, despite hostility from without and backsliding within. The failure of Moses and Aaron to reach the promised land is ascribed in 20:1-13 to lack of faith and obedience on their part. In the same chapter the king of Edom refuses right of way to the Israelites. The Edomites are universally condemned in the Bible, and this incident is said to be the origin of the enmity of Israel towards them. In 21:21-24 the Ammonites also prove unfriendly, as do the Moabites in 22. The hostility of the Israelites towards these neighbours is reflected in the nasty little story in Genesis 19:30-38; but it also reminds us that they were related to Israel, as descendants of Lot - as Edom (Esau) was a descendant of Abraham.

NUMBERS 20

Verses 1-13 are a doublet of Exodus 17:1-7.

1. Notice the pattern of these "murmuring" stories: lack of food or water, the people grumble and threaten Moses (and Aaron), who intercede. God intervenes and provides what is needed, but punishes the people for their lack of faith. Look at Exodus 15:22-25; Exodus 17:1-7; Numbers 11:1-3; Numbers 16:41-50; 20:1-13; 21:4-10. Do all these stories follow this pattern?
2. Does God's punishment of Moses and Aaron (verses 12-13) seem out of proportion to their crime? Analyse verses 9-11 very carefully. Can we, in any case, call GOD to account for his actions?
3. Edom's churlish refusal marks the beginning of a long enmity between Israel and Edom. Compare the rejection of Esau stories in Genesis (25:9 ff) and Malachi 1:1-5.
4. The deaths of Miriam and Aaron are both recorded in this chapter. They have not been presented on the whole in a very favourable light, but look at Micah 6:4 and Sirach 45:7-22, which hint at an alternative tradition not fully preserved in the Bible.

NUMBERS 21

The inspired writer has used a narrative based on ancient war songs. Chemosh (verses 29) was the national god of Moab.

1. Trace on the map the Israelites' progress around Edom towards Moab.
2. The story of the bronze serpent has found its way into the New Testament, cf. John 3:14. What was its original meaning?

NUMBERS 22

Two traditions are combined in this narrative (22-24). Balaam the soothsayer is mentioned several times in the Bible (Numbers 31:8; 16, 2 Peter 2:15-16, Jude 11, Rev. 2:14).

1. The combining of two traditions concerning Balaam makes the story in some ways confusing. Draw out the guidance Balaam receives from God.
2. Can we learn anything from the story of the talking donkey? cf. 2 Peter 2:16. Do animals ever teach us?

NUMBERS 23-24

Ancient poems have been incorporated into the story, some of them anti-Moabite (23), and some from the time of David (24).

1. Make a list of the statements concerning Israel.
2. What do we learn from the story of Balaam a) about the perils and challenges of being a prophet, and b) about the action of God's Spirit even in an unworthy spokesman?

NUMBERS 25

Traditions of Israel's idolatry in Moab are mingled with a Midianite story. Probably at one time Israelites, Moabites and Midianites all frequented the sanctuary at Baal-Peor.

1. This is one of the many stories condemning all contact with foreigners, especially foreign women, because of the danger of children being brought up in idolatry. Why was God's anger so fierce?
2. Phineas is praised for his zeal, and God makes a covenant of peace with him. Read the commentary on this incident (Sirach 45:23-24). What do we learn about the priesthood here?

NUMBERS 26

The census. This list is related to Genesis 46.

1. A census is taken in Moab on the frontiers of the promised land, as a census had been taken at Sinai (Numbers 1). Compare the two lists. Which tribes had grown and which diminished? Notice the references to daughters (verses 33, 46).
2. What was the *theological* reason for the insertion of this list? See verses 63-65.

NUMBERS 27

The problems of inheritance for daughters crops up in many societies. Different solutions occur, more or less equitable.

1. What was the principle underlying the request of the daughters of Zelophehad? (Verses 1-4).
2. What steps did Moses take to provide for the people after his death?

NUMBERS 28-29

This section is based on Leviticus 23. The blowing of trumpets (29:1) was a New Year festival for warriors.

1. List the daily, weekly and monthly festival offerings. Find out how they are kept in modern Jewry.
2. How do these anticipate the Christian liturgical year?

NUMBERS 30

Note the importance attached to vows, in an age when the spoken word was never lightly uttered. Compare Judges 11:30-40 and Eccles. 5:3-4.

1. Woman's inferior status is made clear in this legislation, and the law protects her from burdens she cannot carry, where she is not a free agent. Are there any occasions allowed for in the legislation where she IS independent?
2. What do we learn here about the importance of vows, and of speech uttered before God?

NUMBERS 31

This story follows the incident at Peor (Numbers 25).

1. Why was Balaam put to death?
2. We find it very difficult to understand the theology of the "holy war". Can we spiritualise the account and read it allegorically, or is it better simply to dismiss the chapter as reflecting a mentality of a different age?

NUMBERS 32

This story reflects the situation of the Reubenites and Gadites (Gilead). Their colonisation was peaceful, but the lack of natural frontiers meant they were frequently overrun in later years.

1. Why was Moses concerned at the request of the Reubenites and Gadites? What implications did it have for the unity of the Israelites?
2. What is the principle expressed in verse 20-23? Are there occasions a) in scripture and b) in our own lives when the workings of this principle can be illustrated?

NUMBERS 33-35

The itinerary of chapter 33 seems to be rather artificial, not corresponding to the ancient tradition of a route through Ezion-Geber, and round Moab and Edom. Canaan was given its name by the Egyptians in the thirteenth century BC.

1. Follow the stages of Israel's journey on a map. Which places named contain a story or a lesson that you remember from your reading of Exodus, Leviticus or Numbers?
2. What orders did God give to Moses on the threshold of Canaan?
3. What were the cities of refuge? What do you think of the whole idea of "sanctuary"?

NUMBERS 36

This chapter follows 27:1-11.

1. This chapter illustrates an ancient problem concerning women's rights as heirs: their marriages can lead to the break up of family property. Do you think that the obligation to marry within the tribe is a fair compromise?
2. Israel now stands at the threshold to the promised land. What are the warnings to which anyone on the threshold of a new venture in God's service should pay heed?

AN INTRODUCTION TO DEUTERONOMY

'And Hilkiah the high priest said to Shaphan the secretary, I have found the book of the law in the house of the Lord. And Hilkiah gave the book to Shaphan and he read it. And Shaphan the secretary came to the king, and reported to the king..... Hilkiah the priest has given me a book. And Shaphan read it before the king'. (2 Kings 22).

Most scholars believe that the scroll discovered in the Temple during the reign of Josiah was an early edition of the Book of Deuteronomy which was brought to Jerusalem after the fall of Samaria in 721 BC. The reason why it is believed that the scroll was Deuteronomy and not the Holiness Code or the Book of the Covenant is its insistence on one sanctuary.

The Code of Laws (12-26) is introduced by two homilies purporting to have been delivered by Moses on the threshold of the promised land, and the laws are rounded off by the conclusion to the second homily (26:16-28:68). The first homily (1:1-4:43) is a summary of Israelite history from Sinai to the arrival at the Jordan. It dates from the period of the exile, which is predicted as a punishment for sin. The second homily (4:44-11:32) serves as an introduction to the Code of Laws, and concludes them at 26:16-28:68. It also summarises past history, and is in origin a cultic catechism on the code. Both homilies are therefore a theological statement on the message of the Pentateuch: God's choice of Israel and the gift of the land. The third homily (29-30) once more reviews the events of the Exodus and contains a covenant formula and a warning against the dangers of idolatry. Chapters 31-34 conclude the Pentateuch with commissioning of Joshua, the Song of Moses, the blessing of the tribes, and the death of Moses.

DEUTERONOMY 1

Moses begins his discourse, reviewing Israelite history from Sinai to the Promised Land. The Anakim were legendary giants (cf. Genesis 6:4).

1. Go carefully through the discourse picking out the successive sins of the Israelites at each stage of the journey.
2. Notice that the writer attributes the sending of spies (verse 22) to the suggestion of the people, not to God's orders (Numbers 13:1-2). What is Moses' responsibility here? See verse 23 and 29-31.
3. What is the explanation here of Moses' exclusion from the promised land (verse 37)? Compare Deuteronomy's account with Numbers 20:12-13.

DEUTERONOMY 2

The people's journey from Kadesh to the borders of Canaan is described. Seir (v.1) is associated with the sons of Esau, the Edomites.

1. God is here represented as having given land not only to Israel but to Esau (verse 5) and to the sons of Lot (verse 9). What does this tell us about God's care for all people? Yet the Amorites are seemingly excluded from God's protection. Why?
2. What do verses 24 and 31 teach us about faith and trust in God's promises?

DEUTERONOMY 3

Whereas the conquest of Sihon is historical, Og the king of Bashan is a figure from legend - another giant like the Nephilim (Gen. 6:4) and the Anakim (Deut. 1:28).

1. How did the conquest of Sihon and of Og disprove the fears of forty years before? Compare 1:28 with 2:36 and 3:4-6. What may we learn from this about timidity in God's service?

2. Consider Moses' prayer and God's reply (verses 23-27). What does this teach us about true dialogue in prayer?

DEUTERONOMY 4:1-43

This first discourse of Moses ends with a strong theological statement of the distinction between the 'statutes and ordinances' (vv 1, 5, etc) ie, the Deuteronomic Code, which is to be elaborated in chapters 12-26, and the Ten Commandments.

1. What is said about the word of God as revealed in the Law?
2. How is God's intimacy with his people emphasised?
3. Against what sin are the people warned?

DEUTERONOMY 4:44-5:33

The second discourse begins (5:1 - 11:32) and continues from 26:16 - 28:68, after the block of law called the Deuteronomic Code (12-26). It is similar in structure to the first discourse, and forms a kind of commentary on the Code.

1. Notice the emphasis on the immediacy of the law for every succeeding generation (5:3). What does this say to all of us who read the scriptures and take part in the liturgy? Does Old Testament speak to us as well as to the Jews?
2. Compare this version of the Decalogue with that in Exodus 20. What is the significance of the difference?

DEUTERONOMY 6

This chapter contains the Shema (vv 4-13), the great Jewish creed, recited every day by orthodox Jews.

1. The commandment to *LOVE* God is the profoundest insight of the Jewish faith into the nature of God. Jesus calls this the first and greatest commandment (Matt. 22:37). What kind of love can be *COMMANDED*?
2. Jesus said "Where your treasure is, there will be your heart also" (Matt: 6:21). Comment on this in the light of verses 10-15.
3. What does this chapter tell us about the importance of religious education in the family?

DEUTERONOMY 7

The apartness of Israel is emphasised here, because the author, writing at the time of the monarchy, knows the dangers to which the people are exposed in their contacts with their neighbours.

1. Notice the theme of divine election, very strong in Deuteronomy, especially verses 6-8. Apply this to our own call as Christians. Does it mean that those not called are not loved by God?
2. In what sense can God's promise of blessing (verses 12-15) be said to be of universal application? What about suffering? Is it always a punishment, as the Deuteronomist seems to believe? What did Jesus say? (Luke 13).
3. What do we learn in this chapter about courage and trust in God's promises?
4. What reason does the writer give for the slowness of the conquest of the land? See verse 22, and cf. Exodus 23:29.

DEUTERONOMY 8

The testing time in the desert is succeeded by the temptations of the promised land.

1. The time in the desert is represented as an ordeal (cf. Numbers 14:26-35 where it was a punishment). In what did the testing time consist?
2. What are the temptations of prosperity? Is this chapter relevant for us today? In what ways?

DEUTERONOMY 9

Moses addresses the people, giving an account of the Golden Calf episode from his own point of view, emphasising the travail of an intercessor.

1. What is the great snare for all people who are conscious that they have been chosen? Study carefully verses 1-6 and compare with Luke 18:9-14.
2. What incidents does Moses recall in this chapter? What aspects of the people's history does he emphasise?
3. Notice that Moses refers to the day of the Assembly (verse 10). What was it that formed the people into an Assembly, a congregation?

DEUTERONOMY 10

The language (10:12ff) is that of covenant treaties made between kings. It includes curses and blessings (11:16ff).

1. Compare 10:12 with 6:5. What is the underlying reason for loving God? See verse 15.
2. What attributes of God are here described?

DEUTERONOMY 11

1. What rewards and punishments are specified in this chapter?
2. We have almost entirely ceased to view events in our personal lives or in the lives of members of our families, community or nation in the light of rewards for obedience to God or punishment for disobedience. Is there any sense in which this kind of theology is still valid? See Luke 13:1-5, 34-35 for New Testament teaching.

DEUTERONOMY 12

The law of the unique sanctuary aimed at protecting the pure worship of Yahweh from contamination by Canaanite cult associated with other shrines. The Northern sanctuary was originally at Shiloh, but by the time of Josiah the shrine was solely at Jerusalem.

1. Pick out the references to rejoicing in worship.
2. Notice the warning against worship of Canaanite gods. What was particularly abominable about their practices? Does this have any relevance for us today?

DEUTERONOMY 13

This chapter contains important warnings against idolatry, and the dangers from false prophets.

1. What are the temptations described in this chapter? Are we open to any of them?
2. What do you think was the underlying problem (hinted at in this chapter) that faced a nomadic people encountering a settled agricultural people for the first time?

DEUTERONOMY 14-15

There is probably a warning against Baal fertility rites in 14:1 - when the god "died" at the end of the summer. The laws concerning the tithe vary in the different codes. The Deuteronomic Code shows frequent concern for the poor.

1. What provision was made for the poor in these laws?
2. Compare the regulations for tithing with those in Numbers 18:25-32.

DEUTERONOMY 16-17

The celebration of Passover to include the feast of unleavened bread dates from the time of Josiah. From a family meal, it became an annual pilgrimage to Jerusalem.

1. What is meant by the "bread of affliction"? How did Jesus give it new meaning at the Last Supper?
2. Draw out from these chapters the laws governing civil cases and the appointment and conduct of judges.
3. What advice is given to kings or other secular rulers?

DEUTERONOMY 18

Prophecy is of great antiquity, and is found among all the countries of the ancient middle east. It is here described as an institution from the time of Moses. The true prophet will speak in Yahweh's name.

1. What practices were forbidden to God's people? See verses 9-14. Are these laws still applicable today? Why?
2. What were the rules for testing and discerning true prophecy? With verses 15-22 compare Deut. 13 and Jeremiah 28.

DEUTERONOMY 19

These laws cover the fifth to the tenth commandments.

1. How do verses 1-13 illustrate in practice the commandment *THOU SHALT NOT KILL*? Does the Code consider intention?
2. How does verse 14 provide an illustration of the seventh commandment (thou shalt not steal), and verses 15-21 of the eighth?
3. What safeguards are there for the poor and under privileged in this chapter?

DEUTERONOMY 20

The excuses listed by Jesus in his parable of the banquet (Luke 14:16-20) are taken from this chapter - those exempted from conscription.

1. Why were certain categories of people exempt from war?
2. Why were conquered cities near to the Israelites to be treated less mercifully than those far away? What do we learn about conservation in this chapter?

DEUTERONOMY 21

The problem of identifying a murderer is solved, not by pursuit, investigation and trial, but by ridding the land of blood guilt through an ancient rite. It is taken for granted that the murderer would not dare to pronounce the words uttered in vv 7-8. God is not mocked. Rebellious children are not tolerated (vv 18-21).

1. What rights did women have? See verses 10-17, and compare verses 18-19.
2. Why was disobedience to parents treated so severely? Have we gone too far the other way nowadays?
3. What use does the New Testament make of verses 22-23?

DEUTERONOMY 22

The laws in the Deuteronomic Code are frequently notable for their humanity and for their advance on the other Codes.

1. What rules governed a) the rights of others to their property, and b) the rights of other creatures? Do we take b) seriously enough?
2. What laws safeguarded chastity and honesty in sexual relations? Has Christianity improved on this?

DEUTERONOMY 23

A physical defect was viewed as symbolic of an interior fault. This explains the harsh attitude towards eunuchs, bastards and foreigners. Their exclusion from the cult signifies a respect for God's holiness, rather than a moral judgement. Ammonites and Moabites are often scorned, though later writers (Isaiah 15:5 and Ruth) show a more developed mentality.

1. How do purity and hygiene reflect God's holiness? Can we draw any principles from this chapter?
2. Eunuchs were excluded from the assembly, but cf. Isaiah 56:4-8 for a more compassionate ruling. What is New Testament teaching about outcasts of all kinds?

DEUTERONOMY 24

The law concerning divorce remained in force until the time of Jesus (Matt. 5:31-32; 19:7). However, concern for the individual and especially for the poor is remarkable in this chapter.

1. Draw out further laws defending the poor, the needy and the foreigner in this chapter. What rights did they have?
2. What did Jesus teach concerning divorce, going beyond this passage (verses 1-4) and referring back to Genesis 2:24?

DEUTERONOMY 25

The levirate law is mentioned several times in the Bible. It is also found among the Assyrians and the Hittites.

1. What application does Paul make of verse 4? See 1 Cor. 9:9; 1 Tim. 5:17, 18.
2. What provision is made to safeguard prisoners from torture or abuse?
3. The levirate law is frequently mentioned, cf. Genesis 34, Ruth, and Matt. 22:23 ff. What was its real purpose?

DEUTERONOMY 26

This chapter contains the second great "credo" of the Jewish faith (the other two being Deut. 6:5-13 and Joshua 24). This one emphasises the gift of the land, the first fruits of whose produce are offered to Yahweh. The second discourse, interrupted at 4:44 by the Code, is resumed at v.16.

1. Sum up the obligations listed in this chapter.
2. What were the blessings promised to those who kept the covenant?

DEUTERONOMY 27

This chapter interrupts the discourse that has just been resumed. Verses 1-8 and 11-26 consist of cultic traditions associated with the shrine at Shechem, incorporated here by the author as a conclusion to the covenant document.

1. Put the "curses" in the order of the Ten Commandments.
2. Notice that the crimes mentioned were done in secret. What does this teach us about interior sins or intentions?

DEUTERONOMY 28

The second discourse concludes with blessings and curses, as is usual in material of this kind.

1. To what extent do the Blessings (verses 1-14) still apply to us? Can they also be spiritualised?
2. The curses (verses 15-19) describe a situation that is the opposite of that described in verses 1-14. Then the paragraphs succeed each other, building up a frightful picture until the climax is reached at verse 49. Which calamity did the writer have in mind?

DEUTERONOMY 29

This chapter sees the beginning of Moses' third discourse: the covenant at Moab.

1. What warning is contained in this discourse? See verses 4, 18-20. How can one stubborn person be a root "bearing poisonous and bitter fruit"?
2. Notice the universal nature of this covenant (verses 10-11, 14-15).
3. For what purpose is revelation given according to verse 29? cf. James 1:22.

DEUTERONOMY 30

The third discourse is concluded in the style of the Wisdom writers.

1. How is the character of God revealed in this chapter?
2. How will Yahweh form his people?
3. Read carefully verses 11-14 and compare Romans 10:5-13. How are Law and Gospel alike?

DEUTERONOMY 31-34

These four chapters form a conclusion to the whole Pentateuch.

DEUTERONOMY 31

Joshua is chosen as leader in succession to Moses; the reading of the Law (vv 9-13) is to serve as a cultic witness to the covenant, as the Gospel read during the liturgy of the Christian assembly brings Christ's presence among his people.

1. List the different ways in which the Lord, through Moses, sought to save the people from backsliding.
2. What was it that gave Joshua (and gives us) strength and courage?

DEUTERONOMY 32

The Song of Moses echoes the Psalms, and Deutero-Isaiah, so it probably dates from the exile.

1. Make a list of the titles and attributes of God in this poem.
2. How is Israel described?
3. What was God's purpose in chastising Israel?

DEUTERONOMY 33

This Blessing seems to belong either to the time of David or to the schism.

1. Compare what is said of each tribe with Genesis 49.
2. Which tribe has the greatest blessings?

DEUTERONOMY 34

Moses' death is recounted, followed by a short panegyric.

1. Compare what is said of Moses here with Numbers 12:3.
2. Ponder the character of Moses as prophet, intercessor and lawgiver.

AN INTRODUCTION
TO
THE BOOK OF JOSHUA

If we read this book with such works as 'The Iliad' or 'Beowulf' or 'Sorhab and Rustum' in mind, we shall be less disconcerted by its simplistic and idealised account of the conquest of Canaan. It is a great epic; a celebration of a nation's victory, not factual reporting as we understand history. It contains various traditions, some very ancient, woven together probably during the exile. Chapters 2-9 draw on a group of traditions connected with the Benjaminite shrine at Gilgal; chapters 10-11 contain two records of battles, Gibeon and Merom, associated with the conquest of the south and of the north. Chapters 13-21 can be described as a geographical treatise made up of lists taken from various sources, not earlier than the time of Solomon, and some as late as the reign of Jehoshaphat of Judah. Chapters 22-24 preserve memories of Joshua's last days and of an assembly at Sechem.

Who was Joshua? He is mentioned several times in Exodus and in Numbers, and once in Deuteronomy. In Exodus 24:13 he is described as Moses' servant and in Exodus 33:11 we are told he was the son of Nun. In Numbers 13:8 his name is given as Hoshea son of Nun from the tribe of Ephraim, and he is listed among the spies sent out to reconnoitre Canaan. In verse 16 we are told that Moses changed his name to Joshua. With Caleb (14:6-7) he tried to persuade the people to attack Canaan at once. In Numbers 27:18 ff. he was appointed Moses' successor and leader of the conquest of Canaan. From the Book of Joshua we learn that he was buried 'in his own inheritance at Timnath-serah, which is in the hill country of Ephraim, north of the mountain of Gaash'. (Joshua 24:30).

JOSHUA 1

This chapter written in the style of Deuteronomy, serves as a link with all that has gone before.

1. Look up all that is said of Joshua in Exodus 24:13 ff.; 33:11; Numbers 11:26-30; 13:16; 14:5 ff. What opinion do you form of his character?
2. What are the promises God makes in this chapter? What is the condition? See verse 8.
3. What is the meaning of the name Joshua? What does his story therefore typify?

JOSHUA 2

Two traditions are combined in the story of the conquest of Jericho: a) the story of Rahab and the spies (Joshua 2 and 6:22-25); b) the crossing of the Jordan and the capture of Jericho (Joshua 3-4 and 6). Shittim (verse 1) was directly opposite Jericho.

1. Look up the other references to Rahab: Joshua 6; Matt. 1:5; Hebrews 11:31; James 2:25. What was her outstanding quality? What indications are there that she "knew" the Lord?
2. What does the whole episode tell us about God's providence?

JOSHUA 3

The crossing of the Jordan is described in the style of epic poetry.

1. Draw out the parallels between the crossing of the Jordan and the crossing of the Red Sea (Exodus 14).
2. What titles are accorded to God in this chapter? See verses 10 and 11. What do they emphasise?
3. What does the ark symbolise in this chapter? Follow its progress.

JOSHUA 4

The crossing is achieved, and the people camp at Gilgal (= ring of stones). It was between the Jordan and Jericho, and became an important Benjaminite shrine.

1. In what way could this chapter be said to represent a liturgical commemoration of an event rather than a straightforward chronicle?
2. Note the emphasis on 'twelve'. What does this signify?

JOSHUA 5:1-12

The religious significance of the crossing of the Jordan into the promised land is emphasised by the circumcision of the Israelites and the celebration of Passover.

1. Gilgal became a celebrated shrine until at least the time of Saul. What two events are associated with it here?
2. The desert period, symbolised by the manna, ended with the arrival at Gilgal. What will be the new challenges of an agricultural way of life (verses 11-12)? How do we mark new stages in our lives?

JOSHUA 5:13 - 6:27

The conquest of Jericho is celebrated in a liturgical, poetic style. There is no archaeological evidence for an assault on Jericho during the period usually assigned, i.e. the thirteenth century BC, for Jericho seems to have been already largely a ruined city then. It is more likely that the Rahab story (Joshua 2,6:22-25) points to an infiltration of the area by Israelites, whose descendants are linked to Rahab.

1. Compare Joshua's experiences (verses 5:13-15) with those at 1:2-9 and 5:2,9.
2. Verse 6:1. Does this verse in any way suggest an attitude of mind common enough? What can bring about 6:20?
3. The story of the conquest of Jericho is typically a 'holy war' story, with its war cry (verses 5, 16) and the 'devotion to destruction'. Such a mentality is far from our own - though remember the crusades! - and can make reading such parts of Old Testament a problem for us, but what are the theological lessons we can draw from these chapters?

JOSHUA 7

Two stories are combined in this chapter: that of Achan (vv 1, 16-26), a Judean from Achor in Judah, far away to the south, and the repulse of the Israelite armies at Ai.

1. Compare Joshua's prayer (verses 6-9) with that of Moses (Numbers 14:13-20). What is the central argument in each prayer?
2. What was the sin that contaminated the community? Do we take sin seriously enough? Compare Isaiah 59:1-2.

JOSHUA 8

The story of the capture of Ai is only historical in a very general sense.

1. Follow the plan of campaign on a map. How far do you think the stratagem described may reflect ancient tradition of the whole conquest? Can this story be in any way 'spiritualised'?
2. The capture of Ai is succeeded by a dedication ceremony (verses 30-35). Look up Deut. 11:26-29 for the background. What was the purpose of this service?
3. Compare Moses with Joshua in this chapter. See especially verses 9, 18, 31, 34.

JOSHUA 9

The Gibeonites were a non-Canaanite enclave in the region of Jerusalem (verse 17). They wished to make an alliance with the invaders. See 2 Samuel 21:1-9.

1. Why did Joshua and the leaders disobey the rules for war? How did they get out of the awkward situation they had created for themselves?
2. The Gibeonites were to prove useful allies (10:2, 11:19). Does the writer draw a moral, or does he let the facts speak for themselves?

JOSHUA 10

An independent narrative of the conquest of the southern area of Canaan. It contains much ancient material - poetry, legendary events not originally connected with Joshua, rather in the way stories have accumulated round the figure of Arthur in ancient British historical legend.

1. Use a map to follow this campaign - the conquest of southern Palestine. What lessons for our faith are contained in this chapter? See verses 6 ff.
2. In verses 12-13 an ancient poem is quoted. The editor has taken it literally (verse 13). What are we to make of it?
3. Note the stereotyped account of the conquest (verses 28-39). Many of the towns mentioned (Libnah, Lachish, Eglon) were not, in fact, conquered until much later. What does this tell us about the Book of Joshua?

JOSHUA 11 - 12

A parallel narrative of the conquest of the north of Canaan is found in Chapter 11. Chapter 12 is the work of the editor, summing up the account of the conquest of the land by Joshua.

1. How did the Israelites win the battles of Merom (verses 6-9)? Follow the northern campaign on a map. To what does the writer attribute Joshua's victory?
2. If we transpose these events to the spiritual level, how can we apply Moses' orders to Joshua to our own battles with sin and evil? Does New Testament have any further teaching? cf. Matt. 18:8, 9; Ephes. 6:10-18.

JOSHUA 13 - 14

The material in these chapters is based on sections in Deuteronomy (3:12-17) and in Numbers 32. It attempts to relate the whole area of Palestine to the sons of Jacob. The picture is idealised, since little is known of the real origins of these tribes.

1. Consider God's challenge to Joshua (13:1). Should we be discouraged if we find, as we grow older, that there is still much to be done, many battles still to be fought? What encouragement does God give in verse 6? What does it require from us?
2. What do we learn of Caleb? Look up also Numbers 13:6, 30; 14:6-9, 24, 30.

JOSHUA 15 -17

Judah was to become a separate kingdom for a time (under David and Solomon) uniting the whole land, and, after the division into two kingdoms under Solomon's successor, surviving as a kingdom under the Davidic dynasty until 587 BC. The origins of the Calebites are obscure,Ephraim was also destined to have an important history, giving its name in some periods to the northern kingdom.

1. What was Achsah's complaint? How should we deal with aridity in prayer and in the spiritual life?
2. Using a map discover the boundaries of a) Judah (15:1-63) and b) of the sons of Joseph (16:1-17:18). Why did the Josephites complain? How did Joshua respond?

JOSHUA 18 - 19

The apportionment of land to the seven remaining tribes is given a solemn liturgical setting, based on Shiloh, the principal sanctuary during the time of the Judges.

1. Look up on a map the various territories assigned to the tribes. Which are the most important? Then look at Genesis 29:32 - 30:24. Is there any connection between the status of the sons of Jacob/Israel and the fortunes of their descendants?
2. Notice that Simeon has no territory assigned to him, except within the inheritance of Judah (19:1). Read Genesis 34 for a possible connection.

JOSHUA 21

A systematised account of the provision of cities of refuge and of towns of the Levites.

1. Compare 20:1-9 with Numbers 35:9 ff. and Deut. 4:41-43.
2. What is the theological meaning of 21:43-45? How do we experience this in our own lives?

JOSHUA 22

This narrative incorporates an ancient tradition of rivalry between the shrines in Shiloh and in Gilead in Transjordania.

1. What do you think of the argument used by the Transjordanian tribes to justify their shrine? Can centralising of worship go too far?
2. For the reference in verse 17, see Numbers 25:1-9. What kind of an altar were the Transjordians setting up? See verse 34. Can this story teach us anything?

JOSHUA 23

The chapter concludes the career of Joshua with a farewell discourse after the fashion of Moses (Deuteronomy 31). Chapter 24 is a later addition to the whole book.

1. List the admonitions of Joshua to the children of Israel. In what ways are they of universal application?
2. Compare this farewell discourse with that of Moses (Deut. 31) What were the main preoccupations of both men?

JOSHUA 24

The covenant at Shechem was made not only with the incoming tribes from Egypt but also with those descendants of Abraham who had remained in Canaan and not been in Egypt. All were now bound together to the covenant with Yahweh.

1. Why was Shechem chosen as an assembly place? See Genesis 12:6, 7; 33:18, 19; Joshua 8:32-35.
2. What did the people promise? How was the covenant symbolised?
3. What have you learned of the personality of Joshua?

AN INTRODUCTION
TO
THE BOOK OF JUDGES

There are some well-known characters in this book: Gideon and his fleece, the daughter of Jephthah, Deborah, and above all, Samson and Delilah. They are on the whole, a rough lot, and the Bible does not gloss over the less edifying aspects of their lives and fortunes, but the stories have been preserved from very ancient times, when the Israelites were struggling to establish themselves in the land of Canaan. According to the Book of Joshua the conquest was achieved in three rapid campaigns: according to Judges 1 the process was considerably more complicated, and often by infiltration rather than by conquest. Facts are sketchy, but traditions are preserved of various charismatic leaders, called 'Judges' in English, but which really should be translated 'leader' or 'prince'. These led the people against pagan oppressors at different times and in different parts of the land. Thus Othniel (3;7-11) appeared in southern Palestine (Judah), Deborah and Barak were in the highlands of Ephraim (4:4, 5), Gideon in Manasseh (6:33), Jephthah in Gilead in Transjordan (11:1) and Samson in Zorah, west of Benjamin.

The book as we have it is made up of three parts: Chapter 1, which is an ancient document listing the state of the tribes at Joshua's death; chapters 2-16, the stories of the judges embedded in a theological commentary; two appendices concerning the migration of the Danites and the crime at Gibeah, chapters 17-21.

PRELIMINARY EXERCISE

Read carefully Judges 2:6-23; 3:7-11; 4:1-3; 6:1, 7; 10:6-10; 13:1

Notice the continual pattern of wrongdoing, punishment, lament, salvation. The sacred author has used the historical traditions at his disposal to write a theology of history based on the theme of man's infidelity and God's saving action. The stories themselves (some very ancient and not very edifying) are independent of this theology. In the Book of Judges we have the first volume of what scholars call the Deuteronomic History which extends through 1 and 2 Samuel and 1 and 2 Kings.

JUDGES 1:1 -2:5

An ancient document giving a more realistic account of the conquest of the land than the glorified, simplified epic of Joshua.

1. Look up all the remaining Canaanite strongholds on the map.
2. There is some evidence that Judah and Simeon were long established in the south, and perhaps did not even come from Egypt. Does anything in this chapter support this?
3. What charges did the Lord bring against the Israelites? What warning was given?

JUDGES 2:6-19

The sacred writer makes a theological statement on the meaning of events in the history of the chosen people, according to his own religious outlook.

1. Examine in general the history of any country you know (our own?), and ask yourself if the teaching in this chapter can in any way apply.
2. Do the same with the history of the Church.
3. Does this cycle in any sense occur in your own life?

JUDGES 2:20 - 3:31

The so-called "Judges" are listed as twelve in all, corresponding, supposedly, to the twelve tribes of Israel, but few details are given of six of them.

1. What explanation is given for the survival of the foreign nations in Canaan? Compare Exodus 23:29, Deut. 7:22 and Wisdom 12:3-22.
2. What is meant by a judge in this book?
3. Compare the work and achievements of Othniel and Ehud.

JUDGES 4

This story is given in prose in Chapter 4 and in poetry in Chapter 5. It refers to a victory by the tribes of Zebulun and Naphtali in the North West against the Canaanite general, Sisera. The date is 12th century BC, and the events are certainly historical.

1. Who was Deborah? What functions did she exercise? Compare her with Miriam (Exodus 15:20) and with Huldah (2 Kings 22:14).
2. Which tribes were involved in this victory? What conclusions do you draw from this?

JUDGES 5

The Song of Deborah is one of the oldest passages in the Bible, contemporary with the events described and celebrated. This means that it probably comes from the 12th century BC.

1. What is its central theme? Which tribes followed the call to battle? Which ones stayed at home? Which are not mentioned at all?
2. Draw out the picture of God in the minds of the ballad-makers indicated in the Song.
3. Recite the whole poem aloud if possible.

JUDGES 6

The narrative of Gideon and Abimelech (6-9) concerns a) Gideon's military exploits against the Midianites, and b) the religious crisis that overwhelmed a nomadic people confronted with an agricultural way of life. Did Yahweh reign in Palestine, or did the gods of the Canaanites?

1. Notice Gideon's forthright discussion with the angel of the Lord. Are we equally honest in prayer?
2. Gideon's first test comes in his own household (verses 25-32). What do we learn from this about human respect?
3. God allowed Gideon to "test" him twice. What does this tell us about God?

JUDGES 7

The story of Gideon's victories over the Midianites is continued.

1. God now tests his army. What reasons are given?
2. Camels used in warfare could be the equivalent of tanks today against bows and arrows. What is the lesson for us all in this chapter? Do you know any modern stories of a similar loss of morale in an apparently invincible enemy?
3. Notice the transformation of Gideon from 6:13, 15 to 7:15. In what ways does the narrative emphasise the work of God in Gideon?

JUDGES 8

This chapter records Ephraim's early claims to ascendancy (vv 1-3) and further campaigns of Gideon.

1. Gideon shows courage and resolution in crisis, but a failure of nerve in time of peace. In what other ways does he show deterioration in this chapter?
2. How did idolatry creep in again?

JUDGES 9

This story was inserted here because Abimelech was a son of Gideon by a Shechemite woman, though he was not a judge, but a Canaanite king. Jotham's fable is the earliest example in the Bible.

1. What is the point of Jotham's fable?
2. What is the moral of the story of Abimelech? In what way is his end similar to that of Sisera? See verses 53-55, and cf. 5:24-27.

JUDGES 10

Three more judges are listed, of whom little is known. Tola ruled in Ephraim, and Jair and Jephthah in Gilead.

1. What do we learn about the prayer of lament, and perseverance in prayer in this chapter?
2. Follow on a map the places named in this chapter. List the enemies of Israel.

JUDGES 11-12

The (to us) repugnant story of Jephthah's sacrifice of his daughter is recorded without comment by the sacred writer. Three more judges are briefly listed in Chapter 12: Ibzan of Bethlehem, Elon of Zebulun and Abdon of Ephraim.

1. Notice the two aspects of a choice of a judge (11:9, 29).
2. What were Jephthah's qualities a) as a leader, and b) as a man of faith?
3. What do you think of Jephthah's vow? Does the New Testament give any light on rash words?
4. Compare this story with Genesis 22. What is meant by Jephthah's daughter's request?
5. Compare Jephthah's treatment of the Ephraimites (12:1-6) with that of Gideon (8:1-3). What light do these incidents throw on a) the struggle of Ephraim for supremacy, and b) the characters of Gideon and Jephthah?

JUDGES 13-16

The story of Samson is a collection of anecdotes of folk-tale quality, that have been used by the sacred writer to illustrate the action of the Spirit in a 'judge', ie. one designated and called by God to 'save' his people.

JUDGES 13

The story of Samson contains much ancient, legendary material.

1. Samson's birth is foretold in a manner similar to John the Baptist. What will his mission be?
2. Compare the scene (verses 8-20) with a) Abraham's hospitality to angels (Gen. 18) and b) Jacob's experience at the Jabbok (Gen 32:30). How do we experience God as we read of these events?

JUDGES 14

Samson contracts a marriage common among ancient peoples, where the bride stays among her own people and the husband pays her occasional visits.

1. The theology of the Holy Spirit is very primitive in these stories. Is there any way in which we can transpose it onto a supernatural plane?
2. What kind of a man is Samson? Draw out what we learn of him from these episodes.

JUDGES 15-16

The stories are really a succession of anecdotes, coming from an oral tradition of a local hero famous for his exploits against the Philistines.

1. Look on the map for the area dominated by the Philistines.
2. What impression is given of the women in Samson's life?
3. In what way can Samson be described as a "saviour" of his people?

JUDGES 17-18

This ancient story is concerned with the sanctuary at Dan: its origin and its priesthood, presented unfavourably.

1. In 17:1-6 draw out all the evidence that the author disapproves of Micah and his shrine.
2. How are the origins of the priesthood at Dan described? See 17:7 ff, 18:14 ff. Notice especially 18:30-31.

JUDGES 19

This terrible story has echoes of the story of Lot in Genesis 19. It is originally a story against the Benjaminites, and as a cloak for denigrating Saul, Gibeah having been his capital.

1. Notice the emphasis on the failure of hospitality. What other crimes occur in this story?
2. What was the attitude a) of the Levite, and b) of the old man towards the concubine of the one and the daughter of the other? Does the writer in any way indicate that their behaviour is reprehensible?
3. Gibeah is mentioned several times in the account, and see Hosea 9:9 and 10:9 for echoes of this story.

JUDGES 20

Two separate accounts have been clumsily combined, leaving a rather incoherent text.

1. The Benjaminites put loyalty to their own tribe before loyalty to the moral law, and refused to deliver their fellow townsmen to justice. This led to civil war. Are there any occasions when we have a similar dilemma? Give examples.
2. What does this chapter teach about perseverance in prayer, even in times of apparent refusal on the part of God?

JUDGES 21

Two different accounts of provision for the future of the tribe of Benjamin are juxtaposed (verses 8-14, and 15-23).

1. What festival was celebrated at Shiloh?
2. To what does the author attribute the lawlessness of Israel as reflected in these last chapters? Do you think this is an adequate explanation?

AN INTRODUCTION TO THE BOOK OF RUTH

The voice I hear this passing night was heard
In ancient days by emperor and clown:
Perhaps the self-same song that found a path
Through the sad heart of Ruth, when, sick for home,
She stood in tears amid the alien corn.

J. Keats.
Ode to a Nightingale.

Ruth's fidelity and steadfastness, her devotion to her mother-in-law, her sensitive acceptance of her husband's people and their customs all have inspired poets and storytellers through the ages, but the book, in fact, has some curious aspects. The law of levirate marriage by which a man was obliged to wed the childless widow of his brother and name their eldest son as a descendant of that brother seems strange to us, and Naomi's advice to Ruth in 3:1-5 seems provocative, to say the least, but the book describes ancient customs, and though some scholars believe it to be part of the protest literature that emerged in reaction to the reforms of Ezra which excluded all foreign wives, most are of the opinion that it was composed during the time of David (c.950 BC). Ruth is presented as the greatgrandmother of David, and Matthew included her in the genealogy of Christ.

RUTH 1

The artificial names, the vague dating (v.1) and the echoes of poetry, all indicate that this is a work of historical legend, rather than of strict history.

1. The names in this story all have meanings. Naomi means "sweetness", Mahlon "sickness", Chilion "pining away", Orpah "she who turns away", and Ruth "the beloved". Show how this sets the scene, and how God guides events.
2. What are the characteristics of Orpah and of Ruth?

RUTH 2

Boaz as goel or redeemer (verse 20) had the duty of preventing alienation of the clan's land (cf. Lev. 25:23-25), and, if the nearest relative, of marrying the childless widow of Mahlon. (Deut. 25:5-10).

1. Trace the stages of Boaz' wooing of Ruth.
2. The poor had the right of gleaning (Lev. 19:9-10). Do you get the impression from this chapter that this right was always and everywhere respected?

RUTH 3

The story records ancient courtship rituals, still in use in country districts in England in the 18th century.

1. In what ways did Ruth indicate that she was willing to carry on the line of her husband's family?
2. What kind of man was Boaz?

RUTH 4

According to the custom, Ruth's son by Boaz would be legally the son of Naomi and Elimelech, and their heir.

1. What picture of marriage and family emerges in this story?
2. What is the meaning of Boaz' transactions with the 'next of kin' (verse 1)?
3. Compare the two genealogies in verse 17 and in verses 18-22. Why do you think the second one was added?

AN INTRODUCTION
TO
1 and 2 SAMUEL

If you are using the Douai or the Knox Bible, you will look in vain for these books! In the Vulgate, of which these are translations, there are four books of Kings, so 1 and 2 Samuel correspond to 1 and 2 Kings, while 1 and 2 Kings become 3 and 4 Kings. The Hebrew Bible ascribes them to Samuel as their author. They are among the most interesting of the historical books, containing many well known stories, such as the Witch of Endor, David and Goliath, and the call of the child Samuel.

1 and 2 Samuel are one book, telling the story of the monarchy from Samuel (the last of the judges) and Saul, the first king, to the last days of David. Within this history are inserted the story of the ark (1 Samuel 4-7; 2 Samuel 6) and the so-called succession narrative (2 Samuel 7-20; 1 Kings 1-2).

The dominating figures are Samuel, then Saul and above all, David. Samuel is introduced even before his birth, as a child of promise. He was chosen by God at Shiloh, the ancient shrine of the ark. He was recognised as a prophet, and served as a judge and a military leader. Saul, the first ruler to unite all the tribes, was installed as king, and his erratic personality dominates the rest of the book, but it is above all David who appears as a full length portrait, first of all in the collection of stories in 1 Samuel 16 - 2 Samuel 5, and still more vividly in the court narrative (2 Samuel 7-20) which seems to have been written by a contemporary.

David left a united kingdom to his successor, and his reign was looked back upon almost as a golden age, but the various tribes were not really united, and there were wide differences between the populous hill country of Ephraim and Manasseh on the one hand, and isolated Judah in the south. David conquered the Canaanite city-state of Jerusalem, and brought the ark there, but there was a religious as well as a national division between north and south that was only exacerbated by the building of Solomon's temple and the use of slave labour from the north.

1 SAMUEL 1

The first three chapters are centred on the sanctuary at Shiloh.

1. What name is given to God (verse 3)? What does it signify? Does it add anything to our understanding of God?
2. Examine the prayer of Hannah, and its effect on her (verse 18). What can we learn from her?
3. Compare the birth narrative of Samuel with that of a) Samson (Judges 13) and b) John the Baptist (Luke 1). What is the constant theme?

1 SAMUEL 2

The Song of Hannah, which says virtually nothing about either Hannah or Samuel except a very general reference in verse 5, was inserted into the text by the editor.

1. What is the main theme of this Song? In what way is it suitable on Hannah's lips? Compare it with the Song of Mary (Luke 1:46-55). What features have the two Songs in common?
2. In verses 13-14 we are told that at Shiloh the priest could take a random thrust at whatever meat was being prepared for sacrifice. What were the abuses of which Eli's sons were guilty? See verses 15-16. Compare this whole passage with Leviticus 7:29-36 and Deut. 18:3-4. What differences are there? Of what other crimes are Eli's sons accused?
3. In what ways is Samuel contrasted with the sons of Eli?

4. God rewards Hannah's generosity (verse 21). Compare her as a mother with Eli as a father.

1 SAMUEL 3

A typical prophetic call, such as Moses and Jeremiah received (cf. Exodus 3 and Jeremiah 1).

1. Trace the spiritual development of Samuel in this chapter, noting especially verses 1, 7, 10, 19-21. Can I discern a similar development in my own life history?
2. What test was Samuel given? How did he conduct himself?

1 SAMUEL 4

The ark now takes centre stage.

1. The ark was a symbol of God's presence among his people (see especially verse 4). Yet it here proved unavailing. Why? Do *WE* ever make the mistake of trusting to symbols, without an accompanying change of heart?
2. Eli and his two sons were all dead, but there was a gleam of hope at the end (verse 21). What does this teach us about punishment? See further 14:3, 18.

1 SAMUEL 5

Ashdod on the west coast was a Philistine stronghold. Dagon was a very ancient deity of West Semitic origin. He seems to have been a storm god.

1. Look up the place names on a Bible map and follow the progress of the ark.
2. The ark contained the tables of the Law, and was therefore a sign not only of Yahweh's presence but also of his visitation in judgement. What is the theological meaning of the scene in verses 1-5?
3. What further signs of judgement a) on Israel and b) on the Philistines can be seen in this chapter?

1 SAMUEL 6

The story of the ark is continued in this chapter, to be resumed in 2 Samuel 6.

1. Draw out the various references to purgative rites in the story of the return of the ark. See especially verses 3-4, 7, 14-15, 17-18. What is their real significance? Can we learn anything from the advice of the Philistine priests and diviners?
2. The plague seems to have spread from Philistia to Bethshemesh (verse 19). What explanation for this visitation is given by the sacred writer?

1 SAMUEL 7

The narrative now returns to Samuel. Verse 2 should be translated 'the whole house of Israel longed for Yahweh' (NJB) or 'There was a movement throughout Israel to follow the Lord' (REB) not 'mourned' as in RSV and NIV. Mizpah was an old place of prayer for Israel cf. 1 Maccabees 3:46.

1. What meaning do the rites mentioned in verses 5-6 have? What do they symbolise for us?
2. What lessons do we learn from the account of Yahweh's victory over the Philistines? What was the role of Samuel? What does EBENEZER mean?
3. How would you sum up the lessons of this chapter? What secure advantages had Samuel's rule gained for the Israelites?

1 SAMUEL 8

The idea of a monarch, proposed in this chapter, meets with objections from Samuel who points out the dangers of autocratic rule.

1. What were the offences of Samuel's sons? What contrast do you note between 7:15-17 and 8:1-3? What is the universal lesson of this contrast?
2. Draw out the echoes in this chapter of the temptation of Eve (Genesis 3), cf. especially verses 19-20. What was the basic sin of the people in demanding a king?
3. What do God's interventions (verses 7, 22) signify?

1 SAMUEL 9

This tradition comes from an independent source. Samuel is here described, not as a judge, but as a seer.

1. Comment on verse 2, in the light of Genesis 39:6; 1 Samuel 16:12; Esther 2:7; Exodus 2:2. Is the quality to be interpreted in a purely physical sense?
2. What is the significance of verse 8 in the narrative? What other indications are there that divine Providence is at work?
3. What signs are there that Saul is more than a dutiful young man?

1 SAMUEL 10

The consecration of Saul follows the pattern for the designation of all the kings of Israel: anointing by a prophet or in Judah by a priest, thus marking the sacred character of the king as servant (or son) of Yahweh; acclamation by the people.

1. What were Saul's tasks as king to be (verse 1)? In what way do they apply to all rulers?
2. What is meant by verses 6 and 9? a) Was this openness to the spirit always a good thing in Saul's case (cf. 16:14, etc.)? b) In what sense can these verses be said to describe a Christian experience?
3. In what terms did Samuel introduce the election of a king? See verses 17-19. Does this imply that the king is a gift from God or a punishment? Why did Saul hide?

1 SAMUEL 11

This story is independent of the preceding chapter, with no reference to Saul's having been made king at Ramah. It derives from Gilgal.

1. Compare the story in verses 1-13 with Judges 10:17 - 11:33. In what ways do both stories follow a similar pattern? What are the important differences?
2. What were the qualities of Saul revealed in this chapter?
3. Look up Jabesh-Gilead on the map. The people of Jabesh never forgot what they owed to Saul. cf. 1 Samuel 31:11-13.

1 SAMUEL 12

Like Moses and Joshua, Samuel makes a farewell discourse, reviewing events and his part in them.

1. In what way did Samuel insinuate that the people had made an unwise move in choosing a king? How did he show his own power with God? Did other prophets demonstrate their power in similar ways? cf. verses 16-18 with 1 Kings 17:1.
2. What role did Samuel promise he would exercise in the future (verses 19 ff.)? How does he compare a) with Moses and b) with later prophets?

1 SAMUEL 13

The text is confused, but verse 3 seems to be the key to the narrative of verses 2-15. Saul's son Jonathan's assassination of the Philistine governor (we follow JB here) seems to be an act of rebellion which initiated a long war between the Philistines and the Israelites.

1. What connection between kingship and obedience to God is underlined by the story in verses 2-15? Why did Saul have to wait for Samuel to offer sacrifice? What is the modern theology of relations between Church and State?
2. Notice the serious dependence of the Israelites on the Philistines (verses 19-22) and the great danger in which they therefore found themselves. In these circumstances what ought they to have remembered? (Verses 12, 14, 15). In similar occasions, do we have faith in God, or in armaments, treaties, or insurance companies?
3. How does the writer build up the contrast between Philistine might and Israelite weakness?

1 SAMUEL 14

Philistines and Israelites were encamped face to face across the Michmash Pass, Saul and his men at Gibeah.

1. What does the story of the Battle of Michmash Pass teach us about faith? What effect did Jonathan's courage have on the Hebrews? See verses 21-22.
2. Note the evidence of Saul's rash headstrong temperament. Why did he impose a fast on the soldiers? How is Jonathan shown in contrast? What do we learn from this episode of the theological value of commonsense? Are there other examples in the Bible of the God- given use of good judgement?
3. What do we learn of Jonathan? Why was he not the chosen heir to Saul, despite his gifts? Compare the stories of Ishmael and of Esau in Genesis.
4. List Saul's victories, and find the places on the map.

1 SAMUEL 15

Agag is mentioned in Numbers 24:7; the Kenites were a tribe of metal workers or smiths who inhabited the deserts of Israel and Judah. They must have made a covenant with the Israelites. (Kindness - v.6 - = covenant loyalty).

1. The first king of Israel must punish Israel's ancient enemies. Such is the reasoning behind the injunction in verses 1-3. cf. Deut. 25:17-19. What parallel unpalatable duties might have to be undertaken by a modern ruler? Note the influence of Samuel. Who would be his modern counterpart?
2. Wherein lay Saul's mistake? What explanation did he give of his actions? (verse 24). What light does this throw on the whole episode?
3. Compare verses 22-23 with Isaiah 66:2-4; Amos 5:21-24. What is the theme of all three oracles?

1 SAMUEL 16

An independent account of David's anointing by Samuel (verses 1-13) is followed by the old story of David's rise to power.

1. What is meant by verses 13 and 14? What meaning are we to attach to the sequence: anointing (by a prophet) and the coming of the Spirit? What is the analogy with the sacraments of baptism, confirmation and ordination?
2. What important details in the story of David's first appearance at court (verses 14-23) are introduced by the writer to emphasise the contrasting fortunes of Saul and of David? What is the theological meaning of these details?

1 SAMUEL 17

Two traditions are fused in this chapter: the old narrative, part of the David Saga is found in verses 1-11, 32-40, 42-48a, 49, 51-54; an independent account (verses 12-31, 41, 48b, 50, 55-58) which was introduced fairly late - some think during the fourth century BC, though the narrative itself may be ancient.

1. In what way is the story of David and Goliath a typical story of the battle between good and evil? What are the lessons of this story?
2. Notice Eliab's impatience with his younger brother (verse 28) and David's reply (verse 29). Are we ever tempted to think and speak like Eliab? If so, what kind of things stir us up? Is there any similarity to the effect Joseph had on his elder brothers?

1 SAMUEL 18

Some scholars believe that the covenant (verse 3) between David and Jonathan implied a conspiracy against Saul. The covenant language (love, loyalty etc) has political overtones. There is also the possibility that David's marriage to a daughter of Saul (verses 17 ff.) would make him heir, rather than Jonathan.

1. David aroused deep affection in Jonathan (verses 1-3), in Michal (verse 20), and in the people (verses 5, 16). In Saul he inspired anger (verse 8), fear (verse 12), awe (verse 15). To what does the sacred writer ascribe the effect that David had on others? See verses 12, 14, 28. Think about the whole story of David's rise to power in the light of these verses.
2. Trace the deterioration in Saul's character.
3. What do we learn of Saul's family life in this chapter? (Verses 14:49-51). Look up all we know thus far of Jonathan.

1 SAMUEL 19

A different version of David's relations with Saul's children.

1. How did David come to attract such devotion and loyalty from two of Saul's children? Is any explanation given in these chapters? What impression have you formed, thus far, of David?
2. Compare the scene in verses 18-24 with 10:9-13, of which it is almost a parody. How do you interpret the accounts of Saul's mental illness?

1 SAMUEL 20

A parallel account with the events in the preceding chapter.

1. David had received help from Michal (19:12ff.), from Samuel (19:18), and now he turns to Jonathan (20:1). What is the significance for the narrative of these sources of support for David?
2. Notice Saul's warning to Jonathan (verse 31). What do you think of Jonathan's reaction (verse 34)?
3. What do we learn from these scenes concerning God's handling of events?

1 SAMUEL 21

The priests at Shiloh had taken refuge at Nob after the disaster of Chapter 4. Ahimelech was the son of Ahitub, the brother of Ahijah, Saul's chaplain, son of Phineah, son of Eli. (14:3).

1. What use does Jesus make of the incident (verses 1-6) in the New Testament? See Matt. 12:3-4.
2. Note from this chapter that there is room for humour and even comedy in the Bible! Does David's flight to the Philistines teach us anything about God's use of circumstances? In what way?

1 SAMUEL 22

The story of the priests at Nob is concluded in this chapter. David is now an outlaw.

1. What were David's motives in gathering a company of people in distress? Why did he seek guidance at this point?
2. Can David be said to have any part of responsibility for the massacre of the priests at Nob? cf.21:2ff. How does he acknowledge this? Are we ever so magnanimous?
3. Notice the courage of Ahimelech. God's vengeance on the house of Eli continues (3:14), but is there a gleam of hope?

1 SAMUEL 23

Further stories of David's exploits in southern Judah.

1. How is this chapter connected with the last one? What significance is intended by the sacred writer?
2. In what ways did God's protection cover David? What is the meaning of the ephod? Do *WE* find signs of God's protection or guidance in material objects or is this superstition? Can a distinction be made?
3. Why is the story of Jonathan's encouragement of David and his belief in his destiny (verses 16-17) and their renewal of covenant (verse 18) inserted here? What does it tell us about the intentions of the author?

1 SAMUEL 24

One account of David sparing Saul.

1. In what ways are David and Saul contrasted in this episode? How does the author depict the nobility of the one and the meanness of the other?
2. For David, Saul was still 'the Lord's anointed'. Do we have a similar respect for all Christians as "anointed" in Christ? How should this respect be demonstrated?
3. Analyse Saul's feelings in this episode.

1 SAMUEL 25

Sheep shearing was a festive occasion, when rich farmers were expected to be generous. 'Nabal' means 'foolish, senseless'.

1. Is there any difference between David's tactics (verses 4-8) and a demand for "protection money"? What does this teach us about God's forbearance with human nature? Can you think of any other examples a) in the Bible, b) in your own experience?
2. Notice David's words to Abigail (verses 32-34). In the light of the last question, what is there about David that makes him more than a common outlaw and freebooter?
3. Read this story in the light of Wisdom teaching, especially the Book of Proverbs. Who is the fool in the story, who the wise person? What is David's role?

1 SAMUEL 26

Another, older tradition of David sparing Saul (see chapter 24). There is a play on the word 'call' in verses 14 and 20 where 'partridge' in Hebrew is the 'calling bird'.

1. Notice what is said of Abishai and Joab (of whom we shall hear more), and look up 1 Chronicles 2:13-16 for their relationship to David.
2. On what grounds did David appeal to Saul?

1 SAMUEL 27

David now leaves Israel and enlists in the service of a Philistine prince.

1. David had put himself in an ambiguous position from which he hoped to extricate himself by cunning and prevarication. Give an example of each. What caused this desperate situation? See verse 1.
2. Look up all we know of Achish (21:10-15, this chapter, 28:1-2 and 29). How do you account for his attitude to David?

1 SAMUEL 28

One of the most brilliant narratives in Old Testament, worthy of a great tragic writer.

1. Draw out the numerous elements of doom in this story.
2. Does it give any authoritative teaching on life after death? cf.Luke 16:23.
3. Does Saul's total despair (verse 15) show loss of faith, or merely a mood of deep depression? Do WE believe Saul to be doomed? Why is the story of the Amalekites (verse 18) raked up here? cf. Chapter 15.
4. Look up the Chronicler's verdict on Saul (1 Chronicles 10:13-14). Is it too harsh?

1 SAMUEL 29

The narrative follows on from 1 Samuel 28:2.

1. What circumstances saved David from either fighting against his own countrymen or losing the support of Achish? What did he mean by verse 8?
2. What light does this whole Philistine episode throw on his character?

1 SAMUEL 30

David builds up support among the southern clansmen, friends who will later support his claim to the throne.

1. Contrast David's situation at this point with that of Saul.
2. Was David's generosity to the men who had been too exhausted to follow him (verses 21 ff.) magnanimity or policy or both? What was its theological basis (verses 23-25)? Notice also the sharing of booty among the towns of Judah. What picture of David's position is being built up by this author?

1 SAMUEL 31

The death of Saul is tersely recounted.

1. Saul's tragedy reaches its final consummation in this chapter. Review his life, his aims, his achievements and his mistakes.
2. Look up Chapter 11 for the story of Saul's rescue of the men of Jabesh-Gilead.
3. The Chronicler (1 Chronicles 10:13,14) gives a very unfavourable summary of Saul's life and death. Compare it with the defeat recorded in Chapter 4. Would New Testament teaching in any way soften this doctrine of God's vengeance?

2 SAMUEL 1

It is essential that David disclaim all responsibility for Saul's death (though he will profit from it). His blood must not cry for vengeance on David or on David's descendants.

1. Did David sincerely mourn Saul and Jonathan? What evidence is there in this chapter?
2. Read aloud David's lament for Saul and Jonathan. What are your feelings as you read it?

2 SAMUEL 2

Saul's death and that of his sons left Israel without a king. The natural division between Judah and the other tribes was opened up, and David was proclaimed king at Hebron (in Judah) while a son of Saul, Ishbosheth (or Ishbaal) was made king of Israel and Transjordan, but as a puppet of Saul's army commander, Abner.

1. How did David make allies in the period following Saul's death? See verses 4-7.
2. The death of Saul led to civil war between Judah and Israel. Make a character study of Joab and Abner, and cf. Chapter 3.

2 SAMUEL 3-4

Events leading to David becoming king of the whole of Israel are recorded by the sacred writer, using an ancient narrative.

1. Compare David's family life (3:2-5) with that of Saul. What was the great weakness of David's?
2. Abner's taking of Saul's concubine implies he is claiming Saul's throne. What touches reveal Ishbosheth's character?
3. How did David turn events in his own favour?

2 SAMUEL 5

1. What events led to David being chosen king of all Israel?
2. How did he succeed in taking the stronghold of Zion, and why?
3. Do WE allow the "Lord of breaking through" (verse 20) into our lives? What is the reason for David's success? See verses 10 and 12.

2 SAMUEL 6

The narrative of the ark is resumed.

1. What was a) the theological and b) the political motive for bringing the ark to Jerusalem?
2. Is it permissible to read the events described in verses 6-11 as follows:? Uzzah had a sudden attack while walking beside the ark. This was interpreted as a judgement on him for touching the ark, but David noticed that the presence of the ark brought blessings to Obed-edom and all his household. What do you think? Are there similar Old Testament stories that can be explained in the same way?
3. Compare the characters of David and of Michal. Have you ever felt like Michal?

2 SAMUEL 7

In this chapter begins the Succession Narrative written, it seems, by a member of David's court (Nathan?). Its themes are a) the crisis in the succession caused by Michal's childlessness (6:23), for, as Saul's daughter she would have united the two dynasties; and b) the Messianic origins of David's dynasty.

1. David wished to build a 'house' for Yahweh, who responded by promising him a "house" or dynasty. Follow these two themes through the chapter.
2. Trace the Messianic element. To whom do verses 12-14 refer? To Solomon, or to Christ, or to both?
3. Compare this chapter with Luke 1:26-38.

2 SAMUEL 8

A summary of David's campaigns.

1. List David's conquests, noting on the map the extension of the Davidic kingdom. What is the theological purpose of this chapter?

2. Look up the following members of David's household (verses 15-18): Abiathar (1 Samuel 22:20; 1 Chronicles 6:8, 52-53; 1 Kings 2:26-27,35.); Jehoshaphat (1 Kings 4:3); Zadok and Benaiah (1 Kings 1:8,26,etc.). Note the continuity with Solomon's reign.

2 SAMUEL 9

The first obstacle to David's seizure of Saul's throne is the existence of Jonathan's son Mephibosheth (Meribaal).

1. Read carefully the words and note the activities of Ziba. You will meet him again! In what way did he gain by the transaction?
2. Did David mean what he said about Saul's family? What was the position of Mephibosheth (Meribaal)?

2 SAMUEL 10

David extends his empire through victories over the Ammonites (in modern Jordan) and over the Syrians (Aramaeans).

1. What made Hanun's behaviour inexcusable?
2. What light does this chapter throw on Joab as a commander?

2 SAMUEL 11

The story of David's sin is incorporated into the account of the Ammonite Wars.

1. Where should David have been? See verse 1. At what stage did he sin?
2. Why did David try to persuade Uriah to go home?
3. Contrast verse 27 with 8:6,14. In the following chapters note down the consequences of David's adultery for the kingdom.

2 SAMUEL 12

The story of David's sin and repentance is concluded, and the account of the Ammonite wars resumed.

1. How did Nathan open David's eyes? What was David's response? Read Psalm 51.
2. Why should Bathsheba's child have died? See Q.2 on 2 Sam. 6.

2 SAMUEL 13

The birth of Solomon (2 Samuel 12:24) by no means settles the question of the succession. The writer records the elimination of Amnon, Absalom and Adonijah in turn. This chapter shows the fall of Amnon.

1. Notice the attention to psychological exactitude in the story of Amnon and Tamar. Compare the reaction of Amnon with that of Shechem in Genesis 34.
2. What were the reactions of a) Tamar, b) David, c) Absalom to the rape of Tamar?

2 SAMUEL 14

Absalom's mother was a Geshurite (2 Sam. 3:3), so he fled to his kinsfolk in Geshur.

1. Why do you think Joab intrigued to get the king to recall Absolom?
2. What details do we learn concerning Absalom? Why did David delay so long in receiving him after his recall?

2 SAMUEL 15

Absalom exploits the divisions between the northern tribes and Judah.

1. Notice carefully David's actions when he hears of Absalom's rebellion. Who are his friends at this juncture?
2. How did David plan his campaign? Did he seek God/s help?

2 SAMUEL 16

The story of David's flight is continued.

1. What light does Ziba's account of Mephibosheth's reaction shed on 2 Sam. 9:1-13?
2. David's behaviour in defeat always shows his greatness of soul. cf. 12:13, 16:10-11. What can we learn from David?

2 SAMUEL 17

The narrative increases in pace and in complexity.

1. How was David rewarded for his previous generosity? For Shobi look up 10:2, for Machir 9:4, for Barzillai 19:32.
2. Sort out who Amasa was from 17:25-26 and 1 Chron. 2:16-17. What relation was he a) to Absalom and b) to Joab?

2 SAMUEL 18

The death of Absalom brings a crisis in David's kingship.

1. What do you think of Joab's actions in this chapter?
2. Look back over Absalom's life. Did David have any responsibility for his fall from grace?

2 SAMUEL 19

The drama continues, and the war ends, leaving David once more in control, but an older man with less energy than formerly.

1. Consider Joab's advice to the king, and David's response. Are we always so honest with each other?
2. What signs are there in this chapter of continuing ill-feeling between Judah and the northern tribes?
3. What are we to make of Mephibosheth's response to David's victory? Was he sincere? cf. 16:1-4.

2 SAMUEL 20

The seeds of the destruction of David's kingdom under his grandson are being sown.

1. Why would the Benjaminites be especially antagonistic to David?
2. Compare the murder of Amasa with that of Abner (3:22 ff).
3. Compare the list of David's officials with 8:15-18. Notice one chilling addition.

2 SAMUEL 21-23

Chapters 21-24 are independent of the Succession Narrative and contain various traditions. Chapter 21 should probably follow Chapter 8.

1. This ancient song (23:1-7) gives us David's 'throne names': he is called son of Jesse, the man who was raised on high, the anointed of the God of Jacob, the sweet psalmist of Israel. Comment on each one.
2. Compare 23:3-4 with 23:5. What reasons are given for David's happiness and prosperity? Is there any conflict between the words of the song and the facts of David's career?

3. Consider David's response to the courage and loyalty of his followers.
4. Look up what is said in Chapter 23 about Abishai, Benaiah, Asahel, Uriah the Hittite, and compare it with what we know of them elsewhere.

2 SAMUEL 24

This narrative probably relates to events early in David's reign.

1. Compare 24:1 with 1 Chronicles 21:1. How does the Chronicler's theology show development on the problem of evil, suffering and sin?
2. Why was the census considered sinful?
3. Follow on a map the places covered by the survey.
4. How would you explain, theologically, the connection between the census and the pestilence?

AN INTRODUCTION TO 1 and 2 KINGS

This is again one work, the climax of the Deuteronomic history. It begins with the final section of the Succession Narrative (1-2). Then comes a long account of Solomon's reign, of his buildings, his wisdom, and his weaknesses. At his death, the kingdom was once more divided, and the author tells the story of each reign from Jeroboam I until the fall of Samaria in the case of the northern kingdom (Israel), and from Rehoboam until the fall of Jerusalem in the case of the southern kingdom (Judah). But the author is a theologian, not primarily a historian. His purpose is to demonstrate that Israel through all her kings had been unfaithful to the covenant, and therefore deserved the fate that befell her in 721 when the Assyrians deported thousands and destroyed the nation.

With regard to Judah, while their infidelity also brought punishment in the destruction of the Temple and of the city of Jerusalem by the Babylonians in 587, the author returns repeatedly to the promises made to David, and understands them to be not annulled but transformed.

This view of history is, of course, selective. Two of Israel's greatest kings, Omri and Jeroboam II, are dealt with in 15 verses! Every king of Israel, even those who reigned for a very short time, is described as unfaithful to the covenant; very few of the kings of Judah are commended, and these for their devotion to the Temple, rather than for their statesmanship.

However, besides his selective use of the annals of the kings of Israel and of Judah, the author draws largely on prophetic sources, and many of his most vivid stories are drawn from these circles, especially the ninth and eighth century accounts of Elijah and of Elisha. Without him, we would know virtually nothing of these great prophets.

1 KINGS 1

The Succession Narrative is resumed. The last of Solomon's rivals, Adonijah, is to be eliminated.

1. Reflect how God used such varied circumstances to bring about his design - the accession of Solomon, far from being the eldest son, to the throne of David. Make two lists, one of David's supporters, the other of Adonijah's. How far did personal rivalries decide the choice of faction?
2. Trace the physical and mental decline of David in this chapter. What should it teach us?

1 KINGS 2

The Succession Narrative is concluded in this chapter. The terrible task laid on Solomon to avenge his father's enemies was believed to be a sacred duty, according to the ideas of the time, lingering on in the story of Hamlet, for example.

1. What were the injunctions laid on Solomon by his father? Look up Barzillai 2 Sam. 17:27 ff. and 19.31 ff; for Shimei 2 Sam. 16:5 ff. and 19:16 ff. Why did Solomon have to slay Joab and Shimei if his father had spared them?
2. What big mistake did Adonijah make?

1 KINGS 3

The Succession Narrative and the stories of David's youth provided the sacred writer with plenty of colourful material. For the reign of Solomon he has to rely on the usual records and

chronicles, with a few legends. The theological preoccupations of the Deuteronomist immediately become prominent, with an emphasis on the evils of sacrificing 'at the high places'. See verse 2.

1. Solomon's name is associated above all with wisdom. What was the quality he prayed for (verse 9) and what was God's response?
2. How does the story of the two harlots illustrate Solomon's qualities as a ruler?

1 KINGS 4

The narrator uses lists from the royal archives to tell the story of Solomon's reign. He has no document comparable with the Succession Narrative.

1. Check the two lists of David's officials (2 Sam. 8: 15-18 and 2 Sam. 20: 23-26) with 1 Kings 4:1-6. Which of his father's officials did Solomon retain?
2. The writer gives an idyllic picture of life under Solomon. Are there any signs even here that it is not likely to last? What kind of wisdom is described? See verses 32-34.

1 KINGS 5-7

The building of Solomon's temple is the centre piece of his reign. His palace was equally magnificent.

1. What preparations did Solomon make for building the Temple? Notice 5:6, 15.
2. From chapters 6 and 7 work out the shape and dimensions of the Temple.
3. What theological notes are added to the account in 6:1,7,11-13?

1 KINGS 8

Solomon now completes his father's work by bringing the ark into the new Temple.

1. Verses 1-13. How was God's presence among his people symbolised? What symbols do we use in the Christian church?
2. Verses 15-21. In what way does Solomon emphasise God's eternal fidelity? How does the Church throughout the ages experience God's fidelity? cf.Matt. 16:18.
3. Verses 23-53. a) How does Solomon's prayer reconcile the transcendence of God (verse 27) with his presence in the Temple? b) What sins and disasters are listed? Can we make this prayer our own?
4. Verses 54-66. Can these verses be applied to the history of the Church? What gave the people of Israel their confidence in God?

1 KINGS 9

The writer once more uses material from the royal archives.

1. What warning is contained in Solomon's second vision of God?
2. Are there other elements in this chapter that warn us that all is not well?

1 KINGS 10

Sheba was in Arabia. The queen probably came to make a trading agreement with Solomon.

1. What were the reasons for the Queen of Sheba's visit?
2. What were Solomon's temptations? Are we in this century in the same kind of danger?

1 KINGS 11

The seeds of decline are discovered by the writer in the influence of foreign wives over a complaisant Solomon. It is perhaps more true to say that decline was inevitable, given the deep

divisions in the kingdom, and the over stretching of what was, after all, a small country. Israel's greatness lasted for less than a century.

1. List the causes of Solomon's decline. Why were foreign marriages so dangerous?
2. Trace Solomon's relationship with God (cf 3:1-14, 9:2-9, and 11:9-13).
3. Study carefully the background of Jeroboam. What part did the prophet Ahijah play? Compare Samuel's intervention with Saul and David.

1 KINGS 12

The underlying tension between Judah and Israel came to a head at Rehoboam's accession.

1. Rehoboam is presented as a 'foolish' son following a wise father (cf.Sirach 47:23). Is there anything to be said in his favour? Or did he make a difficult situation worse?
2. Why did Jeroboam set up new shrines at the ancient sanctuaries at Dan and Bethel? Is there anything to be said for a 'state church'. as, for example, was set up in several countries at the Reformation?

1 KINGS 13

The mention of Josiah's name makes this prophecy rather suspect. It probably originally consisted of verse 3 only.

1. Notice that there is a distinction made between a man of God and a prophet. Which in this story is of a lower grade?
2. What is the moral of the story and what is its theological purpose?

1 KINGS 14

The Books of Kings now record the histories of the divided kingdoms.

1. Why was Jeroboam and all his dynasty doomed, according to the author of Kings?
2. What facts are we given concerning the reign of Rehoboam? What light do they throw on the state of the kingdom and on Rehoboam's character?

1 KINGS 15

The sacred historian now records in parallel the history of the two kingdoms. This chapter deals with Abijam and Asa of Judah, and Nadab and Baasha in Israel.

1. Notice that Abijam and Asa were descended from a daughter of Absalom. Asa is approved by the historian. Why? What else do we learn about him?
2. How was Ahijah of Shiloh's prophecy concerning the house of Jeroboam fulfilled?

1 KINGS 16

The story of the kings of Israel is continued, with the successive reigns of Baasha, Elah, Zimri, Omri and Ahab.

1. Omri was one of the greatest of Israel's kings, so much so that in Assyrian records Israel is referred to as 'the land of Omri' long after his death. What do you learn of his accession to the throne, and of his achievements as king from this chapter?
2. Why was Ahab very especially condemned?

1 KINGS 17

Into the heavy chronicle of the kings of Israel is now inserted the great story of Elijah, taken from annals preserved in prophetic circles.

1. How can we learn faith and trust in God from the stories in this chapter?
2. What use did Jesus make of the story of the widow? See Luke 4:25-26

1 KINGS 18

The famous story of Elijah on Mount Carmel.

1. What is symbolised by the prophet's sudden disappearances? See especially verse 12.
2. Until now the prophets have been represented as supporting, guiding and warning the king. They are now (verse 17) seen as confronting him. On what issue does Elijah confront Ahab and Israel in this chapter? Are there prophets in our day?
3. Compare the scene described in verses 20-46, especially the people's attitude, with Exodus 24.
4. Read Sirach's summing up of Elijah's career (Sirach 48:1-11) and compare it point by point with the events described in this chapter.

1 KINGS 19

The call of Elijah at Horeb (Sinai) recalls Exodus themes.

1. Elijah 'went in the strength of that food forty days and forty nights' (verse 8). Consider this passage as describing a 'type' of the manna and of the Eucharist. Why did Elijah go to Horeb (Sinai)?
2. What were the tasks given to Elijah? Were they all carried out by him?
3. Compare verses 19-21 with Luke 9:61. What did Jesus imply by referring to this passage?

1 KINGS 20

This chapter records battles between Syria and Israel during the reign of Ahab.

1. What part is played by prophets in this chapter? In what light is Ahab now seen?
2. Compare verse 34 with the account of Omri's reign in 1 Kings 16: 23-28. What does it add to our information?

1 KINGS 21

The story of Naboth's vineyard.

1. Elijah now confronts the king on an issue of social justice. What is at stake? Is there an underlying principle for us all?
2. What impression have you formed of Ahab from chapters 20 and 21?

1 KINGS 22

Israel and Judah are now allies, as Ahab's daughter Athaliah has married Jehoshaphat's son Jehoram (2 Kings 8:18).

1. In what way were the prophets at Ahab's court suspect? Why did Ahab not want to consult Micaiah? Are we ever guilty of the same fault?
2. Jehoshaphat is praised by the historian (verses 43-46). What light does this chapter throw on his character? See especially verses 4-5, 7-8.

2 KINGS 1-2

Stories from the Elijah and Elisha collections, preserved in prophetic circles.

1. Why did Ahaziah consult Baal-ze-bub? Where is Ekron?
2. Did Elijah die? Look up the later references to him in the Bible, especially Malachi 4:5, Sirach 48: 9-11, Luke 1:17, Matt.17 1-13.
3. The mantle of Elijah falls on Elisha, the great miracle-worker. Compare 2 Kings 2:19-22 with Exodus 15:22-27. What is the significance of these miracles?

2 KINGS 3

War between Moab, and a coalition of Israel, Judah and Edom.

1. Compare this story with 1 Kings 18, where a water miracle also reveals God's power. What symbolism is conveyed by God's gift of water?
2. Follow the Moabite campaign on a map. Why did Israel need the help of Judah and of Edom?
3. What is the significance of the Israelites' withdrawal (verse 27)? Were they afraid of the god of Moab, or outraged at child-sacrifice, or was there another reason?

2 KINGS 4

Miracles from the Elisha collection.

1. What can we learn from the faith of the woman (verses 1-7)? What encouragement does Christ give us to trust God?
2. Elijah and Elisha both raised the dead to life (1 Kings 17:1-24 and 2 Kings 4:8-34). What are a) the similarities and b) the differences with regard to Jesus' three such miracles? cf.Mark 5:40-42; Luke 7:11-17; John 11).
3. Compare and contrast Elisha's multiplication of the loaves with Jesus' feeding miracles.

2 KINGS 5

The famous story of Naaman the Syrian, quoted by Jesus in Luke 4.

1. Notice that God guides the Syrians (verse 1) as he guides the Israelites. What other signs of this doctrine are there in this chapter?
2. What use did Jesus make of this story? See Luke 4.
3. What have we learnt about the character of Gehazi? cf. 2 Kings 4:18 ff. and 5:20 ff.

2 KINGS 6-7

Elisha and the Syrian Wars.

1. What do we learn from Elisha's faith and vision (6:15-20), his compassion and justice (6:22) and his influence on events?
2. The king evidently believed that Elisha's trust in God was going too far during the siege (6:31). What are we to learn from the outcome (7:3-18)?

2 KINGS 8

The writer now concludes his prophetic narratives, with short summaries of the lives of two kings of Judah, Jehoram and Ahaziah.

1. Draw out Elisha's many interventions in politics (2 Kings chapters 3, 6, 7 and 8:7-15). Are they in some ways ambiguous? What does this teach us about God's use of very human instruments?
2. What do we learn of the kings of Judah mentioned in this chapter?

2 KINGS 9

This blood thirsty story is recounted without theological comment, because the writer thinks of Jehu as a religious reformer, but the prophet Hosea thought otherwise (Hosea 1:4).

1. Notice the doom that fell upon the house of Ahab and why. Does our understanding of modern history (eg. the fall of the Third Reich) gain from reading these Bible stories?
2. Ponder the effects of royal marriage alliances on the kingdoms of Israel and of Judah.

2 KINGS 10

The story of Jehu is concluded.

1. Trace the course of Jehu's rise to power, and his reign in Samaria. His brutality horrifies us, and, in fact, his dynasty will fall in its turn (Jeremiah 1:4-5).
2. John Wesley quoted verse 15 in a letter concerning his relationship with Catholics. Can we too find nuggets of gold in the most unpromising chapters in the Old Testament?

2 KINGS 11

Jehosheba was the wife of Jehoiada the priest (2 Chronicles 22:11)

1. The story now passes to Judah. How were Jehosheba and Jehoiada God's instruments in reviving true worship in Judah?
2. What would have been the 'testament' or "covenant" (JB) put into the hands of Joash at his coronation? What evidence is there that this revolution was 'popular', whereas Jehu's was a 'coup'?

2 KINGS 12

The whole chapter is devoted to the activities of Jehoash of Judah.

1. How were the repairs to the Temple to be financed?
2. The account of Joash's reign is incomplete. Look up 2 Chronicles 24 for further details.

2 KINGS 13

The writer continues his chronicle of the two kingdoms: Jehoahaz of Israel, and Jehoash his successor, during whose reign Elisha dies.

1. What evidence is there that during the reign of Jehoahaz of Israel the country was greatly impoverished? What reason is given for this?
2. What is signified by the events recorded during the last illness of Elisha?

2 KINGS 14

Two kings: Amaziah of Judah and Jeroboam II of Israel.

1. The historian's refrain is repeated faithfully for each king, but the information given in this chapter for Amaziah and for Jeroboam II seems to contradict it. Pick out instances in each case.
2. What evidence is there that Jeroboam II was a very able ruler?

2 KINGS 15

The long reign of Uzziah of Judah coincided with a series of short reigns in Israel.

1. Notice the comparative stability of Judah, whereas Israel had a succession of kings in a short space of time. Why was this?
2. What evidence do we have that a great power has arisen and is threatening Israel?

2 KINGS 16

The reign of Ahaz in Judah. This account is supplemented in Isaiah chapters 7 and 8.

1. In what respects was Ahaz a strong contrast to his father Jotham and to his grandfather Azariah? What signs are there that he lacked political wisdom?
2. How do you react to the fact that it was the King (Ahaz) who consecrated the new altar in the Temple, and not Uriah the priest? What does this tell us about Temple worship in Judah at that time?

2 KINGS 17

This chapter marks the end of the kingdom of Israel (Samaria).

1. Note the stages by which the people of Israel fell from grace, especially verses 9-18.
2. Explain the theology of verses 24-41. Why did the settlers wish to worship Yahweh?

2 KINGS 18

The narrator is now concerned only with the kingdom of Judah.

1. What were the qualities and virtues of Hezekiah?
2. What arguments were used by the Assyrian officials to break the morale of the people of Jerusalem?

2 KINGS 19

This chapter is repeated in Isaiah 37, with some differences.

1. What actions did Hezekiah take in this crisis?
2. Study the prayer of Hezekiah (verses 15-19). Notice how he lays the affair before God. Do we look in the Bible for models of prayer? Can you find others?
3. What title is given to God by a) Hezekiah and b) Isaiah?
4. Of what sin is Assyria accused? What happened to Sennacherib's army?

2 KINGS 20

The events in this chapter occurred before the Assyrian invasion. This chapter is repeated in Isaiah 38-39.

1. Isaiah is called in as a healer. What methods does he use?
2. What do we learn of Hezekiah's character from these episodes?

2 KINGS 21

The reigns of Manasseh and Amon marked a low point in the religious history of Judah.

1. What were the crimes of Manasseh?
2. What was the punishment? See also Jeremiah 15:4. In what way do very evil rulers leave effects many years after them? Have there been any examples in this century?

2 KINGS 22

The Book discovered in the Temple was almost certainly Deuteronomy.

1. What was Josiah's first task? See verses 3-7. What does this teach us about priorities?
2. Why was the prophetess Huldah consulted?

2 KINGS 23

The finding of the Law led to religious reform and to extension of Judaean influence into the Northern Kingdom, where Assyrian influence was in decline.

1. How did Josiah set about reform? What do we learn of the state of religion in Judah from this chapter?
2. See Jeremiah's comment on the extent and success of Josiah's reform (Jer. 3:10 and Jer.11: 1-17)
3. Josiah was killed at the Battle of Megiddo at the age of 39. The prophetess Huldah had foretold this as a blessing (22.20). Why?

2 KINGS 24

The last years of the Kingdom of Judah are described in more detail by the prophet Jeremiah.

1. Jehoiakim is frequently mentioned by Jeremiah. See Jer. 23:13-19 for an unfavourable comparison with his father Josiah. What information does this add to that recorded in this chapter?
2. What was notable about the deportation to Babylon in Jehoiachin's reign?

2 KINGS 25

The writer gives a rapid account of the fall of Jerusalem and the end of the Kingdom of Judah.

1. The great Deuteronomic History, which began with Judges, ends with the sack of Jerusalem, the destruction of the Temple and the end of the monarchy. What lessons does the historian draw from this saga?
2. What star of hope glimmers right at the end?

AN INTRODUCTION
TO
THE BOOKS OF CHRONICLES

If you are using the Douai or Knox Bible these books are there called Paralipomena 'of things left out'. Having read the great work of the Deuteronomist, one may be surprised to find another historical work covering much the same ground, but, if we read these books carefully, we find considerable differences. To begin with, they only deal with the history of Judah; secondly, they omit the succession narrative which so enlivened 2 Samuel; thirdly, they show great preoccupation with the Temple, its building, its liturgy and its staff. The author of Chronicles was a Levite of Jerusalem, writing about 300 BC, and his aim is to edify. He presents a theology of Israel - the community of God's faithful people with whom God has made a covenant, renewed in the person of David.

In his selection of sources, he focuses on the history of David - omitting his sin with Bathsheba - on the preparations for and building of the Temple, which he sees as having been begun by David and completed by Solomon. The later kings are assessed according to their fidelity to the Temple and to the example set by David, and while the story of the fall of Jerusalem is recorded, the work ends with Cyrus' permission to rebuild the temple.

There are beautiful prayers in this book and some inspiring passages. One of my favourites is 2 Chronicles 7:14, and another is 2 Chronicles 15:12. It has been called a dull, and even a forgotten book, but it repays study. Its theology is more developed than that of Kings, and modern scholars are beginning to note its historical value. I love it. I read it again and again, and find something new nearly every time.

1 CHRONICLES 1

The use of genealogies to write history is frequent in the Bible, even in the New Testament (cf. Matt. 1 and Luke 3). Here the author selects carefully from Genesis to recount the history of the ancestors of Abraham.

1. Among the sons of Shem, trace the line that ends with Abraham.
2. Compare the lists in this chapter with Genesis 5.

1 CHRONICLES 2

The Chronicler begins with Judah because he is largely concerned with David, who was of the tribe of Judah.

1. Why is Achar (verse 7) called the troubler of Israel? Look up his story in Joshua 7.
2. Make a list of familiar characters found in verses 9-20.
3. From verse 42 what indication is there of the home of the Calebites? Find further geographical details in verses 50-53, looking up the names on the map.

1 CHRONICLES 3

The list now reaches David and his household, his descendants to the exile and beyond.

1. Make a list of all the women mentioned in this chapter, and check out how much you know of each one.
2. Compare verses 10-24 with Matt. 1:6-16. How much do we learn of Jesus' ancestors in this chapter?

1 CHRONICLES 4

An alternative genealogy of the Judah tribes, possibly a later version but using ancient material.

1. In what way can Jabez be an inspiration to us? See verses 9-10.
2. What types of people were the descendants of Shelah of Judah? See verses 21-23. Would they have been Canaanites? See Genesis 38.
3. Where did the Simeonites settle? See verses 24-43. What else do we know of Simeon? See Genesis 34.

1 CHRONICLES 5

Lists of Reuben, Gad and the half-tribe of Manasseh - the tribes in Transjordan. To these have been added the lineage of Levi.

1. What two reasons does the Chronicler give for the displacement of Reuben as first-born?
2. Trace the fortunes of the Reubenites, the Gadites and the half-tribe of Manasseh as recounted in this chapter. In what way does their history mirror that of the whole of Israel?

1 CHRONICLES 6

The line of Levi is continued.

1. In what way does the Chronicler associate the priesthood of his day with the worship in the desert? See verses 31-50.
2. What do we learn of the Levites in this chapter?

1 CHRONICLES 7

Census lists for Issachar, Benjamin, Manasseh, Ephraim and Asher - all northern tribes.

1. List the tribes mentioned in this chapter, and locate them on a map of Northern Palestine.
2. List the women mentioned, and look up Bilhah (verse 13) in Genesis 30:6-8.

1 CHRONICLES 8

Another list of the Benjaminites, which introduces Saul. At last the story is beginning to get going!

1. What indications are there in this chapter that Benjamin was an important tribe?
2. Look up 2 Sam. 1:22; 1 Chron. 12:2; 2 Chron. 14:8 and compare with 1 Chron. 8:40. What do all these verses tell us about the Benjaminites?

1 CHRONICLES 9

This chapter, containing a list of returned exiles to Jerusalem, seems to have been added to the book at a later date.

1. The Chronicler pictures Jerusalem as populated by all the tribes. New Testament speaks of a heavenly city, a new Jerusalem (Hebrews 12:22 and Rev. 21:2). In what way is Jerusalem a) a symbol of the Church, and b) of heaven?
2. The Chronicler concludes his genealogies with that of Saul (verses 35-44), repeating a list he had already given in 8:29-40. What is he conveying by placing Saul's family here?

1 CHRONICLES 10

The Chronicler recounts the story of Saul as a prelude to the history of David and his descendants.

1. The story is told briefly and in entirely negative terms. Draw out each stage in it.

2. Study carefully verses 13-14. What particular failings of Saul are emphasised?

1 CHRONICLES 11

The story of David now begins. The Chronicler selects material from the Books of Samuel.

1. This is theology, using, rather than recording, history. What aspects of the story of David's accession and of his conquest of Jerusalem are brought out?
2. What instances are given of the loyalty and courage of David's followers? Can they in any sense be an example for Christian disciples?

1 CHRONICLES 12

This chapter has no parallel in Samuel.

1. What qualities does the Chronicler emphasise in those who followed David? What did David demand from them?
2. How did the Spirit inspire Amasai?

1 CHRONICLES 13

Having shown the whole of Israel united round David, the Chronicler now centres his interest on the sanctuary.

1. Compare verses 1-3 with the account in 2 Sam. 6:2-11. What has the Chronicler added?
2. Describe David's emotion during the scene.

1 CHRONICLES 14

A brief account of David's household and campaigns, selected sparingly from 2 Samuel. The Chronicler is concerned largely with the cult.

1. How does God intervene in David's life? Is there any parallel in mine?
2. Why were the Philistines alarmed at David's becoming king?

1 CHRONICLES 15

The Chronicler emphasises the part played by the Levites in the ceremonies connected with the ark.

1. To what does the Chronicler attribute the disaster at Perrez-Uzzah (13:11)? See verse 13. Is this different from the reason given in 2 Samuel 6?

1 CHRONICLES 16

The Chronicler quotes from three psalms (Pss 105,96 and 106) to illustrate the Temple liturgy as he imagines it to have been in David's time, even before the building of the Temple.

1. What do we learn from this chapter about joy in the service and worship of God?
2. List the causes for thanksgiving in the psalms quoted, ie. Psalms 105, 96 and 106.

1 CHRONICLES 17

The Chronicler has taken over Nathan's prophecy in 2 Samuel 7 in its entirety.

1. What do we learn from this passage of the importance of the Messianic hope based on David's dynasty?
2. Consider David at prayer. Follow the course of his prayer from his position at the outset (verse 16) through blessing, thanksgiving and praise to his final petition. Use this form of prayer to celebrate God's action in my life.

1 CHRONICLES 18

Only David's military victories are recorded by the Chronicler.

1. To whom is attributed David's military success? Is this glorification of war, or a genuine faith attitude on the part of the writer?
2. Compare the list of David's officials with that at 2 Samuel 8:15-18. What differences or clarifications do you find?

1 CHRONICLES 19-20

Selected material from 2 Samuel.

1. Look up David's campaign on a map.
2. Compare these two chapters with 2 Samuel 10-12,21. What omissions or amendments has the Chronicler made? Why?

1 CHRONICLES 21

This episode, taken from 2 Samuel, has been placed here by the Chronicler, as an introduction to the building of the Temple, as it refers to the building of an altar on the eventual site of the Temple.

1. Notice the developed theology of Satan and of angels in verses 1-16. How does it compare with 2 Samuel 24?
2. Meditate on the gesture of Ornan and compare him with the rich young man (Matt. 19:16-22). Which is a model for Christian discipleship?

1 CHRONICLES 22

This chapter has no counterpart in 2 Samuel or 1 Kings, but it may incorporate historical material from another source.

1. List the preparations made by David for the building of the Temple. Can we in any way apply their spirit to our own lives? Note especially verse 2.
2. What qualities does David pray for his son Solomon to be given?

1 CHRONICLES 23

The Chronicler always shows great interest in the Levites, whose function of bearing the ark is to become obsolete with the building of the Temple. Their new role will be to assist the priests at liturgical celebrations.

1. Contrast the spirit shown here in building a temple for the worship of God with that described by Malachi (Malachi1:6-14). Which spirit is most prevalent today? Which is my habitual frame of mind?
2. What were the duties of the Levites? See verses 25-32. Are my duties those described in verse 26 or those in verses 28 ff? If the latter, am I content?

1 CHRONICLES 24-27

The details concerning the order of services and functionaries of the Temple probably reflect a much later period, but the Chronicler insists that all derives from the time of David.

1. Notice the meaning of the word 'to prophesy' (25:1, 2, 3 etc) in the understanding of the Chronicler. What other meaning has the word?
2. Is there any sense in which all this ritual can be said to have remained in our liturgy? In what sense?
3. Study the account of David's personal advisers (27:32-34). How many of them can we identify?
4. What do 27:16-31 tell us about David's kingdom?

1 CHRONICLES 28

This chapter continues the narrative from Chapter 22.

1. Who is the real author of David's plans for the Temple? Consider verses 1-2, and verse 8. What is symbolised, and what is its significance for the whole project?
2. What were the two charges laid on Solomon (verses 9, 10, 20, 21). Translate these into your own life pattern.

1 CHRONICLES 29

The story of David's reign fittingly concludes with his gift for the construction of the Temple and his prayer of blessing.

1. What were the main sources of finance for the building of the Temple? What does this tell us about the intentions of the contributors?
2. Consider David's prayer. What does it tell us of David? What does he say of God?
3. This is David's last testament. What lessons do we draw from it about old age?
4. In what way does the Chronicler's account of Solomon's accession (verses 21-30) mirror the story of the covenant (Exodus 24)?

2 CHRONICLES 1

The Chronicler emphasises the glory and wealth of Solomon, as he emphasised the success and achievements of David.

1. Notice how the Chronicler emphasises the continuity of the Davidic dynasty and of the Temple with the Mosaic institutions. List the different references.
2. In what way does the Chronicler use the story of Solomon's vision to emphasise the glory of the new reign?

2 CHRONICLES 2

The preparations for the building of the Temple.

1. Show how the Chronicler makes use of Exodus 26 and 31 in describing the preparations for the building. What is he seeking to convey?
2. Consider verses 4-6. What advance theologically is shown on 1 Kings 5:5?
3. Who were to be the actual workmen? (and cf. 1 Kings 5:13).
4. 'The glory of the Lord filled the house of God'. How is this true a) of the ecclesia - assembly, and b) of our own hearts?

2 CHRONICLES 3-5

The building of the Temple and the transferring of the ark are described.

1. Why do you think the Chronicler, after giving so much information concerning the preparations, gives relatively little space to the account of the actual building, and indeed, abridges 1 Kings?
2. What is said at the singing at the dedication of the Temple (5:11-13)? What place should singing have in our worship?
3. What do you think is a) the literal and b) the symbolic meaning of 5:14?

2 CHRONICLES 6

This chapter is based on 1 Kings 8.

1. The Temple is the sign of God's presence among his people. In what sense are our Churches a similar sign?
2. At the feast of a Dedication of a church what different modes of God's presence are celebrated? In the new covenant who is God's temple? (cf. 1 Cor. 3:16-17). Do we live this?
3. What is the essential quality for our prayer to be genuine? See especially verse 28.

2 CHRONICLES 7

The Chronicler's own conclusion to the account in 1 Kings 8. He re-introduces a theophany.

1. What was God's great promise (verse 14)? Do we take this to heart? Do we make it the basis of prayer for ourselves, for the Church, for our country?
2. Apply God's warning to the individual soul, and compare with Jesus' teaching (Matt. 12:43-44).

2 CHRONICLES 8-9

The account of Solomon's reign is concluded, with all references to the great king's weaknesses omitted.

1. Why did Solomon move Pharaoh's daughter into a separate house? Because she was a foreigner, or because she was a woman?
2. How does the Chronicler interpret God's glory?
3. What aspects of Solomon's character and of his reign have been omitted by the Chronicler? What does this indicate about his purpose?

2 CHRONICLES 10-11

The account of the division of the kingdoms is based on 1 Kings 12, but the Chronicler introduces independent material concerning Rehoboam (Chapter 11).

1. What were the reasons for the division of the kingdom? Were there any advantages for Judah?
2. Why do you think the number of Rehoboam's wives (not mentioned in Kings) is dwelt on? Does the Chronicler present Rehoboam as *merely* a 'foolish' king?

2 CHRONICLES 12

The account of Rehoboam's reign is concluded.

1. What was the contribution of the prophet Shemaiah? Do we learn new facts not recorded in Kings? Read the chapter in the light of verse 15.
2. How does the Chronicler summarise Rehoboam's character and reign? Do you think he is quite fair to him, given verses 6,12?

2 CHRONICLES 13

It is well to compare each reign with the information given in Kings. For this chapter see 1 Kings 15:1-8. The Chronicler records only the history of the Kings of Judah.

1. In what ways did Abijah set his confidence on the legitimacy of Judah's worship? Do his arguments in any way apply to claims made in Christian terms in our own day?
2. What gave the armies of Judah victory over the Israelites?

2 CHRONICLES 14-16

The reign of Asa of Judah is recorded, with new material not found in 1 Kings.

1. Compare the small space given to Asa in 1 Kings 15:9-24 with that devoted to him by the Chronicler. What are the virtues of this king that are highlighted in chapters 14-16?
2. What are the different points of Azariah's message? See 15:2-7.
3. The people made a covenant together (15:12) to seek the Lord God. Can we take inspiration from them? How could this text be used for marriage liturgy? Can you think of any other occasions in which Christians could make such a covenant?
4. To what does the Chronicler attribute Asa's fall from grace? See chapter 16. How often do we fall in similar ways?

2 CHRONICLES 17

For Jehoshaphat, see 1 Kings 15:24. This king is portrayed as an ideal warrior for Yahweh.

1. What was the fundamental reason, according to the Chronicler, for Jehoshaphat's success?
2. How did he instruct the people in the Law? Can the modern Church learn from him?

2 CHRONICLES 18

This chapter is based on 1 Kings 22.

1. Compare verses 18-22 with Job 1:6 ff. What kind of a picture of God and his heavenly court was in the mind of the authors? What truths do they both seek to convey?
2. Compare the account in 1 Kings 22:29-34 with Chron. 18:28-34. What characteristic details are added by the Chronicler?

2 CHRONICLES 19

The prophet Jehu is nowhere else mentioned. The reforms of Jehoshaphat are based on an independent source.

1. What evidence is there in these chapters of Jehoshaphat's organising abilities?
2. What values does he inculcate in his subjects at all levels?
3. What is the principle that Jehoshaphat had violated, according to the prophet Jehu? See verses 1-3. How should we interpret this principle today?

2 CHRONICLES 20

Compare 1 Kings 22:41-49. The Chronicler adds material from another tradition.

1. What was Jehoshaphat's first recourse when trouble came?
2. Compare the king's prayer with that of Solomon (6:1 ff.) and with that of Hezekiah (2 Kings 19:14 ff). What points are found in all three prayers?
3. Notice that Jehoshaphat did not forget to give thanks. What forms did his thanksgiving take? Compile a thanksgiving liturgy from elements in this chapter.

2 CHRONICLES 21

The reign of Jehoram is described, based largely on 2 Kings 8.

1. List the reverses suffered by Jehoram. What reasons are given by the Chronicler?
2. Compare this account with 2 Kings 8:16-24. Make a list of the crimes added by the Chronicler.

2 CHRONICLES 22

The story of Ahaziah is based on 2 Kings 8 and 11.

1. How far can the low state of Judah under Kings Jehoram and Azariah be attributed to Jehoshaphat's action recorded in 18:1? How is this underlined in this chapter?
2. How was the principle enunciated in 19:1-3 vindicated in this chapter?

2 CHRONICLES 23-24

The details inserted by the Chronicler into the record in 2 Kings 11 are of great interest and historical value.

1. Notice the Chronicler's emphasis on Davidic institutions in chapter 23. See verses 3,9,18. In what ways does his version of events differ from the author of 2 Kings 11? Does his interpretation shed light?
2. What was the principal cause of Joash's decline?

2 CHRONICLES 25

The Chronicler gives new information (vv 5-16), elaborating on 2 Kings 14, and throwing light on a campaign against Edom.

1. Notice the influence of prophets. What advice was given in each case? What principles lay behind the advice in verses 7-8 and 15?
2. What kind of man was Amaziah? See verses 2-4, 7-10, 14-16.

2 CHRONICLES 26

Uzziah was one of Judah's great kings. The Chronicler gives us information of considerable interest, supplementing 2 Kings 14-15.

1. Compare the account of Uzziah (Azariah)'s reign in 2 Kings 15:1-7. List the information given by the Chronicler concerning Uzziah's campaigns.
2. 'He loved the soil'. This is an unusual comment. What evidence is there of Uzziah's aims and interests?
3. What sin led to his downfall?

2 CHRONICLES 27-28

The reigns of Jotham and Ahaz are recorded in 2 Kings 15-16 and in Isaiah 7-9. However, the Chronicler writes from a somewhat different perspective.

1. What is the reason, do you think, for the Chronicler's somewhat different verdict on Jotham from that of 2 Kings 15:32-38?
2. Compare the accounts of the Syro-Ephraimite War (28:5 ff.) with 2 Kings 16, noting the differences. In what ways is the Chronicler's verdict even darker than the earlier writer's?
3. Oded's influence caused an act of almost unprecedented generosity. What can we learn from this?
4. Give some examples of Ahaz' lack of faith.

2 CHRONICLES 29

Hezekiah, with Asa and Jehoshaphat is one of the Chronicler's favourite kings. For a different view, see Isaiah 22.

1. What can we learn from the example of Hezekiah's public confession on behalf of the nation? Does our nation need a liturgy of penance or healing today?

2. How does the cultic purification of the Temple reflect a true desire for right worship of God? Note especially verses 10,30,31,36. Is there still a place for public acts of penance?

2 CHRONICLES 30

This is a very important chapter with signs of the influence of Hosea. cf. v.9 with Hosea 3:1-5, and the use of prophetic language of 'seeking' God (v.19) and 'returning' (v.9).

1. Notice that Hezekiah wanted to involve the whole of Israel as well as Judah in the Passover. What was the response from the North?
2. Notice Hezekiah's remarkable emphasis on purity of heart rather than on mere outward legal purity (verses 18-20). What did Jesus have to say on these lines (cf. Matt. 15:1-20)?

2 CHRONICLES 31

Hezekiah is portrayed as performing the functions of a true king, in succession to David and Solomon.

1. Notice Hezekiah's thoroughness in every way. What was the secret of his success? See verses 20-21.
2. What can we learn from this chapter a) about tithing and b) about the careful use of supplies given to charity?

2 CHRONICLES 32

The account of Hezekiah's reign is concluded, with some interesting side-lights on his character.

1. What were Hezekiah's preparations against the invasions of Judah? Are they in character?
2. Study the Chronicler's comments (verses 24-26,31) on the events dealt with at length in 2 Kings 20. How does he sum up the less favourable aspects of Hezekiah's character?

2 CHRONICLES 33

The account of Manasseh's captivity is not in 2 Kings 21, nor is it mentioned in extant Assyrian records, but this does not mean it did not happen. In fact, there is a hint in an Assyrian text that several vassal princes were taken to Assyria, and Manasseh may have been among them.

1. Make a list of Manasseh's activities (verses 3-9). By reintroducing Assyrian religious practices, he was evidently trying to curry favour with a very great power. Can you think of any modern parallels?
2. In what ways did God intervene in Manasseh's life?
3. What signs of Manasseh's repentance are given?

2 CHRONICLES 34

The Chronicler's chronology of Josiah's reign may be more accurate than the order in 2 Kings 22-23.

1. Notice the order in which Josiah undertook reforms - first political extension of power from Judah into Israel (verses 3-7) - then religious - the purification of the Temple (verses 8-13). What light does this throw on the account given in 2 Kings 22-23?
2. In what way does the prophetess Huldah proclaim God's hatred of sin?

2 CHRONICLES 35

The Chronicler's account of the Passover is based on Deuteronomy 16, and probably on the celebrations that took place in his own time. He gives additional information on the death of Josiah.

1. Draw out the details of Passover described in 10-18. In what ways does the Chronicler associate the ceremonies with a Messianic banquet? Does this chapter in any way throw light on the New Testament accounts of the Last Supper?
2. Study the account of Josiah's death. In what way does it explain 2 Kings 23?

2 CHRONICLES 36

The Chronicler summarises very briefly the material contained in 2 Kings 23-25 and in Jeremiah 37-39. He is above all a prophet of hope, so does not emphasise the darker aspect of history.

1. In the indictment of the kings in this chapter, on what sin does the emphasis lie? Compare Jeremiah 22:10-30. What dimension is supplied by the prophet?
2. In what particular matters did Zedekiah fail?
3. On what note does the Chronicler end his account? How does this reveal his central theme?

AN INTRODUCTION TO EZRA – NEHEMIAH

The Chronicler continued his work, after passing over in silence the period of exile in Babylon, with the story of the return to Jerusalem and the rebuilding of the Temple. For this he drew on memoirs composed by Ezra the scribe and Nehemiah the high commissioner of Jerusalem, but he has taken extracts from them without apparent regard for chronological order, and this has proved very confusing to historians. However, his intention was not to write history, but to present the events in such a way as to make his own point clear: that the Temple was rebuilt and Jerusalem reconstructed against all the odds.

The main subject for Ezra 1-6 is the rebuilding of the Temple under Darius; the successive returns from Babylon are all simplified and told as one series of events; Sheshbazzar (Ezra 1: 8-11 and 5: 14-16) the governor of Judah is ignored to throw Zerubbabel, grandson of King Jehoiachin, into prominence; various hostile attacks from Samaritans are grouped together. Ezra and Nehemiah are portrayed as working side by side. Thus this is a book full of hope. Ezra, the father of Judaism, dominates it with his doctrines of the chosen people, the Temple, the Law. Nehemiah restored and repopulated Jerusalem, trusting in God through all difficulties.

This book, together with the prophecies of Zechariah, Haggai and Malachi, remains as a lasting source of confidence for the Church, the people of God. However long the exile, the future is full of promise.

EZRA 1

The kings of Persia were very generous to the temples of all their subject peoples, and seem to have equated Yahweh 'the God of heaven' with the god whom they too worshipped.

1. In what ways does God move in the events of history to bring about his purposes?
2. What practical steps were taken by Cyrus in planning the rebuilding of the Temple in Jerusalem?

EZRA 2

This list is also found in Nehemiah 7, with small differences. It is used here for the history of the return of the Jews from exile.

1. Who were Zerubbabel and Joshua (verse 2)? cf.Haggai 1:1 and Matt. 1:12. What was the value of the list of names? cf especially verses 59-63.
2. What impression is the Chronicler conveying by the details in this chapter?

EZRA 3

The full ritual is described, in celebration of the return to Jerusalem.

1. We are told (verse 2) that the returned exiles built the altar, though the altar in the Temple (cf. Jeremiah 41:5) had not been destroyed by the Babylonians. What does this tell us about the importance of a fresh start? Why were the Jews afraid of the 'peoples of the lands' (verse 3. cf.4:4)?
2. Compare verses 10-11 with 2 Chronicles 5: 11-13. What did the writer intend to re-inforce by this comparison?
3. What were the emotions aroused by the rebuilding? See verse 12. Can you think of any experiences of restoration or reconstruction in your own life? What is the message of such events?

EZRA 4

The Persians had organised Samaria into a province to which Judah was attached. The 'adversaries' referred to in verse 1 and the 'people of the land' in verse 4 would have been the descendants of the mixed population that had remained in Israel and Judah during the period of the exile, who had collaborated with the foreign rulers.

1. Verses 1-5. What can we learn from this passage concerning religious disputes? Was Zerubbabel right, in your view, to refuse any help from local people?
2. Verses 7-24. The local Persian authorities objected to the rebuilding of Jerusalem. What arguments did they use? What is the theological purpose of the selection of material for this chapter by the author? What impression is he trying to give?

EZRA 5

The date is 520 BC.

1. The early fervour of the returned exiles had evaporated, and the buildings lay in ruins for about twenty years. How did God reanimate the project?
2. Notice the importance of prophetic influence (verses 1-2; 6:14 and cf. Haggai 1-2 for further details). In what way are prophets needed in the renewal of the church today?

EZRA 6

The Chronicler describes the completion of the Temple and the celebration of Passover. The date is 515 BC.

1. What forces joined together to allow the rebuilding of the Temple to get under way at last? What does this teach us about God's use of people and events?
2. What means were used to celebrate the re-dedication? What is the keynote?

EZRA 7

Some sixty years have elapsed since the end of chapter 6.

1. Notice the descent of Ezra from Aaron and Eleazar. What else are we told about him? See especially verse 10.
2. What were the main provisions for Judah and Jerusalem made by Artaxerxes?

EZRA 8

The list of heads of families seems to have been inserted to emphasise the legitimacy of the Jerusalem priesthood, 'the sons of Aaron'.

1. What preparations did Ezra make for his journey? See especially verses 15-16, 21, 28, 36. How should we prepare for great ventures in our lives?
2. Would it have been wrong for Ezra to have asked for an escort? See verses 22-23. What do you think?

EZRA 9

Ezra's rigidity over foreign marriages seems to us excessive, but the majority of the returned exiles were probably single men, who, by marrying Gentile wives, would be less likely to pass on their faith in Yahweh to their children, especially as the land had been under foreign occupation for more than a century.

1. What was Ezra's reaction to the news of the Jews' infidelity to God?
2. Similarly, should we feel horror at the sinfulness of our century? Can we take example from Ezra and intercede? What is the essential preliminary to all intercession? cf. verses 3 and 6.

EZRA 10

Ezra's measures against foreign marriages are recorded, and the chapter ends with a list of culprits, which includes many priests!

1. Why was Ezra so severe about foreign marriages? Are there circumstances when Christians should forbid marriages with non-Christians?
2. What do we learn from this episode of the cost of repentance?
3. Are there any signs in the Bible of a different attitude to foreigners?

NEHEMIAH 1

Nehemiah was cupbearer to the Persian King, Artaxerxes 1 (464-423 BC).

1. What was the situation in Jerusalem (about 446 BC)?
2. What can we learn from Nehemiah's prayer for his people? Note its structure, his knowledge of scripture (cf. Deut. 7 and 2 Chron. 6).

NEHEMIAH 2

Jerusalem had been sacked by the Babylonians in 587 BC, and its Temple destroyed. The walls seem to have been in ruins ever since, and the province of Judea governed from Samaria.

1. Notice Nehemiah's faith as he speaks to the King, asking God's guidance (verse 4). Do we consciously seek God when engaged in difficult or crucial conversations?
2. What do we learn of Nehemiah in this chapter? How did he cope with setbacks?

NEHEMIAH 3

This information is clearly historical, based probably on a contemporary document.

1. Follow the construction of the walls of the city on a map of Jerusalem.
2. What can we learn from co-operation described? Were there any backsliders?

NEHEMIAH 4

The Samaritans were jealous of the returned Jews, and alarmed at the restoration of Jerusalem. The antagonism between Jews and Samaritans which continued until the time of Christ, sprang from national and religious causes, the Samaritans being descendants of Assyrian and other peoples planted in the Northern Kingdom from 721 BC. They were not recognised as fellow Jews. A Northern Ireland situation!

1. Notice the effect on the morale of the Jews of the opposition of their neighbours (verse 10). How did Nehemiah deal with this crisis?
2. What do we learn from the attitude of the builders, each with one hand at work and one on his weapon (verse 17)? What does this teach us about vigilance against spiritual enemies?

NEHEMIAH 5

Nehemiah's difficulties as governor are recounted vividly.

1. What social evil did Nehemiah put right and by what means? What should be our attitude to social problems?
2. What qualities made Nehemiah an excellent governor? See especially verse 15.
3. What do we learn of his reactions to injustice? Does he come across as humane, or boastful?

NEHEMIAH 6

This chapter continues the story begun in Chapter 4. It hints at a hope that Nehemiah would become king.

1. Nehemiah's enemies now intrigue against him, offering to confer with him, and, at his refusal, spreading rumours against him. Nehemiah is unmoved. What is the source of his strength? What may we learn from his refusal to enter into any parleyings with danger? Contrast Genesis 3:1-5.
2. The prophet Shemaiah seems to have been in Tobiah's pay. What test of true prophecy did he fail? cf: Deut. 18 and Jer 23.

NEHEMIAH 7

The list in Ezra 2 is repeated here.

1. Why was Hananiah put in charge of Jerusalem? See verse 2.
   What qualities did Nehemiah value in leaders?
2. What steps were taken to repopulate the city? See verse 5.

NEHEMIAH 8

This chapter follows Ezra 8:36 chronologically. It celebrates the birth of Judaism, the religion of the Jews based on study of and observance of the Torah (Law).

1. With what did the great religious revival begin? Compare the scene a) with our own liturgical readings from scripture and b) with a modern revivalist meeting.
2. What were the reactions of the people to the reading of the Bible ? cf. Psalm 119: 71.

NEHEMIAH 9

This chapter follows Ezra 10:44. The sin of contracting a foreign marriage is expiated by public penance. The psalm quoted is Psalm 78. The material is taken from Genesis and Exodus.

1. Compare this scene with a Christian penitential rite or with a revivalist rally.
2. Meditate on God's great saving acts, as in this lament. Transpose the scene to your own life.
3. Go through the lament, underlining what we learn of God's forgiving heart. Does God act only in PUNISHMENT when we sin?

NEHEMIAH 10

The list is taken from the Temple archives.

1. List the obligations the people undertook in renewal of covenant. What were their priorities?
2. What elements would we include in a covenant renewal? Make a list a) for parish or diocesan renewal, and b) for interchurch renewal.

NEHEMIAH 11-12

Further material from the Temple archives.

1. Jerusalem was still underpopulated. By what two methods was this problem overcome? cf:11:1.2. Am I willing to be chosen, or even to volunteer for service in the community, or do I opt for a quiet life?
2. How did the people celebrate the dedication of the wall? (12:27 ff.) Follow their route on a plan of Jerusalem.
3. What general impression is given of Judah and its people under Nehemiah's governorship?

NEHEMIAH 13

The Chronicler concludes his work with a summary of Nehemiah's achievements.

1. Tobiah and Sanballat had succeeded in gaining access to the interior of the Temple (cf. verses 4-5 and 28). What does this symbolise? cf. Matt. 12: 43-45.
2. What actions did Nehemiah take to ensure a) regular support of the Levites, and b) respect for the Sabbath?
3. Why was he so severe about mixed marriages?

AN INTRODUCTION
TO
THE BOOK OF ESTHER

> But at Purim the more noise the better. As the Rabbi recounted the famous story of Esther, we booed with all our might every time the name Haman was mentioned, and cheered loudly for Esther and Mordecai. Cheder once inflicted a Purim play on the parents. Mr. Rosenberg gave me permission to join another class for the great event. I was so excited. Stardom at last! And then I realised I was only wanted as a walk-on extra, a Babylonian soldier. They are not even mentioned in the story.
> *(Michele Guinness. Child of the Covenant. Hodder and Stoughton).*

The story of Esther may have some basis in history, but it is really a festal legend always read on the feast of Purim. Like Judith, it tells of the deliverance of Israel through a woman. Like Daniel and Joseph, it is the oppressed who win through in the end. In the Hebrew version, God's name is never mentioned, though his guidance of events is implicitly understood. The Greek additions are more overtly religious in tone. They provide us with the prayers of Mordecai and of Esther. The Hebrew text was probably composed during the second century BC; the Greek text seems to date from about 114 BC. An appendix to this text refers to *ESTHER* having been sent to the Jewish community in Egypt from Palestine. There is reference in 2 Maccabees 15:36 to a Day of Mordecai which probably refers to Purim.

We are using the Hebrew version with the Greek additions, as they are familiar from their liturgical use.

ESTHER

The Greek text presents the meaning of the story in the guise of a dream. Susa was a city near Babylon, winter residence of the Persian kings.

What is the apparent meaning of Mordecai's dream? What are signified by the dragons, the little spring and the vine?

ESTHER 1

Ahasuerus is not an historical figure, neither is Vashti.

1. What do you think of Vashti's conduct? Do you sympathise with her, or with the king? Why?
2. Pick out the ironic touches in this account.

ESTHER 2

Esther is a Babylonian name (Ishtar), as is Mordecai (Marduk). Hadasseh (v.7). is a Hebrew name, meaning 'myrtle'. The story has reminiscences of Daniel 1.

1. Note the details that emphasise Esther's natural beauty and simplicity.
2. How is Divine Providence moving in these events?
3. What is the character of Mordecai? See verses 7, 10-11, 22.

ESTHER 3

Agag (v.1) is the name of an enemy of Saul (1 Samuel 15:7-9), chosen to emphasise the antagonism of Haman towards Mordecai, a descendant of Saul's tribe (son of Kish 2:5). The Greek text inserts the text of Ahasuerus' edict between vv 13 and 14.

1. What is the reason for Haman's antagonism towards Mordecai? What signs are there that Haman was insecure?
2. Notice the complaints made against the Jews (verses 8-9). Should they likewise be made of Christians? What do you think?

ESTHER 4

The Greek text inserts Mordecai's and Esther's Prayers after v.17.

1. Mordecai makes no secret of his grief. Is this courage, wiliness or fool-hardiness? What more do we learn of his character in this chapter?
2. Notice the arguments he uses to persuade Esther to intervene with the king. What makes her relent? (verse 14). Who gives her this courage?
3. What more do we learn of Mordecai's motives from his prayer? (See Greek text).
4. Study Esther's prayer, reflect on it and make it your own when facing an ordeal, especially the last verse.

ESTHER 5

The short, rather bald, Hebrew text is supplemented by an emotional account in the Greek of Esther's mission to the king.

1. How does the Greek author build up the drama of this scene, culminating in the change of mood on the part of the king?
2. Pride before a fall. Notice the lively account of Haman's elation.

ESTHER 6-7

The fall of Haman is rapidly told.

1. The situation now moves rapidly. Haman is trapped into honouring Mordecai. Who strikes a note of warning to Haman?
2. How is the story of Haman's fall illustrated in Wisdom literature, eg. Psalm 7:16, 35:7-8, Proverbs 26:27, Eccles 10: 8 etc.? Does history also furnish examples?

ESTHER 8

The Hebrew text is supplemented by an insertion of the decree of revocation between vv 12 and 13.

1. What opinion have you formed of Ahasuerus? Is he to be taken seriously? See Greek text for an excuse for his conduct.
2. Contrast the situation of the Jews at the end of Chapter 8 with that at the beginning of the story.
3. In what particulars does the Greek text show more advanced theology?

ESTHER 9-10 and EPILOGUE

The feast of Purim is described, and an epilogue added in the Greek text referring back to the Greek Prologue.

1. Notice the style in these chapters: exaggerated numbers, very rhetorical account. What does this tell us about the author's purpose?
2. See verses 9: 19-22 with the account of the liturgy of rejoicing. What detail could be a foreshadowing of the Offertory at Mass?
3. Mordecai explains his dream. Did your own explanation match this?

AN INTRODUCTION TO THE BOOK OF JOB

'Why do bad things happen to good people?' ... 'Why?' ... 'What have I done to deserve this?' ... 'Am I very wicked that such things happen to me?' ...

These are the questions posed in the Book of Job. The received wisdom was that evil is a punishment for sin. If your sufferings were great, your sins must have been even greater. God is just. He would never punish the innocent. The author of Job faces this question, in all honesty. In the persons of Job's 'comforters' he presents and demolishes the traditional arguments; in the figure of Job, he dares to face the issue. Job is innocent - and yet he suffers every kind of deprivation. Why? Job refuses to bow to the inevitable, and admit to being a great sinner, which he knows he is not; he refuses to curse God, as his wife suggests; he refuses to sulk or to doubt God; instead, he has it out with him, in words that perhaps go deeper into the mystery of God's relationship with man than any other book in the Old Testament.

This book is part of Wisdom Literature. Its author is unknown, its date probably the beginning of the fifth century BC. Job is not a Jew, but from the land of Uz, in Edom, famous for its sages (Jeremiah 49:7, Obadiah 8, etc). Job is mentioned twice elsewhere in the Bible (Ezekiel 14: 14,20 and James 5:11).

JOB 1-2

The first two chapters and the last seem to be a folk-tale, into which the great poetic drama has been inserted.

1. How does the writer a) build up the picture of Job's prosperity, and b) of his misfortunes?
2. What do you understand by the figure of Satan? Do you find it disconcerting? cf. Zechariah 3:1 ff., 1 Chronicles 21:1
3. How does Job react to his misfortunes? See 1:20-22, 2:8-10

JOB 3

The dialogue between Job and his 'Comforters' now begins.

1. Compare this chapter with Jeremiah 20:7-18. What are the main points in common?
2. Notice that Job does not complain of his losses and afflictions. What is the real cause of his anguish? What does this tell us of his real quality?

JOB 4-5

Teman is also in Edom.

1. What is Eliphaz' central theme? What did he learn from his wisdom?
2. Do we ever find ourselves consoling sufferers with words similar to those used by Eliphaz? Pick out some examples.
3. What is the danger of relying too much on one personal religious experience? How can we avoid this?

JOB 6

Job replies to Eliphaz.

1. Job reacts against Eliphaz' use of the word 'Vexation' (5:2). He feels it is utterly inadequate to express his sense of calamity, and agrees that his words have been rash (verse 3). What does he ask for from his friends?
2. What leads us to believe that Job's suffering is largely spiritual?

JOB 7

Job now addresses God: 'Remember' (verse 7) is in the singular.

1. What picture does he draw of human suffering?
2. How does he appeal to God? List a) his appeals, and b) his accusations against God.

JOB 8

Bildad now takes up the argument.

1. To what authority does Bildad appeal? See verses 8,20.
2. Notice his cruel reference to the loss of Job's children (verse 4). What other hint is there that he believes Job to be at fault?

JOB 9

God's goodness is known through revelation. The sacred writer has deliberately placed his story outside the covenant people.

1. Look at verse 24, which is a key statement in this book. How does Job reach this point?
2. How can we know that *our* moral judgments are the same as God's?
3. Notice the mention of an umpire or arbiter (verse 33). Make a note of each reference to this idea, and see how fresh features are added to it: 16:8; 17:3; 19:25; 33:23-24.

JOB 10

Job's monologue continues, addressed rather to God than to Bildad.

1. What is Job's main desire in this chapter? Can we make it our own?
2. On what grounds does Job base his appeal to God?

JOB 11

Zophar now speaks.

1. What is Zophar's reaction to Job's plain speaking?
2. What is Zophar's main argument? Notice the sharp rebuke (verse 6), the steps to repentance (13,14) and the picture of blessedness (15-19). Why did he fail to convince Job?

JOB 12

Job replies to Zophar, using Wisdom themes.

1. What is Job's retort (verses 2-3)?
2. Job now compares the traditional wisdom (verses 7-12) with God's wisdom (13-16). What aspects does he mention?
3. Then Job turns the received wisdom of orthodoxy onto its head (16b-25). Have we ever known or experienced the kind of situation that Job describes?

JOB 13

Job's discourse continues.

1. With what does Job reproach his friends? (verses 1-12).
2. He now calls on *GOD* to give an account of himself. What does he request of God? (verses 21-23).
3. What is his greatest strength? (verse 18). Is this arrant conceit, profound honesty or great faith in God's justice?

JOB 14

Job accuses God of injustice.

1. Job now accuses God of injustice to all mankind. What does he plead in our defence? What is man's greatest sorrow?
2. Is there any hint in this chapter that Job hopes for a life beyond the grave?

JOB 15

The series of dialogues begins again, with Eliphaz.

1. Read Eliphaz' first speech again (4 and 5). Compare the tone and the approach with this chapter. What aspect does he now emphasise?
2. What is the source of knowledge, according to Eliphaz?

JOB 16

Job takes the argument onto another plane. He appeals to God's sense of injustice.

1. What image of God does Job present in verses 7-17?
2. He looks for a mediator, an umpire, a witness in his contest with God. Who is that witness (verse 19)? cf. John 14:16 for the NT fulfilment of this remarkable insight.

JOB 17

Job continues his lament.

1. Since his friends have let him down, and God himself accuses him unjustly, Job calls on his Adversary to be the pledge or guarantor himself. Follow this idea through into the passion of Jesus, especially in the Agony (John 12: 27-36) and in the Crucifixion (Mark 15:34).
2. Apply verses 6-10 to Jesus in his passion.
3. Make a list of the images Job uses to express his state of mind.

JOB 18

'Light' and 'lamp' normally in the Bible refer to descendants.

1. Show how Bildad interprets Job's fate as the result of wickedness. Which of his misfortunes does he mention?
2. What references to pagan beliefs can be found in this chapter?

JOB 19

Go'el (verse 25) can be translated as Defender, Redeemer, Vindicator.

1. What did Job's friends really attempt in their arguments? See verses 1-5.
2. Job lists his complaints against God. What are they (verses 6-12)? With what consequences (verses 13-22)?

3. What scriptural justification did the writer of Job have for the remarkable hope expressed in verses 25-27? cf. Hosea 11, Psalm 19:14 etc. Do we too have this hope?
4. Meditate on verses 26(b)-27 and make them your own.

JOB 20

The Bible often refers to the 'giants' of old (Genesis 6: 1-4, Genesis 11, Isaiah 14: 12-14, etc.)

1. In what sense can Zophar's central theme that pride inevitably leads to a fall, be said to be true? What example can you think a) in the Bible, and b) in modern history?
2. Of what particular crime (verse 19) does Zophar accuse wicked men, and by implication, Job?

JOB 21

Job responds to Zophar.

1. Place Zophar's views of the state of the wicked beside Job's; cf 20:6-28 with 21:6-26. At what points do they a) agree, and b) disagree?
2. What answer can be given to the problem of the suffering of the innocent, and of the apparent well-being of the evil a) in Job's terms, and b) in terms of our own faith?

JOB 22

Eliphaz begins by repeating the substance of his dream (cf.22:2-4 with 4:17-20).

1. Of what sins does Eliphaz accuse Job (verses 5-9)?
2. Why is it that Eliphaz' advice to Job to repent (verse 21) is so wide of the mark? How limited is Eliphaz' own religious experience? cf. Psalm 77 verses 3-10. Do we trust too much in our own experience to the exclusion of other teaching?

JOB 23-24

Job, finding no understanding from his friends, continues his monologue of lament.

1. 23:2-14. Pick out the signs in this part of the speech that Job is reaching a new confidence, see especially verses 6, 7, 10.
2. Draw out the images in 24: 1-12 that show Job's new sense of solidarity with the poor and downtrodden.

JOB 25-27

There is some confusion in the text here. We follow RSV.

1. How do Bildad and Job speak a) of God's holiness, and b) of his power?
2. Does 27:7-22 add any fresh ideas about the wicked?

JOB 28

This hymn in praise of Wisdom has been inserted as a sort of interlude.

1. Verses 1-11: What do we learn about mining in this section? What fascinates the author?
2. Verses 12-22: Where shall Wisdom be found? Do we reflect enough nowadays? There is an African proverb - 'Western man thinks too much'. Do we, in fact, ever think about Wisdom?
3. Verses 23-28: 'The fear of the Lord, that is wisdom' (verse 28). This is the theme of all the Wisdom books. Is it the foundation of all my thinking?

JOB 29

Job's apologia. He describes his past happiness.

1. What was the most golden aspect of Job's prosperous past? See verses 2-4. What insight does this give into Job's present anguish?
2. What was the foundation of Job's prosperity?

JOB 30

The contrast with his present situation is starkly presented.

1. In what ways does Job now feel degraded? See verses 1-14.
2. What does Job say about a) his illness and b) his mental suffering?

JOB 31

Note the high and sensitive standards of morality in this chapter.

1. List the sins of which Job declares himself to be innocent.
2. In what sense can this whole chapter be said to be Job's speech for the defence?

JOB 32

The intervention of Elihu seems an interpolation by another hand. Has he been introduced as the 'umpire' for whom Job longed? Buz is mentioned among Abraham's relatives (Genesis 22:21) and Ram is an ancestor of David (Ruth 4:19). So he is an Israelite!

1. On what grounds does Elihu challenge the other three? See especially verse 8 and JB translation of verse 3.
2. Elihu is young (verses 4,6). Is there any precedent in the Bible of God speaking through young people?

JOB 33

Elihu continues his attach on Job. He summarises his arguments used hitherto in the debate.

1. Job had said that God treated him unjustly (33:8-11). What reply does Elihu make to this on God's behalf? See verses 12-13. Do we ever console sufferers in this way?
2. In what ways does Elihu say that God speaks, and for what purpose? See verses 14-33.

JOB 34

Elihu seems to classify Job as a 'scoffer' (Proverbs 21:24). He parodies his laments.

1. Elihu again quotes Job (verses 5-6). How does he answer him?
2. Elihu further comments on Job (verse 9). What does he then declare about God? Is his accusation about Job (verse 35) fair?

JOB 35

Elihu continues his attack on Job.

1. Elihu reproaches Job for accusing God of injustice (verse3). How does he refute this? See verses 5-8. Is it true that our sins are unimportant?
2. Are we grateful enough for the "songs in the night"? Do we have enough faith to *TEST* God in time of trial as Job did?

JOB 36-37

Elihu seems to echo here much of what Eliphaz has already said (Job 22). He then praises God's power and greatness.

1. 'The godless in heart cherish anger' (36:13). How should we deal with anger? Can we take a lesson from Job? See verse 18.
2. Read carefully what Elihu says about thunder (36:29-37:5). Is there a deeper meaning here?
3. In what ways (37:14-24) does Elihu anticipate God's words in Chapters 38 ff?

JOB 38

God now speaks, and he speaks as Yahweh (the Lord). The covenant-God is speaking therefore not only to Job (a non-Israelite) but to the chosen people.

1. Compare verse 1 with Zechariah 9:14 ff and notice the context. What adjectives docs Zechariah apply to God who 'marches forther in the whirlwind'? What questions does God now ask of Job?
2. What examples of God's handiwork are depicted? Point out the imagery in verses 4-13.

JOB 39

God's discourse continues.

1. God now turns to the animal kingdom (38:39ff). Which creatures are described?
2. Pick out two of the most living descriptions. Do we regard nature in all its living energy? What do we learn about the Creator?

JOB 40-41

A second speech from God begins at 40:6.

1. Job had begged God to answer him and let him justify himself. See 13:3; 23:4; 31:37. God proves Job's littleness. What is Job's response? Is it adequate?
2. God now introduces two creatures of immense strength: the hippopotamus (40: 15-24); the crocodile (41). What does God intend that Job should learn from these animals?

JOB 42

The long poem is concluded and the folk-tale is resumed.

1. Job's undeserved suffering has led to the vision of God, (verse 5). Can we ever say that we have known this too, or met those who have? Give examples.
2. What is the ultimate teaching of the Book of Job?
3. The story is concluded with the fable with which it began. Notice especially God's rebuke to the comforters, and the fabulous restoration of Job's fortunes. Does this spoil the effect of the book, in your view?
4. The comforters are discredited. If we are honest, we may have agreed with some of their arguments. In what way has the Book of Job affected my attitude towards God, suffering, traditional Church teaching?

YAHWEH
YOU YOURSELF
ARE MY LAMP
MY GOD
LIGHTS UP
MY DARK
NESS
PS:18

AN INTRODUCTION TO THE PSALMS

The Psalter is the hymnal of Christians and of Jews. It has been called Israel's 'soul-book'. The psalms are divided into five books, of which two are largely Davidic psalms (3-41 and 51-72). Some derive from the psalter of the sons of Korah, some of Asaph. The inscriptions were added much later, and one can only guess at the origins of most of the psalms. However, one of David's throne-names was 'the singer of Israel's psalms' (2 Samuel 23:1) and clearly Jeduthun and Asaph collections relate to Temple worship. There are also pilgrim songs, laments, royal psalms, processional hymns, psalms of praise and of petition. They have been sung continuously since the days of Solomon's temple (about 966 BC). They express every mood and every need. Jesus himself used them, and so, as St. Augustine says, Christ's voice can be heard in all the psalms. They are prayed officially in church and in synagogue; they are prayed by individuals, who can always find one or other of them to suit every mood.

The numbering followed will be that of all modern Bibles. However, the Grail translation, used in the Book of Hours and in the Divine Office follows the Vulgate numbering where the corresponding number follows it in brackets.

PSALM 1

Psalms 1 and 2 form an introduction to the Psalter. Psalm 1 is a post-exilic Wisdom psalm.

1. Three types of bad company: the wicked, the sinners and the scoffers. The good man will avoid their influence, and spend his time in what way?
2. Compare Jeremiah 17: 7-8 and Matthew 7: 13, 14 with this psalm.

PSALM 2

A royal psalm composed for the occcasion of the king's accession.

1. Read this psalm through picturing the original scene.
2. Now apply it to Christ in his resurrection (verses 1-6) and his eternal begetting by the Father (verses 7-8). Notice its use in New Testament (Acts 13:33; Hebrew 1:5; 5:5; 2 Peter 1:17).

PSALM 3

An individual lament.

1. What is the situation of the psalmist?
2. Consider its use a) as a morning prayer, and b) in the liturgy for Holy Saturday.

PSALM 4

An individual lament. Evening prayer.

1. Show how the psalmist expresses trust and confidence.
2. What is his state of mind as he goes to sleep?

PSALM 5

A morning prayer.

1. The psalmist catalogues certain types of sinners. What are they?
2. Compare verses 7-8 with Luke 2: 41-45. Did these words inspire the young Jesus?

PSALM 6

A penitential psalm.

1. Read this psalm as a prayer in sickness. Learn it by heart for such use!
2. Re-read it, picturing Jesus reciting these words in Gethsemane.

PSALM 7

A lament.

1. Why does the psalmist feel so injured?
2. Look at the imagery used to describe evil (verses 14-15). What kind of evil is meant?
3. Note verse 17 for the end of a prayer. Why is it not always mine?

PSALM 8

A hymn of praise.

1. What is man's destiny, according to the psalmist?
2. Apply the psalm to Christ, and cf. Hebrews 2: 6-8.

PSALM 9

A thanksgiving song.

1. What truths about God are revealed in this psalm? Make a list.
2. For what is the psalmist giving thanks?

PSALM 10

A lament.

1. Make a list of the aspects of evil mentioned in this psalm. See especially verses 7-8, for vivid imagery.
2. What would be the equivalent behaviour and attitude today? Is it prevalent?
3. How far is verse 4 the key of this psalm? What encouragement do you find in verses 12-18 if you are ever tempted to echo verse 4?

PSALM 11

A song of trust.

1. 'If the foundations are destroyed' (verse 3) what does the just do? What do WE do when the foundations of our faith are attacked?
2. Look up Genesis 19 for the story behind the imagery of verse 6. What is the psalmist saying about God's justice?

PSALM 12

A liturgical lament.

1. 'With flattering lips and a double heart they speak' (verse 2). The psalmists were very insistent on the evil of misuse of the tongue. Are we ever 'two-faced'? What circumstances make it a temptation? What does verse 4 mean?
2. Notice the references in psalms 11 and 12 to the children of Adam. What lies behind each reference? (See 11: 4; 12:1; 12:8).

PSALM 13

An individual lament.

1. Use this prayer when prayer itself is dry and one's heart feels empty. Imagine Christ praying it during his agony and passion. (St. Augustine reminds us that Christ's voice can be heard in all the psalms).
2. What leads the psalmist to trust and hope?

PSALMS 14 and 53

1. Contrast verse 1 with verse 2b. The fool denies the very existence of God; the wise man SEEKS God. Trace the fortunes of the 'fool' in this psalm. Can it ever indeed be said that godless people live in 'great terror'?
2. What, on the contrary, befalls those who seek God?

PSALM 15

A liturgical entrance psalm.

1. Compare the qualities of the righteous with the Beatitudes of Jesus (Matthew 5: 1-12). What are a) the similarities and b) the differences?
2. Note the emphasis on truth once again in those who seek God, and cf. Psalm 14.

PSALM 16

A psalm of trust.

1. Pray this psalm in your own name, especially verses 5-8.
2. Look up Acts 2:27 and 13:35 for its use in the New Testament, and then re-read it with Christ's resurrection in mind, so that it becomes Christ's prayer to his Father after his resurrection. Does it help you to enter into the Christ -consciousness?

PSALM 17

An individual lament.

1. This too can be a prayer of Christ. Why? and cf. verse 15. How far can it be my prayer?
2. What language is used to describe God? See especially verses 6, 7, 8 and 13.

PSALM 18

A royal psalm of thanksgiving. The setting seems to be the Temple: verse 10 refers to the cherubim or winged creatures above the ark. (Exodus 25:18).

1. Go through this psalm as if the imagery referred to the believer's unconscious (verses 16-19). Ask God to enlighten your darkness (verse 28) and to do battle with the enemies that war against the soul.
2. Now re-read the psalm as a prophecy of the passion, death and resurrection of Christ.

PSALM 19

A hymn of praise. God is celebrated as Creator of the universe and particularly of the sun (verse 4b) and author of the Law. In the ancient East the sun symbolised justice.

1. How does the psalmist proclaim the mystery of God a) in creation; b) in his Word?
2. Apply verses 4b-6 to the incarnation and resurrection of Christ.
3. From what sins does the psalmist ask to be purified? Make an examination of conscience on verses 11-14.

PSALM 20

A royal psalm. Verses 1-5 are sung by the people: verse 6 by the king; verses 7-9 by the people.

1. Do we emulate the people's trust and confidence? Is our heart's desire (verse 4) to overcome the enemies of our soul and to enjoy God's love? How do we obtain this grace? See verse 2.
2. What are the "horses and chariots" by which we set store?

PSALM 21

A royal psalm of thanksgiving. Possibly this psalm was sung for a coronation or an anniversary of accession. Verses 1-7 are addressed to God; verses 8-12 to the king.

1. Read verses 1-7 in praise of Christ the Messiah. To what mystery is it especially appropriate? What is Jesus' 'heart's desire'?
2. When Jesus comes as judge, how will he triumph over evil?

PSALM 22

A lament.

1. Read verses 1-21 and imagine Jesus praying them on the cross. Compare Mark 15: 22-37; Matthew 27: 33-50 and John 19: 23-24 and 28-30.
2. Read verses 22-31 in the light of the resurrection.
3. Can we in any way make this psalm our own?

PSALM 23

A psalm of trust.

1. Verses 1-4. Notice how the imagery can apply to our life of prayer. Take it through verse by verse with this in mind.
2. Verses 5-6. How can these verses be applied to Holy Communion?
3. This psalm is used at weddings, funerals, first communions. Why? How many metrical versions of it do you know?

PSALM 24

A processional hymn. This psalm possibly refers to the transfer of the ark (2. Samuel 6: 12-16).

1. What virtues are extolled in this psalm?
2. What does it mean to 'seek the face of God'?
3. Read this psalm in the light of the ascension of Christ.

PSALM 25

An individual lament.

1. This psalm is suitable for the opening of a penitential season (Lent or Advent) or for someone going into retreat. Note the emphasis on trust and on desire to know God's ways (verses 3 and 4). What other attitudes are essential to the believer as he/she renews friendship with God?
2. What truths about God lead the psalmist to trust and confidence?

PSALM 26

An individual lament.

1. Do we dare to pray 'Test my heart and my mind'? What could be the outcome?

2. Compare the categories of evildoers (verses 4-5) with Psalm 1. What nuance has been added?
3. This psalm was once used at the lavabo at the Offertory at Mass. Why?

PSALM 27

An individual lament.

1. In what ways are we to understand the psalmist's prayer to 'dwell in the house of the Lord' (verse 4) and to 'seek his face'?
2. What are the seven petitions the psalmist makes in verses 7-14? Can we make them our own?

PSALM 28

An individual lament.

1. What particular aspect of evil is mentioned in this psalm (verse 3)? Are we ever guilty of this?
2. The psalmist expresses deep gratitude at the answer to his prayer (verse 6). What does this experience lead him to declare? cf.the prayer of Hannah (1 Samuel 1: 9-18).

PSALM 29

A hymn to the Lord of the storm.

1. Apply this psalm to the Word of God.
2. In what sense can it be said to describe Jesus' baptism?

PSALM 30

A thanksgiving song.

1. Can we make this psalm our own, letting it express our different experiences in prayer? See verses 2, 3, 5, 6-7, 8 and 11.
2. Read this psalm as Christ's prayer to his Father at his resurrection.

PSALM 31

A thanksgiving song. This psalm may have been inspired by Jeremiah 6, 20, 46, 49. Luke 23:46 puts verse 5 onto the lips of Jesus on the cross.

1. Pray this psalm on behalf of the persecuted or the mentally ill.
2. Draw out the expressions of trust in God.

PSALM 32

Though known as the second penitential psalm, this is really a Wisdom psalm with a didactic purpose, a commentary on Proverbs 28:13.

1. What are the effects of concealment of guilt? The psalmist uses the image of a parched field. Can unacknowledged guilt be said to dry up the *HEART*? Can you think of an example?
2. Use this psalm as prayer of thanksgiving after Confession.

PSALM 33

A hymn of praise. This psalm begins (verse 1) where Psalm 32 left off (32:11). It is a typical psalm of praise, with Call to worship (verses 1-3), motives for Praise (verses 4-19) and Recapitulation (verses 20-22).

1. What are the effects of God's word? Compare Genesis 1.

2. In the frightening times in which we live, can we draw strength from verses 10-17? What is meant by the expression 'the thoughts of his heart'? (verse 11).

PSALM 34

A wisdom psalm.

1. What is the advice given by the psalmist to his 'sons'?
2. List the blessings God gives to his people.

PSALM 35

An individual lament.

1. The psalm falls into three parts (verses 1-10, 11-18, 19-28) each part ending with a cry of thanksgiving. Summarise each section by an appropriate heading.
2. What are the various evils which beset the psalmist?

PSALM 36

An individual lament.

1. What are the characteristics of sin (verses 1-4)?
2. Note the repetition of the idea of the faithful covenant love of God for his people. What indicates this?
3. God invites us to share in the 'abundance of his house' (verse 8). What is the spiritual meaning of this? cf. John 6:35 and 4:14; 7:37.

PSALM 37

A wisdom psalm.

1. Perhaps your reaction on reading this psalm is 'It's too good to be true'! How far can our own attitudes contribute to the state of affairs promised by the psalmist? (See verses 1, 3, 4, 5, 7, 8). How can we make verses 4-5 our watchword?
2. How far did Jesus use this psalm in the Beatitudes? cf. Matthew 5:1-11.
3. In what ways have we experienced the truth of verses 35-36 in the events of this century?

PSALM 38

The third penitential psalm. Sickness was often believed to be the result of sin.

1. This psalm can be read as referring to Christ's passion.
2. List the evils that afflict the psalmist, and then gather evidence of his trust in God.

PSALM 39

Another lament of a sick man.

1. Contrast the attitude of the sick man in this psalm with that of Psalm 38.
2. To whom does he address his lament and in what terms? Do we tell God all we feel? What does verse 13 mean? (cf. verse 10).

PSALM 40

A hymn of thanksgiving followed by a cry of distress.

1. What do verses 1-5 tell us about perseverance in prayer, even when it is dry and desolate?
2. Verses 6-8 are applied to Christ in Hebrews 10:5-9 with a variant reading of verse 6 from the Greek. What does this reveal to us about Christ's desire to become man?

3. What do verses 13-17 tell us about prayer? and cf. Jesus' advice (Luke 18:1) in view of verses 1-5!

PSALM 41

Thanksgiving psalm for one who is gravely ill.

1. Consider the vivid picture in verses 5-8. Are we ever guilty of malicious gossip?
2. Draw out the ways in which the psalmist's faith in God has sustained him.

PSALM 42-43

Lament of a Levite in exile. Mount Hermon is in Jordan, to the North, on the Syrian border.

1. The psalmist is in exile among Gentiles who taunt him. In what terms does he express his longing for God?
2. Do we ever feel exiled in a secularised world? If so, can we draw strength from the same source? See 42:5, 8, 11; 43:5.

PSALM 44

A community lament. This psalm, contrasting past victories with a desolate present, probably refers to the destruction of Jerusalem in 587 BC. Verses 17-22 may have been added in the Maccabean period.

1. What does the psalmist draw from the history of the conquest of the land? See verses 1-3 and cf. Joshua 24:12. How does he contrast it with the present situation (verses 9-16)?
2. The people declare their innocence. Are there times when, like Job, we honestly feel we do not deserve the calamities that befall us? Can we then pray verses 17-26? Put them into our own words.

PSALM 45

A royal psalm, composed for a royal marriage.

1. What is said of the bridegroom? Apply each verse to Christ (verses 2-9).
2. Read verses 10-15 with a) the Church in mind, and b) the individual soul. What is the essential quality of the bride of Christ, the Christian?

PSALM 46

A song of Zion. This psalm may have originally celebrated the defeat of Sennacherib (2 Kings 18 and 19).

1. Compare verses 1-3 with Genesis 1: 1-2. How does the Holy Spirit deal with the waters that 'roar and foam', the chaos within our unconscious?
2. Apply the imagery of verses 4-7 to the Church, indwelt by grace, by the Holy Spirit.
3. The waters purify the city, making wars to cease (verses 8-10). Allow these words to penetrate our own hearts, purifying, cleansing, stilling.

PSALM 47

The first of the psalms of kingship.

1. Draw out the historical references in this psalm (verses 3,4 and 9). What further victories has God won in Christ?
2. Apply this psalm to the ascension of Christ.

PSALM 48

A song of Zion. This psalm, like Psalm 46, may refer to the defeat of Sennacherib.

1. This psalm was probably a pilgrim song. Picture the pilgrims to Jerusalem singing it as they arrive in the holy city. What are they exhorted to hand on to the next generation?
2. Apply the psalm to the Church, not triumphally, but gratefully. See especially verses 9 ff.

PSALM 49

A Wisdom psalm.

1. What is the difference between the fate of the foolish (verse 14) and of the wise who trust God (verse 15)? Does the psalmist refer to an afterlife? cf. the story of Enoch (Genesis 5:24) and of Elijah (2 Kings 2:1) where the word for 'receive' (laqah) is the same.

PSALM 50

A prophetic liturgy. The original setting was probably a covenant renewal.

1. What does God ask from his faithful ones (verses 5-15)? Are they to renounce their sacrifices, or offer them in a different spirit? See especially verses 14-15. Is this a summons to us to increase our dependence on God, to ask him to deepen our faith, to worship with more honesty and depth?
2. What does God say to the wicked? What sins are especially mentioned?

PSALM 51

The fourth penitential psalm.

1. Read this psalm prayerfully under-lining the verses that emphasise our need for inner purity, and our incapability of purifying ourselves.
2. The psalmist asks for wisdom (verse 6) and for a new spirit (verse 10). Who is the author of these gifts? See verse 11. What does this mean in Old Testament terms?
3. We are all, in some sense, part of the terrible 'blood guiltiness' of the world (verse 14). We have only to think of the violence, murder, war, abortion, careless driving, etc. that mar our society to realise that our century is drenched in blood. What answer does the psalmist give to this situation? Can a Christian add more?

PSALM 52

A wisdom psalm.

1. What are the characteristics of the evil man? In what does he put his trust?
2. What image describes the one who trusts God. What is the difference between the evil man and the wise one?

PSALM 53 is the same as PSALM 14

PSALM 54

An individual lament.

1. What experience could be expressed by this psalm? What do we learn from it of the severity of a trial of faith?
2. How do we know when God has come to our help? cf. 1 Samuel 23:19 ff.

PSALM 55

An individual lament. This psalm seems to be inspired by Jeremiah 4:19; 9:1 ff.

1. What characteristics of evil do we find in this psalm?
2. What consolation does the psalmist find? Which is better, verses 6-7 or 22? Are we sometimes tempted to the former?
3. Read this psalm as Jesus' prayer on the way to Calvary, but cf. verse 15 with Mark 14:21.

PSALM 56

An individual lament. This psalm may refer to Hezekiah during the siege of Jerusalem, 701 BC.

1. 'When I am afraid, I put my trust in thee' (verse 3). What results does this act of trust have for the psalmist? Can I make verse 3 my own prayer in times of stress?
2. Read 2 Kings 19-20 and Isaiah 38: 3-5 for a possible background to this psalm.

PSALM 57

A lament. Verses 7-11 recur in Psalm 108: 1-5. How far can one read this psalm as a prophecy of the arrest, trial, death and resurrection of Christ?

PSALM 58

A lament. 'The gods' (verse 1) - either members of the heavenly court who assist Yahweh in governing the world, or, perhaps more likely, the gods of the nations, who are thought of as subject to Yahweh.

1. What evils come from the rule of the 'gods' of this world? See verses 3-5. Notice the vivid imagery in verses 4-8 and the deliberately violent language of verse 10.
2. Contrast the justice of the 'gods' (verse 2) and of God (verse 11). Can this psalm in any sense be applied to our contemporary situation?

PSALM 59

An individual lament.

1. Draw out from this psalm the different ways in which the psalmist calls on God. What do we learn about God from the titles given to him in these verses?
2. What are the characteristics of the 'enemies'?

PSALM 60

National liturgy of lament. This psalm is probably a lament for the destruction of Jerusalem in 587, when the country, long divided, was plundered by its neighbours as well as by the Babylonians.

1. Notice the prayer pattern of this poem. What does the nation do first (verses 1-5), second (verses 6-8), third (verses 9-12)?
2. Compose a liturgy of lament on the same pattern.

PSALM 61

An individual lament. A Levite in exile from the Temple.

1. In what ways is this a prayer for when one feels dry, abandoned, 'in exile' from God?
2. What consolation is offered to the psalmist?

PSALM 62

A Wisdom psalm of trust.

1. What verses in this psalm reveal the hollowness of all created things?
2. Notice the different aspects of prayer in verses 1, 5 and 8. What is the psalmist's conclusion (verses 11-12)?

PSALM 63

An individual lament. This psalm is part of Lauds (Morning Prayer) on the first Sunday of the month and on Solemnities.

1. Trace the course of the psalmist's different stages of prayer. Can we begin meditation with verse 1? What is the 'dry and weary land'?
2. What leads on to the state of joy in verse 5? But does temptation come, and in what form? (verse 9). Make verse 8 the foundation of our faith.

PSALM 64

An individual lament.

1. Do we ever 'whet our tongues like swords' or 'aim bitter words like arrows' (verse 3)? Do we ever take pleasure in malicious gossip? Are we ever, in our secret hearts, pleased at what is bad news for others? Let us pray that we may, in the light of God's Spirit, discover the depths of our own hearts (verse 6).
2. Are there any occasions in the gospels when Jesus 'shoots his arrow' at those who are cruel and malicious in their talk? See. for example, Luke 5: 30-31; Luke 6: 6-11; Luke 19: 1-10 etc.

PSALM 65

A hymn of thanksgiving for the harvest.

1. Draw out all the blessings God gives through the fruits of the earth.
2. Go through the psalm interpreting the blessings spiritually. For what should we give thanks in the order of grace?

PSALM 66

A liturgy of thanksgiving on behalf of the community.

1. Verses 1-12 recall God's gracious deeds at the Exodus and at the Jordan (verses 6, 12) and during a more recent ordeal - possibly the defeat of Sennacherib.
2. Verses 13-20. An individual comes to offer a sacrifice of thanksgiving. What is my offering?

PSALM 67

A harvest song.

1. Mark the number of occasions in this psalm when 'all nations', 'the peoples' are mentioned. What is the significance of this?
2. What blessings of creation are celebrated in this psalm?

PSALM 68

A hymn of thanksgiving for the enthronement of the ark in the Temple. This psalm is obscure in some places. Zalmon (verse 14) is in Bashan (verse 15); 'the beasts that dwell in the reeds' (verse 30) refers to Egypt.

1. Read this psalm with the history of Israel in mind. What features a) of God's character, and b) of sacred history are revealed?
2. Ephesians 4: 8-10 makes use of verse 18 with reference to Christ's ascension. Re-read the psalm with this in mind.

PSALM 69

Two laments have been combined here: the first, verses 1-6 and 13-15 speak of the waters of the deep; the second, verses 7-12 and 16 ff. is a cry of distress from one who suffers for his zeal.

1. Verses 1-6 and 13-15. There are times when our fears, our sense of being attacked by 'enemies', our depression ... can take hold of us, and we seem drowned in deep waters. What help does the psalmist seek when such is the case?
2. Verses 7-12 and 16 ff. Several New Testament writers have quoted this psalm in relation to Jesus' sufferings. Read it with this in mind, but how did he react to the taunts and cruelty of his foes? cf. Luke 23:34 with the psalm, especially verses 22 ff.
3. Is there any legitimate place in the Christian life for the violent imprecations found in such psalms as this?

PSALM 70

This psalm is a doublet of Psalm 40:13-17.

PSALM 71

A prayer in old age.

1. Read this psalm as a prayer for the aged, or from one in old age. A few years ago it would have seemed far-fetched, but nowadays there are many lonely and even persecuted old people. Draw out all the expressions of trust, and make a list of them.
2. How can we take comfort, as we grow older, in the memory of all that God has done in our lives? See verses 17-21.

PSALM 72

A royal psalm. This psalm is dedicated to Solomon and draws inspiration from the promises to David (2 Samuel 7).

1. This century has seen more than one attempt to create an ideal state where all live in peace and the poor are provided for. Why have these attempts failed so dramatically? See verse 1-2 and 15.
2. Read this psalm as a description of the kingdom of Christ. What are its chief characteristics?

PSALM 73

A thanksgiving hymn.

1. In what terms does the psalmist state his problem? (See verses 2-14). What is the most galling aspect of the prosperity of the wicked?
2. This mystery is frequently discussed in the Bible. What answer challenges and in the end convinces the psalmist? Does it convince me?
3. Draw out the different stages of the psalmist's experience of God. What does he mean by 'glory'? (verse 24).

PSALM 74

A liturgical lament for the Temple. This psalm probably refers to the sacking of the Temple by Nebuchadnezzar's armies.

1. Notice the details of the sacking in verse 4-8, and the final note of abandonment (verse 9). What considerations rouse the congregation to prayer and trust?
2. Pick out the allusions to the Creation and to the Exodus and crossing of the Jordan. What further wonders do Christians have to celebrate? Are they prefigured in any way in this psalm?

PSALM 75

The occasion of this psalm is perhaps a harvest festival.

1. Compare Isaiah 65:8 with verse 8 of this psalm. What is meant by the 'cup of wrath'? From whom will judgment come?
2. How are the wicked characterised? See verses 4-5.

PSALM 76

An eschatological hymn. The historical reference is probably to the retreat of Sennacherib in 701 BC. See 2 Kings 19:35 for the reference in verses 5-6.

1. Consider the scene. The greatest army of the ancient world - and the most cruel - the army of Sennacherib - is at the gates of Jerusalem. Then suddenly plague strikes. The people of Judah and Jerusalem are saved. See Isaiah 22 for the celebrations on this occasion. Who, according to Psalm 76, is the author of salvation? Notice the way in which the psalmist turns the historical moment into a great eschatological vision of the final judgment (verses 6-7).
2. What is the theme of judgment (verse 9)? Are there any occasions when God really and dramatically intervenes in history, or in our own lives?

PSALM 77

Meditation on Israel's past. This psalm probably dates from the difficult days after the return from exile.

1. In what terms does the psalmist describe his state of depression? What is the cause of his grief? (See verse 10). What scenes in Israel's past does he call to mind? See verses 16-20.
2. At times of lowness or dryness, do we recall the Lord's mighty works in our lives? What scenes do we recall?

PSALM 78

A credo psalm.

1. Verses 1-8. What is the purpose of studying history, according to these verses? What note is set in verse 8?
2. Verses 9-31. Make a list of the events in Israel's history remembered in these verses. Notice that Israel in verse 9 is called Ephraim, thus stressing the sins of the Northern Kingdom.
3. Verses 32-41. Distinguish between true and false repentance. What is God's response?
4. Verses 42-53. Compare the account of the plagues with that in psalm 105: 28-36.
5. Verses 56-64. What evils befell the people because of their idolatry? What evils are happening to our generation because of idolatry?
6. Verses 65-end. God works his purpose out despite man's sin. Compare what is said of God's attitude in this section with verses 38 and 39.

PSALM 79

A national lament for the capture of Jerusalem and the destruction of the Temple in 587 BC.

1. A chastened people laments the destruction of the sanctuary. To what does the psalmist ascribe the disaster?
2. What argument does he use in calling on God for redress?

PSALM 80

A national lament. The Greek title of this psalm is 'concerned with the Assyrian' and the references to the northern tribes in verses 1 and 2 make it seem likely that this psalm refers to the Assyrian devastation of the Northern Kingdom in 721 BC. Verse 1: God is pictured as 'enthroned upon the cherubim' of the ark.

1. Look up Isaiah 5:1-7 for another example of vine imagery, and compare with verses 8-13. Jesus uses similar imagery, cf. Luke 20:9-18.
2. What signs of hope are there in this psalm?

PSALM 81

A liturgy for the feast of Tabernacles.

1. Picture the scene described in verses 1-5. God reveals himself in the Liturgy. Does he speak to us in the same way, or is he always an unknown voice (verse 5)?
2. What is God's word to his people? See verses 6-10. How do they respond (verse 11)?
3. What do we learn of God's heart in this psalm?

PSALM 82

A warning against the judges. See note on psalm 58.

1. This scene is similar to that in Job 1:6 ff. What is God's indictment of pride and powerful rulers? Do we, if we have any power of any kind, remember our duty to the weak and the needy?
2. What is it about the abuse of power that puts those responsible into the state referred to in verse 5?
3. What answer does the New Testament give?

PSALM 83

A lament against Israel's enemies. All those mentioned except Assyria were neighbours of Israel.

1. Look up the stories behind verses 9-11, i.e. Judges 4 (Sisera and Jabin); Judges 7:25 (Oreb and Zeeb): Judges 8: 10-21 (Zebah and Zalmunna).
2. Pick out the images (verses 13-15) describing the fate of Israel's enemies.
3. What is the aim of the psalmist's prayer - the destruction or the conversion of the enemy?

PSALM 84

A song of Zion. A pilgrim song. Verse 6 refers to the valley of the Nettle Tree which was the last stage of the pilgrimage.

1. Make a list of the titles given to God.
2. What are the virtues of the pilgrim? And what is his reward?

PSALM 85

A prayer for peace and justice.

1. Read this psalm in the light of the New Testament. Why is it suitable for an Advent liturgy?
2. What are the characteristics of the restored 'land'? In what sense can we say that God's glory dwells in our land? cf. John 1:14 ff.

PSALM 86

A lament.

1. What are the characteristics of the psalmist?
2. St. Augustine says that Christ's voice is heard in all the psalms. Can we hear him at prayer to his Father in this one?

PSALM 87

A song of Zion. Verse 4: Rahab means Egypt; 'my springs' (verse 7) refers to sources of the river.

1. Read this psalm as a prophecy of the church of God. Note its universalism. Does this mean that all nations will eventually belong to the Church?
2. Notice the words used to describe membership in verses 4-6. How can the Church be mother of all peoples?

PSALM 88

A lament.

1. Read this poem a) as a description of the people of Israel during the exile or at the time of the holocaust in Nazi Germany, and b) as a prophecy of Christ's passion.
2. What references are there to Sheol? (There are at least six). Yet the psalmist still clings to God (verse 13). The psalm ends in darkness. Is there any consolation in this type of prayer for those in great pain or suffering? Compose a suitable liturgy for those in grief.

PSALM 89

A royal psalm.

1. The psalm emphasises God's faithfulness and steadfast covenant. Draw out the references to it.
2. What two great acts of God are remembered in verses 9-10?
3. What are the promises God makes to his Messiah?
4. Can we make verses 38-end our own prayer for the Church and for the world?

PSALM 90

A Wisdom psalm. This psalm is the only one in the psalter attributed to Moses, perhaps because of references to Genesis, and its similarities to Deuteronomy 32.

1. In what way could this psalm be said to be a meditation on Genesis 6: 1-7?
2. Newman, in his Dream of Gerontius, puts this psalm onto the lips of the souls in Purgatory. Why is it so appropriate for them?
3. What is meant by a heart of wisdom (verse 12)? cf. Proverbs 1:7; Ecclesiastes 11:8
4. Is there a New Testament application of this psalm? cf. Luke 12: 15-21.

PSALM 91

A psalm of trust. There are four divine names in the first two verses: Elyon (the Most High), Shaddai (the Almighty), Yahweh (the Lord), and Elohim (God)

1. What are the perils that beset us? See verses 3-6. In verse 13 how are we delivered? By magic (as in Egypt) or by faith and trust?
2. There are three voices in this psalm: the psalmist (verses 1-13); the individual addressed (verse 2) and God (verses 14-16). What promises does God make, and what reassurance does he give?
3. This psalm was quoted by Satan (Matthew 4:6) in what sense? In what sense did Jesus interpret it?

PSALM 92

A Wisdom psalm of thanksgiving.

1. What are the principles of God's working? See verses 6-8. For what blessings does the psalmist give thanks?
2. Why do you think this psalm is entitled A Song for the Sabbath?
3. Verses 12-15 can be a source of inspiration as we grow older. Compare Zech. 8:3.

PSALM 93

A hymn of praise.

1. What are the two kinds of law celebrated in this psalm?
2. Draw out the meaning of each stanza: verses 1-2: How is God's sovereignty described? verses 3 and 4: What is meant by 'the floods'? verse 5: The Torah partakes of what unique aspect of God?

PSALM 94

Wisdom psalm.

1. What is the source of the psalmist's confidence?
2. What characteristics are ascribed to the wicked?

PSALM 95

A processional hymn. This psalm is used as the Invitatory psalm at Matins in the Roman breviary - the Divine Office.

1. What two motives for praise are given in verses 3-7 ff?
2. Look up Numbers 14 and 20 for the references to Massah and Meribah, and then see what the New Testament makes of this psalm - Hebrews 3:7-11.

PSALMS 96, 97 and 98

Three psalms of kingship.

1. Go through these three psalms, counting the number of references to 'the earth' or to 'the peoples'. What conclusions do you draw?
2. What are the signs of God's univeral kingship?
3. Do we think enough of the eschatological hope of a new heaven and of a new earth? Count the number of references in these psalms.

PSALM 99

A psalm of kingship.

1. What names are given to God in this psalm?
2. Compare the scene in this psalm with Luke 9: 28-36. What are a) the similarities, and b) the differences?
3. What relationship with God is indicated in verses 6-8?

PSALM 100

An invitation to praise. This psalm is also one of the Invitatory psalms. It was probably recited on entering the sanctuary.

1. What are the motives for praising God given in verses 3 and 5?

PSALM 101

A royal psalm. This psalm is a sort of 'coronation oath' taken by the king at his accession.

1. What are the virtues of a ruler listed in verses 1-3 and 6? What kind of person is condemned?
2. How can we apply this to our own lives and conduct? See especially verses 5. Am I ever one of these?

PSALM 102

The fifth penitential psalm.

1. Contrast the wretched state of the psalmist (verses 1-11) with the vision of faith (verses 12-16).
2. Read this psalm as a vivid account of the ups and downs of our life and moods, and especially of our life of prayer.

PSALM 103

A thanksgiving psalm.

1. List the blessings described in this hymn. Are they given to all of us?
2. Pick out the references to God's steadfast love. How is it demonstrated? What is or should be our response? What is meant by fearing the Lord?

PSALM 104

A song in praise of creation.

1. Read this psalm and compare the order of creation with Genesis.
2. What picture are we given in verses 21, 27-30 of God's relationship with his creation? What attitude should this inspire in us?
3. What relation has man to the rest of creation? See verses 14ff,23, 33-35.

PSALM 105

A credo psalm.

1. Go through the psalm, dividing it into sections under the following headings: patriarchs, Egypt, plagues, wilderness, conquest. What aspect of salvation history is repeatedly stressed?
2. What does verse 15 mean? Re-read Genesis 20:7 and 26:11. What light does the psalmist throw on these incidents?
3. Compare verses 7-10 with verse 42. What confidence should we too have in God? Why were the people told to remember (verse 5)?

PSALM 106

An historical psalm.

1. The priest (verses 1-6) makes present the past and associates the people of God with national repentance. Look up the scenes referred to: verses 7-12 - Exodus; verses 13-33 - wilderness; 34-39 - conquest of the land; verses 40-46 - Judges to exile.
2. Compare this psalm with the penitential liturgy in Isaiah 63:7 - 64:11.
3. What were the sins that made God change his attitude to Israel? cf. verses 13, 21, 24 and 25. Are we ever guilty of any of them? What consequences do they bring?
4. Find a parallel in our own lives for each of the sections named in Question 1. Make our own confession of guilt and faith.

PSALM 107

A thanksgiving litugy.

1. Look at the four dramatic situations described in a) verses 4 and 5, b) verses 10-12, c) verses 17 and 18, and d) verses 23-27. What in each case led to God's saving intervention?
2. Can you find any parallels in the gospels for the situations described in a), c) and d)?

PSALM 108

This psalm is a repetition of psalm 57: 7-11 and psalm 60: 5-12

PSALM 109

An individual lament. This psalm consists of a) verses 1-5 Prayer of the psalmist; b) verses 6-19 his accusers curse him; c) verse 20: summary; d) verses 21-31 Prayer of the psalmist. The curses are highly coloured in the eastern way!

1. Verses 1-5. What does the psalmist say of his own innocence?
2. Verses 6-19. Of what do his enemies accuse the psalmist? Is there any underlying accusation? What leads us to accuse and 'curse' others?
3. Verses 21-31. What is the burden of the accused man's prayer? Can we share it?

PSALM 110

A royal psalm.

1. Read this psalm as a court poem celebrating the king's coronation.
2. Now look carefully at its Messianic meaning, and read it again as applying to Christ who is Lord (verse 1), King (verses 2, 5-6), Son of God (verse 3), Priest (verse 4).
3. Meditate on verse 7 as foretelling Jesus' passion and resurrection.

PSALM 111 and PSALM 112

Psalm 111 is an alphabetical psalm, and so is Psalm 112. One praises God; the other celebrates the virtuous man.

1. Psalm 111. What gracious acts of the Lord are proclaimed in this psalm? Follow salvation history in verses 4-7. What are the 'works', 'food', 'heritage' and 'precepts'?
2. What gracious acts has God done in *MY* life?
3. Psalm 112. 'We shall be like him' (1 John 3:2). In what ways, according to this psalm, does the just man resemble God (as described in Psalm 111)?
4. Comment on verses 7 and 8. Are there 'evil tidings' you fear? What is the answer?

PSALM 113

The opening hymn of the HALLEL (Psalms 113-118) sung at Tabernacles and at Passover. It is sung at Vespers on the eve of great feasts.

1. Why is this psalm a fitting one to open the celebration of the great feast of our redemption?
2. What great blessings are promised behind the imagery of verses 7-9?
3. Who are 'the poor' and the 'barren woman'?

PSALM 114

This psalm with Psalm 113 is sung at the beginning of the Passover meal.

1. What mysteries are celebrated in this psalm? cf. Exodus 14 and Joshua 3.
2. Whose presence is 'understood' in verses 3-6 and revealed in verse 7? How does this happen in my life?

PSALM 115

A choir song of the Temple liturgy.

1. What are the idols of modern man? In what or in whom do I trust?
2. What answer does psalm 115 give to the question 'Where is their God?'

PSALM 116

A psalm of praise.

1. From what kind of trouble has the psalmist been delivered?
2. Consider this psalm as suitable a) for a funeral, b) for an offertory procession and c) for Confirmation.

PSALM 117

1. What are the two great attributes of God extolled in this psalm?
2. What are the virtues Paul sets above all others (1 Cor. 13:13)? What conclusions do you draw?

PSALM 118

A thanksgiving liturgy. This psalm has three sections: verses 1-4 - a thanksgiving liturgy of choruses (Israel, priests, God-fearers); verses 5-21 - a king's hymn of thanksgiving added to a victory song (15-18); verses 22-29 - a processional liturgy probably used at the feast of Tabernacles.

1. Apply this psalm to Christ in his passion (verses 5-14) and his resurrection (verses 15-18), and his ascension (verses 19-29). What aspects of each mystery are celebrated?
2. Draw out the reasons for trust in God given in this psalm. What are his 'deeds' (verse 17)?

PSALM 119

An alphabetical psalm in praise of the Torah.

Verses 1-24.

1. Pick out the synonyms for the Law in these verses.
2. Is this mere legalism? See verses 9, 10 and 11.
3. Make verse 18 your prayer before beginning any Bible study.

Verses 25-48.

1. How is the depression of the psalmist lifted? See verses 25 and 28.
2. What is true liberty according to the psalmist?

Verses 49-80.

1. What are the characteristics of the 'godless' (verses 51, 69 and 70)? What does the psalmist learn from them?
2. Each section begins with a statement about the Lord. How is the experience of the believer in his life with God to be used in prayer, in suffering, in daily living?
3. How should the commandments affect our relations with others? See verses 63, 74 and 79.

Verses 81-104

1. What is the psalmist's state of mind as described in verses 81-88? How has he been supported by his meditations on God's Torah?
2. In what does the psalmist place his hope in verses 89-96?
3. Verses 97-104. How do these verses illustrate the importance of obedience in making progress in knowledge and understanding of the truth?

Verses 105-128

1. The psalmist has sworn an oath (verse 106) to obey God's commands, but he is 'sorely afflicted' (verse 107). Wherein lie his difficulties? What upholds him?
2. What features of temptation are described in verses 113-130?
3. For what graces does he pray?

Verses 129-152

1. How does the psalmist describe God's word? Make a list of all the expressions he uses.
2. What images of urgent desire are found in this section? What other emotions are expressed?

Verses 153-176

1. What troubles still beset the psalmist? Do they correspond to any of the problems or temptations that I face?
2. Are you encouraged by this long psalm to persevere in your study of scripture? What are the fruits of meditation on God's word? See verses 161-168.

PSALMS 120-134

Songs of Ascent - probably by pilgrims to Jerusalem.

PSALM 120

Meshech is in the Caucasus, Kedar in the Syrian desert.

1. What leads one to believe the psalmist is in exile? Make this a prayer of an exile from God 'who is our home'.
2. What does this psalm teach about the use of speech?

PSALM 121

1. Notice the emphasis on hope. As the pilgrim looks at the mountains surrounding Jerusalem, he is inspired with trust in God's presence there. Make this an 'everyday' prayer.
2. What images does the psalmist use to describe God's care for us?

PSALM 122

1. Picture the sense of deep joy as the pilgrim arrives at the gates of Jerusalem, city of peace. What are the sources of his hope? See verses 3 and 5. Make this a prayer for peace.
2. What was special about Jerusalem? cf. Deuteronomy 12:5-7. Are there special places of pilgrimage in our lives?

PSALM 123

1. This song probably recalls the returned exiles subjected to contempt and hostility from the Samaritans (cf. Nehemiah 4: 4 ff). Does this situation echo any experience of my own?
2. What is the best antidote to discouragement, according to this psalm? Take out one encouraging prayer from it, and learn it by heart.

PSALM 124

1. How does the psalmist's experience of escape from dangers strengthen his faith?
2. Work out the meaning of each of the images in this psalm.

PSALM 125

1. What did the mountains signify to the psalmist?
2. Compare this psalm with Deuteronmy 33: 27-29. What qualities do we need to understand the message of these two passages?

PSALM 126

1. The returning exiles can hardly believe their good fortune. Notice the imagery in verses 4-6.
2. What kind of hope does the thought of God's intervention inspire? What 'memories' does a Christian have to inspire even greater hope?

PSALM 127

1. This is a Wisdom psalm. What is its theme?
2. Apply verse 2 to my own life situation.

PSALM 128

1. What is the secret of true prosperity? What spiritual blessings are represented?
2. What do you think of the picture of family life in these two psalms (127 and 128)? How can it be realised today?

PSALM 129

1. This psalm refers to Israel's sufferings in Egypt. What is the meaning of the imagery in verses 6-8? What response should we make to painful memories?
2. What truths concerning Christian life in the world are set forth here?

PSALM 130

1. This psalm is customarily recited for the dead. What makes it appropriate for this? It probably was originally sung by the deportees as they went into exile. What are the three sources of hope mentioned?
2. What can we learn from the psalmist's attitude to prayer?
3. This psalm is sung at Vespers on Christmas Day. Why?

PSALM 131

1. Another psalm of hope. What are the dispositions of soul of the psalmist? What New Testament virtues does he exemplify?
2. This is a very good psalm for recitation at the beginning of prayer time, and before going to sleep. Why? Is this my habitual state of mind with regard to life's events, or do I rebel against God's Providence?

PSALM 132

A royal psalm. Ephrathah was Bethlehem, David's city. The psalm describes the procession of the ark from Ephrathah (verse 6) to Jerusalem (verse 13).

1. What name is given to God in this psalm? What does it mean? Does it have any significance for me?
2. What are the blessings promised to David's line? How are they fulfilled in the Church?

PSALMS 133 and 134

These two psalms refer to the Temple priests and levites.

Psalm 133.

1. In what way do oil and dew symbolise brotherly unity? What symbols would we use?

Psalm 134.

1. The pilgrims as they left the Temple (verses 1 and 2) called to the priests on the night watch, and the priests responded with a blessing (verse 3). Do we ever think of those who pray and work for us during the hours of night? Make this psalm our own family night prayer. It is sung in the Divine Office on Saturdays at Compline.

PSALM 135

A psalm of praise.

1. Who are called to praise? What is the significance of verses 19-21? cf. verse 2?
2. What are the motives given in verses 1-5 for praising God? Can we make them our own?
3. Find headings for each section: verses 6-7; 8-9; 10-12; 13-14; 15-18. What aspects of salvation history have been omitted?

PSALM 136

A psalm of praise - the Great Hallel. This psalm was recited at Passover after the lesser Hallel.

1. What names are given to God? See verses 2, 3 and 26. In what ways are these names demonstrated in this psalm?
2. Make a Christian litany of salvation with the same refrain as this psalm.

PSALM 137

Song of the exiles.

1. The last three verses of this psalm are omitted from the Divine Office, thus leaving only a sweet sad song of exile. Look up Ezekiel 35:5,10; Lamentations 4:21, 22; and Obadiah 10-14 to see what the Edomites did to Jerusalem.
2. Has bitterness and revenge any legitimate place in our prayer?

PSALM 138

1. What are the specific reasons given by the psalmist for thanking God?
2. How does he interpret the experiences of his life in relation to God's activity? How much of this psalm can I make my own?

PSALM 139

1. Pray this psalm in your own name. Why does it lead to peace and confidence, never to fear? Compare Luke 22:61.
2. Read the psalm again as Christ's dialogue with his Father at his resurrection. Note especially verses 5, 6a, 13, 14 and 18b. Compare with the Entrance Antiphon (Introit) for Easter Sunday in the Roman Missal.

PSALMS 140 and 141

Two laments.

Psalm 140.

1. How does the psalmist convey an atmosphere of distrust and confusion? What action does he take? In what circumstances could I make this prayer my own?

Psalm 141.

1. What are the temptations that beset the psalmist? How does he deal with them? What is the meaning of verse 2?

PSALMS 142 AND 143

Two laments.

Psalm 142.

1. In what different images does the psalmist express his confidence in God? Make verse 3 your own in times of dryness or depression. (v. 4 'I look to the right' for defending counsel).

Psalm 143.

1. What are the two sources of grief to the psalmist in verses 1-3? What two sources of comfort can be drawn upon? See verses 5-8.
2. Draw out the references in this psalm to the covenant love of God for the psalmist.

PSALM 144

A hymn for war and victory.

1. List the attributes of God mentioned in this psalm. Which ones do I experience especially?
2. What are the blessings of the Messianic reign? Transpose these into spiritual key.

PSALM 145

A hymn of praise.

1. Look in verses 4ff. for the motives given for praising God.
2. What features of God's character are mentioned in this psalm?

PSALM 146-150

A third Hallel. These five psalms are recited by Jews every morning.

PSALM 146

1. In verses 3-4 the psalmist warns against trusting human beings or institutions. Why is this such a mistake? Whom should we trust?
2. Verses 5-9. How does the Bible portray God's acts as detailed here? How do these verses describe Jesus' 'doing good'?

PSALM 147

1. This psalm is chosen in the Divine Office for feasts of our Lord. Why do you think this is so? What particular verses seem best to describe Christ?
2. The psalm can be divided into three sections a) 1-6; b) 7-11; and c) 12-20. What attribute of God is referred to in each one?

PSALM 148

1. Show how each part of creation is called to praise God. cf. Genesis I.
2. What motives for praise are given in verses 5-6 and 13?

PSALM 149

1. Who are especially called to worship in this psalm?
2. What motives for praise are suggested in verses 4, 7-8? Can we spiritualise this?

PSALM 150

1. This hymn of praise answers the questions where (verse 1), why (verse 2) and how (verses 3-5). What are the answers given?
2. Do we keep the balance in our minds and in our worship between God's presence 'in his sanctuary' and in his 'mighty firmament'? Where else is he present, and how?

AN INTRODUCTION TO THE BOOK OF PROVERBS

'God gave Solomon wisdom and understanding beyond measure, and largeness of mind like the sand on the seashore, so that Solomon's wisdom surpasses the wisdom of all the people of the east, and all the wisdom of Egypt. For he was wiser than all other men, wiser than Ethan the Ezrahite, and Heman, Calcol, and Darda, the sons of Mahol; and his fame was in all the nations round about. He also uttered three thousand proverbs; and his songs were a thousand and five. He spoke of trees, from the cedar that is in Lebanon to the hyssop that grows out of the wall; he spoke also of beasts, and of birds, and of reptiles and of fish'. 1 Kings 4:29-33.

Solomon was the first of the sages of Israel, and we note what was understood by a sage in the list above: a knowledge of proverbs, of natural history, of herbs. It is fairly certain that many of the proverbs in the Book of Proverbs date from his reign. Other sages mentioned in the above text are also found elsewhere in the Bible: Psalm 89 is attributed to Ethan, and all four of them are included among the descendants of Judah in 1 Chronicles 2:6. Heman is also listed among the Temple singers (1 Chronicles 6:33).

The proverbs of Solomon are found in Proverbs 10:1 - 22:16; another ancient collection ascribed to the reign of Hezekiah is found in Proverbs 25-29. Proverbs are included from other sources: the words of Agur, Proverbs 30:1-14 and of Lemuel - Proverbs 31:1-9, both from Massa in North Arabia. There is also evidence in Proverbs 22:17 - 23:11 of Egyptian influences which are based on the maxims of Amen-em-opet.

Proverbs treat of life's problems, not philosophically, but from experience. They offer practical advice for a successful life, especially to those setting out in world of the court. To this the collection, of concrete individualist maxims, has been added a long preface (Proverbs 1-9) modelled on Egyptian Counsels of a Father to his Son, but showing a growing doctrine of Wisdom, of which the beginning and end is the fear of the Lord.

Look among the proverbs: there are pithy, short sentences; there are profound insights; there are vivid descriptions. Among my own favourites are:

Trust in the Lord with all your heart,
and do not rely on your own insights. 3:5

There is one whose rash words are like sword thrusts,
but the tongue of the wise brings healing. 12:18.

The spirit of man is the lamp of the Lord,
searching all his inmost parts. 20:27

and I enjoy the descriptions of the sluggard, especially 22:13 and 24:30-34, and of the effects of drinking (23:29-35), but, best of all, I make this my prayer:

Give me neither poverty nor riches;
feed me with the food that is needful for me,
lest I be full, and deny thee, and say
"Who is the Lord?" or lest I be poor and steal,
and profane the name of my God. 30:8-9.

PROVERBS 1

This chapter forms an introduction to the whole collection of Wisdom literature. It is ascribed to Solomon, as the Psalter is ascribed to David and the Pentateuch to Moses.

1. Pick out all the words describing Wisdom in verses 1-6. What, according to verse 7, is the climax of the introduction?
2. Look at the lively scene in verses 10-19. Who is the recipient of the warning? Against what is he warned?
3. Wisdom is personified. What is her character?

PROVERBS 2

An independent poem.

1. Divide the poem into stanzas (verses 1-8; 9-15; 16-19; 20-22) giving a title to each.
2. Compare verses 4-5 with Matthew 13:44,45. In what way does Jesus' teaching show an advance on Solomon's?
3. What are the principal snares against which the young man is warned? See verses 12-15, 16-19.

PROVERBS 3

The benefits of Wisdom are enumerated.

1. Look at verses 3-4 and compare them with Deuteronomy 6:7-8. Notice the emphasis on God's covenant love and faithfulness. How is this developed in 1 Corinthians 13?
2. Learn verses 5-7 by heart and make them a daily guide.
3. What advice is given in verse 27-30 about treatment of others?

PROVERBS 4

The choice of Wisdom. How it is applied to every day living.

1. Contrast the ways of the righteous and of the wicked (verses 10-19).
2. Have a personal check. Make use of verses 20-17 beside Ephes. 6:10-17.

PROVERBS 5

Adultery is contrasted with fidelity in marriage.

1. What advice does the Wise Man give about resisting temptation? How does St Paul complete this (Romans 7:21-25)?
2. What picture of marriage is given in verses 15-19? Is it a complete one?

PROVERBS 6: 1-19

Lively descriptions of the sluggard and the trouble-maker.

1. What advice is given in this chapter a) to those in debt, b) to those tempted to indolence, and c) to those inclined to listen to trouble-makers?
2. Do another check - verses 16-19.

PROVERBS 6: 20 - 7:27

The imprudent young man is warned against the adventuress.

1. What is said about the cost of adultery? Does it apply today?

2. Trace the course of temptation as described in 7:6-23. Can you reverse the picture and mak the girl the victim? What have you learned from this exercise about the different dangers tha confront men and women?
3. What Bible stories illustrate the Wise Man's teaching?

PROVERBS 8

Wisdom, personified, speaks out.

1. Compare the personification of Wisdom in verses 1-21 with that in 1:20-33. What more have we learned about her? What does she offer?
2. Verses 22-31. How far can this passage be seen as a prophecy of the Word of God, the second Person of the Trinity? Compare John 1:1-6.
3. Verses 32-36. Note the 'Beatitudes' of Wisdom. Compare them with Matthew 5:3-10 and compare verse 35 with John 10:20-28. What is the crucial difference between the Old Testament and New Testament outlook revealed in this passage and in John 10:20?

PROVERBS 9

Dame Wisdom and Dame Folly are contrasted.

1. Compare Dame Wisdom (verses 1-13) with Dame Folly (verses 14-18). To what elements in human nature do they appeal?
2. Notice how Jesus has used a similar device in Luke 14:15-24. What a) does Dame Wisdom offer at her banquet, and b) does Jesus signify by the banquet in the parable?

PROVERBS 10

The collection of proverbs that follows (10:1 - 24:22) is the oldest in the book probably dating from the tenth century BC. Several show Egyptian influence.

1. What do we learn about the sluggard in this chapter?
2. Compare 10:8 with 9:8-9. What do you make of this advice?
3. What is the lesson of verse 18?

PROVERBS 11 and 12

Righteousness and true security.

1. Gather the advice of right use of speech in these chapters. See especially 11:12,13; 12:14,16-19.
2. What are the advantages of kindness a) to the recipient and b) to the author?
3. Comment on 12:25.

PROVERBS 13

Wisdom reveals herself in wise instruction.

1. What is said in this chapter about good teaching? What are its chief benefits?
2. Do you agree with verses 2, 6, 11 and 21?
3. Comment on verse 24.

PROVERBS 14

1. Do you agree with verse 10, and with verse 30?
2. What advice is given concerning the right use of material goods?

PROVERBS 15

1. Draw out the comments on wise talk. See especially verses 1, 4, 23.
2. What do we learn about God in this chapter? Draw up a list of all the attitudes ascribed to him. Is the source revelation or reason?
3. What advice for good living do I find?

PROVERBS 16

1. Make verse 3 your golden rule. How is it explained in verse 4a?
2. What is the meaning of verses 1-2? Can you think of any applications? How is the maxim further explored in verse 9 and in verse 33?
3. Apply verses 10, 12-15 to Christ the king a) during his life on earth, and b) in the kingdom to come.

PROVERBS 17

1. What advice is given concerning social relations?
2. Draw out comments on family life. Which do you find the shrewdest, which the most helpful?
3. Learn verses 9 and 14 by heart. What New Testament passages comment on them?

PROVERBS 18

1. Go through this chapter for comments on the fool's attitude and behaviour. Is he merely silly?
2. Comment on verses 3 and 12 in the light a) of your own experience, and b) of recent events on the world scene.

PROVERBS 19

1. Compare verse 2 with Romans 10:2. How does Paul throw light on this proverb?
2. Comment on verse 3 in the light of contemporary attitudes, and even of our own. Are we challenged by it?
3. Draw out advice for families from this chapter. Reverse verses 13 and 14 to give the wife's point of view!

PROVERBS 20

1. What is said of the sluggard? Do we need this advice in any area of our own lives?
2. What comments are made on desire for revenge and on rash vows?
3. What is the meaning of verse 27?

PROVERBS 21

1. Comment on verses 9 and 19. For a wife, what kind of husband would be the equivalent of the 'contentious and fretful' woman?
2. Consider verses 13, 15 and 26 in the light of our obligations to seek justice for all and to share our possessions.

PROVERBS 22

At verse 17 a new collection of proverbs begins (22:17 - 24:22). This collection reflects the influence of the Egyptian 'Wisdom of Amenemope', possibly from the twelfth century BC.

1. Take verses 4 and 11 as watchwords for your own life. Why was verse 11 used for the office of virgin saints?
2. What four pieces of advice are given in verses 22-28? Do any of them apply to me?

PROVERBS 23

This chapter contains a brilliant cartoon of a drunkard.

1. Draw out the advice about behaviour at table. Can verses 6-7 be applied more generally? In what ways?
2. Against what two snares is the young man warned? Read carefully verses 27-28 and 29-35.

PROVERBS 24

Another collection begins at 24:23.

1. How should we apply verses 11-12? cf. Genesis 4:9 and Luke 16:19-31. In what way am I challenged?
2. Consider verse 27 as advice to young people thinking of getting married. Does it apply in any way to my own situation?

PROVERBS 25

This is the fourth collection (25:1 - 29:27). It dates from the eighth century BC.

1. Compare verses 6-7 with Luke 14:7-11, and verses 8-10 with Matthew 5:28; 18:15. Does their Old Testament origin throw any light on Jesus' words?
2. What is the meaning of verses 16 and 27? Do you agree?

PROVERBS 26

1. Find examples of irritating behaviour in this chapter.
2. What advice is given about speech? See especially verses 4-5, 20-26,28. Which advice do I most need?

PROVERBS 27

1. What warnings are given in this chapter?
2. What is the meaning of verse 19? Do you agree?
3. What advice is given in verses 23-27? How does it apply to us nowadays?

PROVERBS 28

1. What rewards are promised to those who keep the law? See verses 4-7.
2. What is said in this chapter about confession of sin?
3. What sins are exposed in this section?

PROVERBS 29

1. What warnings for those in authority do you find in this chapter?
2. What advice to parents is contained in verses 1, 15, 17?
3. Comment on verse 18.

PROVERBS 30

This fifth collection seems to be either from an Ishmaelite or an Edomite source.

1. What is the burden of Agur's hymn (verses 1-6)?
2. Compare verses 7-9 with New Testament teaching.
3. What can we learn from the animals? See verses 25-31.

PROVERBS 31

The sayings of Lemuel (verses 1-9) seem to come from an Ishmaelite collection. Verses 10-31 are an alphabetical poem.

1. What advice is given to a ruler? See verses 3, 4-7, 8-9. Could it be bettered today?
2. What do you think of the perfect housewife? In what spheres does she excel? Has she anything to teach us today?

AN INTRODUCTION TO ECCLESIASTES

The questions that concerned the writer of Job were also the preoccupations of the Preacher (Ecclesiastes); but while the Book of Job is a great drama, the writer of this book is a sceptic. He has tried the various Wisdom schools and found them wanting - in fact, he parodies the Book of Proverbs:

Be not righteous overmuch, and do not make yourself overwise;
why should you destroy yourself?

Be not wicked overmuch, neither be a fool;
why should you die before your time? 7:16-17

Bread is made for laughter,
and wine gladdens life,
and money answers everything. 10:19

To the optimism of Proverbs, he replies with the warning that death comes to all, and he sets the scene in 1:2: *FUTILITY* (REB and NJB), Vanities (RSV and JB), Meaningless (NIV), Emptiness (NEB), Useless (GNB)... Enough said! But, interestingly enough, the word so variously translated, *HEBEL*, which means air, breath, also occurs in Genesis 4 in the name Abel. In fact, there are several echoes of Genesis 1-4 in Ecclesiastes, with its sentence of futility and of recurring seasons. Compare Ecclesiastes 1:3-11 with Genesis 1 and 3:17-19. In the New Testament Paul takes up the theme of futility in Romans 8:18-25.

The book is divided into two parts, each with a prologue. The first part (1-6) centres on the boredom of the Preacher with all endeavour - pleasure, work, promotion - all end in death. The second part (7-12) introduces another theme - mockery. The old aphorisms are parodied, and the futility of man's endeavour is made into a joke. But the Preacher has some useful advice to give, despite his cynicism.

When times are good, be happy;
but when times are bad, consider.
God has made the one
as well as the other. 7:14 (NIV).

and

Behold, this alone I found, that God made man upright,
but they have sought out many devices. 7:29.

The Preacher's central doctrine is a simple one: make the most of life (5:18-20, etc) live heartily, actively, responsibly, remembering the Creator, and caring for the aged.

The book is written in late Hebrew by a Palestinian Jew, probably during the third century BC. It was known to Ben Sira (Sirach).

ECCLESIASTES 1

After his prologue setting his theme (verses 1-11) - boredom with the futility of all things - the Preacher begins a short autobiography (verses 12 ff).

1. Compare verses 1-11 with Genesis 1 and with Genesis 3:17-19. What comment is the author making?
2. The author speaks in the name of Solomon. What facts does he give of his life?

ECCLESIASTES 2

The Preacher's experiences illustrate his theme.

1. In what way is Solomon's experience a commentary on the ideals put before many if not most people today?
2. How does the author make fun of traditional wisdom? Note especially the proverbs he quotes, and comment on them. (cf. verses 14, 24, 25).
3. What is the special pain of the Preacher (verses 17-23)? Is there advice here for a workaholic? Of what nature?

ECCLESIASTES 3

A poem on life and death is followed by a series of scattered reflections.

1. Verses 1-9. What philosophy lies behind this passage? Does it explain our experience or reflect it? Does revelation add anything?
2. Comment on verse 11. In what way does this great mystery add to the pessimism of the author?
3. The same idea keeps recurring (2:24, 3:13,22). Is it a) a wise response, and b) an adequate one? Do we ever have moods in which we share the author's pessimism? What consolation do WE find at such times?

ECCLESIASTES 4

Social problems are discussed with some sensitivity.

1. Show how verses 1-3 are an expansion of the idea contained in 3:16-17. How does the Preacher differ from Job 3:11-23; 10:18-22?
2. Comment on verse 4. How is the balance restored? See verses 8-12.
3. Compare verses 5-6 with Proverbs 6:9-12. What accounts for the difference in tone?

ECCLESIASTES 5

Some advice to worshippers is followed by some proverbs concerning money.

1. What advice does the Preacher give on worship? How does it compare with Matthew 6:7?
2. Study the Preacher's central doctrine, contained in verses 18-20. Go through it point by point, examining my own life in the light of it. Am I in danger of sometimes neglecting commonsense? What are its limits?

ECCLESIASTES 6

The author repeats and enlarges on his central doctrine.

1. The author develops the ideas contained at the end of chapter 5. What are the situations he envisages? See verses 2-3.
2. Comment on verses 3-6. Compare the Preacher's musings with New Testament teaching.
3. Do you agree with verse 7? How far is it a commentary on contemporary life?
4. Compare verse 10 with Job 9:32-35. What is the Christian's answer?

ECCLESIASTES 7

A new prologue to the second half of the book, on the theme of laughter. The author parodies the traditional teachings of Proverbs.

1. Compare verse 1 with Proverbs 22:1. What does the Preacher do to the proverbs he quotes (or misquotes)? What is his underlying purpose?

2. What do you think of the pessimism in verses 2-6?
3. How far can verse 14 be taken as a watchword? Compare with the Beatitudes (Matthew 5:3-10). Comment on verses 15-16.
4. Verses 23-29. Draw out what the Preacher is trying to express. Does New Testament have a response to verse 25? cf. Romans 8.

ECCLESIASTES 8

Public life and politics.

1. What is suggested in verses 1-8 about a) the way to conduct one's affairs, and b) the problems that are inevitable?
2. How does the author express what we call the problem of evil and the mystery of innocent suffering? See verses 12-15. How does he summarise his findings?

ECCLESIASTES 9

The Preacher returns to his central doctrine.

1. Read verses 1-6 and then look at 3:11. Do you think this is in any way an answer? Are there occasions when we feel no further than the Preacher in our response to life? What commentary do you find in New Testament? cf. Romans 11:33.
2. Consider verses 7-12 as the story of most people's lives. Is it your story?
3. What do you think of the story in verses 14-16?

ECCLESIASTES 10

This is an interlude chapter - a collection of proverbs, many of them parodies on Proverbs.

1. Draw out the proverbs concerned with careless talk.
2. Pick out the proverbs that are clearly parodies on Wisdom literature.
3. List the absurdities the author has observed.

ECCLESIASTES 11

A positive chapter, containing the Sage's advice.

1. The advice in this chapter comes under two headings: challenge life's uncertainties and live heartily; live responsibly. Sort out the sayings under each heading.
2. Comment on the advice to a young man, and compare it with Proverbs.

ECCLESIASTES 12

The Book ends with a description of old age, and an epilogue repeating the theme.

1. What do you think of the picture of old age in verses 1-7? What is lacking?
2. Verses 9-13. What do we learn of the author from these verses?
3. What have you learned from the Preacher? Is his message totally negative, or has he taught you anything about prayer?

AN INTRODUCTION
TO
THE SONG OF SONGS

What is one to make of this Canticle? Is it a series of love songs? What is the meaning of the reference to Solomon? Is it to be interpreted mystically or literally? If literally, why is it in the Bible? It has been beloved by many saints: St Bernard wrote a long commentary on it, so did St John of the Cross; St Therese of Lisieux quotes it repeatedly.

We give a suggested interpretation here, but, in the questions which follow, we invite the reader to see in the Canticle the expression of Christ's love for his Church, and for the individual soul.

Song I. 1:1-2:7.

The first speaker (2-4) seems to be a girl who has been brought to the king's palace. She is praised by her companions in verse 4b, but is shy because of her darkened skin - evidence of her country origins. She has been working in the sun. In verse 7 she addresses her lover, who seems to be a shepherd. He praises her in extravagant terms. A dialogue of love follows between them.

Song II. 2:8 - 3:5.

This song is divided into a description of a day in the countryside (2:8-17) and a night of dreams (3:1-5). In verse 14 the lover asks the girl to sing to him and verse 15 is probably her song, taken up by a chorus. Possibly the dream of 3:1-5 represents the girl, kept in Solomon's harem, pining for her rustic lover.

Song III. 3:6 - 5:1.

Solomon's wedding procession is described in 3:6-11. In 4:1-15 the bridegroom or rustic lover or Solomon - praises the bride. The imagery of a garden locked, a fountain sealed, clearly points to a virgin bride, exclusively for her husband, either Solomon, or, perhaps more likely, the shepherd lover.

Songs IV. 5:2 - 6:3.

Presumably 5:2-8 is a dream, indeed a nightmare. If the girl is now in Solomon's palace, and yearns for her lover, such a dream, with its elusive qualities, frustration and violence, is not surprising. By 6:2, we seem to be back to reality. She knows where her lover is.

Song V. 6:4 - 8:4.

This seems to be Solomon praising his bride, describing how he first met her and fell for her (verses 11-12). The companions (are they other women in the harem?) seem to be recalling the girl from her dreams of her shepherd lover, and Chapter 7 is perhaps the attendants preparing her for her marriage to the king. In 7:10 the bride interrupts to deny Solomon and to reaffirm her preference for her shepherd. In verse 11 she seems to have escaped once more to the countryside, where she can meet her true love once more.

Song VI. 8:5-14.

The lovers are re-united, and the marriage is celebrated by the villagers. Verses 8-10 refer to the guardianship of chastity by the family. The bride re-affirms her own chastity (I am a wall - verse 10), and to her bridegroom she brings wholeness (peace, contentment). Solomon is welcome to his harem and to his possessions (verse 11). She is happy in giving her own fullness to her lover in marriage (verse 12).

SONG OF SONGS 1:1 - 2:7

1. The bride says she is dark (1:5) but comely, and that the king has brought her into the secret chambers of his heart (1:4). What light do these images throw on our devotion to the heart of Jesus? What makes us 'dark' even though basically comely?
2. What is the meaning of 2:3-6? In what way can it be an image of our life of prayer? Who is symbolised by the apple tree?

SONG OF SONGS 2:8 - 3:5

1. On what occasions has Christ said to me, 'Arise, ... and come away'? Have I responded?
2. Do we ever experience the sense of abandonment at prayer expressed in the dream (3:1-3)? Can the church community (my mother's house) support me at times of dryness in prayer? What helps most?

SONG OF SONGS 3:6 - 5:1

1. Consider 3:11 as a prophecy of Christ's 'wedding' with humanity at his incarnation cf. Hebrews 10:5-7. What is the note struck here?
2. Several verses in Chapter 4 are used in the office of Mary the Virgin (especially verses 7 and 12). They are also applied to virgin saints. What mysteries do they celebrate and foreshadow? Can they in any sense be applied to all Christians?

SONG OF SONGS 5:2 - 6:3

1. 'My head is wet with dew' (verse 5:2) has been applied to Christ in his Passion. Make this application for the whole verse, and cf. Psalm 110:7a. Does the symbolism in any way add to your understanding of Christ's suffering? How would you express it?
2. What does this Song teach us about perseverance in prayer?
3. Trace the dynamics of prayer through the whole Song.

SONG OF SONGS 6:4 - 8:4

1. Verses 6:4 and 10 have been applied to the Church, and cf. Revelations 12:1. What truths could this imagery be seeking to convey?
2. Verses 6:12-13 are very obscure. They have been variously translated. Do they describe temptations to backsliding or to distractions in prayer?
3. Read Chapter 7 as a description of a newly baptised Christian. What virtues are here celebrated?
4. Consider 2:16, 6:3 and 7:10 as stages in a) human love and b) in our love for Christ.

SONG OF SONGS 8:5 - 14

1. What do verses 5-7 teach us about love? How would you characterise it? Does New Testament go further?
2. "Then I was in his eyes as one who brings peace" (verse 10). Examine this verse as a description a) of a wife; b) of one consecrated to Christ. Is it true of me?
3. Verses 8-10. What are the values of chastity in Christian teaching and tradition? What role should the family play in the protection of young people? Do you think that these values could be restored in the modern world? How?

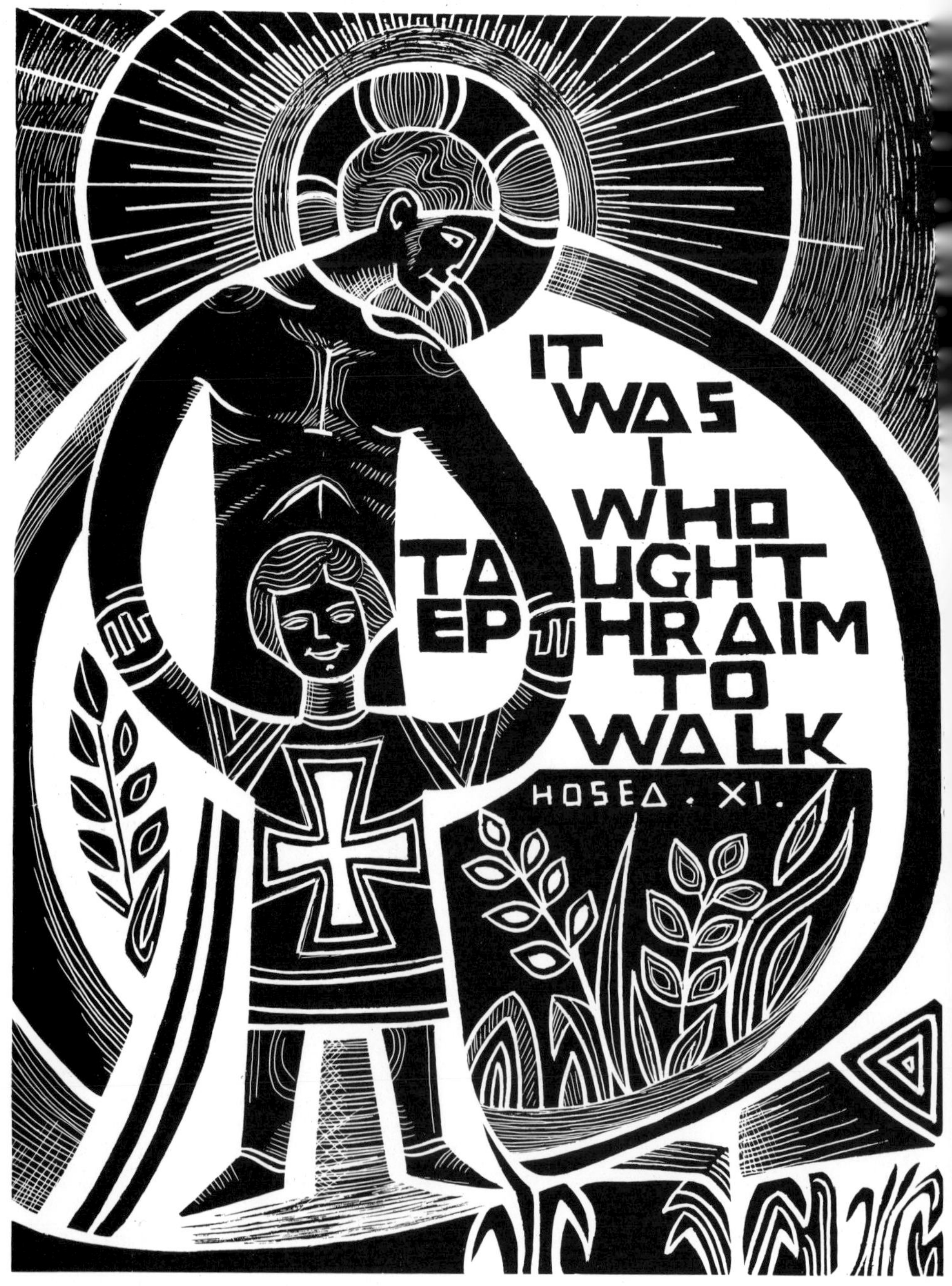
IT
WAS
I
WHO
TAUGHT
EPHRAIM
TO
WALK
HOSEA . XI .

AN INTRODUCTION TO THE BOOK OF ISAIAH

'Bind up the testimony, seal the teaching among my disciples. I will wait for the Lord, who is hiding his face from the house of Jacob, and I will hope in him'.

Thus wrote the prophet Isaiah when the king Ahaz refused to listen to his warnings and advice. He would write down his prophecies so that later generations would know that he was proved right. The prophet whose oracles are (largely) contained in chapters 1-39 is known as Isaiah of Jerusalem. He was born about 765 BC and his prophetic ministry covered the years 740-700 BC. His call came during the last year of King Uzziah's long reign (6:1), and he was influential at court during the reigns of Jotham, Ahaz and Hezekiah. The story of the reigns of these is related in 2 Kings 16:1-20 (Ahaz), and 2 Kings 18-20 (Hezekiah). It was a period of some prosperity in Israel and Judah, but this very wealth led to gross inequalities. The political situation was volatile,and in 733 Israel and Syria rebelled against the great power of Assyria, and tried to force Judah into alliance with them. In spite of Isaiah's warnings, Ahaz appealed for help to the notorious ruler of Assyria (Tiglath-Pileser III) who attacked Damascus, the capital of Syria, and Samaria, the capital of Israel, at the same time turning Judah into an Assyrian satellite. Isaiah withdrew from public affairs (8;16-18) after his failure with Ahaz. In 721 Assyria annexed the whole of the Northern kingdom, and Samaria itself fell, thousands of its inhabitants deported to Assyria. In 716 Hezekiah succeeded Ahaz in Judah, and he tried to reform the Temple worship which had been much infiltrated by Assyrian religious practices during Ahaz' reign. However, Hezekiah, trying to free the country from the Assyrian yoke, turned to Egypt for support, against Isaiah's advice. Sargon of Assyria actually invaded Judah in 711, after which Isaiah once more withdrew from public life. In 705, Hezekiah rebelled against Assyria, and Sennacherib, Sargon's successor, ravaged Palestine in 701, besieging Jerusalem. By a miracle (plague?) the Assyrian armies withdrew. We know no more about Isaiah; the Jewish tradition has it that he was martyred under Manasseh, Hezekiah's successor.

Isaiah of Jerusalem is one of the great prophets and thinkers of all time. His insights into the holiness of God, into God's Providence in history, into the meaning of secular events rank him among the philosophers as well as among the men of God. He is, of course, best known to Christians for his Messianic vision. First of all, during the Syro-Ephraimite war, when weak-kneed Ahaz trembled before his northern neighbours, Isaiah saw the coming of Emmanuel - God-with-us - to judge, and to heal (Isaiah 7-8). Later, disheartened by the futility of most of David's successors, he foresaw a King of the stock of Jesse who will bring wisdom into his understanding of his office, filled with the Spirit of God, ruling in justice and equity (Isaiah 9 and 11). However, while it is right to search the scriptures for prophecies of Christ, prophetic literature is above all, important for its proclaiming of the gospel - the good news that Jesus emphasised - that events have a meaning, that in the end justice will triumph, - indeed that God is in control. Therefore all that Isaiah and the other prophets say is not for their own time only, but is re-interpreted in every age - is the Word of God for us today, just as it was in their own time. Jesus' coming did not blot out the Old Testament scriptures, it fulfilled them.

Isaiah of Jerusalem mentioned disciples (8:16). These must have collected his oracles and perhaps formed a school of Isaian thought and tradition - underground during the reign of Manasseh - but alive in some way, for his traditions were passed on through the changing fortunes of the kingdom of Judah. In 587 BC Babylonian armies besieged the city, destroyed the Temple, put the king Zedekiah to death and deported many thousands of the people to Babylon, where they remained until 521 BC. During this period of exile, other prophets arose to interpret events to the people. Among them was an unnamed prophet, in the tradition of

Isaiah, known to scholars as Deutero-Isaiah. He preached in Babylon between 550 and 538 BC. His book is often called the Book of Consolation. Chapters 40-48 proclaim that God is about to restore the exiled Jews to their land: that Jerusalem's 'time of service is ended, her iniquity is pardoned, that she has received from the Lord's hand double for all her sins'. (40:2).

A series of great poems follows, proclaiming the good news, and incorporating the first of the so-called Servant Songs (42:1-7). Chapters 49-55 prepare the exiles for their return to Jerusalem, offering persuasion and encouragement to the timid and disheartened. The other three Servant Songs (49:1-7); 50:4-9; and 52:13 - 53:12) deepen the theology of suffering, of death and of resurrection. A new exodus, even more wonderful than the first one, will bring the people home to a renewed Jerusalem.

The final part of the Book of Isaiah (56-66) is a collection of oracles - sometimes called Trito-Isaiah - which were addressed to the restored community after the return from exile, about the time of Haggai and Zechariah 1-9. It does not seem that one author is responsible for all, as there are: prophecy, catechesis, prophetic liturgy, psalms, prayers - all gathered into an interesting anthology which could be entitled Return to the Land. There is advice on fasting (58), encouragement for groups formerly excluded from worship (56), warning to sinners (56:9-12 and 59 and 65), visions of eschatological hope (62-63, 65:17-25).

ISAIAH 1

Isaiah speaks in the Temple during Sennacherib's invasion of the country and siege of Jerusalem (701 BC).

1. Of what sins does Isaiah accuse the people? What would be their equivalent in the Church today?
2. By what names does the prophet refer to God?
3. What is the double purpose of God's judgement revealed in verses 24-31? Can it be linked to verses 16-20?

ISAIAH 2

The new title (verse 1) introduces a collection of oracles in chapters 2-5. Verses 2-5 also occur in Micah 4:1-3 and verse 4 is re-interpreted in Joel 3:10.

1. What vision of the kingdom of God is contained in verses 2-5?
2. This early prophecy (probably 735 BC) was uttered when Judah was rich and prosperous under Uzziah and Jotham. In what ways is it relevant to our own land and century? See especially verses 6-8. What sin is especially condemned? See verses 11, 12, 17, 22.

ISAIAH 3

This oracle probably dates from the anarchic situation during the reign of Ahaz.

1. In what ways could the prophet be describing the anarchy in many countries today? Why is the situation so bad? see verses 8, 12, 14-15.
2. Why is the prophet so harsh to the women of Jerusalem? In what sense can it be said that the attitude and behaviour of women is an index of the moral health of a people?

ISAIAH 4

This short chapter introduces the theme of the vineyard. The "branch" (verse 2) refers to God's work of recreating his people, through the "remnant".

1. What hope for the future is contained in verses 2-6?
2. Contrast verse 4 with verses 5 and 6. In what ways is the experience of the desert an inspiration to the prophet?

ISAIAH 5

The Song of the Vineyard, a poem originally recited at a grape harvest. The curses are a common prophetic device for getting a message across.

1. Verses 1-7. Work out the allegory in this song. Compare Christ's use of it in Matthew 21:33-45. Of what does God principally accuse the inhabitants of Jerusalem and the men of Judah?
2. Verses 8-24. Of what six crimes are the people accused, and how will they be punished? What are the twentieth century equivalents of these sins?

ISAIAH 6-12

Chapters 6-12 are designated the Book of Emmanuel in JB. They contain memoirs of the prophet, oracles concerning the Syro-Ephraimite war, and some Messianic oracles.

ISAIAH 6

The call of Isaiah took place in the Temple in 740 BC.

1. In verses 1-4 try to imagine the scene. What does the prophet tell us of God? On what ideas and images does he draw to describe the indescribable? What is the keynote of his vision?
2. What is Isaiah's reaction? (cf Luke 5:8-11). How is he cleansed? What use is made of this scene in the liturgy?
3. Can we respond like Isaiah (verse 8)? Or are we more like Moses (Exodus 4:10) or Jeremiah (Jer. 1:6)? What is the meaning of verses 9-10? What use is made of them in New Testament? see especially John 12:40.

ISAIAH 7

The Syro-Ephraimite war. Rezin of Syria (Aram) and Pekah of Israel hoped to force Judah into a coalition against Assyria. In spite of Isaiah's warnings Judah's King Ahaz appealed to Assyria for help against his northern neighbours (Syria and Israel). Assyria attacked them, and put Ahaz under tutelage. In this chapter Ahaz is reviewing his fortifications when the prophet meets him accompanied by his little son Shear-Jashub, who has a prophetic name meaning 'A remnant shall return'.

1. Verses 1-9. Isaiah urges Ahaz to be calm and to trust in God, not in foreign alliances. What grounds does he give for his optimism? See verse 9.
2. Verses 10-25. This obscure passage can be read at two levels: a prophecy of reverses for Israel and Syria (verse 16, the birth of a child in the Davidic line, and, later, the devastation of Judah by Assyria (verses 18-end); a Messianic prophecy concerning Emmanuel. How has this prophecy been understood a) in New Testament (cf. Matthew 1:23) and b) in the liturgy and in Christmas carols?

ISAIAH 8

A collection of oracles largely concerned with the uncertain period during the Syro-Ephraimite war. Waters of Shiloah symbolise God's protection.

1. Isaiah's second son is named Maher-shalal-hash-baz - 'The spoil speeds, the prey hastens'. What does this portend? (Verse 4). What two examples of lack of trust on the part of the people does the prophet give? See verses 6,19. Are we guilty of the same lack of trust in our personal and in our political lives? Give examples.
2. Compare the different uses of the idea of 'Emmanuel' in this section. (See 7:14, 8:8, 10). Is it always a prophecy of hope? Can God-with-us also imply judgement?
3. What is the state of mind of the prophet at this time? See especially verses 16-20.

ISAIAH 9

Zebulun and Naphtali were devastated by the Assyrians in 732 BC (See 2 Kings 15:29).

1. What use does the New Testament make of verses 1-7? See Matthew 4:13-16 and John 12.
2. The prophecy gives the Messiah's 'throne-names' (verse 6). What do they tell us about Christ?
3. Of what sins does the prophet accuse the Northern kingdom? See verses 9-10, 13, 17, 20-21. What is their equivalent today?

ISAIAH 10

Verses 1-4 seem to complete the 'woes' of Chapter 5:8-25. The rest of the chapter refers to Sennacherib's invasion of Palestine in 701 BC. In verse 9 Isaiah refers to cities ravaged by the Assyrians - the Nazis of the ancient world. The last section (verses 27-34) is a powerful description of the advance of the Assyrian armies on Jerusalem.

1. How does this chapter teach us a) that God uses Assyria (therefore all similar armies) as an instrument of judgement, b) that God will punish the pride of the avenger, and c) that all events are in God's hands?
2. What is promised to the 'remnant'? See verses 20-27. How can we apply the doctrine of this chapter to our own age?

ISAIAH 11-12

The prophet was so disheartened at the record of David's descendants that he turned to a fresh source of hope - a new shoot of Jesse's line, Jesse being David's father. No good government can come from a tainted stock. The whole line needs renewal.

1. Notice the restoration of creation and of world history in Chapter 11. See especially verses 6-9 and 10-16.
2. a) What aspect of the kingdom of God is especially brought out in Chapter 11? b) List the gifts bestowed upon Christ. What will be the characteristics of his reign?
3. Chapter 12 consists of two psalms (verses 1-3, and 4-6). What are the graces celebrated?

ISAIAH 13-23

A collection of oracles against foreign nations, some of them not from Isaiah of Jerusalem.

ISAIAH 13:1 - 14:23

1. For what sins was Babylon destroyed? See verses 13:11 and 14:13-14.
2. In what sense can Babylon be said to typify the "evil city"? cf. 1 Peter 5:13 and Revelations 18.
3. The fathers of the Church applied 14:12-14 to the fall of Satan (Lucifer). Why?

ISAIAH 14:24-32

The prophecy against Assyria probably dates from 701 BC, the time of Sennacherib's invasion of Palestine.

1. Note how God's purpose and power are emphasised in verses 24-27. Do we read the events of our own lives and of our own generation with this truth in mind?
2. With verse 29 compare Proverbs 24:17 and 25:21. Are we inclined to rejoice at the misfortunes of those who have afflicted us? Do we see them as people in their own right? What should we do about unforgiving feelings?

ISAIAH 15-16

Moab was a neighbour of Judah. It was famous for its vineyards, cf. 15:8, 9, 10.

1. Consider the severity of the judgement on Moab, and the prophet's sympathy with the sufferings of the Moabites, especially 15:5. Are we ready to lament the sorrows of others, even of our enemies? Think of an example in ordinary life a) of unforgiveness and its consequences, and b) of forgiveness.
2. Study the Messianic promises in 16:5. What virtues are ascribed to the Messiah? How are they fulfilled in Jesus?

ISAIAH 17-18

Chapter 17 contains an early oracle against Syria and Israel (cf.chapter 7).

1. What is the chief sin of the Israelites? cf. 17:7-8, 10-11. How can this be said to describe our Western civilisation?
2. Chapter 18 refers to Egypt which had an Ethiopian (Cushite) ruler at that time. What is Isaiah's message to Egypt? See verses 2b-6. What is God's attitude, according to the prophet?

ISAIAH 19

This remarkable chapter shows the Lord treating Egypt as he treats Israel, visiting her to judge, to cleanse and to renew.

1. Verses 1-15. What three forms does judgement of Egypt take?
2. There are five oracles in verses 16-25, each beginning "In that day". Express each one in your own words.
3. The language of the Pentateuch is used in verses 19-22. Distinguish each section: Patriarchs, Exodus, Judges.
4. Learn verses 24-25 by heart, and apply them to a contemporary situation.

ISAIAH 20

Ashdod, a Philistine town, was captured by Assyrian troops in 711 BC, because, instigated by Egypt, it had revolted.

1. What was the meaning of Isaiah's acted parable?
2. What is Isaiah's constant teaching about reliance on Egyptian or any foreign alliances? Do we heed it today?

ISAIAH 21

Babylon was eventually overwhelmed by the Persian empire (Elam, Media). Verses 1-10 describe the fall of Babylon, whose officers are all unsuspecting (verse 5) to the Persians, while the Judean exiles long for news (verses 3-4, 6-7).

1. Contrast the feelings of the Babylonians with those of the exiles. Can we picture this scene as in any way relevant to twentieth century events? What is God's attitude? See verses 6, 10.
2. Verses 11-16 contain short oracles against Edom and against Arabia. Edom asks how long the night (of foreign domination?) will last. What is the answer? Is it an answer I receive for my own life? If so, what is my reaction?

ISAIAH 22

Jerusalem, under siege from Sennacherib, was suddenly released by the withdrawal of the Assyrian troops, decimated by plague. See 2 Chronicles 32:21.

1. What was a) the people's and b) Isaiah's reaction to the city's sudden reprieve?
2. What was the people's chief fault? See verses 11 and 13. Why is God so severe (verse 14)? Compare 6:10 and John 12:37-41.

ISAIAH 23

This is the last of the oracles against the nations. Tyre was a great Phoenician seaport.

1. What was Tyre's sin? Compare her fate with that of some of our own great ports. Have we anything to learn from this chapter?
2. The oracle ends on a positive note. Tyre was resilient. What lessons can we learn from verses 15-18?

ISAIAH 24-27

These chapters, consisting of poems and laments, are known as the 'little apocalypse' of Isaiah. They are similar in style to Daniel and Zechariah 9-14.

ISAIAH 24

1. Trace the influences of the Flood story (verses 4-6, 18b-19) in this chapter. What does the symbolism convey?
2. The chapter ends with a reference to Exodus 24:9 ff (verse 23). What is the significance of this?

ISAIAH 25

1. From what sorrows and perils are the people rescued?
2. What is the symbolism of the banquet on the mountain? Note especially verse 9. In what way do we 'wait' for our God to save us?
3. Look up the New Testament references to this banquet (Luke 22:18; Matthew 26:29; Mark 14:25; Revelation 19:9). How do they develop the idea?

ISAIAH 26:1-19

1. a) Read these verses as a dialogue between God and his people. In what way is it our experience too? b) Pick out all the words and phrases that emphasise trust in God.
2. What is the lesson of verses 10-11?

ISAIAH 26:20 - 27:13

Leviathan (27:1) is a symbol of evil itself.

1. Compare 27:1 with Genesis 3:14-15 and Revelation 12-13. What is the meaning of God's struggle with the fleeing serpent and the dragon?
2. What does the reversal of Isaiah 5:1-7 (cf. verses 2-6) signify?
3. What is the message of the oracle in verses 27:12-13?

ISAIAH 28

This oracle must date from the destruction of the northern kingdom in 721 BC. The prophet denounces drunkenness and debauchery (verses 1-8); his opponents retort (verses 9-10); he warns them (verses 11 ff.)

1. In what did the people of Jerusalem place their trust? See verses 15, 18. What had God promised? (verses 6, 12, 16-17).
2. What instead was God's "strange" deed, his "alien" work? Can we see this judgement at work in our century?
3. What is the meaning of the parable in verses 23-29?

ISAIAH 29

Prophecy dating from before the siege of Jerusalem in 701 BC.

1. What is meant by a 'famine of the Word'? See verses 9-13, and cf. Amos 8:11-12. Is such a situation happening today?
2. What is the cause of the transformation in verses 17-23? Can we take to heart verse 24?

ISAIAH 30

This prophecy is concerned with Hezekiah's envoys asking for Egyptian help against the Assyrians (703 BC).

1. Verses 1-7. The prophet condemns reliance on Egypt and mocks the difficulties of the envoys (verse 6) on a fruitless journey. How much of our lives is spent on useless activity, and in reliance on insecure securities? How many times is God's advice mentioned in verses 1-3?
2. Trace in verses 8-17 the results of two things: reliance on God, or on 'Egypt'.
3. What blessings has God in store for his people? See verses 18-28. How is the promise of a Teacher fulfilled in Christ? Are we sensitive to his holy Spirit (verse 21)? What signs follow dociliity to his promptings?
4. Compare verses 25-30 with 2:11-17. What is the message of each?

ISAIAH 31

The Assyrian army was utterly ruthless and very strictly disciplined, inspiring terror wherever it went.

1. What are the symbols of power mentioned by the prophet? What would be their equivalent today? What would Isaiah say to us about our trust in weapons (for defence!)?
2. What are the arguments the prophet uses to persuade Judah and her rulers to trust God and not foreign alliances?

ISAIAH 32

The first part of this chapter is a description of good government after the style of the Wisdom school.

1. Compare verses 1-8 with Proverbs 16:10-13 and Proverbs 31:3-9 and show how verse 5 is a reversal of Ecclesiastes 10:5-7.
2. Contrast the situation foretold in verses 10-14 with that in verses 15-20. Which describes the situation in our lives, in our church, in our country?

ISAIAH 33

This chapter is a prophetic liturgy, like many of the psalms. The people lament, call on God, and he answers.

1. What is the spiritual state of the people as described in verses 7-12?
2. What does God promise a) concerning the historical situation (cf. verse 19), and b) concerning the Messiah?

ISAIAH 34-35

These two chapters are similar in style to chapters 24-27. They date from post-exilic times. At the time of the fall of Jerusalem in 587 BC Edom took advantage of Judah's misfortunes and invaded in the wake of the Babylonians. This was not forgotten by Judah.

ISAIAH 34

The first part of the oracle describes the outburst of divine wrath (1-8); the second part the resulting destruction (9-17).

1. Verses 1-8. What is the theology that lies behind the imagery?
2. Verses 9-12. Compare the desert state of Edom with Genesis 1:2 and 19:24-28. What underlies the deliberate use of "creation" language and references to patriarchal times?
3. Verses 13-17. Edom becomes the territory of wild beasts. What is meant by the reference to the 'book of the Lord' (verse 16) and to the work of the Spirit? Can such imagery be applied to any great theological questions that concern us today?

ISAIAH 35

1. Go through the chapter carefully, comparing it with chapter 34, and noting each example of a reversal of imagery. Compare also verse 2 with 33:9. What is the theological purpose of these contrasts?
2. What are the blessings promised to the returned exiles? Why are they called "redeemed" (verse 9)?

ISAIAH 36-39

These chapters reproduce 2 Kings 18:13,17 - 20:19.

ISAIAH 36

1. What did the Rabshakeh (cupbearer) offer the Judeans?
2. What interpretation did he put on Hezekiah's reforms (verse 7 and cf. 2 Kings 18:4)?

ISAIAH 37

1. What reassurance did Isaiah give to the king's servants?
2. In what way can Hezekiah's prayer (verses 16-20) be a model for our own prayer when in trouble?

ISAIAH 38-39

1. In what sense can Hezekiah's prayer be said to be the prayer of one who hopes, but does not fully believe? Do we ever feel like that?
2. How does God respond?
3. Compare 2 Chronicles 32:25,31 with Isaiah 39. What light does it throw on Hezekiah's motives and actions?

ISAIAH 40-55

This book is often called the Book of Consolation. It was composed in Babylon by a disciple of the Isaian school between 550 and 538 BC.

ISAIAH 40

The theme is of preparations for a processional triumph. God himself will lead his people out of exile, as he led them out of Egypt.

1. What four aspects of God are presented in this chapter? See verses 8,10,11,12. How are these aspects brought together in Christ?
2. Many people feel worthless, unloved, perpetually guilty. What strength and consolation for them is to be found in verses 1-2 and 27-31?

ISAIAH 41

The deliverer mentioned in verse 2 is Cyrus, king of the Persians, who defeated the Medes in 555, and in 539 entered Babylon. He ordered the rebuilding of the Temple in Jerusalem, and allowed the exiles to return.

1. Notice the repetition of consoling words from Yahweh to his people. Draw out the promises he makes to them. How do they apply in our personal lives?
2. The nations (verses 1-2) and then the gods (verses 22-24) are put on trial. For what are they called to account? Have we trusted in idols? Of what nature?

ISAIAH 42

Four songs in this chapter: the Servant (1-4); a victory song (5-9); a hymn of praise (10-17); the song of the blind servant (18-25).

1. First Song of the Servant of Yahweh (verses 1-4). Apply this song (as New Testament does cf. Matthew 12:15-21) point by point to Jesus.
2. Victory song (verses 5-9). What illustrations of the power of God's Word are found in this song?
3. Song of redemption (verses 10-17). What images are used to convey God's redeeming action? Can this imagery be applied to Christ's victory over sin? See verses 13, 16.
4. Song of the blind servant, Israel (verses 18-25). The prophet denounces God's chosen people as deaf and blind (verses 18-20). Can this ever be said of the people of God nowadays? Can we think of examples in which the sufferings of Christians comes about as a result of sin in the Church?

ISAIAH 43

Oracles of salvation, reflecting Biblical themes: (Daniel, Exodus, Patriarchs).

1. Many times in the New Testament (especially Luke 24:27, 44) we are told that the story of Jesus is contained in the scriptures (Old Testament). Show from verses 1-13 how the story of Israel *is* the story of Jesus, the beloved Son of God, precious in God's sight, redeemed after great suffering. Can verses 1-13 be my story too?

2. Of what sins is Israel accused in this chapter? See especially verses 22-24.
3. What new thing (verse 19) is God doing? Is he doing it again in our day?

ISAIAH 44

Another oracle of salvation. The exiles are saved for a great future. Verses 9-20 are a taunt-song against idolatry.

1. Verses 1-5. What do we learn of God's blessings promised to those he has chosen? Are *WE* open to receive his grace, symbolised by 'streams on the dry ground' (verse 3)? What occasions in my life have been marked by the outpouring of the Spirit?
2. Verses 6-8. How do we witness to the mighty action of God in people and in events?
3. Verses 9-20. In what way does the prophet taunt the idol worshippers? Can we honestly say that *WE* have no idols? Consider carefully verse 19. Do we take time to consider our attitude to the material things on which we set our heart?
4. Verses 21-28. What is the climax of God's creating and redeeming activity according to the prophet? How are these verses a foretelling of the Christian gospel?

ISAIAH 45

Cyrus is introduced in similar terms to 2 Chronicles 36:23. God uses him as his instrument for the salvation of his people. The chapter is remarkable for its universalism.

1. How does the story of Cyrus remind us that God's sovereignty is over all mankind, even over those who do not know him? What does this teach us about respect for everyone? What are the 'treasures of darkness'?
2. In what sense can verse 8 be an Advent hymn?
3. In verses 14-25 what are the reasons given for all nations turning from idols to the living God?
4. Does verse 15 or verse 19 express your experience of God at present? Have you known both at different times?

ISAIAH 46

Bel and Nebo were Babylonian gods. They were carried in procession on festivals. The prophet foresees the Babylonians fleeing before the Persians, carrying their idols on beasts into captivity.

1. Compare the God of Israel - Our God - (verses 3-5) with the powerless idols of Babylon (verses 1,6-7). Do we trust wholly in God, or do we place our security in possessions? What idols would we be tempted to take if *WE* had to flee in a hurry?
2. Can you think of occasions when verses 8-13 have been fulfilled in events, or in your personal life?

ISAIAH 47

A lament for Babylon.

1. What sins led to Babylon's disaster? Contrast her situation in verses 7 and 8 with that described in verses 1-3.
2. Babylon was famous for astronomers and mathematicians as well as for soothsayers. The prophet warns her not to trust in them. What would be the equivalents for the twentieth century? Find a modern example for each of verses 10, 12, 13.

ISAIAH 48

This chapter is addressed to the exiles who still have doubts that they *will* return to Judah.

1. Do we deduce from this chapter that the exiles had been led to trust in Chaldean magicians and fortune-tellers? See verses 6-8, 14. What is the mood of the prophet? Do we refuse to acknowledge God's action in our lives? On what occasions? In verse 5 is God speaking to *me*?
2. What picture is given in verses 17-21 of what Israel *could* have been if she had obeyed God? On what occasions in my life does God make water flow from the rock for me?

ISAIAH 49

Verses 1-6 are the second of the Servant Songs. "Israel" in verse 3 is a gloss.

1. Read these verses (1-6) as applying a) to a second Jeremiah, b) to Christ, and c) (cf. Acts 13:47) to the individual Christian. Then apply them to Israel and to the Church, the new Israel. What is the central theme in all these applications?
2. Verses 7-13. In what way do these verses sum up the vocation of Israel and , eventually, of the Church of Christ? See especially verses 7 and 8. Do we recognise the 'desolate heritages' in the empty churches and dispirited Christians of many countries in the West? What hope is contained for them in this oracle?
3. Verses 14-26. What response does God give to the discouraged exiles? Under what two images does the prophet express God's love for his people?

ISAIAH 50

The third Servant Song is from verses 4-9.

1. What is God's final accusation to Israel? See verses 1-3. What historical events does he evoke to reassure the exiles?
2. The servant speaks like a sage (verse 4). Compare this verse with John 12:49. Is my prayer one of listening for God's Word, and my life one of uttering it at God's command?
3. The Servant suffers opposition and even persecution (verse 6). What categories of believers cause his suffering? Contrast verses 10 and 11.

ISAIAH 51

Verses 1-16 is a poem in five stanzas: (1-3, 4-6, 7-8, 9-11, 12-16). Verses 17-23 are another poem in the style of Lamentations 3.

1. Look up the following references: Deuteronomy 16:20; Genesis 12; Jeremiah 7:34 and Ezekiel 33:24 and find their echo in the first three stanzas of the poem (verses 1-8). On what past blessings and promises does the prophet base his hopes?
2. Trace the Creation and Exodus themes in verses 9-11 and find their echo a) in the situation of the exiles and b) in your own life.
3. Compare the situation of Jerusalem (verses 17 ff) with that of Babylon (47:1-3). Contrast verse 20 with verse 21. What brings about the transformation?

ISAIAH 52:1-12

The prophet now addresses Jerusalem, soon to be restored and re-peopled.

1. Note how verses 3 and 6 emphasise God's sovereign freedom in redeeming his people, and Israel's nothingness. What does this teach us concerning God's grace?
2. The Book of Consolation is a 'Gospel'. What is the Good News announced by the herald?

ISAIAH 52:13 - 53:12

This is the fourth Servant Song.

1. 52:13-15. God praises the Servant. Apply his words to Jesus and look especially at John 19:5 as a commentary on 52:14.
2. 53:1-9. The community speaks announcing the fate of the Servant. Look up 2 Chronicles 26:20-23 for the condition of a leper. Follow Jesus' sufferings in his Passion and Death as foretold in these lines. What interpretation is put on the Servant's sufferings?
3. 53:10-12. Who are the 'offspring' (verse 10)? What benefits does the Servant's death bring them?

ISAIAH 54

There is an abrupt change of mood and of metaphor in this chapter. Jerusalem is likened to a barren and forsaken wife restored to her husband.

1. Draw out patriarchal themes in this chapter (the barren wives, Noah). What use does the prophet make of them?
2. What picture of God do you find here? What name is he given? See especially verses 5, 8 and 10, and note that El Shaddai means "God of the mountain".
3. What is the 'heritage of the servants of the Lord' (verse 17)? What benefits do they enjoy? Do we accept these benefits, or neglect them?

ISAIAH 55

The climax to Deutero-Isaiah. It echoes Wisdom's invitation (Proverbs 9).

1. Compare the invitation in verses 1-2 with Proverbs 9:1-6 and also with John 6:32-35. What IS the banquet? See verses 3,6.
2. The punishments of Genesis 3:17-19 are reversed in verse 13. What does this mean in every day language? Can you give any examples that prove the truth of verses 8-9?

ISAIAH 56-65

This collection seems to be the work of Deutero-Isaiah's disciples and may be a re-interpretation of his writings, collected and in part written after the return from exile.

ISAIAH 56

The post-exilic community is exhorted to abandon its exclusiveness and to welcome all those who hold fast to the covenant.

1. Foreigners and eunuchs, hitherto excluded, are now welcomed into the redeemed community (verses 3-6). What groups do these represent in today's Church?
2. What use does the New Testament make of this chapter? cf. Matthew 21:13 and John 10:16.
3. Verses 10-12 are a lively description of lazy Judean leaders. What attitudes are represented? Do we, as leaders, ever fall into these sins?

ISAIAH 57

This chapter contains a judgement scene. Verses 3-10; charge of idolatry and sorcery; verses 11-12: judgement. Verses 14-21 are a poem showing God's care for the poor.

1. What practices are condemned in verses 3-10? What would be their modern counterpart? What is the root cause of the people's infidelity?
2. What does God promise those who are contrite of heart? What does this chapter teach us about God?

ISAIAH 58

The theology of fasting. This chapter is used in the Lenten liturgy.

1. What evidence is there of the people's hypocrisy in verses 1-5? What are the real evils from which they should 'fast'?
2. List the practical advice given. How far does our observance of Lent take its inspiration from this chapter, or do we just 'give up something'?
3. What blessings are promised? How should we celebrate Sunday?

ISAIAH 59

A penitential liturgy: prophetic preaching of repentance (verses 1-8); confession of guilt (verses 9-15); divine pardon (verses 15c-20).

1. Verses 1-8. Show how the prophet illustrates his statement in verses 1-2 by images portraying deep human depravity. List the sins named or hinted at.
2. Verses 9-15. The people acknowledge their responsibility for the situation. Can we think of occasions when these verses are true in our own times, when sin has blinded us to God's light on a situation?
3. Verses 15c-21. In what terms is God's redeeming action described? Can this be applied to our own life situation? How is it fulfilled in Christ? Learn verse 21 by heart.

ISAIAH 60

Midian, Ephah and Sheba were all peoples descended from Abraham (Genesis 25:1-4). So were Kedar and Nabaioth (Genesis 25:13).

1. What is the theological purpose of the references to Abraham's descendants? How does Matthew 2:1-12 echo this passage?
2. What spiritual realities are hidden under the imagery of the return to Jerusalem of the exiles?

ISAIAH 61

This chapter echoes the Servant Songs of Deutero-Isaiah.

1. The prophet is called (verse 1) to proclaim the good news. What is this gospel? Draw out the various aspects expressed in verses 1-3. Does the Church always proclaim and act upon this gospel?
2. Jesus quotes these words in Luke 4:18-19. How did he act upon them during his ministry?
3. What are a) the duties and b) the blessings of the priestly people whom God has called into covenant with him? See verses 5-9 and cf. Exodus 19:5-6 and Deuteronomy 33:8-10.

ISAIAH 62

The glory of Jerusalem is proclaimed in a wedding song - the marriage of Yahweh with his bride - Zion.

1. Trace the theme of 'watchman' through this chapter (verses 1, 6, 7). What was the duty of the watchman? cf. Ezekiel 22:30; Isaiah 21:6 ff.
2. Look up 1 Kings 22:42 and 2 Kings 21:1. Then compare the marginal version of the names given in verse 4. What is the significance of the name changes? See also verse 12 and compare Isaiah 7:3, 8:3 and Hosea 2:25. Are there any occasions when "new names" are given in Christian usage?

ISAIAH 63:1 - 64:11

63:1-6 are a fragment of a poem in the shape of a dialogue between God and the prophet; 63:7 - 64:11 are a lament on the history of Israel.

1. 63:1-6. Read the section with two optics in mind: a) taking the text literally as applying to God's judgement of the 'world' (typified by Bozrah, the capital of Edom), who could be able to 'help'? (verse 5); b) applying the verses to Christ (as does the liturgy) what insight do they give into the sufferings of the Messiah?
2. 63:7-14. What is the doctrine of the Holy Spirit in this passage? Note three aspects (verses 10, 11, 14). How do these aspects anticipate the teaching on the Holy Spirit in New Testament?
3. Consider the movement of this long lament: praise, supplication, prayer for help and for forgiveness. What leads the people to plead with God (63:15 ff.)? What would a Christian add?
4. What do we learn about pleading with God from Chapter 64? Of what ills does the prophet complain?
5. Read verse 64:4 and note carefully its meaning in the context. Then look up 2 Corinthians 2:9. In what way has Paul enlarged on its meaning?

ISAIAH 65

An apocalypse. God's anguish at his unresponsive people.

1. What picture of God is conveyed in verses 1-2, 12? Do we ever think of God's point of view when we grumble? Why was God unable to forgive the people (verse 3)? How do these verses reveal the inevitability of judgement if man misuses his free will?
2. Consider the parable in verse 8, and compare it with the parables of the weeds and the dragnet (Matthew 13:24-30, 38-43; and 13:47-50). What hope is contained in verses 8 and 9?
3. What is to be the lot of God's chosen people in the new age (verses 17-25)? What in contrast will befall those who forsake God (verses 11-15)? How are we to interpret these blessings and curses?

ISAIAH 66

The conclusion of the apocalypse and of the whole book.

1. How can verses 1-2, together with other warnings against trust in the Temple (cf. Jeremiah 7) be applied to the Church?
2. What would be the twentieth century equivalent of the practices and attitude condemned in verses 3-4?
3. Therese of Lisieux found great inspiration for her little way of spiritual childhood from verses 10-13 (cf. Autobiography of a Saint, chapters 30, 31. Harvill Press). In what way can we too make them a foundation for our walk with God?

AN INTRODUCTION TO THE BOOK OF JEREMIAH

> One finds in the records that Jeremiah the prophet ordered those who were being deported to take some of the fire, as has been told, and that the prophet after giving them the law instructed those who were being deported not to forget the commandments of the Lord, nor to be led astray in their thoughts upon seeing the gold and silver statues and their adornment. And with other similar words he exhorted them that the law should not depart from their hearts. (2 Macc. 2:1-3).

Thus was the prophet Jeremiah honoured, indeed reverenced, centuries after his death, as is shown in this legend recorded during the second century BC. Jeremiah's ministry lasted from his call in early life during the reign of King Josiah (626 BC) through the reigns of Jehoiakim and of Zedekiah 'when the people of Jerusalm went into exile' in 587 BC. The story can be read in 2 Kings 22-25 and in 2 Chronicles 34 and 35.

The early years of his ministry, before Josiah's reform (622) were a time of religious decadence and syncretism, following the terrible years of the reign of Manasseh (Jeremiah 15:4). Even the reform, which the prophet certainly supported (Jeremiah 11), was not really accepted wholeheartedly by the people (3:6-10), and after the premature death of Josiah at the age of thirty-nine, a period of confusion and uncertainty was followed by the reign of the unpleasant king Jehoiakim, whom the prophet lampoons in 22:13-27, and whose personality is revealed in a brilliant vignette in 36:20-26. He was succeeded by his son Jehoiachin (Jechoniah) who reigned for only three months. In 598 the Babylonians against whose depredations of the land his father had rebelled, laid siege to Jerusalem, and took Jehoiachin prisoner. He was taken to Babylon, where he remained a prisoner for the rest of his life - a focus for nationalist hopes in Judah. His uncle Zedekiah took the throne in Jerusalem. A weak, vacillating man, he had, nevertheless, a great respect for Jeremiah and consulted him on three occasions, but he was too afraid of his own advisers and of the people to accept Jeremiah's counsel, which was to make terms with the Babylonians. Instead he rebelled against Nebuchadnezzar, who besieged Jerusalem for eighteen months, until a breach was made in the wall and his troops poured in, captured the king and put him to death. They set fire to the Temple and to the royal palace, and destroyed almost the entire city. Most of the people were deported to Babylon, and of those left, many fled to Egypt, among whom was Jeremiah.

His life, therefore, was one of almost unmitigated tragedy. Indeed his name has come into the language in the form of a noun - jeremiad - a lament. But his sufferings never destroyed his faith, nor embittered his temper. He poured out his feelings to God in the sections known as **Confessions** (11:18 - 12:6; 18:18-23; 20:7-18), and this intimacy formed him into a balanced, wise and kindly man. Note his gentle reply to the false prophet Hananiah (28:6), his dignity under persecution, his ability to make and to keep friends - Baruch, the family of Shaphan (who supported Josiah's reform), Ebed-Melech, Gedaliah.

The text is not in chronological order, and some of the oracles to the nations in 46ff are probably not by Jeremiah. Baruch's biography of the prophet and his account of events has been incorporated into the collection.

JEREMIAH

Jeremiah was born about 646 BC of a priestly family at Anathoth in Benjamin. Although not far from Jerusalem, Anathoth of Benjamin was closer in mentality and in theology to the Northern tribes, rather than to Judah. Jeremiah belongs with Hosea, to the heritage of the 'Rachel tribes'. His roots lay in the priesthood of Shiloh rather than in the Zionist tradition of Isaiah. His prophetic ministry was certainly influenced by the tensions that underlay the Deuteronomic insistance on one shrine only, at Jerusalm. This displaced the local shrines and the local priests. Though he supported Josiah's reform, it caused misunderstandings with his family (11:21).

JEREMIAH 1-6

The first collection of oracles belongs mainly to the reign of Josiah (2 Kings 22 and 23).

JEREMIAH 1

The call of Jeremiah in 626 BC. The prophet was about twenty.

1. Look up 1 Kings 2:26-35 for the background history of Jeremiah's family. He seems to have been descended from Abiathar.
2. Jeremiah was called by God from the earliest days of his existence (verse 5). How far can this be said of every Christian? How should we respond?
3. Compare Jeremiah's call with those of Isaiah (Isaiah 6) and of Ezekiel (Ezekiel 2:1-3: 15). What three things are distinctive about Jeremiah's? See especially verses 5, 8 and 19.
4. Verses 11 and 12. There is a pun in this vision: almond branch (shaqed) is punned with watching (shoqed). What is the underlying meaning of the vision?
5. Verses 13-19. How is the political situation described in these verses?

JEREMIAH 2

Hosea's influence is strong in this chapter. Unlike the Pentateuch tradition which emphasises Israel's shortcomings in the wilderness period, Jeremiah and Hosea (cf. Hosea 2) portray it as a 'honeymoon' period when Israel was beloved of and faithful to Yahweh.

1. Verse 13. What is the fountain of living waters? Compare this allusion with Isaiah 55:1 and with John 4:14 and 7: 37-39. Is there a progression? What is the broken cistern in spiritual experience?
2. Trace the course of Israel's backslidings in this chapter. Is it true of me? If so, what is the remedy?

JEREMIAH 3

Jeremiah longed for the return of the Northern kingdom from exile and apostasy. Josiah's reform, extended to Israel (2 Kings 23:15-20), inspired verses 6-10.

1. What opinion did Jeremiah have of Judah's conversion? Why does he compare Judah unfavourably with Israel? Is there any evidence that Jesus took a particularly severe attitude towards hypocrisy and insincerity? Is my conversion genuine, or only a matter of feelings or externals?
2. What are the conditions of forgiveness in this chapter and in 4:1-4?

JEREMIAH 4

An early oracle from 625 BC.

1. An invasion from the north (perhaps Assyria) is foretold. What purpose does the prophet discover in the disaster? See verses 8, 12 and 18.
2. The prophet identifies himself with the suffering people (verse 19). Has he any hope?

JEREMIAH 5

Early oracles inspired by the state of Judah before Josiah's reforms.

1. Catalogue the sins of which Judah is accused.
2. What evidence of false prophets' lulling the people to a spurious confidence do you find in chapters 4 and 5?

JEREMIAH 6

An invasion of Judah is foretold, still in vague terms.

1. What various means did God use to bring the people to repentance? Why did they not succeed? See verses 7, 10, 13 and 14 etc.
2. Look at verse 16. When is it apposite in our spiritual lives?
3. Trace the mission of the prophet in this chapter, especially verses 10, 11, 17 and 27. What is my mission?

JEREMIAH 7 - 20

These chapters largely contain prophecies made during the reign of Jehoiakim, Josiah's son. There is a vivid picture of him in chapter 36.

JEREMIAH 7

The divine protection of Jerusalem and of the Temple during the Assyrian siege under Sennacherib in 701, led the people and their rulers to think that the Temple would never be destroyed. Jeremiah was sure this was a dangerous illusion. The Temple itself could become an idol.

1. List the acts of virtue required of the people of Jerusalem (verses 5-6). To what is priority given? Am I challenged by these verses? If not, is it because I have grown complacent?
2. Look up 1 Samuel 4 for the destruction of Shiloh. What are the modern equivalents of Shiloh and the Temple? Is our worship also in danger of being as insincere as that of Jeremiah's first hearers?

JEREMIAH 8

These poems date from 605 BC when Jehoiakim was king.

1. In chapter 7 Jeremiah warned against insincere worship and false confidence in the Temple rituals. He now warns against misinterpretation of scripture (verse 8-9). What forms does this danger take today? What other indictments are made in verses 4-7? What remedy against backsliding do I find suggested?
2. What does this chapter reveal of Jeremiah's state of mind? See especially verses 18-22. Do we grieve for the sorrows and sins of our generation, or do we echo the false prophets (verse 11)?
3. Verses 13-17. What insight is given in this poem into the feelings of God? How do the people react to suffering? Is such an attitude common today? Is there any sign of hope in this chapter?

JEREMIAH 9

The prophet laments the moral corruption of the people.

1. What specific sins are condemned by the prophet? See verse 2-6, 8, 14. Which of them are prevalent today? Note the reference to the ancestor Jacob in verse 4 and cf. Hosea 12:2-4.
2. What is the heart of true religion (verse 24)? Compare Micah 6:8 and James 1:27. In what way does Jeremiah go deeper than the other two writers?

JEREMIAH 10

A satire on idolatry, after the manner of Deutero-Isaiah. This chapter probably does not come from Jeremiah.

1. Verses 1-16. In this satire on idolatry, in what ways does the prophet show the futility of idol worship? How does it compare with faith in the living God?
2. Verses 17-22. Compare the atmosphere in this section with 9: 9-21. What is the danger referred to? Who are the shepherds (verse 21) and why are they stupid? Is there any sense in which these verses can be applied to the world situation today?
3. Verses 23-25. What does Jeremiah mean when he says that the "way of man is not in himself"? Does he mean that man is fundamentally helpless before God's might, or that it is not in man to find of himself the grace to follow the right path? Can we make verse 24 our own prayer?

JEREMIAH 11

In 622 Josiah undertook a major religious reform (2 Kings 22 and 23), supported by the priests and prophets, including Jeremiah, but this entailed the abolition of local shrines, so angered Jeremiah's family at Anathoth (verse 21).

1. Jeremiah accuses the people of having broken the covenant relationship with God through their idolatry (verses 1-13). Why does he say that God will no longer listen to them? (See verses 9-13). Is there any occasion in the New Testament when Christ can only respond by silence?
2. Verses 18-22. What personal sufferings does the prophet describe?

JEREMIAH 12

Part of Jeremiah's 'Confessions' cf. 11:18-22

1. Jeremiah complains to God. What is the significance of God's reply (verses 5 and 6)? Are there any occasions in our lives when our prayer strengthens us without, seemingly, giving an answer?
2. What aspects of God are revealed in this chapter? Compare verses 7-13 with verses 14-17.

JEREMIAH 13

The prophets quite often used acted parables to teach the people. cf. Isaiah 20. The sign of the loincloth is such a parable, rather than a vision.

1. To understand the point of the parable of the loincloth, compare verses 4 and 6 with 2:18. How does this one verse throw light on the others? Why were foreign alliances always condemned?
2. What is the meaning of the parable of the jar (verses 12-14)? How does it reinforce the message of the first parable?
3. Verses 15-17. Do we take sufficiently to heart the warning contained in these lines? Are we using the light we have to 'give glory to the Lord' by our generous service?
4. Verses 18-27. What punishment awaits the people of Judah for their idolatry (verse 22)? Is there any hope for them? See verses 23 and 27.

JEREMIAH 14: 1-15:4

Lament in time of drought: verses 2-6 description of famine; 7-9 lament; 10-12 God replies; 13-16 complaint of Jeremiah: 17 and 18 famine; 19-22 lament; 15:1-4 God replies.

1. Why is God's first reply to the people's plea (verses 10-12) so severe? Is their repentance sincere?
2. The people continue to lament (verses 19-22) and God's second response (15:1-4) is even more uncompromising. What is the root cause of all the evil in Jerusalem? See 15:4. Are there occasions in our experience when only severe hardships can purify an individual or a nation?

JEREMIAH 15: 5-21

A crisis in the prophet's ministry.

1. What complaints does the prophet make? See verses 10-12, 15-18.
2. God's reply (verses 19 and 20) is even more disconcerting than at 12:5. How well did Jeremiah know himself? See especially verse 19. What new element is added? Are *we* ready to face up to the challenges of real dialogue with the living God?

JEREMIAH 16

The prophet's life itself was symbolic. cf. Ezekiel 24: 15-24; Hosea 1:3.

1. What was the purpose of Jeremiah's celibacy (verse 2)? See verses 3-10. What other restrictions were laid on him? See verse 8. Are there similar restrictions in my life as a Christian? Do I resent them or use them?
2. Contrast the situation described in verse 13 with that in verse 15. How is all this fulfilled and resolved in verse 21?

JEREMIAH 17

This chapter is a hotch-potch of Wisdom sayings, Oracles, 'Confessions' (verses 12-18) and teaching on the sabbath, put together by an editor.

1. Verses 1-4. How does Jeremiah emphasise the deeply engraved reality of Judah's sinful idolatry? Do we encounter similar deeply rooted attitudes today?
2. Verses 5-11. What teachings are contained in these verses? Compare verses 5-8 with Psalm 1; verses 9 and 10 with Mark 7:20-23; and verse 11 with Luke 12:16-21.
3. Verses 19-27. Compare these verses with Nehemiah 13:15-22. What is the theological meaning of sabbath rest?

JEREMIAH 18

Look up Sirach 38:29-30 for a description of a potter at work.

1. Verses 1-12. Using the analogy of the potter (see verse 4), what does Jeremiah teach about God's design and human free will? How does his teaching differ from that of Paul (Romans 9: 20-24)?
2. Verses 13-17. Is there a lesson for the Church in this oracle? Have the 'people of God' forgotten him and 'gone into bypaths'? Can you think of any examples? Do we take seriously enough verse 7?
3. Verses 18-23. Are Jeremiah's complaints the sign of a vengeful nature or a healthy outlet?

JEREMIAH 19-20

Two incidents are combined here: the scene at the Potsherd Gate (19:1, 2b 10-11a, 14-20:6); a discourse at Topheth (19:2a, 3-9, 11b-13).

1. The broken flask: 19:1, 2bb, 10-11a, 14-20:6. What was the significance of Jeremiah breaking the flask? How was it interpreted? How was the warning received?
2. Topheth: 19:2a, 3-9, 11b-13. What was the evil that Jeremiah condemned? Does it exist today under another name? Do we take seriously enough the warning contained in verse 13?
3. 20:7-18. Trace Jeremiah's varying mood in this passage. What was the crisis that brought on the outburst? See verses 8-10. What do we learn from our glimpses of the prophet at prayer? Is ours as authentic, or do we hide ourselves even from God?

JEREMIAH 21-24

This group of prophecies dates from the reign of Zedekiah.

JEREMIAH 21: 1-10

The Pashhur of verse 1 is not the same man as the Pashhur of 20:1-6.

1. Zedekiah hoped the city would be reprieved (verse 2). Why was he so confident?
2. What was God's advice through Jeremiah? Imagine such advice being given, for example, in Paris in 1940 when Hitler's armies were already in France. Why do we so rarely search scripture for political advice?

JEREMIAH 21:11 - 23:8

A collection of oracles addressed to the royal house of Judah.

1. What was the programme the kings were invited to adopt (21:12, 22:3)? Do we expect OUR governments to adopt it or do we expect them to serve OUR interests?
2. 22:10-12. Look up 2 Kings 23:29-34. Which kings are mentioned in these verses?
3. 22:13-19. Jeremiah compares Jehoiakim with his father Josiah. Of what does he accuse Jehoiakim?
4. 22:20-30. Look up 2 Kings 24:6-16 and 25:27-30 for the career of Coniah (Jehoiachin). Then reflect on verse 21. Do we ever have cause to regret that we did not listen in times of prosperity?
5. To restore the flock demoralised by indifferent or poor or absent shepherds, what does God promise to do?

JEREMIAH 23:9-40

A collection of tracts against false prophets.

1. What accusations does Jeremiah make concerning the immorality of the prophets of his day (verses 13-15)?
2. What are the criteria of genuine prophecy? With this chapter especially verse 22 compare Deuteronomy 18:22; Jeremiah 28:9 and Deuteronomy 13: 1-6.
3. What kind of false prophecies were current in Jeremiah's time? See verses 17, 27 and 32.

JEREMIAH 24

The people used to bring the first fruits of their crops to the Temple.

1. Who are symbolised by the good figs? This theme will recur more and more in Jeremiah. What effect would it have had on the people of Jerusalem?
2. Who are the bad figs? Does this mean that God is totally abandoning the people in this category? See Jeremiah 42:10-12.

JEREMIAH 25

This chapter is a summary of Jeremiah's prophecies contained in the scroll dictated by Jeremiah to Baruch (chapter 36). The list of oracles against the nations (verses 20 ff.) follows the order of the oracles grouped in chapters 46-51.

1. Consider the number of years (verse 3) during which God, through his prophet, has been warning his people. What prophecy from chapter 1 is about to be fulfilled?
2. Note carefully verse 29. How is the punishment of Jerusalem connected with the warnings against the nations? What is the punishment of today's Church, in your view, and what are the warnings to the nations? Re-read the chapter in the light of these considerations.

JEREMIAH 26-29

Extracts from the biography of Jeremiah, attributed to Baruch.

JEREMIAH 26

The sermon preached in 7:1-15 is summarised in this chapter. Ahikam, son of Shaphan, was the son of king Josiah's secretary (2 Kings 22:3) who had supported religious reform. The family of Shaphan was always well disposed to Jeremiah.

1. Compare verse 3 with 2 Chronicles 36:15. What does this tell us of God's unfailing love and desire for the salvation of his people? What was the obstacle?
2. Notice the two groups of people (verses 7, 8, 10,16 and 17). Which group favoured Jeremiah? What arguments did they use?
3. What side-light do verses 20-23 throw a) on King Jehoiakim and b) on Jeremiah's danger?

JEREMIAH 27

Five kings of the surrounding nations seek Judah's help in attempting to throw off the Babylonian threat.

1. To what three groups of people is this oracle of doom address? What does it teach about Yahweh's sovereignty? What is the symbolism of the yoke bar?
2. Why did Jeremiah encourage submission to Nebuchadnezzar? See especially verses 5-7. Try to imagine the situation as it appeared a) to the coalition states, b) to Zedekiah, and c) to the people of Jerusalem? Was it likely that many of them would heed Jeremiah?

JEREMIAH 28

This chapter reflects the hopes that were pinned on the king in captivity in Babylon, Jeconiah, son of Jehoiakim.

1. Notice Jeremiah's dignity and quiet courage (verses 6-7). To what might it be attributed?
2. Compare the two prophets. Which would have counted on popular support? What can we learn from this encounter?

JEREMIAH 29

A large number of the inhabitants of Jerusalem had been deported to Babylon with King Jeconiah (2 Kings 24:12-16). These had been unsettled by reports that they would soon be able to return. Jeremiah warns that their exile will last for seventy years.

1. What signs are there that Jeremiah had powerful support in Jerusalem among people of position and influence? Compare verse 3 with 2 Kings 22:8.
2. What advice did Jeremiah give to the exiles in Babylon? What especially is the significance theologically of verse 7?
3. What was the effect of Jeremiah's letter on the exiles? Is it predictable? Have we the courage to speak out when we feel called to do so, or do we only speak the truth to those who agree or who want to hear it?

JEREMIAH 30-31

These chapters are called the Book of Consolation. 30:1-31: 22 were originally written foretelling the return of the Northern exiles from Assyria; 31:23-40 were added after the fall of Jerusalem - a message of hope to all.

JEREMIAH 30

1. Verses 1-11. How is the contrast made between the distress of the people and the promised outcome? What is the hope offered?
2. Verses 12-17. Jeremiah grieves over the sufferings of his fellow-countrymen, and promises that God will bring redress. How does the poem assuage suffering even before the conclusion promised? What do we learn from this about comfort for those in sorrow?
3. Verses 18-24. What blessings are promised? How can they be understood with regard to the people of God, the new Israel?

JEREMIAH 31

1. Verses 1-6. Notice the covenant language, especially in verses 2-3. How are God's faithfulness and everlasting love echoed in the virtues poured into the hearts of Christians by the Holy Spirit? (Romans 5:1-5).
2. Verses 7-14. The return of the exiles is described in terms of the exodus. a) Draw out the references, especially verses 7, 9, 11; and b) compare this new exodus with the salvation won for us by Christ.
3. What is the original meaning of verse 15? What use did Matthew 2:18 make of it? Who was Rachel? Where was her tomb?
4. What does this chapter show us a) of God's tenderness, and b) of Jeremiah's own attitude (verse 26)?
5. What are the features of the new covenant, set forth in verses 31-34? Upon what guarantee does Yahweh base it? cf. verses 35-37.

JEREMIAH 32-33

This collection dealing with Judah's restoration has been added to the Book of Consolation, which was originally concerned with Israel only.

JEREMIAH 32

The circumstances of Jeremiah's imprisonment are described in Chapter 37.

1. Contrast the situation of Jeremiah in prison and of the city under siege with the plans for the future, symbolised by his purchase of a field. What is the meaning of this acted parable?
2. What are the promises God makes (verses 36-44)?
3. Read through the whole chapter, interpreting it in the light of either a situation in your own life, or in the light of world events of this century. Have we yet experienced the blessings?

JEREMIAH 33

This prophecy belongs to the same collection as Chapter 32.

1. Verses 1-13. What blessings are promised to the restored city? What do they symbolise?
2. Verses 14-26. What blessings are to be bestowed on the house of David? Are they in any sense realised in the Church? How are the people's doubts (verse 24) dealt with?

JEREMIAH 34-35

'hree incidents from Baruch's memoirs conclude the prophecies of consolation.

JEREMIAH 34

'he siege of Jerusalem has not yet begun, but the Babylonians are fighting in the south (588 BC).

. Verses 1-7. What hope for Zedekiah is contained in this oracle? On what conditions?

2. Verses 8-22. Jeremiah, in the prophetic tradition, defends the poor, in this case slaves fraudulently released and then taken back into slavery. What lessons has this passage for industrial relations today?

JEREMIAH 35

For the Rechabites, look up 1 Chronicles 2:55 and 2 Kings 10:15-17. They were a survival from nomadic times.

1. In what sense can this story be said to be an acted parable? What is its point?
2. Is there room in Christianity for 'alternative life-styles'?

JEREMIAH 36

The scroll mentioned in this chapter is probably summarised in Chapter 25. This incident probably took place soon after the events described in Chapter 26 cf. 26:1 and 36:1.5.9.

1. Notice the characters mentioned: Baruch (verse 4), Gemariah (verse 10), Micaiah (verse 11), Elishama, Delaiah, Elnathan, Zedekiah son of Hananiah (verse 12); Jehudi (verse 14), Jehoiakim the king (verse 20), Jerahmeel, Seraiah, Shelemiah (verse 26). What part did each play? Put them into two columns - those who supported the king and those who defended Jeremiah. Compare Chapter 26. Do any of the names recur? What impression do you form of the king's character?
2. What have you learned from this chapter a) of the transmission and publication of prophecy and b) of the complex background of Jeremiah's ministry?

JEREMIAH 37-38

An Egyptian army had temporarily forced Nebuchadnezzar to lift the siege of Jerusalem.

JEREMIAH 37

1. What are the circumstances (see verse 5) which led Zedekiah to hope for a reprieve such as the city had enjoyed in 701? What is the prophet's response?
2. Why was Jeremiah trying to leave the city?
3. What do we learn of Zedekiah and his feelings for the prophet in this interview? Compare verses 17 and 21 with 36:22-24.

JEREMIAH 38

1. Compare the attitude of Pashhur and the other princes (see also 21:1) with that of the Ethiopian eunuch, Ebed-melech. Are we prepared to risk our reputation, job, even our life, for our friends?
2. Trace the course of Zedekiah's agony in this chapter. Does he believe Jeremiah? Do you think Jeremiah would have been tempted to encourage him?

JEREMIAH 39

The chronology of this chapter is confused, but it is largely based on 2 Kings 25.

1. Jeremiah's prophecies concerning Jerusalem and its king are fulfilled. What is the theological lesson of Zedekiah's fate? Why did Ebed-melech survive? (verse 18).
2. On the face of it, Jeremiah comes out of the war very well (verses 12-14). What do you think his feelings were?

JEREMIAH 40

The story of Jeremiah is followed in this chapter by an account of the assassination of Gedaliah, based on 2 Kings 25. Mizpah was eight miles from Jerusalem, and a former Israelite sanctuary.

1. What signs are there in this chapter that Jeremiah was right in his assessment of the situation and that co-operation with the Chaldeans would have brought peace?
2. What kind of man was Gedaliah? Why are men of his sort so often at a disadvantage?

JEREMIAH 41

The writer continues the story of events following the fall of Jerusalem.

1. What evidence is there in this chapter that there were still worshippers of Yahweh in the northern kingdom?
2. Who was Ishmael? See 40:7-8, 13; 41:1. What lay behind his killing of Gedaliah?

JEREMIAH 42

Jeremiah intercedes for the people, and seeks God's will and guidance for them.

1. What were the underlying fears of those left in Judea (42:11 and 16)? What led them to seek help from Jeremiah? Did they expect him to confirm their intention of going to Egypt?
2. Read carefully verses 20 and 21. Are we sometimes lacking in faith in God's guidance? How do we seek it?
3. What qualities of Jeremiah are revealed in this chapter?

JEREMIAH 43

The last mission of Jeremiah.

1. Why did Azariah and Johanan not accept Jeremiah's word from the Lord? Have I ever been guilty of such backsliding?
2. What did Jeremiah prophesy concerning Egypt? See Ezekiel 29:17-20.

JEREMIAH 44-45

Chapter 44 describes the last episode of Jeremiah's ministry.
Chapter 45 is a footnote concerning Baruch. It stands as his signature to the biographical fragments.

1. What was a) Jeremiah's message to the people (44:2-14) and b) their reply? What does this show of their spiritual condition, of their faulty reading of history and of their blindness to events in Jerusalem? What is the basic reason for their attitude? Are we ever guilty too?
2. What do we know of Baruch? With Chapter 45 compare 36:4 and 10; 43:3 and see 51:59 concerning his brother.

JEREMIAH 46-51

This collection of oracles is introduced and summarised in Chapter 25.

JEREMIAH 46

Two poems concerning Egypt: a) verses 2-12 the battle of Carchemish in 605; and b) verses 13-28 - the invasion of Egypt by the Babylonians in 588.

1. What attitudes of Egypt led to her downfall? See especially verses 8 and 11.
2. Egypt is deserted by her gods (verses 15 and 25), by her mercenaries (verses 16 and 21) and her king is humiliated (verse 17). What is the lesson of this oracle? See verses 25 and 26. Is there any glimmer of hope for Egypt?

JEREMIAH 47

Oracle against the Philistines, who were attacked by the Egyptians. Caphtor (verse 4) is Crete. Gaza and Ashkelon were Philistine cities on the West Coast of Palestine.

1. Remember all that the Bible tells us about the Philistines. Though their name is recalled in 'Palestine', their cities have all vanished today. What does this fact and this chapter tell us about the fate of once proud and prosperous nations?
2. Comment on the theology of verses 6 and 7. Is it relevant to events in our own time?

JEREMIAH 48

Chemosh (verse 7) was the national god of the Moabites.

1. Of what sins is Moab accused? (See verses 7, 11, 14, 26-30).
2. Is there any hope for Moab? What attitude does the prophet take?

JEREMIAH 49

The Ammonites seized Gilead in 721BC. Milcom was their god (verse 1). Edom was famous for its sages (verse 7). The Edomites took advantage of the fall of Jerusalem to occupy cities in southern Judah (see Obadiah 10-14). Kedar was a nomadic Arabian tribe. Elam was on the NE of the Persian Gulf.

1. What were the sins of Ammon and of Edom? Note that, according to Genesis, the Ammonites, Moabites and Edomites were all related to the Israelites (Genesis 19:37 and 38; 36:19).
2. Are we told the sins of Damascus, Kedar or Elam? How are their reverses in war interpreted by the prophet? Is this a univeral law?
3. What does this chapter teach about the Lord of History? Do we believe that God acts through events, or do we trust in our idols? What form do they take?

JEREMIAH 50

This long oracle was composed by a disciple of Jeremiah about 538 BC, just before Babylon fell to the Persians, who were famous as bowmen.

1. Verses 1-7. What excuse is Babylon represented as making for her treatment of Israel? How is Israel's restoration described?
2. Verses 8-20. The theme of Israel's rescue is developed. Which verse sums up her salvation by God's grace?
3. Verses 21-32. What was the ultimate sin of Babylon? Has she a counterpart in the world today?
4. Verses 33-46. What names are given to God in this section? What images are used to describe his actions?

JEREMIAH 51

Further oracles against Babylon.

1. What were the sins of Babylon that called down on her such terrible vengeance? In Revelation, Babylon becomes a symbol of ancient Rome. Of what city or empire is she a symbol today?
2. See verses 15-19 and compare the fate of Babylon's gods.
3. Verses 59-64. Note that this incident took place in 593 BC. At this time Jeremiah was convinced that Babylon would conquer Judah and Jerusalem, and *YET* he also foresaw her fall. What accounts for this remarkable prophecy?

JEREMIAH 52

This chapter is a repetition of 2 Kings 24:18 - 25:30, and is parallel with Jeremiah 39:1-10.

1. Compare verse 3 with Jeremiah 7:15; and verse 6 with Jeremiah 14:15-18; versc 13 with Jeremiah 7:14; verses 18 and 19 with Jeremiah 27:19-22.
2. What is the value of the little footnote (verses 31-34) about King Jehoiachin?

AN INTRODUCTION
TO
THE BOOK OF LAMENTATIONS

One of the reasons why Jeremiah has often been depicted as filled with gloom, is because Lamentations has been ascribed to him, though, in fact, it bears the marks of a different, and later, period. Jeremiah would never have asserted (2:9) that prophecy was silent, nor would he have praised Zedekiah (4:20) or trusted Egypt (4:17). It was probably written in Palestine after the fall of Jerusalem, and reflects or was even part of a liturgy that took place in the ruins of the Temple, when large numbers of the population had been deported, and most of the temple worship had ceased.

Chapters 1, 2 and 4 are a dirge for the dead, Chapter 3 is an individual lament and Chapter 5 is a collective lament.

LAMENTATIONS 1

This dirge seems to have been composed after 597, when the Temple was pillaged, (verse 10), the king, Jehoiachin and his nobles departed, and the Judahites humbled by the king of babylon.

1. What details are given of the state of the city? Is the appeal to God's compassion or to his justice?
2. What is the tone of the dirge? Resentment or honest sorrow? Do we accept suffering in a spirit of submission or do we allow it to embitter us?
3. Consider verse 12 as a commentary on Christ's crucifixion.

LAMENTATIONS 2

This dirge belongs to the period after the destruction of the Temple in 587.

1. Note the reversal of all that God has done in the past for Israel: verses 1, 2, 3, 6. Trace the fortunes of the different classes of people - princes (2, 6, 9) priests (6, 7) prophets (9, 14) children (11, 12, 19).
2. What example do we have of confident, persevering prayer in this chapter? See especially verses 18-22. Do we pray like that when disaster strikes, or do we sink into lethargy (verse 13)?

LAMENTATIONS 3

This individual lament expands (verses 40-47) into a collective lament.

1. Follow the dynamic of this individual lament: bitter suffering, expression of hope in God, renewed depression, new hope.
2. What leads to the sudden change in verse 21? Note especially verse 18, where God is called 'Yahweh' for the first time in this lament. What is the source of hope implied by this Name? What is the source of *MY* hope?
3. Can we ponder this chapter when overwhelmed by the sight or news of the world's suffering? See especially verses 31-39, 48 ff.

LAMENTATIONS 4

The nation mentioned in verse 17 was Egypt whose Pharaoh sent an army to assist Judah, but whose troops were chased away by the Chaldean troops in 587.

1. Verses 1-11. Draw out the details of famine and dereliction in these verses. What reason is given for the people's sufferings?
2. Verses 12-22. Which classes of people are singled out? Compare the fate of the prophets with Jeremiah's warnings (Jeremiah 23:9-40 and 27-29).
3. Compare this writer's attitude to Egypt (verse 17) and to Zedekiah (verse 20) with Jeremiah's (Jeremiah 37:5-8 and 38:21-23).

LAMENTATIONS 5

This lament was probably composed somewhat later (verses 2,7).

1. Contrast the present disposition of the people with their attitude in Jeremiah's time (Jeremiah 5:12). What signs of hope are there in this bleak picture?
2. Have we anything to learn from Lamentations about intercession for and identification with the sufferings of today?
3. Re-read the whole of Lamentations, remembering that traditionally they are read in Holy Week. Pick out the passages that could apply to Christ in his Passion.

AN INTRODUCTION
TO
THE BOOK OF EZEKIEL

'I sought for a man among them who should build up the wall and stand in the breach before me for the land, that I should not destroy it; but I found none'. Ezekiel 22:30.

Who was Ezekiel? Did he write all, or substantially all, of the book that bears his name? Did he preach in Palestine as well as in Babylon? Why are some passages so brilliant and some so banal? Scholars have argued endlessly over these problems. For the clarity of this study, we have adopted the view that the book of Ezekiel as we have it contains the work of two prophets - Ezekiel, who prophesied in Palestine until the fall of Jerusalem in 587 and was carried off to Babylon where he preached to the exiles; and another, unnamed prophet, a disciple, whose visions are described in 1:4-28 (the vision of the throne chariot) and in chapters 40-48.

Ezekiel was, in many ways, an enigmatic figure. Despite the brilliance of his visions, and the precision of his writing, we do not come to know him as we come to know Jeremiah. His doctrine breaks new ground. Instead of recalling God's promises to his people through the patriarchs and the Mosaic covenant, he saw the preservation of Israel not as the fulfilment of promise, but as vindication of God's honour - his Name. (Ezekiel 20). Retribution was no longer collective, but individual (chapter 18). Inner conversion was essential - a new heart and a new spirit (18:31 and 36:26). He is the prophet of a new and deeper spirituality, and also, in his style, of a new tradition, the apocalyptic. His strange visions prepare us for Daniel, and for the Book of Revelation.

He preached first in Jerusalem (2:3), and after a while in some village north of the city to which he seems to have been banished (3:25-27; 24:25-27). When he was sent into exile he took his writings with him, and continued his ministry in Babylon.

A redactor has combined his oracles with those of a disciple, placing the vision at the beginning of his Babylonian ministry (1:1-3) at the beginning of the entire book, as a fitting introduction.

EZEKIEL 1

The editor has combined two introductions: in the first one (verse 1), the prophet speaks in the first person, perhaps prefacing the vision of the throne chariot (verses 4-28); in the second, Ezekiel is referred to in the third person (verses 2-3). This dates the oracle: 593 BC.

1. What was the significance for Ezekiel and for the other exiles of Yahweh's appearance in Chaldea (verse 3)?
2. Compare the vision in verses 4-14 with 2 Samuel 22. On what other occasions in scripture does God appear in a storm (verse 4)? What is the meaning of storm theophanies?
3. How is God described? cf. Isaiah 6:1. What is the overall impression?

EZEKIEL 2:1 - 3:3

This vision of the scroll interrupts the chariot vision.

1. How is Ezekiel's experience of God described? What do we learn of God's nature from this chapter?
2. What was the commission given to the prophet? What is the symbolism of the scroll? cf. Revelation 10:8-10.

EZEKIEL 3:4-27

The chariot vision is continued at 3:12. The theme of the prophet as watchman is central to the Book of Ezekiel.

1. Verses 4-8. What is the spiritual state of the people? Why were they in this state?
2. Verses 9-15. What effect did the visions have on Ezekiel? How does he try to describe it?
3. Verses 16-27. Ezekiel is sent as a 'watchman'. What response does he get from the people? How do you explain the 'cords' and the 'dumbness'?

EZEKIEL 4

Like Jeremiah (13,18), the prophet preaches through mime.

1. What events were foretold by Ezekiel's mime? He is later described as a 'propounder of riddles' (17:2) and a 'maker of allegories' (20:49). What was the purpose of his miming?
2. In what way can visual aids be used in modern preaching? Do you think the liturgy of the Word would gain by such aids?

EZEKIEL 5

The mime of the siege is continued.

1. Compare verses 1-2 with verse 12. What is the meaning of the mime?
2. What will happen to the remnant (verse 3)? From your reading of Jeremiah and Lamentations how far was Ezekiel's acted prophecy fulfilled? What do we know of the "remnant"?
3. Why was God's judgement so severe?

EZEKIEL 6

This chapter and the next one summarises Ezekiel's sermon themes.

1. Verses 1-7. The 'high places' were the scenes of fertility rites, sacred prostitution, etc. What are their equivalents today?
2. Verses 8-10. What sign of hope is described here? Do we encourage a humble and repentant attitude to disaster, or do we express resentment and bitterness?

EZEKIEL 7

1. What is the main theme of this chapter? Give a personal heading to each paragraph.
2. Take each of the sections (verses 1-13; 23-27) and apply them to this century.
3. We are inclined to blame 'the world' for its violence and other sins, but these words are addressed to God's people. Are there ways in which the Church is guilty of injustice and of pride? Are we in any way party to this?

EZEKIEL 8

This vision took place in 592 BC. The idol mentioned in verses 3 and 6 was probably the statue of Astarte, a sex symbol set up in the Temple by Manasseh. Tammuz was an Assyrian Babylonian god.

1. Contrast the experience of Ezekiel in verses 1-4 with that of the elders in verses 10-12. What effect does degradation of sex (verses 3 and 6) have on the mind and imagination? How are we purified?
2. The women wept for Tammuz and the priests (verse 16) worshipped the sun. Find modern equivalents for Tammuz and the sun.

EZEKIEL 9

Only the guilty are punished. This is an important aspect of Ezekiel's message.

1. Compare the protecting mark on Cain (Genesis 4:15) with that on those referred to in verse 4. What difference is to be understood between these two signs from God? (NB. the word for *mark* in Hebrew is *taw* which is a X). What mark is on Christians?
2. 'Begin at my sanctuary' (verse 6). The guilty elders in the Temple (8:16) are the first to be judged. What should this teach us about our own attitudes and responsibilities? We live close to the Holy of Holies. What tempts us to adopt the posture of the elders (8:16)?

EZEKIEL 10

Two visions seem to have been conflated: the 'glory of the Lord' and the throne chariot.

1. Follow the movement of the 'glory of the God of Israel' from 8:4 to 9:3 to 10:4 to 10:18-19. What is symbolised by this movement? Can the indwelling glory in our personal temple (1 Corinthians 6:19) ever be withdrawn? By what cause? Can it be restored?
2. The city is to be purified by fire (verses 6-7), a symbol of the Chaldean armies. In what sense can such a terrible event as foreign invasion be called purifying?

EZEKIEL 11

This chapter follows Chapter 8 (before the destruction of Jerusalem).

1. What is to be understood by the reference to the flesh in the cauldron (verses 3,7,11)? What was the sin of Jaazaniah and Pelatiah?
2. What was the attitude to the exiles of those who remained in Jerusalem? See verse 15. How would you characterise it?
3. Compare Ezekiel's message to the exiles (verses 16-20) with that of Jeremiah (Jeremiah 29:4 ff.) What are the means by which their regeneration is to be accomplished (verses 16, 19)?

EZEKIEL 12

The exile is foretold in mime.

1. The exile is predicted in mime (verses 1-16) and conditions described during the siege. What warning does the prophet underline and repeat? See especially verses 2-3. What word is a refrain?
2. 'The day grows long, and every vision comes to naught' (verse 22). To what is the proverb taken to refer? What attitude does it reveal? What was the prophet's response? Compare 2 Peter 3:4 and the response (2 Peter 3:8-9).
3. 'The vision that he sees is for many days hence, and he prophesies for days far off' (verse 27). Do we console ourselves with words like these, and put away all thought of God's intervention? What does Jesus say? cf. Luke 12:35-40.

EZEKIEL 13

The problem of false prophecy is also discussed in Jeremiah 23:9-40; 27.

1. The false prophets saw visions of peace 'when there is no peace' (verse 10). What warning does Ezekiel give? Why are those who try to smooth over problems so much condemned? What, according to Ezekiel, is the role of the true prophet? (verse 5). Do we listen to false or true prophets today? How do we distinguish?
2. Do we ever think there is peace in our own hearts, where there is no peace? Are we 'daubing' our souls 'with whitewash'? What remedy do we have for this situation? See verse 13.
3. The prophetesses seem to have been supplying charms and veils to ward off evil or to cure illnesses. What would be their counterpart today? Why is it wrong to trust in such things?

EZEKIEL 14

The doctrine of individual responsibility is central to Ezekiel's teaching, cf. Chapters 18 and 33.

1. Verses 1-11. Are we ever in danger of being blinded and deceived by the 'idols in our hearts'? In what ways? Give examples.
2. Verses 12-20. Compare this oracle with Genesis 18:23-33 and 19:29 when Abraham interceded for Sodom. Are we ever discouraged, when we pray in sinful situations and seem to get no answer? Does this passage provide a theological response?
3. Verses 21-23. What do these verses tell us about God's underlying purpose in visitations of judgement?

EZEKIEL 15

The parable of the vine.

1. What is the meaning of the allegory? If Jerusalem is the wood at the centre of the vine (verse 6), what are the two ends that have been consumed by fire (verse 4)?
2. What use does Jesus make of this same image? Compare John 15:1-17, and especially John 15:6 with Ezekiel 15:1-5.

EZEKIEL 16

A long allegory on the history of Jerusalem/Judah.

1. Verses 1-14. Follow the details of the allegory, applying them to Israel's history.
2. Verses 15-34. Of what sins is Judah accused? Could the Church be accused too? Verses 35-52. Jerusalem/Judah is compared unfavourably with Samaria and with Sodom (verses 46-47). What sin is especially condemned? See verse 49.
3. Verses 53-63. God three times remembers the covenant with his people. What does this remind us of God's fidelity to us? Note verses 60, 62, 63. What lesson for our own history can we take from this allegory?

EZEKIEL 17

The allegory has two parts: historical events (verses 1-21); messianic restoration (verses 22-24).

1. Ezekiel explains the allegory in verses 11-21. Work out each element. What sin is he specifically rebuking (verses 15-19)? What does this teach us about a) integrity and b) the theology of events? cf. Jeremiah 27:6-8 and 2 Chronicles 36:12, 13. Do we always give sufficient attention to the human virtues?
2. Trace the messianic theme in verses 22-24.
3. Compare verses 22-24 with Matthew 13:32. What is a) similar and b) distinct about each parable?

EZEKIEL 18

A development of the doctrine sketched in Chapter 14.

1. Verses 1-4. What fundamental principle is stated in verse 4? What form of equality is expressed?
2. Verses 5-9. Look at the catalogue, and distinguish ritual from moral principles.
3. Verses 10-20. Ezekiel says that each one is responsible for his or her own acts, and will be rewarded or punished accordingly. Is there any truth, however, in the older doctrine that the sins of the fathers are visited on the children?
4. Verses 21-29. Do these verses contain a warning for us? What is the conclusion for the 'just'? See verses 30-32.

EZEKIEL 19

A lament for the kings of Israel.

1. Identify the kings in this lament. The clues are contained in 2 Chronicles 36. What is the lesson of the whole chapter?
2. Compare this lament with Jeremiah 23:10-12, 24-30. Do we regularly pray for 'kings and for all who are in high positions'? (1 Timothy 2:2). Or do we simply criticise them?

EZEKIEL 20

The prophet's theology of history.

1. Verses 5-31. a) What is the reason given by Ezekiel for Israel's sufferings in Egypt? In what way does this differ from Exodus 1? b) What is the meaning of verses 25-26? Is it irony or primitive theology?
2. Verses 32-44. verse 32 is addressed to the elders (verse 1). What are God's plans for his people? Note especially verse 35. What is meant by verse 37? To what two conclusions (verses 42-44) will God eventually bring his people Israel? Is Chapter 20 *IN ANY WAY* the story of my life?

EZEKIEL 20:45 - 21:32

A collection of four oracles, loosely connected by war imagery.

1. Find the interpretation of 20:45-49 in 21:1-7. Despite the teaching of 14:12 and 18 on individual responsibility, the innocent do suffer with the guilty. What are the prophet's feelings? See verses 21:6-7.
2. The ballad of the sword (21:8-17). Note the use of a sword dance, but what is its meaning?
3. Verses 18-27. Nebuchadnezzar is seen consulting his oracles (verse 21). Shall it be Ammon or Jerusalem? Who really decides?

EZEKIEL 22

The sins of Jerusalem are indicted.

1. Verses 1-16. What are the principal sins for which Jerusalem is indicted? Measure the city's moral standards by the Decalogue. Then measure contemporary society's standards by this chapter.
2. What will be the punishment? See verses 17-22. Can you see any signs of punishment for contemporary evils in contemporary events?
3. What is meant by verse 30? Compare Genesis 18:22-33, and 19:29. Am I called to 'stand in the breach' before the Lord for the land? What can we all do?

EZEKIEL 23

This third review of Israel's history (cf. chapters 16, 20) is another allegory this time of two sisters, Oholah and Oholibah. Their names are a play on the Hebrew word 'tent', recalling the tent in the desert.

1. Verses 1-32. Trace the history of Samaria and of Jerusalem in these verses. Note that verses 12-13 probably refer to the reign of Ahaz (cf. Isaiah 7-8) and verses 14-15 to Hezekiah (Isaiah 39).
2. What were the origins of Israel's idolatry (see verses 8, 19, 27 and especially verse 35)? Has there been a pattern in my life of allowing material things to take possession of my heart?

EZEKIEL 24

The siege of Jerusalem is announced (January 588 BC).

1. Compare this chapter with 11:3-13 and with Micah 3:3. What is the meaning of the allegory of the pot? Have the Church or society, in your view, ever reached the point where they need the purification described by Ezekiel?
2. Ezekiel's wife, 'the delight of his eyes' died (verse 16) and he was ordered not to mourn for her. Why not? How is she a sign of the devastated Temple? (See verse 21). The people of Judah had made almost an idol of the Temple (cf. Jeremiah 7). Are we Christians ever in danger of making an idol of the Church? How are we purified?

EZEKIEL 25-32

Prophecies against Ammon, Moab, Edom, Philistia, Tyre, Sidon, Egypt.

EZEKIEL 25

1. What was especially blame-worthy about the behaviour of the Ammonites (verses 3,6), the Moabites (verse 8), the Edomites (verse 12) and the Philistines (verse 15)? What word is used twice of their attitude of heart?
2. Are there occasions when we behave in similar fashion? What should we do about unkind gossip, delight in others' misfortune, resentment against them - when we find such feelings in our own hearts? See Col. 1:21-23.

EZEKIEL 26

The date is 586 BC, just after the fall of Jerusalem. Tyre, a former ally of Judah, deserted her during the siege and fall of Jerusalem.

1. What was the ground of God's vengeance on Tyre? See verse 2. Trace the stages of her downfall: 13 years siege by Nebuchadnezzar (verses 7-14), final destruction under Alexander the Great (verses 15-18), complete invasion by the sea.
2. What may we learn from the fall of Trye?

EZEKIEL 27

Second lament for Tyre. Kittim (verse 6) means Cyprus.

1. Work out the allegory of Tyre as a great ship. What happened?
2. What was Tyre's sin? See verse 3 and also verse 13. Examine my own life in the light of these two verses.

EZEKIEL 28

Laments for the prince of Tyre and for Sidon.

1. What was the sin of Tyre's prince? (verse 2). What kind of wisdom did he possess?
2. Note the alternative creation and fall stories in this chapter, especially verses 13-17. Compare with Genesis 2 and 3. What features have these stories in common? What great differences are there?
3. What is said of Sidon? Note the encouragement for Israel at the end of this chapter.

EZEKIEL 29

Oracle against Egypt uttered in January 587 BC. Judah under attack from the Babylonians, had asked for help from Egypt.

1. Compare the allegory (verses 3-7) with its explanation (verses 8-12). What are the sins that caused God's judgement to fall on Egypt?

2. There is some hope for Egypt in verses 13-16; but a humiliating hope. Are there occasions in our lives when we need to become more 'lowly'?
3. Why did Nebuchadnezzar invade Egypt? See verses 17-19. What do you make of this oracle? What is the theology that lies behind it (verse 20)?

EZEKIEL 30

Another oracle against Egypt.

1. Verses 1-19. 'Her proud might shall come to an end' (verse 18). Egypt trusted in her might and in the Nile, source of her life and fertility (verse 12). Why did she fall, according to the prophet? and cf. Job 9:4.
2. Verses 20-26. Jeremiah and Ezekiel both warned Judah not to put any trust in Egyptian help. Do we remember this lesson today? What contemporary situation is represented by "Egypt"? Is there an 'Egypt' in my own life on whom I rely?

EZEKIEL 31

A further utterance against Egypt in the form of a parable of a cedar tree.

1. Look carefully at the allegory and pick out its various aspects, noting especially the references to Eden and the garden of God. What further meaning has the allegory in relation to Genesis 2 and 3?
2. How does this chapter reinforce the lesson of Chapter 30? What is the reason given for the tree (Egypt's) destruction, and what effect is this intended to have on other nations?

EZEKIEL 32

Another parable against Egypt. The Pharaoh is a dragon!

1. Verses 1-16. Pharaoh is likened to a dragon rather than to a lion! (verse 2).Note the reference to some of the plagues of Egypt (verses 6 and 7-8). What other echoes of Exodus do you find in this passage?
2. Verses 17-32. Trace the picture of the under-world, its inhabitants (look up the place names on a map), their situation.

EZEKIEL 33-39

These prophecies all belong to the period after the fall of Jerusalem.

EZEKIEL 33

The mission of the prophet is reiterated and confirmed.

1. Verses 1-9. What warning is given to 'watchmen'? What class of people is meant by this term?
2. What was the mental and spiritual state of the people? See verse 10. How did the prophet respond? Are we sometimes tempted to let our sins and shortcomings get the better of us? What should we do to reawaken hope?
3. What was the principal sin of the righteous man against which the prophet warns (verses 12-13)? How does New Testament teaching complete Ezekiel's ?
4. What is implied by the attitude expressed in verse 24? Have the Judeans learnt anything from their recent terrible experiences (cf. 2 Kings 25:22-26). What does Ezekiel warn them is still to come?
5. The news of the fall of Jerusalem (verses 21-22) vindicated Ezekiel as a prophet and many were attracted to his sermons (verse 30). What, however, were their dispositions (verses 31-32)? Do we sometimes respond no more than this to a scripture reading or a sermon? What word for us is there in verse 33?

EZEKIEL 34

This theme of replacement of unworthy shepherds by God himself and his Messiah marks the beginning of a new theocratic movement. The kings of Israel and Judah will reign no more.

1. Of what faults does Ezekiel accuse the rulers (shepherds)? How did their behaviour contrast with that foretold of the Lord's shepherding?
2. How did the sheep behave to each other?
3. Interpret spiritually the blessings of the Messianic age.

EZEKIEL 35

Oracle against Edom.

1. What were the sins of Seir (Edom)? See verses 5, 10, 12. What was to be their punishment? Are we ever guilty of any of these attitudes to our neighbour?
2. Edom (Seir) according to Genesis was Jacob's twin brother, yet he took advantage of Judah's distress at the time of the Babylonian invasion. Trace the story of Edom's relations with Israel in: Numbers 20:14-21; Obadiah 8, 9, 19, 21; Ezekiel 36; Malachi 1:2-3. Is there any hope for Edom? See Isaiah 21:11-12.

EZEKIEL 36

Israel's revenge on Edom is foretold.

1. Summarise the blessings promised to Israel in verses 8-15. Are we inclined, when disaster strikes, to take the attitude of Israel's neighbours (verse 2), or do we humbly trust in God?
2. Look carefully at verse 24-32. How is such a transformation to be brought about? See verse 27. Do we trust in the power of God's Spirit to change our hearts? Do we pray for our enemies? What New Testament teaching is anticipated here?

EZEKIEL 37

The most famous of all Ezekiel's visions - the valley of the dry bones.

1. Verses 1-14. What was the morale of Israel at the time of this vision? See verse 11. Then note the stages by which the bones are resurrected. Note especially verse 4. How do we preach to 'dry bones'?
2. The vision signifies (verses 11-14) the revitalisation of the Messianic people and their return from exile. What, further, does it mean for us? See especially verses 13-14.
3. Verses 15-28. This prediction was very far from being fulfilled in the historical return from exile. The Northern tribes were never reunited with Judah, and conditions were certainly not those of verses 24-28. Of what, therefore, is the prophet speaking? See verses 26-27.

EZEKIEL 38-39

This poem has strong apocalyptic features. cf. Isaiah 24-27, Daniel 7-12, Zechariah 9-14, Revelation. Meshech and Tubal were in Asia Minor. Magog is an invented name. Gog is a type of barbarian warrior. Chapter 39 is a detailed account of the defeat of Gog.

EZEKIEL 38

1. Contrast verses 10-12 with 4 and 16. What were the causes of Gog's invasion and how are they described?
2. Compare verses 18-23 with 37:25-28. In what two ways will God bring the nations to know that he alone is God?
3. Compare verses 11 and 14 with 1 Thessalonians 5:3. What warnings are contained for us in this vision?

EZEKIEL 39

1. Verses 1-20. Considering Gog as an embodiment of evil forces, how and by whom is he defeated, and what is meant by the cleansing of the land after the battle? Give examples of long term effects of evil that need much time to purify.
2. Verses 21-29. This passage forms a conclusion to the whole section which began at Chapter 33. What is meant by 'I hid my face from them' (verse 23)? How does this apply a) to the people of Israel, and b) to me? Consider the great blessing that is contained in verse 29. How is it further realised in the New Testament? In my life?

EZEKIEL 40-48

This final section, from the school of Ezekiel, (cf. Introduction), contains a programme for the religious and political rehabilitation of Israel - a founding charter for the post-exilic community - in the form of a vision of a new Temple.

EZEKIEL 40

The year is 573 BC. The prophet's vision of Jerusalem.

1. Look carefully at verse 4. What responsibilities does the angel lay upon the prophet? Does our Bible study (look..., hear..., set your mind..., declare...) take these responsibilities seriously? What practical steps should we take?
2. Notice the elaborate gates (verses 6-16), the only means of entry. The prophet insists that the Temple be kept pure from foreigners and sinners. How far is this the spirit of New Testament?

EZEKIEL 41

The vision of the Temple.

1. Only the angel went into the 'holy place' (verses 3, 4). The prophet did not follow him. Is there a 'holy of holies' in our churches? Are Christians excluded?
2. Draw a diagram of the building as described in 40-41.

EZEKIEL 42

Supplementary details concerning the Temple.

1. Notice the emphasis on 'holy things' in verses 13, 14, 20. What is meant by the term 'holy'? What do 'holy' things symbolise? Has the incarnation in any way changed the notion?
2. The Temple is as yet empty. Are there parallels today to this temple, prepared for the worship of God, yet empty?

EZEKIEL 43

The Lord returns to the Temple, and the altar is consecrated.

1. The glory of God returns to the Temple (cf. 10:18-19; 11:22-23). Compare 1 Corinthians 3:16-17. How are the people of God his temple? How does the glory of God dwell in the individual Christian?
2. The altar is like a ziggurat towering above the priest. Compare this with a) Jacob's ladder (Genesis 28:11-19) and b) the cross of Jesus. The words 'I will accept you' (verse 27) connected the way back to God with blood shed in sacrifice (verse 20). What is the special symbolism of the peace offerings (verse 27)?

EZEKIEL 44

The priests of the line of Zadok were the descendants of the priest who replaced Abiathar, of the ancient priesthood of Eli (1 Kings 2:35). The Levites had looked after the local shrines and

were frequently tainted with idolatry. When Josiah abolished these shrines, the Levites wer supposed to serve in turn at the Temple. They were not very keen to return to Jerusalem afte the exile (Ezra 8:15-19). This is the background to this chapter.

1. Holiness is still measured by externals. What are the interior dispositions that these regulation symbolise?
2. Who is an alien in God's sight? (verse 9).
3. How is faithful service rewarded and infidelity punished? See verse 10-16.
4. The priests were to have no inheritance but to trust in God only. What is the New Testament teaching'

EZEKIEL 45

The land is to be divided, with a portion set aside for the Temple and for the prince.

1. Part of the land of Israel was to be 'set apart for the Lord'. What portion of my day, of my room, of my life is given over entirely to him?
2. The prince is given his own property, and exhorted to oppress the people no more. How should this principle be applied today? What is said about justice in this chapter?
3. What is said three times to be the purpose of the sacrifices? What does this mean? What is the relationship of this principle to Jesus' sacrifice?

EZEKIEL 46

Various regulations relating to the Temple.

1. 'When they go in, the prince shall go in with them' (verse 10). Apply these words to Christ. Compare the prince's service on the sabbath (verse 2) with that on weekdays. What limitations were placed on the prince?
2. Practical arrangements for boiling meat (verses 19-24) had to be made. What in your view, is the place for practical arrangements in modern liturgies? List the various aspects. How would participants be chosen?

EZEKIEL 47

This famous passage (verses 1-12) is reflected in Revelation 22:1-2.

1. Verses 1-12. From where did the river come? What is symbolised by its increasing depth?
2. Where did the river flow? (See verses 8-9). What did it bring? See especially verses 12 and cf. Exodus 15:26-27. Are there desolate and barren parts of me that need the river?
3. Verses 13-23. What Gospel principle is foreshadowed in verses 22-23? cf. Ephesians 2:11-13.

EZEKIEL 48

The ideal division of the land by Ezekiel is totally unrealistic and unrealisable, based on geometry rather than geography. It is therefore symbolic, like the heavenly city in Revelation 21.

1. List the tribes of Israel. Notice that Simeon and Reuben, long vanished, are to be restored, and that they once more number twelve. What is the significance of this? cf. Revelation 21:12. Which tribes take precedence? Why?
2. What does the new name of the city (verse 35) reveal about God's relationship with his people? Compare this with Isaiah 7:14, Matthew 1:23 and John 1:14.

AN INTRODUCTION TO THE BOOK OF DANIEL

Daniel in his den of lions, like Noah in his ark, is one of the folk heroes familiar to most children. There is even a story (surely apocryphal) of the child in Sunday school who wept at Daniel's rescue 'because the lions would get no dinner"... The Daniel of scripture is, in fact, a folk hero, though of another kind. He is mentioned in Ezekiel 14:14, 20 along with Noah and Job as a righteous man, and in Ezekiel 28:3 as a wise one. The author of the Book of Daniel uses this mythological figure as his hero in a similar way to the use of Job in the work of that name. There is no question of ordinary history or biography.

The book is divided into two parts: Chapters 1-6 contain pious fables composed for edification, about Daniel and his companions at the royal court in Babylon; chapters 7-12 describe Daniel's visions in which he foresees the successive kingdoms of the ancient world. The Greek Bible has added some deutero-canonical sections: the Psalm of Azariah and the Canticle of the Youths (3:24-90); the story of Susanna (chapter 13), and the stories of Bel and the snake (chapter 14). The book is an apocalypse, written during the persecution of Antiochus Epiphanes, between 167 and 164 BC. It is in late Hebrew, mixed with Aramaic; it shares with Tobit an interest in angels, and it reveals belief in the resurrection of the dead; all these point to a date long after the time of Nebuchadnezzar.

Why is this (to us) strange work among the prophetic books? It gives a prophetic interpretation of history, it encourages those being persecuted for their Jewish faith, it reaffirms the superiority of God's wisdom and reveals him as the Lord of history. It is in the Book of Daniel that the Messiah is represented as "Son of Man", that we receive clear teaching on the resurrection of the body, and that we meet St Michael, and, for the first time, St Gabriel.

DANIEL 1

1. In what ways did the Babylonians seek to plunge Daniel and his companions entirely into their culture? What, for Daniel, was the sticking point, and why? See 2 Maccabees 6:18 - 7:42.
2. In what way can verse 17 be said to introduce the theme for the whole series of stories in Daniel 1-6? Why were visions and dreams so important to the writer? Have they any significance for you?

DANIEL 2

"Chaldeans" here means those practising divination. The greeting at verse 4 was used in the Persian court. The title "God of heaven" (verse 18) was used commonly in Persia (cf. Ezra 5:11 etc.) to designate the God of the Jews.

1. Compare the style of this narrative with Esther, especially verses 5, 12-13 with Esther 3:9, 7:10; and verse 48 with Esther 6:8. How do these details indicate that this is a fable, not history?
2. Compare the story of Daniel in this chapter with that of Joseph in Genesis 41.
3. What do we learn from this story about response to adversity? See especially verses 14-16, 17-18, 19-23.
4. The dream refers to the Babylonian, Median, Persian and Greek empires. What is the stone? cf. Psalm 118:22 and Matthew 21:42-44.
5. Could one reinterpret the dream in terms of this century? In that case, what would be the four empires?

DANIEL 3

This story is clearly not a historical sequence to chapter 2, but another fable in which Nebuchadnezzar once more figures as a tyrant.

1. To unite his huge empire, the king imposes a unified state religion, obligatory for all. Has our century seen any examples of totalitarian 'religion'? What ordeals have been imposed on dissidents, equivalent to the Hebrews' incineration?
2. The Song of the Three Young Men and the Psalm of Azariah are both familiar to those who use the ASB in the Anglican church or the Book of Hours in the Catholic church. How could Azariah's prayer be adapted for intercession for the nation and the Benedicite used as a thanksgiving song?
3. What is the meaning beneath the symbolism of the angelic figure in the flames (verse 25)?

DANIEL 4

1. What is the meaning of the tree? See Ezekiel 17:1-10 and 31:3-14. Who is the 'watcher'?
2. What suggestion does Daniel make to the king to accept the warning contained in the dream? See verse 27. Do we take our dreams seriously?
3. How does salvation come to Nebuchadnezzar? Trace God's dealings with him from 2:38, 47 through 3:29, 4:2, 22-27, 31-32, 34-37. What can we learn from his story?

DANIEL 5

1. What is the moral of this story? See verses 1-3 and 23.
2. Notice the intervention of the queen mother (verses 10-12). What purpose does she serve in the narrative? What does she symbolise? Compare Luke 1:43.
3. Consider the judgement passed in verses 26-28 and compare it with that passed on rulers and regimes in this century. Are we, as a nation, in danger of passing under judgement? See verses 22-23. What should we, as Christians, be doing about it?

DANIEL 6

Darius the Mede is unknown in history.

1. Trace the story of the relations between Daniel and his friends with the courtiers in these stories. Note a) the occasions when Daniel puts them in the shade (1:19-20; 4:7, 18; 5:7, 8, 15; 6:3) and b) the growth of a jealous spirit against the Jews (3:8-12; 6:4, 5, 12, 13, 15). What does this story teach us about ourselves? Is our sympathy with Daniel or with the courtiers?
2. What do we learn about Daniel's life of prayer in these stories? (cf. 2:18-23; 6:10-11). Is his faith indicated?
3. Compare chapter 6 with the alternative version (14:23-42). Which do you prefer and why?

DANIEL 7-12

These chapters contain Daniel's visions.

DANIEL 7

This vision corresponds to the dream of Nebuchadnezzar in Chapter 2.

1. At one, historical, level the vision of the four beasts can be understood to mean the Babylonian, Median, Persian and Greek empires as in Chapter 2. Can we also interpret the dream psychologically, with the clue in verse 3? 'And four great beasts came up out of the sea' of the collective unconscious. Consider especially the characteristics of each beast: intelligence

(verse 4), lust for murder (verse 5), power (verse 6), and especially those of the fourth beast. In what way has our century witnessed the power of the collective unconscious?

2. How is God described in verses 9-10? Draw out each aspect of the vision. How and for what purpose does the author of Revelation use similar language (Revelation 1:14).
3. Who is the son of man (verse 13)? What use does New Testament make of this passage? cf. especially Matthew 24:30, 26:64, etc.
4. What effect did all this have on Daniel?

DANIEL 8

On the symbolism of rams and he-goats see Ezekiel 34:17 ff. and Zechariah 10:3.

1. Work out the allegory: the ram was the Persian kingdom, the he-goat that of the Greeks and the prominent horn Alexander the Great. Then re-apply the allegory to a situation in our own century. What are the outstanding characteristics of the ram, the he-goat and the king (verse 23)? What is the moral?
2. The actual events referred to (verses 20-25) have long passed, though they have often been repeated through history. What is the real significance of Gabriel's intervention (verses 17, 19)? What part does Gabriel play in New Testament?

DANIEL 9

Daniel had access to scripture (verse 2) including Jeremiah's prophecy of the end of the exile. The author is encouraging his readers, enduring persecution under Antiochus Epiphanes, to find comfort in scripture.

1. Work out the structure of Daniel's prayer - address to God, confession of guilt, reference to God's Law, renewed confession and repentance, intercession. Draw up a similar prayer.
2. Is the prophecy of verses 24-27 exhausted by the fall of Jerusalem, or is more implied? Who is the anointed one (verses 25 and 26)? Is there also a reference to the second coming of Christ?

DANIEL 10-11:1

The mysterious conflict between angels is referred to in Zechariah 3:1-2, Jude 9 and Revelation 12:7-12.

1. Note verse 1 - "the word was true" - and - "he understood the word". What word did Daniel receive? What is the meaning of the "great conflict"? Read 2 Kings 6:16-18; Psalm 34:7; Ephesians 6:10-13. What light does Church teaching throw on the spirit world?
2. What encouragement for fasting and other ascetical practices do we find in this chapter? What is their aim?

DANIEL 11:2-45

1. Consider the words in verses 3,16 and 36 "shall do according to his (own) will". Are we happier, in the long run, for a spell of "doing according to our own will"? Notice the sequence of verses 3 to 4, of verses 16 to 17, and especially verses 36-39 through to verse 45. What do we learn from this?
2. What was the "abomination that makes desolate" (verse 31)? How does New Testament use this passage (Matthew 24:15)? What different reactions came from the Jews? See verses 32-35.

DANIEL 12

1. In what way does the teaching of this book go beyond any other in Old Testament in its teaching on the resurrection of the body?
2. Compare verses 10-12 with Revelation 22:6-15. How is the teaching of both supplemented by Matthew 25?

DANIEL 13

This chapter (and chapter 14) is a Greek supplement to the Hebrew text. Like Tobit it is a pious story for edification in the Wisdom style.

1. Trace the way in which sinful desires took hold of the two elders. What was the turning point in their desire leading to crime? (See verses 10-13). What can we learn from this?
2. What is emphasised throughout in the character of Susanna? How does God answer her prayer?

DANIEL 14

These stories are a satire against idolatry. Bel is one of the names of Marduk, the Babylonian god - cf. Isaiah 46:1.

1. The first god is a statue, the second a dragon. What does each symbolise? Are we ever guilty of putting our trust in lifeless machines or of worshipping animals? Why does the Bible so often use satire against idolatry?
2. The Bible has much to say against idolatry. Are we right to read from this a condemnation of all world religions except Judaism and Christianity? Is there a distinction to be made? What are the principles underlying respect for world religions?

AN INTRODUCTION TO THE PROPHECY OF HOSEA

In the old liturgy for Good Friday in the Roman Prayer Book a (to me) mysterious passage was read near the beginning of what was then known as the Mass of the Pre-sanctified:

For he hath taken us, and he will heal us:
he will strike, and he will cure us.
He will revive us after two days: on the third day he will raise us
and we shall live in his sight. (Osee (6:2-3).

I was puzzled that such an apparently clear prophecy of Christ's resurrection should have escaped the scribes and pharisees, and even Jesus' disciples. As far as I knew, no other passage from 'Osee' was ever read in church, and in those days, Catholic Religious Instruction never seemed to get beyond the Pentateuch in Old Testament studies. The Prophets were virtually a closed book to me, and it was many years before I recognised Osee, Abdias, Sophonias and Aggeus, as Hosea, Obadiah, Zephaniah and Haggai, when new translations of the Bible finally discarded the old latin Vulgate.

I had missed a good deal, especially by knowing nothing of Hosea, one of the greatest religious thinkers of all time. He prophesied in the northern kingdom from 750 to 725 BC, at a time of great upheaval. He began his ministry during the prosperous reign of Jeroboam II, and lived to see the assassination of Jeroboam's son Zechariah and the end of that dynasty. A succession of palace revolutions left the kingdom so weak that defeat by the Assyrians and the total collapse of the state became inevitable. Samaria fell in 721 BC.

Hosea saw a zealous but contaminated worship, in fact, if not in intention, idolatrous. Yahweh was coupled with the Canaanite gods - Baal and Astarte - in licentious fertility rites. His own tragic domestic situation (chapters 1,3) led him to experience in some measure God's sense of desertion by his chosen Israel. As Hosea was able to take back the faithless Gomer, so God still loves and will woo and cherish his faithless people. It is a remarkable book, full of bold imagery and great poetry. Unfortunately, it is in a poor state of preservation, so often obscure, and the JB translation departs considerably from other versions. We have followed RSV.

HOSEA 1

1. Study carefully the information given concerning a) Gomer, and b) the three children, noting especially their names. In what way is the whole story symbolic of the covenant story of Israel?
2. Judean editors (verses 7 and 10-2:1) have inserted a commentary and a conclusion. What is the meaning of their intervention? See especially the reversal of the names, and cf. 1 Peter 2:10.

HOSEA 2

For the valley of Achor see Joshua 7 and Isaiah 65:10.

1. At what point is the transition made from Hosea's story to the relations between God and Israel? Of what is Israel accused? See especially verse 13.
2. What is the significance for Hosea of Israel's wilderness experience (verses 14f)? What is the covenant God will make with his renewed people?

HOSEA 3

Another piece of Hosea's biography.

1. What did Hosea do for Gomer? (verses 1-3). What does he promise, for his part?

2. What does God promise his people? (and cf. 2 Chronicles 30:18-20). What is the purpose of the 'many days without king or prince...'? What are the occasions in our lives when we need a period of purification? How is this experienced in the church?

HOSEA 4

1. Notice the emphasis on covenant words (faithfulness, kindness, knowledge (verse 1 cf. 2:19-20). When the covenant is forgotten by the people (verse 2) what is the result for the land? Are these words relevant for us today? Look at verses 1-3 from a psychological and from an ecological point of view.
2. Hosea accuses the priests and prophets of failing in their duty. What specific sins are laid at their door? (verses 4-10). Are church leaders in any way implicated in this scripture?
3. What are the sins of the people (verses 11-13)?

HOSEA 5

Mizpah, Tabor and Shittim were probably shrines where Canaanite rites flourished.

1. Note the contrast between God's knowledge of Israel (verse 3) and their situation (verse 4). What does verse 6 further tell us about their spiritual state?
2. Note the strong language of verse 12. Can it ever be said today that God is like a festering sore in the belly of the nation? What truth is conveyed by this imagery? What do the people try to do? (verse 13).

HOSEA 6

The structure of verses 1-6 is that of a penitential liturgy. Look up Joshua 3:16 and Genesis 31:46-48 for references to shrines at Adam and at Gilead.

1. Verses 1-6. What is the underlying attitude of the people? Are they confident or presumptuous? What is God's response? How is verse 6 used in New Testament (Matthew 9:13 and 12:7)?
2. Verses 7-11. Of what crimes is Israel accused?

HOSEA 7

See 1 Kings 15:25 - 16:28, 2 Kings 15:8-33 and 2 Kings 17:1-6 for background.

1. How does Hosea interpret the anarchy of the time? What is the great error of the people? See verses 7, 10 and 14. Am I ever guilty of this error? On what occasions and in what circumstances?
2. What is God longing to do for his people? What verbs are used in verses 1, 13? What do these words mean in my life?

HOSEA 8

The house of the Lord (verse 1) is not the Temple (Hosea was a northerner) but the land of Israel.

1. Verses 1-10. What accusations does the prophet make against Israel? Was there any connection between idolatry and foreign alliances? How far is all this relevant today?
2. Verses 11-14. What is basically wrong with Israel's religious life?

HOSEA 9

This chapter consists of a group of short oracles probably delivered at the autumn harvest festival.

1. Verses 1-6. Hosea paints a grim picture of the exile ahead. What will be the most serious deprivation of the deportees?

2. Verses 7-9. The people respond that the prophet is a fool (verse 7). What does Hosea assert instead? cf. Ezekiel 33:1-9. Do we treat prophetic figures any better? Who are Hosea's counterparts today?
3. Verses 10-17. Contrast the hopes that God had for Israel (verse 10) with their sin at Baal-Peor (Numbers 25:1-5). What results does sin have (verses 10d and 14). Can you think of any examples of the sterility that is the result of sin?

HOSEA 10

The reference to Gibeah (verses 9-10) is explained in Judges 19. It was also the place where Saul was proclaimed king (1 Samuel 10:23-24). Bethaven (verse 5) refers to Bethel.

1. List the sins of which the people are accused (verses 2,4,13). Do we need to examine ourselves too? What is the remedy proposed by Hosea (verse 12)?
2. What punishment is forseen by the prophet?

HOSEA 11

1. Draw out the different images in verses 1-4 used to describe God's love for Israel. What other image has Hosea used? Which one moves you most?
2. What do we learn of God's feelings in this chapter? See especially verses 4, 8, 9, 12. What do verses 10-11 tell us of God's ultimate intentions for his people?

HOSEA 12

Hosea uses the history of Israel to reinforce his message.

1. Verses 1-6. Look up Genesis 25:21-23 (for verse 3), Genesis 32:24-28 (for verses 3-4), Genesis 28:10-22) (for verse 4), Genesis 29 (for verses 12) for the background to this chapter. Notice that Hosea interprets Jacob's career unfavourably, and applies it to his contemporaries, Jacob's descendants. See especially verse 4 (RSV margin) and verse 6.
2. Verses 7-9. How does Hosea refer to the conquest of the land (trader verse 7 = Canaanite) and to the Exodus?
3. What does Hosea have to say about prophecy? Who is referred to in verse 13? What are the implications of this for Hosea's message? Does the Church today heed her prophets or does she persecute them?

HOSEA 13

The prophet continues to draw parallels from Israel's history.

1. Apply verses 1-3 to our own country's fortunes.
2. Learn verses 4-5 by heart and use them as a prayer, especially for 'dry times'.
3. Trace the history of Israel through chapters 12 and 13. Then find my own life story there. What a) warning and b) consolation do I find?

HOSEA 14

1. What does repentance involve?
2. What is the divine response? Note the evocation of the Song of Songs in verses 5-7. cf. Song 4:11, 2:3 and 4:10.

AN INTRODUCTION
TO
THE PROPHECY OF JOEL

We are familiar with several verses from Joel, because he was quoted by Peter on Pentecost Sunday (Acts 2:17-21), and also because part of Joel is read on Ash Wednesday. The book is first of all about a plague of locusts, one of the worst scourges that can befall humanity. The prophet, of whom we know nothing except his name, was probably a cultic prophet attached to the Temple. He sees the threat of locusts not just as a natural phenomenon, but as the 'day of the Lord' - a visitation of God in judgement. The response of the people must be repentance and prayer. The locusts are God's army which will scourge the people, and lead in the great Day of Yahweh. So the present order is only a preparation for the End.

Joel's message seems to date from about 400 BC.

JOEL 1

Chapters 1 and 2 are a liturgy of mourning and supplication arising from a plague of locusts.

1. How does Joel set the scene? What classes of people are especially concerned? See verses 5, 9, 11, 13.
2. How is Jerusalem to respond (verse 14)? What is meant by 'Sanctify a fast'? Note the repetition of words of lamentation: weep, wail, lament, mourn, cry. Do you think there is a place for such liturgies at times of national disaster? What elements would you include?

JOEL 2

The trumpet or ramshorn (verse 1) was a warning of imminent danger.

1. The army of locusts is likened to an invasion of troops led by God himself (verse 22). Draw out the references to the Day of the Lord. Look up Isaiah 13 and note the similarities of language, especially cf. verse 2 with Isaiah 13:6; verse 6 with Isaiah 13:8 and verse 10 with Isaiah 13:10; and the climax 'Who can endure it'? (verse 11).
2. What are the conditions of true repentance (verses 12-17)?
3. Verses 18-27. God gives an immediate response. What are the blessings he promises? Have such responses from God occurred in recent history? Can they be interpreted spiritually?
4. Verses 28-32. God's long term intentions are revealed. What does New Testament make of the promises? See Acts 2:17-21.

JOEL 3

The new age ushers in the judgement of the nations.

1. Which nations are indicated and for what offences?
2. In verse 10 Isaiah 2:5 is reversed. Why? What, according to verses 17 and 21 is to be the supreme blessedness of God's people? How are these promises fulfilled a) in New Testament, and b) in Christ's people?

AN INTRODUCTION
TO
THE PROPHECY OF AMOS

Amos was the earliest of the so-called 'writing prophets' - and his message was a stern one - God is a God of justice, and he defends the poor from oppression. A nation which amasses great wealth at the expense of its own people is doomed. Amos was not a professional prophet, but a sheep farmer from Tekoa in Judah. He was sent to prophesy to the northern kingdom during the prosperous reign of Jeroboam II (783-743 BC). Like Hosea, his contemporary, he foresaw the downfall of Israel. His words are blunt, his manner uncompromising - the privilege of being God's people brings serious moral obligations.

The oracles of Amos have been rearranged by an editor, beginning with an oracle of judgement on Israel's neighbours. In chapter 9:11-15 the messages of doom are reversed, detail by detail, into a message of salvation. The intention was not to avert judgement - it had already taken place at the fall of Samaria in 721 BC - but to reassure Judah that God's will for his people was that salvation should follow judgement. This is one piece of evidence that the book was used, and seen to have a valid message, in times much later than Amos'. It was also used in public worship: three short hymns are interspersed (4:13; 5:8-9; 9:5-6) praising God in his creation.

Note: The ancient shrines (Bethel, Gilgal, Beer-sheba) that had been associated with the worship of the patriarchs, in Amos' time were used for a corrupt worship of false gods - even for fertility rites. Hence Amos' scathing reference to them (4:4; 5:5, 7:10 ff.).

AMOS 1

1. What are the sins calling for God's judgement: a) of Damascus (Syria), b) of Gaza (Philistia), c) of Tyre, d) of Edom, e) of Ammon? Which nations had attacked Israelites?
2. In each case, what was the punishment?
3. Have any of these crimes been committed in this century? Have they been punished?

AMOS 2

1. Judah and Israel are also condemned. For what sins? See verses 4-8.
2. In what ways have the chosen people failed to live out the covenant (verses 9-10)? What will be their punishment?

AMOS 3

Israel is warned of the coming judgement.

1. What is the heart of the covenant law (verse 2)? How do the images in verses 3-8 warn that the message of the prophet will be one of judgement?
2. How do I respond to the challenge of verse 2? Does it inspire fear or confidence or humility?
3. What sins of Israel are mentioned in this chapter? See verses 10,14,15. Under which categories do they fall? What does this tell us about God's priorities?

AMOS 4

Verse 3 "... into Harmon" means towards Assyria. Bethel and Gilgal were shrines given up to idolatry.

1. In what ways were the women of Samaria especially blameworthy? Compare verses 1-3 with Isaiah 3:16-26.

2. With what calamities does God seek to warn his people (verses 6-11)? Do we ever see disasters as a warning judgement, or do we just complain? What is the climax? See verse 12. What does the phrase mean?

AMOS 5

The shrines to which the people flock represent a superficial, tainted cult. Verses 25-27 are quoted in Acts 7:42-43 in the Greek translation.

1. What are the sins of which the people will not repent? See verses 7, 10, 11, 12. What will be the punishment? Do you think we are guilty of any of these sins? What steps should we take to ensure justice in society and in the church?
2. Amos calls the people three times (verses 4, 6, 14) to "seek the Lord". What are we to understand by this? How do we 'seek the Lord'? Were the people's sacrifices and festivals pleasing to God (verses 21-24)? Why not?

AMOS 6

Calneh, Hamath and Gath were cities that had fallen to the Assyrians.

1. What are the themes of the three Woes (5:18-20; 6:1-3; 6:4-6)? Against what sins is Amos warning the people of the northern kingdom? We are not nowadays guilty of the first. What of the other two?
2. What is meant by verses 9-10? What was the real sin of the Israelites? (verse 12).

AMOS 7

The prophet's visions.

1. What message of hope is contained in verses 1-6? Do we pray enough for the world of our time that God will avert the judgement hanging over us? Notice Amos' plea (verses 2, 5). Can I honestly make it my own?
2. Opposition is roused in Israel against Amos. What kind of man is Amaziah? Notice the account Amos gives of himself (verses 14-15). What can we learn from this episode?

AMOS 8

Further visions.

1. Compare verses 1-3 with 7:7-9. What is the meaning of these two visions?
2. Is there any message for today's multinationals and other huge business interests in verses 4-6? How can we protect poor nations from being undersold?
3. What is the warning contained in verses 11-12? Do we in this country today suffer from such a 'famine'? Are there any hopeful signs?

AMOS 9

Caphtor (verse 7) is the island of Crete. Kir is unknown.

1. Compare the terrible vision of Amos (verse 1) with that of Isaiah 6:1. Is there any indication in the book that Amos' words were eventually heeded?
2. Notice the universalism of Amos' message (chapter 1 and verse 7). What does the doctrine of moral accountability teach us about God's relationship with non- Christians? What implications does this have for my attitude to them?
3. Draw out the hymn that recurs through the book (4:13; 5:8-9; 9:5-6). What is its theme? Why do you think it has been inserted?
4. What blessings are promised after judgement?

AN INTRODUCTION
TO
THE BOOK OF OBADIAH

In 587 BC the Edomites took advantage of the fall of Jerusalem to invade southern Judah. This fragment evidently dates from the time of the exile or soon after the return. Judah is pictured as taking her claim against Edom to God's tribunal. God's verdict (verses 2-9) is followed by a list of Edom's crimes (verses 10-14). Israel's revenge on Edom is seen in terms of the Day of Yahweh. This fragment bears witness to Israel's faith in God's ultimate justice and power.

1. What was Edom's sin (verses 10-14)? Make a list. Are we ever guilty of taking advantage of a brother or sister in any way? Have we ever 'stood aloof'?
2. What will be Edom's punishment? See verses 1-9. How does it fit her crime?
3. The prophet proclaims a vision (verse 1) and speaks in the name of God. What does he see beyond the immediate sins of Edom? See verses 15-21.
4. In what sense does Obadiah comfort his people with hope in God's moral judgements? Are we able to distinguish between our need to face up to our feelings of hatred of those who commit atrocities, and Christ's command to forgive our enemies?

AN INTRODUCTION
TO
THE BOOK OF JONAH

Hosea, Joel, Amos, Obadiah, Jonah, Micah, Nahum ...
Find the odd man out. – Answer: Jonah.

Like Noah, Jonah is a household name, a companion of the nursery. His whale is a marvel to children, like Daniel's lions or the animals in Noah's ark. This is unfortunate, for the book has a serious message, from which the fish incident of chapter 2 tends to distract us. Scholars have wasted much ink determining whether a fish could swallow a man and release him alive, and whether Nineveh could be said to be within walking distance of the Mediterranean! All this is a mistake. The book is a parable, a didactic tale against rigid interpretation of prophecy, and against racism. The great message of Jonah is in chapter 4 not in chapter 2 - and the hero of the narrative is not Jonah but God, who cares for the Ninevites and their beasts. This destroys all confidence in an elite. God caring for everyone is a terrifying notion.

The book was probably written during the fourth century, and represents a rejection of the narrow racism of the post-exilic period, in part a protest against the reforms of Ezra. It is one of the greatest books of the Old Testament, with a message we so often forget - God so loved the world.

JONAH 1

The story purports to be that of the Jonah mentioned in 2 Kings 14:25, but this is an ascription like that of Ecclesiastes to Solomon - a literary device. Tarshish stands for the furthest end of the earth.

1. What indications already in this chapter alert us to a satire on a prophetic call? See verses 3, 9, 10.
2. What are the virtues of the mariners?
3. How does the Lord retain control of the situation?

JONAH 2

The psalm was probably inserted later into the book.

1. Jesus uses this book (Matthew 12:40; Luke 11:30) as a type of his own burial and resurrection. Read the psalm with this in mind, and picture Jesus praying it while in the tomb. What is the symbolism of a) the sea and b) the fish?
2. Why do you think Jonah was used in the early Church in baptismal typology?

JONAH 3

Nineveh was the capital city of the Assyrians, the great enemy of Israel.

1. What does it mean when it says that God repents (verses 9,10)? Balaam said: 'God is not man... that he should repent' (Numbers 23:19). CAN God change his mind?
2. Jesus commended the Ninevites (Matthew 12:24, Luke 11:32). Does this mean that Jesus necessarily implied that the story was historical?

JONAH 4

The book ends with a strong emphasis on God's love for all creation.

1. List the ways in which God's compassionate love is shown a) in this chapter and b) in the whole book.
2. Note the various aspects of the character of Jonah.
3. What is the lesson of the book? Do WE apply it in our attitudes to each other, to criminals, to other nations?

AN INTRODUCTION
TO
THE PROPHECY OF MICAH

Micah is actually quoted in the Book of Jeremiah (Jeremiah 26:18-19). He came from Moreshath-gath, a small village in the hills about twenty-five miles south west of Jerusalem. He was a countryman, who spoke up for the poor farmers who were suffering at the hands of powerful landowners and landlords (2:2). He was a contemporary of Isaiah, prophesying during the reigns of Ahaz and Hezekiah. Some think he was a disciple of Isaiah, and like him, he warned of judgement to come (1:2-9), in the shape of the Assyrian menace. Like Amos, he was suspicious of city life, and saw only evil in Samaria and Jerusalem (1:5). The book falls into four parts, which must be due to an editor: 1:2 - 3:12 - arraignment of Israel; 4:1 - 5:14 - promises to Zion; 6:1 - 7:7 - Israel arraigned; 7:8 - 20 - promises of hope. Micah's prophecy of the birth of the Messiah at Bethlehem is mentioned in the New Testament (Matthew 2:6; John 7:42) and his work will be forever loved because of the great precept of 6:8: to do justice, and to love kindness, and to walk humbly with your God.

MICAH 1

This oracle was uttered as a warning to Samaria before the Assyrian invasion in 721. It was directed against Jerusalem by a later editor.

1. At first sight the language seems very strong, but read the chapter with God's feelings in mind. Why is he obliged to be so severe? See verses 8-9.
2. The text of verses 10-16 plays on the names of twelve towns about to be invaded. Look up the meaning of each name in a commentary.

MICAH 2

Micah preaches to a scoffing unreceptive audience.

1. What sin is condemned in verses 1-5? What will be its punishment? Why is Micah so severe?
2. Verses 6-11 are a dialogue between Micah and his audience. What do the people claim (verses 6-7)? They put their faith in the covenant and we perhaps in our membership of the church. What is the prophet's retort (verses 8-11)? List each point made.
3. Promise (verses 12,13) follows banishment (verse 10). How are God's acts of restoration described? Who is the king?

MICAH 3

The prophet attacks the ruling classes and the false prophets.

1. What classes of people are reproached and for what crimes? Why are they so complacent (verse 11)?
2. Notice the contrast between the true prophet (verse 8) and the false (verses 5-7). What are the signs of the presence of the Spirit?
3. Verse 12 is quoted in Jeremiah 26:18. In what circumstances?

MICAH 4

Oracles of hope - these prophecies may be later than Micah, perhaps post-exlic.

1. Verses 1-3 are also found in Isaiah 2:2-4. Why do you think they are inserted here? Do they get a fresh meaning from their context? cf. 3:12.
2. What categories of people are to become the 'remnant' of the blessed? See verses 6-7. What use does Jesus make of this passage (Luke 14:13, 21)?
3. Jerusalem will be besieged (verses 8-9) and her people deported (verse 10). But what will be the outcome?

MICAH 5

A famous Messianic prophecy, quoted in the New Testament.

1. Contrast the great capital under siege (verse 1) with a little town (verse 2) from whom the saviour is to come. Micah is thinking of the obscure origins of David, but Matthew quotes it of Christ (Matthew 2:6). What are the characteristics of the saviour (verse 4)?
2. How will God purify his people? See verses 10-15. Are we in need of such purification? What would you put on that list?

MICAH 6

The prophets frequently use the image of a trial, with God as the accuser and Israel as the defendant. The mountains are the witnesses. They are the chosen places where God meets his people.

1. God indicts his people in the presence of the mountains. Of what does he accuse them (verses 3-5)? What is Israel's reply (verses 6-7)?
2. Micah sums up the message of Amos, Hosea and Isaiah in verse 8. Identify each one. Is this our blueprint too? The prophets draw on the covenant virtues. How are they realised in the Sermon on the Mount? and cf. Deuteronomy 10:12, 13.
3. The prophet once more mourns over the social evils of his time (verses 9-12). In what ways do they bring their own punishment (verses 13-16)? Who were Omri and Ahab?

MICAH 7

The oracles conclude on the theme of restoration, hope and forgiveness.

1. Note how the details of this passage (verses 1-6) could describe our own century. In what sense does Jesus quote this passage? See Matthew 10:35-36; Luke 12:53.
2. What is the situation of the prophet? (verses 7-10).
3. Sketch the qualities of the remnant (verses 18-20 and cf. 4:7).

AN INTRODUCTION TO THE PROPHECY OF NAHUM

All empires decline and fall eventually, and Assyria was no exception. The great power of the eighth century had waned to such an extent that by the reign of Josiah (640-609 BC) that king was able to make considerable inroads into Assyrian colonies in Israel, and in 612 the Assyrian capital Nineveh fell before the combined assault of the Babylonians, Medes and Scythians.

The fall of Nineveh was celebrated like the fall of the Third Reich in 1945, and Nahum's prophecy expresses frank glee at God's judgement on an evil empire. The vivid description in chapter 2 of the panic in Nineveh as the invading armies arrive ranks Nahum among the great dramatic poets of the Bible. He teaches that lasting kingdoms cannot be built on fraud and force, and that God punishes injustice, violence and idolatry. Beyond this short book we know nothing at all about Nahum. He is never quoted in the New Testament.

NAHUM 1

The theme of God's anger is not a popular one today, but Nahum sees God's wrath as part of his justice. He is 'slow to anger ... will by no means clear the guilty' (verse 2).

1. Verses 2-8 are an acrostic poem developing the traditional theme of the wrath of God. What is the reason for the contrast between the character of God as portrayed in verses 2-6, and as portrayed in verse 7?
2. What threat does God make to Nineveh (verses 9-11, 14), and what promise to Judah (verses 13, 15)?

NAHUM 2

The rest of the oracle is addressed to Nineveh.

1. Describe the approach of the army (verses 3-5) and the disarray in the palace (verses 6-8). What word especially recalls the cruelty of the Assyrians (verses 11-12)?
2. To what ultimately does the prophet ascribe Nineveh's downfall?

NAHUM 3

Verse 8 dates the oracle, as it refers to Thebes in Egypt which fell in 663 BC. The whole chapter is a fierce celebration of God's ultimate justice, triumphing over an evil empire.

1. What sins of Nineveh are listed in this chapter? See verses 1,4.
2. Notice the strong imagery in verses 12-17. What events are described?
3. Look at verse 19. What do you think of the sentiments expressed? Are there, in your opinion, any empires or regimes in this century at whose fall such a verse would be appropriate?

AN INTRODUCTION
TO
THE PROPHECY OF HABAKKUK

There is a strange story in Daniel 14:33-39 (Greek Bible) which used to be read on one of the weekdays of Lent, which I much enjoyed as a child:

> The prophet Habakkuk, who was in Judea, had made a stew; he broke bread into the bowl, and he was on his way to his field, carrying it to the reapers, when an angel of the Lord said to him, Habakkuk, carry that meal you have to Babylon for Daniel, who is in the lion-pit. My Lord, replied Habakkuk, I have never been to Babylon, and I do not know where the lion-pit is. The angel took the prophet by the head, and carrying him by his hair swept him to Babylon with the blast of his breath and set him down above the pit. Habakkuk called out, Daniel, Daniel! Take the meal that God has sent you. Daniel said, You do indeed remember me, God; you never abandon those who love you. He got up and ate; and at once God's angel brought Habakkuk back home again. *(Daniel 14:33-39 REB).*

This apocryphal story witnesses to the popularity of the canonical prophet, though it clearly gives us no actual facts concerning him. Who was he? He lived in Judea, after the fall of Nineveh (612) and the defeat of the Egyptians by the Babylonians at the battle of Carchemish in 605. A new power was beginning to darken the horizon. Habakkuk actually requires of God that he give an account of his ordering of the world. Judah may have sinned, but why should the all-Holy God choose savages like the Chaldeans to punish her? Is this not appearing to support injustice? Habakkuk's punch line - 'the righteous shall live by his faithfulness' (2:4) was taken up by Paul (Romans 1:17) and still more by Luther.

HABAKKUK 1

This short prophecy, more than any other in my opinion, is a wonderful model for genuine prayer of intercession. The prophet complains, by stating the facts of the situation; God replies; the prophet objects to God's reasoning.

1. What is the situation of which the prophet complains? (verses 2-4). What is God's answer? (verses 5-11). Note especially God's 'work' (verse 5).
2. What is Habakkuk's further problem? Do you share his bewilderment?

HABAKKUK 2

Habakkuk, determined to read a satisfactory answer in 'the signs of the times' takes his stand and waits for God's reply, which is somewhat ambiguous. However, the prophet takes heart, and sees justice coming to his enemies in the shape of punishment.

1. What do we learn from Habakkuk about perseverance and faith in prayer (verses 1-3)? What is God's response? What is the original meaning of verse 4? (Note RSV margin and JB) cf. Hosea 2:20.
2. The prophet now predicts the enemy's eventual downfall. What five 'woes' will overtake them? How can these 'woes' be interpreted for us today?

HABAKKUK 3

This psalm was used in the liturgy.

1. What past acts of God are remembered by the prophet? What acts of God does the Christian remember? What is meant by 'in wrath, remember mercy'?
2. Verses 3-15. Pick out the elements that refer a) to creation, b) to the Exodus, c) to the final battle.
3. Why did Habakkuk, though so alarmed by the vision (verse 16) wait *QUIETLY* for the 'day of trouble'? Do you know any other examples in scripture where prayer and the vision of God bring this grace? Do you know of anything like it in your own experience?
4. The last verse emphasises the graces bestowed on the prophet. What are they? Have we received them too?

AN INTRODUCTION
TO
THE PROPHECY OF ZEPHANIAH

Yahweh your God is there with you,
the warrior-saviour God.
He will rejoice over you with song,
He'll renew you by his love,
He will dance with shouts of joy
on a day of festival,
He will dance with shouts of joy for you.

One of the great benefits of the charismatic renewal has been to open up the scriptures to many people, especially through songs. Who, before this song appeared, knew these wonderful lines from one of the lesser known prophets? Zephaniah 3:17 has been variously translated - this hymn is based on the Jerusalem Bible - but all versions agree that this verse celebrates God's love for and joy in his people, renewed by his love.

Several passages in Zephaniah are familiar to us through the liturgy. Luke echoes 3:14 in the story of the Annunciation, and the medieval hymn. 'Dies Irae' is based on 1:15. This used to be sung at funeral Masses. Who was Zephaniah? He seems to have been a member of the royal family (1:1), whose ministry coincided with the early years of Jeremiah, while king Josiah was still young. It was a turbulent period: Judah during the long reign of Mannasseh had fallen under Assyrian influence, and Hezekiah had lost 46 cities to Sennacherib in 701 (cf.. 2 Kings 18:13 ff.).

Zephaniah was a bold preacher (1:2), fearless in his attack on false syncretism (1:4-7), on foppish courtiers, on worldly merchants. He carried his onslaught to Judah's neighbours, but above all on to Jerusalem itself, with a scathing catalogue of the evils of the day (3:1-5). However, he was not without hope that God would raise up a humble remnant, the "anawim" who were to play an increasing part in prophetic teaching, until Jesus himself opened his mouth and said 'Blessed are the anawim - the poor in spirit'.

ZEPHANIAH 1

Jerusalem was still very much under the influence of Assyrian religious practices imported during the reign of Mannasseh.

1. The prophet begins on a note of devastating disaster (verses 2-3). Is this shock tactics or to be taken literally? What explains his strong language? See verse 12.
2. Of what does he accuse the people of Judah (verses 4-8)? What are the modern equivalent sins?
3. What are the accompaniments of the Day of the Lord? What does New Testament say about it? See Luke 17:22-37.

ZEPHANIAH 2

Having called the people of God to a change of heart (verses 1-3), the prophet now warns their enemies of God's vengeance: the Philistines, the Moabites, the Ethiopians and the Assyrians (west, east, south and north).

1. What remedy can be adopted to escape God's anger (verse 3)? Do WE take this warning seriously? How should we respond?
2. What phrases are used to describe the nations coming under judgement? See verses 1, 10, 15. What was especially sinful about Nineveh's attitude?

ZEPHANIAH 3

Zephaniah condemns Jerusalem, but offers hope for the future.

1. Jerusalem comes out worst in this catalogue. List her most grievous faults. What makes her attitude particularly blameworthy? See verse 5.
2. How does God seek to bring Jerusalem to her senses (verses 6-7)? With what result? Do we read 'the signs of the times' and take warning?
3. Verses 8-10. God acts to punish, to purify and to deliver. Apply these three verbs to the work of Christ.
4. What are the results of God's action (verse 11)? What are the characteristics of the redeemed remnant?
5. Verses 14-18. These verses are some of the most remarkable in Old Testament. What do they tell us of the true character of God's love for his people? Note especially the JB translation of verse 17, and the boldness of the imagery. cf. Isaiah 62:5. What New Testament teaching completes the doctrine of renewal by and through God's *LOVE*?

AN INTRODUCTION
TO
THE PROPHECY OF HAGGAI

With the books of Haggai, Zechariah and Malachi we come to the post-exilic period and the end of Old Testament prophecy. In 521 BC Cyrus, Emperor of Persia, conqueror of Babylon, proclaimed the right of all Jews in exile, if they so wished, to return to Jerusalem and rebuild the Temple. This remarkable turn of events is described by the Chronicler in Ezra-Nehemiah. Many Jews took the long journey from Babylon to Judea, but when they arrived there, they found many obstacles (Ezra 4:1-5,24) and the work of reconstruction ceased. The people became preoccupied with rebuilding their own homes, and were inclined to leave the work of restoring the Temple to a more opportune moment.

Haggai preached a straightforward message: put God's Temple before your own concerns and see how God will not be outdone in generosity. He applies the test of experience: bad harvests have not been a coincidence. God has a lesson in them. Learn that lesson, and trust that God will take the restoration into his own charge.

HAGGAI 1

520 BC. Read Ezra 5-6 for the background.

1. What was the attitude of the returned exiles (verse 2)? What was their situation as pointed out by the prophet?
2. What reward did their obedience to the voice of God through the prophet receive?
3. How is the teaching of Haggai reinforced by Jesus in Matthew 6?

HAGGAI 2

We do not usually see catastrophe as a signal for hope, but Haggai teaches (verse 6) that cataclysms will precede the Messianic age of hope and peace (verse 7). Jesus takes up this theme in his apocalyptic discourse (Luke 21:25-28).

1. What disheartened the people? (verse 3). What promise did they receive? What is meant by verse 7?
2. Verses 10-19. How were the two ceremonial questions (verses 11-13) used by Haggai to point to a deeper question? What place have externals in our sanctification?
3. a) What promises did God give? b) Draw out in Haggai references to the redemption of the people from Egypt. c) What is the significance of these references?

AN INTRODUCTION
TO
THE PROPHECY OF ZECHARIAH

Zechariah 1-8 records a series of dreams that seems to have occurred on a single night in February 519 BC (1:7); Zechariah 9-14 begins with a new title and is entirely different.

ZECHARIAH 1-8

The prophetic ministry of Zechariah son of Iddo began two months after that of Haggai. His aim was the same - to encourage the rebuilding of the Temple. He was probably a priest (cf. Nehemiah 12:4,16), and seems to have been a man of great imagination, of profound thought and with a practical sense. He preached hope and encouragement, and interior conversion. His visions are strange, but if one remembers that they were probably dreams, one is more able to accept their strangeness. He was convinced that God was going to break into world history on Judah's behalf. He distinguishes powerfully between repentance and mere remorse, between pessimism and hope.

ZECHARIAH 9-14

This section is different in tone, form and theology. There are no dates. We hear no more of Joshua or Zerubbabel or the Temple. Assyria and Egypt reappear from earlier prophets as symbolic oppressors. These chapters clearly do not belong to the same period as Zechariah 1-8, and it is probable that they date from the late fourth century BC, after Alexander the Great, and were added to the scroll of Zechariah at some later period. The message is that God's people must be purified before they are ready to enjoy his kingdom. Their leader (s) will be a great shepherd, a"pierced one" who will assume the sufferings of the people. This clearly Messianic note is brought out in the frequent use of this book in the New Testament.

ZECHARIAH 1

The prophet's first dream: the horseman; and his second dream: the four horns.

1. What is the keynote of these verses (1-6)? See especially verses 3, 4 and 6 for Zechariah's doctrine of repentance. What lessons does the prophet draw from history?
2. What is the meaning of the dream (verses 7-17)? What verses show it as a message of comfort for Judah?

ZECHARIAH 2

The third dream: the man with a measuring line.

1. Compare verses 1-5 with Ezekiel 41:13. What is the message of comfort for Jerusalem in the dream?
2. The exiles still in Babylon are exhorted to return (verse 6). Why? Are we in need of a command to return from exile and to entrust our lives to God? What kinds of exile are there?
3. What is the message of comfort in verses 10-13? How does it anticipate New Testament doctrine?

ZECHARIAH 3

Zechariah hoped that the priesthood, represented by Joshua, would be restored to the rebuilt Temple, and that Zerubbabel, descendant of King Jehoiachin, would rule as king.

1. Compare this scene with Job 1:6 ff. Why was Joshua wearing 'filthy garments'? What new mission is given to the priesthood (verse 7)? How does this vision anticipate the New Testament?

2. Compare verses 8-10 with Jeremiah 23:5. If the Branch refers to Zerubbabel in one sense, to whom does it ultimately refer? Note that Matthew 1:13 lists Zerubbabel among Jesus' ancestors.

ZECHARIAH 4

The 'two anointed' are Joshua and Zerubbabel.

1. What evidence is there in this chapter that the prophet is discouraged at the slow progress of the rebuilding? See especially verse 10.
2. The dream reassures him by the word of the Lord. See verses 6-9 and cf. Hosea 1:7. Do I sometimes despise the 'day of small things' and feel I am doing nothing of any importance? What comfort should I take from these verses?

ZECHARIAH 5

An ephah was a barrel shaped measure. Shinar refers to Babylon.

1. What is the common meaning of the two strange dreams in this chapter? cf. verse 3 with verse 6. How is the evil in the land dealt with?
2. Can you imagine twentieth century versions of these two visions? What would be the modern 'land of Shinar'? cf. Genesis 11:2.

ZECHARIAH 6

The night ends with Messianic hope.

1. Day is dawning (verse 1). The night of dreams is nearly over. Compare the chariots with their horses with the horsemen of the first dream (1:8 ff.) Both symbolise God's lordship of the whole earth. What message of hope for the exiles is contained in verse 8?
2. Zerubbabel was never crowned king, but how were verses 1, 12-14 fulfilled in the Messiah?
3. The night of dreams ends on a practical, urgent message of hope (verse 8). On what were the promises dependent?

ZECHARIAH 7

The fast (verse 3) was in memory of the destruction of the Temple and of Jerusalem in 587. That of verse 5 was in memory of the murder of Gedaliah (Jeremiah 41). The answer to the question is given at 8:18-19.

1. With what did God find fault in these fasts? See verses 5 and 6.
2. Read carefully verses 9-10. In what does true religion consist? Is it limited to external acts? To what does Zechariah attribute the disasters that befell the people of Judah and Jerusalem? Does he differ in this from the earlier prophets?

ZECHARIAH 8

Hopeful oracles of heaven / the new Jerusalem.

1. Verse 1-8. What is striking about the inhabitants of the new Jerusalem? What kind of people are they? Are we among them?
2. What are the conditions that will bring about this 'sowing of peace' (verse 12) and blessedness? See verses 16-17. What will replace the fasts mentioned in chapter 7?
3. The book ends with another version of Isaiah's and Ezekiel's vision. What is it? (verse 23).

ZECHARIAH 9

This passage seems to have been inspired by the march of Alexander the Great after the Battle of Issus (333 BC).

1. Verses 1-8 are an allegory: the restoration of Judah will come through the destruction of some nations (Tyre and Sidon) and the incorporation of others (Philistines, Syrians). What obstacles stand in the way of the kingdom of God, and what elements of the present situation will be incorporated into it?
2. Verses 9-10. What are the features of the Messianic king realised in Jesus? How does New Testament use verse 9? What are the modern equivalents of verse 10 that will be 'cut off' in the new age?
3. Verses 11-17. What are the blessings promised? How do they foreshadow the promises of Romans 8:18-23?

ZECHARIAH 10

The corner stone, the tent peg and the battle bow refer to the leaders of the people who will eventually emerge to save the people. When things are at their worst, apparently, the prophet sees hope for the future.

1. Verses 1-2. The prophet exhorts us to 'ask rain' from the Lord and not trust to false teachers and diviners. How can we make this apply to our own lives? What is the 'season of the spring rain'?
2. Verses 3-12. List the blessings promised in 3b, 5, 6-7, 8, 10, 12. How does this passage apply to the Church?

ZECHARIAH 11

Verses 1-3 perhaps recall Judges 9:7-15 (Jotham's fable) and serve as a warning note, introducing the allegory of the two shepherds.

1. What is the attitude of the flock in this allegory? See verse 8. What is to be understood by the two staffs? Why are they broken?
2. Verses 12-13 are quoted in Matthew 26:15, 27:9. What Messianic elements do you discover in this chapter?
3. What warning is given to bad rulers?

ZECHARIAH 12

A new prophetic oracle is introduced (verse 1). This section seems to be inspired by Deutero-Isaiah and perhaps dates from the third century BC. Jerusalem will be restored.

1. Verses 1-9. Jerusalem is besieged by the nations, even by Judah (verse 2). Read this section as a prophecy of attacks on the Church from within and from without. What is the outcome? See especially verses 8 and 9.
2. Verses 10-14. A great national leader (Josiah ?) falls in battle and is mourned by the house of David. Look up John 19:37 and Revelation 1:7 to see how New Testament interprets verse 10. Pray for a 'spirit of compassion and supplication' to be poured down on our nation and on the Church today.

ZECHARIAH 13

The last two chapters of Zechariah were read during the liturgy of the feast of Tabernacles in the Temple. cf. John 7:37 ff.

1. What are the sins from which the land is to be cleansed (verse 1)? Can you think of any institutions in the Church (once good) that have degenerated as prophecy has in this period?
2. What ordeal is symbolised in verse 7? How is it applied in Matthew 26:31?

ZECHARIAH 14

The great battle of the end time.

1. Verses 1-5 describe the Day of the Lord. Who will be gathered against Jerusalem (the Church)? When and in what manner will the Lord appear? How are the events interpreted in New Testament?
2. Verses 6-11. Compare these verses with Revelation 22:1-5.
3. Verses 12-21. Compare this last section with Deuteronomy 28:20-22. What is said of the final triumph of Zion, the Church of God? Do we take these promises seriously?

AN INTRODUCTION
TO
THE PROPHECY OF MALACHI

'An oracle of the word of the Lord to Israel by my messenger' (1:). This is the translation of the Hebrew for 1:1. Malachi is not the name of the prophet, who remains anonymous. The Targum reads: 'my messenger, whose name is Ezra'. The oracle certainly dates from the middle of the fifth century BC, around 460. It takes a catechetical form, dealing with six aspects of the Law, queried by a popular objection, and the answer given in a careful message.

The questions dealt with are as follows:

1	**:2 – 5**	**— God's love**
1	**:6 – 2:9**	**— irregularities in worship**
2	**:10 – 16**	**— divorce**
2	**:17 – 3:5**	**— scepticism (1)**
3	**:6 – 12**	**— Temple contributions**
3	**:13 – 4:3**	**— scepticism (2)**

The book ends with a postscript (4:4-6). The Day of Yahweh will purify the priesthood, consume the wicked and secure the triumph of the upright.

The style is plain, but vivid, echoing an actual 'catechism class'. The book gives valuable teaching on tithing, too often neglected, and on divorce. New Testament believes the messenger or angel of 3:1 to be John the Baptist, Elijah come again. Thus Old Testament prophecy, and Old Testament scriptures themselves, come to an end.

MALACHI 1

1. Verses 1-5. What is the attitude of Israel? How does God respond? How are we to react to the statement that God 'hated' Esau? cf. Genesis 25:23.
2. Verses 6-14. What further do we learn about the people's attitude and morale? See verses 7,8,12,13. Are we ever guilty of boredom and slackness in God's service? What does this scripture have to say to us?

MALACHI 2:1-16

1. Of what faults are the priests guilty (verses 2,8)? What will be their punishment?
2. What is said in verses 10-16 of divorce? On what grounds is it condemned? Does New Testament add anything to this teaching?

MALACHI 2:17 - 4:6

1. What examples of a sceptical, scornful attitude on the part of the people do you find in this section? Of what do they accuse God? Do we ever feel like this? How does God respond? (3:1-6).
2. What particular fault does this general attitude of the people lead them to commit (3:9)? Learn verse 10 by heart and put it into practice.
3. How will the people be cleansed? What use has New Testament made of these verses?

DEUTERO - CANONICAL BOOKS

AN INTRODUCTION TO THE BOOK OF TOBIT

We now come to a complication that can be a source of dismay in ecumenical Bible study groups. Every edition of the Bible dos not contain the same books, or in the same order. Catholic Bibles like the Jerusalem Bible, the Knox Bible, or the Douay put Tobit and Judith after Nehemiah; the ecumenical versions of the Revised Standard Version and of the Revised English Bible put them into a separate group called the Apocrypha, between the two Testaments; other Bibles omit them altogether. So, if you compare Catholic Bibles with, say, the New International Version or the Good News Bible, you will find that there are seven more books in the Catholic Bible: Tobit, Judith, Wisdom, Ecclesiasticus (or Sirach), Baruch, 1 and 2 Maccabees. Why is this? These seven books (called Deutero-Canonical in the RC Church) were all written in Greek, are included in the Septuagint (Greek) translation of the Bible, but are not in the Hebrew Bible. They were accepted as canonical by the Jews of the Diaspora and by the early Christians. When in the sixteenth century new translations of the Hebrew Bible were made by the Reformers, these seven books were omitted, and fell into disuse among Protestants.

Tobit is an edifying story, of no historical value, composed about the year 200 BC. It shows no interest in history or geography, but takes themes from the patriarchs and from Jewish piety, especially family life, almsgiving, devotion to the dead, prayer. It shows a developed theology of angels; and the story of Tobias' journey with Raphael has been immortalised in art and in literature. Some of the fathers ascribed to the archangel Raphael (the healer) the moving of the waters in John 5:4. The doctrine of marriage in chapter 8 is a noble one.

TOBIT 1

Tobit in exile in Nineveh.

1. Notice that Tobit's piety consists in strictly observing the prescriptions of the Law. What practices are especially emphasised? How do they compare with the traditional Christian practices of prayer, fasting and almsdeeds?
2. What picture of the life of the exiles is conveyed in this chapter? See verse 17. What impression does this give? From which tribe did Tobit come?

TOBIT 2

Tobit's misfortunes.

1. Compare this chapter with Job 1 and 2. Why does God reward good deeds with trials? Do you sympathise with Anna or with Tobit over the affair of the kid?
2. Can you find examples of faith as well as of good works in Tobit 1 and 2?

TOBIT 3

Tobit's and Sarah's prayers.

1. Analyse Tobit's prayer. In what spirit does he beg God's help? What is striking about Sarah's prayer?
2. Tobit was blinded by a cruel chance, Sarah's life ruined by misfortune and by the cruelty of unfeeling mockery. What is God's answer in this chapter? Compare verse 16 with Genesis 19:29.
3. Consider the psychological reality of the story. What does the demon represent?

TOBIT 4

Tobit's advice to his son Tobias.

1. List the various elements in the advice Tobit gives to his son. What are the special virtues of almsgiving?
2. 'Seek advice from every wise man'! (verse 18). Study verses 18-19. What do we learn from them about how to look for God in all whom we meet and in all that we do? How is this doctrine completed in New Testament?

TOBIT 5

The angel Raphael undertakes to guide Tobias on his journey.

1. What does this chapter teach about angels? Note that AZARIAS means *GOD HELPS* as RAPHAEL means *GOD HEALS*. The angel would have many names.
2. Work out the symbolism in this chapter. What do each of the characters - Tobias, Tobit, Raphael, Anna - stand for?

TOBIT 6

Tobias and the fish.

1. 'The story gives us a clue about how a woman can destroy the deadly effects of the animus: her soul must be filled with a more powerful spirit than that of the destructive animus, and her capacity for Eros and relationships must live'. John A. Sanford. (The Invisible Partners. Chapter Two. Paulist Press).
   In the light of this comment, work out the psychological elements in the story of Sarah.
2. List the details that show Tobias as a model son. Can we learn anything from the teaching of this chapter on marriage and family life? See verses 11, 12, 15, 17.

TOBIT 7

Tobias comes to his kinsman Raguel's house in Ecbatana.

1. Compare this scene with Genesis 29. What are the common aspects? Is the purpose of each story the same or are there important differences?
2. Draw out the unconscious materials in the myth. See, for example, verses 8, 11, 17. How has the writer superimposed a conscious, religious aspect?

TOBIT 8

Tobias' and Sarah's wedding night.

1. What lesson do we learn from the account of the wedding night?
2. Draw out the different points made by Raguel in his prayer.
3. How was Sarah healed? List the mythological, psychological and theological reasons given in the narrative.

TOBIT 9-10

The wedding celebrations.

1. What examples do we find of Tobias' thoughtfulness?
2. What advice do Raguel and Edna give to the young couple? How far could such advice be acceptable today?
3. Draw out the indications of a carefully ordered time scheme in these chapters. What does it suppose?

TOBIT 11

Tobias' return home, and the healing of Tobit.

1. Notice the reference to the dog (verse 4) and cf. 5:16. Challoner comments on this verse: 'This may seem a very minute circumstance to be recorded in sacred history: but as we learn from our Saviour, St Matthew 5:18, there are iotas and tittles in the word of God; that is to say, things that appear minute, but which have indeed a deep and mysterious meaning in them'.
   Douay Bible.
   Is there a deep mystery, or is the writer just reinforcing the domestic character of the story?
2. This chapter is full of blessings. Enumerate them - and in our own lives too.

TOBIT 12

Raphael reveals himself.

1. Explain Raphael's teaching in verses 7-9.
2. What is the theology of angels as explained by Raphael (verses 10-22)? Raphael presents Tobit's prayers and good works to God as it were on a tablet (verse 12). Compare with the teaching in Acts 10:4. Is this theology, or merely a reflection of contemporary thinking?

TOBIT 13

Tobit's canticle of praise.

1. What reasons does Tobit give for the sufferings of the exiles (verses 1-8)?
2. What are the blessings promised to Jerusalem?

TOBIT 14

A recapitulation of the story of the exile and subsequent events (verse 4). Some authorities read 'Nahum' (who foretold the destruction of Nineveh); others read 'Jonah' a prophet associated with Nineveh.

1. Draw out the similarities between Tobit and the patriarchs.
2. Would you say that the story of Tobit and his family is the story of faith, or of reward for good deeds?
3. Go through the book, drawing out the references to the pagan sage Ahikar. What is his significance in the Book of Tobit?

AN INTRODUCTION TO THE BOOK OF JUDITH

See note on Tobit.

This book has been neglected in the modern Church - it is almost entirely ignored in the revised liturgy - but it was once popular, as the frequent occurrence of the name 'Judith' reminds us, and has inspired artists at different times. The book shows no interest in history or geography, and is clearly an allegory - *JUDITH* means *JEWESS*. The woman represents the chosen people, facing a mighty enemy in the person of Holofernes, who represents a typical figure of tyranny and world aggrandisement. Another David and Goliath story, it has a female protagonist, like Esther. It was written in Palestine about 150 BC.

JUDITH 1

Nebuchadnezzar was king, not of Assyria, but of Babylon, and Nineveh was destroyed by his father. Arphaxad is unknown to history.

1. Pick out the details which build up the impression of a whole world against Judah.
2. What touches make the whole story seem 'larger than life'? Does this give a clue as to the real intention of the author? What is it?

JUDITH 2

The power and advance of Holofernes.

1. Compare the scene in verses 1-3 with the modern image of the Super power. Can you think of any twentieth century Nebuchadnezzars who have threatened small states who have had the temerity to stand up to them?
2. What touches hint that this is a deliberate parody of the Last Judgement?

JUDITH 3

The claims of Holofernes.

1. What is the response of the conquered peoples? How does the author convey his contempt for them?
2. What indicates that 'Nebuchadnezzar' is a type of anti-God? Has this century seen any examples of such ludicrous claims by a tyrant? List them.

JUDITH 4

It is clear from verse 4 that the author has no interest in history since he places the return from exile during the reign of Nebuchadnezzar, like putting the battles of World War II into the context of the Boer War!

1. What inspires fear in the Israelites? How are they presented as the people of God, ready to take on the forces of evil?
2. List the preparations that they make. What example do they give us in undertaking spiritual warfare?

JUDITH 5

As Ahikar was a pagan sage for Tobit, so Achior is a figure of pagan wisdom in JUDITH.

1. What interpretation does Achior put on the history of Israel?
2. Notice his conclusion (verses 20-21), and compare Acts 5:33-39.

. Brute force is urged against religious faith. Does this doctrine govern human affairs still? Can you imagine a scenario today where Christians might have to take some very difficult decisions in the event of war?

JUDITH 6

Achior is handed over to the Israelites, who treat him kindly.

1. Draw out the details which highlight Holofernes' arrogance and contempt. See verses 2, 5 etc.
2. Contrast the attitude of the Israelites. What is the significance of their treatment of Achior?

JUDITH 7

Bethulia is unknown. It must simply be the "place" where God does battle with his enemies.

1. Mark the stages by which Israelite morale began to fall.
2. The Israelites are starved of water, which is a symbol of grace. What happens to us if we allow our souls to be deprived of the means of grace (prayer, the sacraments, Christian fellowship)?
3. What echoes of the story of Moses and the Israelites in the desert do you find in this chapter?

JUDITH 8

Judith appears in the narrative and through her words the central doctrine of the narrator is underlined (verses 11-23).

1. Draw out Judith's teaching on prayer and trust in God (verses 11-17). In what way is her faith more filial than that of Uzziah and the elders of Bethulia?
2. In what way did Judith's background prepare her for her role? How is her widowhood significant?
3. Judith teaches a very important truth in verses 25-27. What is it? How should we apply it in time of trial?

JUDITH 9

Judith's prayer reveals an unusual interpretation of some scripture passages. The author has an individual voice.

1. What interpretation does Judith make of scripture? cf. verses 2-4 with Genesis 34.
2. Outline the pleas she makes to God. What new titles are ascribed to the Lord?

JUDITH 10

Judith's preparations for combat.

1. What is the spiritual significance of the preparations made by Judith?
2. David used a staff and a sling against Goliath (1 Samuel 17). What are Judith's weapons? Compare Holofernes with Goliath.

JUDITH 11

Judith meets Holofernes and speaks in language full of ambiguities.

1. Pick out the deliberate ambiguities in Judith's words, and notice the way she uses Achior's words to mislead Holofernes. Is this justifiable?
2. Go through the chapter carefully and note down Holofernes' reply and the author's deliberate irony. Why do you think Holofernes was so easily fooled?

JUDITH 12

The defeat of Holofernes.

1. In what ways does the author emphasise Judith's real and ritual purity? What is a) the ostensible and b) the real purpose of her nightly watches by the spring?
2. Trace the stages of Holofernes' downfall.

JUDITH 13

The story moves rapidly from the beheading of Holofernes to the return of Judith to Bethulia.

1. In this story, the writer is clearly influenced by the stories of Jael (Judges 4:21) and of David (1 Samuel 17:49-51). What lesson does he draw from them, and from Judith's own victory?
2. Take this story as an allegory of a battle with evil, and work out the details.

JUDITH 14

The head of Holofernes is hung on the wall of Bethulia.

1. Achior's conversion and circumcision mark a fitting climax. He is an Ammonite (5:5). Look up Deuteronomy 23:4-5. What does this indicate about the developed theology of the writer?
2. In what ways do these events remind us of the Exodus event (cf. 13:11)? Notice the references to daybreak (verses 2, 11). What is the symbolism?

JUDITH 15

The rout of the Assyrians.

1. Compare this apocalyptic victory scene with Zechariah 14 and with Exodus 12:35-36 for the despoiling of the enemy. What lesson is the author conveying by these deliberate echoes of scripture?
2. Judith, like Miriam (Exodus 15:20), leads the women in dancing and rejoicing. Compare this scene also with Zephaniah 3:14-18. Why is a woman an especially apt symbol for Israel?

JUDITH 16

The song of Judith. This hymn contains echoes of the psalms.

1. What are the saving acts of God celebrated in this song? What characteristics are ascribed to him?
2. Compare Judith's old age with that of the patriarchs. In what significant way does it differ? What light does this throw on the author's values?

AN INTRODUCTION
TO
THE BOOK OF WISDOM

In what book of the Bible is the serpent who tempted Eve called the devil?
In which book of the Old Testament does the word 'immortal' occur? — The Book of Wisdom.

We take it so much for granted that the serpent in Genesis 3 was the devil, that we do not always realise that this is never said until the author of Wisdom (about 50 BC) mentioned it. Nor do we always remember that immortality was a concept unknown to the Hebrew mind until it came into contact with Greek philosophy during the Hellenistic period. So this deutero-canonical work, the latest in the Old Testament, is an important one. It witnesses to the theology of Jesus' life time. It was composed in Alexandria, chief city of Egypt under the Ptolemies, by a Jew whose scripture was the Septuagint. He interprets the scriptures to a Hellenistic world. It is a long-winded book (the Romans too thought the Greeks were too voluble!) but it has an important purpose, drawing together traditional prophetic intuitions, Wisdom themes and Greek philosophy.

The book is divided into three main sections: a dissertation on Wisdom and the destiny of humanity (chapters 1-5); the meaning of Wisdom (chapters 6-9); Wisdom guiding the history of salvation (chapters 10-19) with a long parenthesis on idolatry.

WISDOM 1

All Hellenistic writings were expected to contain a prologue, often a very elaborate one. This work is no exception. The author is a great 'word spinner'.

1. The author draws on the prophetic and wisdom traditions, as well as on Greek philosophy, in his introduction (verses 1-5). Can you discover words or phrases that suggest each source?
2. In what, according to the author, does Wisdom consist? Does he advance on the 'fear of the Lord' theory of Proverbs?
3. Find a) a doctrine of the Holy Spirit and b) of immortality in this chapter? In what ways have New Testament writers drawn on this book?

WISDOM 2

Arguments used against the righteous by 'ungodly men'.

1. Compare verses 1-5 with Ecclesiastes 2:16, 6:12, 8:8 and 9:5. Does the author agree with Ecclesiastes' conclusions? See verses 6-11.
2. In what ways does the 'righteous man' offend the ungodly? How is he a type of Christ?

WISDOM 3

The immortality of the righteous. Verses 1-9 are used in the Lectionary in Services for the Dead.

1. How far does the author show an advance on Old Testament? Compare verses 1-3 with Isaiah 57:1-2, and verse 5 with Deuteronomy 8:2-5. What are the 'wages of holiness'?
2. What despised categories of people will be rewarded? Compare Isaiah 54:1 and 56:3-5.

WISDOM 4

Why do the good die young? The author gives one answer. This passage (verses 7-15) is also used at funerals of young people.

1. What aspects of immortality are found in this chapter? See verses 1, 7, 11-14.
2. How can Enoch (verse 10 - cf. Genesis 5:21-24) be a figure of those who die young? What explanation does the author give for premature death?

WISDOM 5

The wicked will be judged and punished.

1. The author pictures the state of mind of the wicked on the day of judgement. Compare their confession (verses 4-13) with their earlier words (2:1-20).
2. Contrast the fate of the wicked (verses 17-23) with that of the righteous (verse 15-16).
3. Select readings for a) the funeral of a young person, b) the funeral of someone who has died in tragic circumstances, from these chapters.

WISDOM 6

The author now turns to the responsibilities of rulers and kings.

1. What is the highest task of a ruler, and how is it achieved? See verses 11, 12, 14-20.
2. What are the 'secrets' of wisdom that are revealed in this section? Compare with Job 28:20 ff. and Sirach 24:1 ff.

WISDOM 7

In the person of Solomon, the author now describes Wisdom.

1. What account does Solomon give of himself and of his upbringing? Compare verses 17-22 with 1 Kings 4:29-34. What kind of knowledge would a modern Solomon boast?
2. In the eulogy of Wisdom (verses 17 - 8:1) consider especially verses 25-26 and compare them with John 1:9 and Col. 1:15).

WISDOM 8

Solomon's eulogy of Wisdom. The author uses the story in 1 Kings 3:5 - 9 to develop his theme.

1. Why did Solomon long for wisdom (verses 2-8)? What essential quality does a ruler need?
2. Draw out the 'cardinal' virtues from this chapter. What kinds of knowledge (verses 8-9) does Wisdom impart? Why did Solomon turn to prayer? (verse 21). Do we remember this ourselves? cf. James 1:5.

WISDOM 9

This story is told in 1 Kings 3:6-9 and 2 Chronicles 1:8-10.

1. What two reasons are given for Solomon's request for wisdom? cf. verses 5,10. What place should such prayer have in the liturgy? Draw up suggestions for prayers for rulers, for elections, etc.
2. Compare Solomon's prayer in this chapter with its prototype in 1 Kings 3:6-9 and 2 Chronicles 1:8-10. What difference of emphasis do you find in this later writer?

WISDOM 10-19

The rest of the work, with a long parenthesis against idolatry, (13-14), shows Wisdom at work in history. 9:18 introduced this topic.

WISDOM 10

The history of God's action (Wisdom) from the beginning in Adam until the Exodus.

1. Identify the characters from Genesis in verses 1-2, 3, 4, 5, 6-7, 10-12, 13-14, 16.
2. Verses 1-8. In what ways does the author emphasise the almost universal wickedness of the pre-Abraham world? What reason does he give for the destruction of Sodom and Gomorrah? Compare with Genesis 19.

3. Verses 10-12. In what way is the story of Jacob interpreted? See especially the account of his experience at Bethel (verse 10). Compare this with Genesis 28:17, and for the whole treatment of Jacob compare Hosea 12 for a less favourable tradition.
4. Verses 13-21. What is the keynote of the author's account of the Exodus? In what ways has Christian tradition followed the Book of Wisdom in its understanding of events?

WISDOM 11

The author now works out an ingenious comparison between the plagues (which punished the Egyptians - he is writing in Egypt!) and the desert miracles (which rewarded the virtuous Israelites). This is a good example of midrash - an explanation of scripture that seeks to make it understandable to a later generation. The author uses Psalm 107 as a basis rather than the Pentateuch.

1. In verse 5 the author states the theme of his homily. What is it? Take note of its application to the rest of the section.
2. Verses 6-14. Identify the plague and the miracle in these verses. What, according to the author, was the reason for the poisoning of the Nile?
3. Verses 15-26. In what ways are these verses a commentary on Genesis 1? What idea is added and emphasised by the author?

WISDOM 12

Why God allowed the Canaanites to survive.

1. Why was God forbearing with the Canaanites (verse 10)? What reason is given to explain this goodness of God (verses 18-22)? cf. Exodus 23:29; Deuteronomy 7:22; and Judges 2:22 for other opinions concerning the survival of the Canaanites.
2. The author condemns the Egyptians for making idols of animals. What forms of idolatry are prevalent today? Consider verses 23-27 in this light.

WISDOM 13

A digression on the evils of idolatry.

1. Verses 1-9. How does nature speak to us of God? What aspects of his divinity does it reveal? How would you use this argument today?
2. Verses 10-19. Compare this satire with Isaiah 44:9-20.

WISDOM 14

The digression on idolatry is continued.

1. Verses 1-7. Show how the writer uses Noah as the centrepiece of his argument.
2. Verses 8-21. What are the origins of idolatry, according to the author? What is their modern counterpart?
3. Verses 22-31. To what evils does idolatry eventually lead? Compare the catalogue in verses 23-26 with Romans 1:18 ff. Are we free of such ills nowadays? Draw out besetting sins of this age from verses 22-26.

WISDOM 15

The digression is concluded.

1. Verses 1-13. Compare the potter with the woodcutter of 13:11. Why is the former more to be reprobated? To what kind of workman or craftsman today would he be compared?

2. Verses 14-19. The writer returns to the Egyptians. Of what does he accuse them? Which animal is meant in verse 19? cf. Genesis 3:14.

WISDOM 16

The theme is taken up again, of the contrast between the plagues of Egypt and the testing of the Israelites.

1. Work out the contrast between the Egyptian plagues of small animals (frogs, flies, locusts), the Israelite plague of serpents (Numbers 21:6-9) and the miracle of the quails (Numbers 11:10-32). What further light do verses 6-7 throw on Numbers 21:8-9? See further John 3:13-17. How was the full significance of this incident gradually revealed?
2. Verses 15-23. Notice how the liturgy and popular Communion hymns have made use of verses 20-21. Trace further development in John 6:25-34. Draw out the full meaning of 'food of angels' and 'bread of heaven'.
3. Verses 24-29. What instruction is contained in these verses concerning God's word?

WISDOM 17

A brilliant chapter on the plague of darkness.

1. The whole chapter emphasises the darkness in which the Egyptians were plunged. How is this plague symbolic of their exile (verse 2)? Can this word (exile) be applied to many people today who do not know God? What is the chief characteristic of the darkness?
2. What is the meaning of verses 20-21? In what way is it a commentary on the effects of sin?

WISDOM 18

The massacre of the first born is described with great drama.

For verse 24 cf. Exodus 28:15 ff.

1. What does the light symbolise? See verses 1 and 4. What use does John make of this image in his gospel? cf. John 8:12.
2. What interpretation does the author put a) on the death of the first born, and b) on the plague in the desert (Numbers 16:44-50)?
3. What use does the liturgy make of verses 14-15? (cf. 2nd Sunday after Christmas in the Roman Missal). What is the primary meaning of verses 14-16?

WISDOM 19

The book concludes with the crossing of the Red Sea and a final condemnation of the Egyptians.

1. Verses 1-5. How does the writer deal with the mystery of free will and pre-destination in these verses?
2. Verses 6-12. Work out the comparisons between the Creation and Exodus events.
3. Verses 13-17. How does the author show that the Egyptians were even worse than the Sodomites (Genesis 19) and were punished accordingly?
4. Verses 18-22. How does the author harmonise the miracles with Greek science and philosophy?

AN INTRODUCTION
TO
ECCLESIASTICUS or SIRACH

This book is a hotch-potch of proverbs, history and good advice. Ben Sira, the author, is religious, theological, eloquent and repetitive. He has collected many proverbs, and turned them into a spiritual anthology. He revived the ancient meaning of Wisdom as 'skill': the doctor has it (38:2); the craftsmen and designers have it in some measure (38:31), but the higher wisdom needs leisure - for the study of the Law (39:1-11). Sirach's piety is centred on the Law - the covenant, worship and the priesthood. His famous men are listed according to these criteria, so Aaron receives more attention than Moses, and the high priest Simon, otherwise unknown to us, is for Sirach the climax of history!

God's wisdom is revealed in the wonders of his creation - chapters 42-43 contain one of the most lyrical passages in the Bible.

The book was written originally in Hebrew, of which only part remains, and translated into Greek. It was written about 190-180 BC. It is an attempt to restore traditional wisdom identified by the writer with the Law (Torah) in the face of spreading Hellenisation.

There are a number of echoes of Sirach in New Testament, especially in Matthew, Luke and James. Compare Sirach 4:1-10 with James 2:1-4, 15-16; Sirach 11:14-19 with Luke 12:16-21 and Sirach 11:23 with Matthew 6:25-26. It is also a favourite of some of the Victorians, for example George Eliot mentions it in *ADAM BEDE*.. 'On some mornings when he read in the Apocrypha, of which he was very fond, the son of Sirach's keen edged words would bring a delighted smile, though he also enjoyed the freedom of occasionally differing from an Apocryphal writer'. Chapter 51.

SIRACH 1

This chapter, an introduction to the whole book, is a collection of proverbs on the theme of Wisdom.

1. What, for Sirach, is the origin of Wisdom? How does he describe it?
2. Count the number of references to the fear of the Lord (verses 11-20). Is there any advance on Proverbs here? See Proverbs 1:20.

SIRACH 2

Sirach's version of a theme familiar in the Psalter - the testing time for one who serves God.

1. Verses 1-6. What response does Sirach give to those who ask why trials come? In what way does he differ from the accepted wisdom of Old Testament? Does he in any way anticipate New Testament?
2. Verses 7-11. What threefold reassurance is offered to those who fear the Lord? What help are they to receive from scripture?
3. Verses 12-18. Contrast the fainthearted with those who fear the Lord.

SIRACH 3

Advice on family matters and on the value of meekness.

1. Verses 1-16. In these days, with many people living to a great age, how can we best put into practice Sirach's counsel on duty to parents? See especially verse 13.
2. Verses 17-31. Against what dangers does Sirach warn in this passage? Are we in any similar danger? What is the remedy?

SIRACH 4

Justice and charity; respect for others.

1. Verses 1-10. Comment on verse 3 'Do not add to the troubles of an angry mind' in the light of contemporary grievances.
2. Verses 11-30. What distinction does Sirach make between true Wisdom and humility and a modest bearing? What other advice does he give to his Jewish contemporary in a Hellenistic setting, that is equally suitable for Christians in a secularised culture?

SIRACH 5

Nine 'Do nots'.

1. Verses 1-8. What warnings are given to the rich? Do they lie behind Jesus' attitude to wealth? cf. Matthew 19:24. What is the greatest danger that lies in wait for a rich man?
2. Verses 9-15. Compare Sirach's teaching on straightforward speech with Proverbs 10.

SIRACH 6

Sirach has more to say on friendship than any other Biblical writer.

1. Verses 1-17. What are the characteristics of a true friend? Draw out of the text the different examples of a 'fair-weather' friend. Is there anyone to whom I am such?
2. Verses 18-37. What advice is given to a young person seeking wisdom? In what does it ultimately consist? See verses 32-37.

SIRACH 7

Various maxims - the duties of a man who sincerely wishes to serve God.

1. Verses 1-17. Consider the advice in these verses about making one's way in the world. How can it be applied to the Christian life? What warnings to church goers are contained in verses 9-10?
2. Verses 18-36. What does Sirach say about the traditional duties of a righteous man? Go through the section point by point, applying each piece of advice to your own life. What does New Testament add?

SIRACH 8

Prudence.

1. Draw out the practical advice in this chapter, commenting especially on verses 15-16.
2. What does Sirach have to say about tradition?

SIRACH 9

Sirach is very severe on women, even more so than Proverbs or Ecclesiastes.

1. Verses 1-9. Find examples in the Bible of the faults against which Sirach cautions in this section. cf. Proverbs 5 and 7:6 ff.
2. Verses 10-18. Caution is Sirach's watchword. List examples and comment on them.

SIRACH 10

The evils of pride and the merits of humility.

1. Verses 1-18. Find examples in the Bible, in history or in contemporary life of the fate of the proud as described by Sirach. What motives does he propose for humility?

2. Verses 19-31. According to Proverbs, the fear of the Lord is the beginning of wisdom. How does Sirach build on this insight?

SIRACH 11

Sirach returns frequently to the idea of trust in God. However, he also once more emphasises prudence - a human, but also a 'cardinal' virtue.

1. Verses 1-28. In what way does Sirach's teaching anticipate New Testament? cf. verses 14-19 with Luke 12:16-21 and verse 23 with Matthew 6:25-26.
2. What notion of eternal reward lies behind verses 26-28? (Compare RSV with NJB).
3. Verses 29-34. How can Sirach's advice be reconciled with the laws of hospitality? What place do prudence and commonsense have in the Christian life? Is there any gospel counsel on the same lines as verses 29 and 34?

SIRACH 12

Sirach's advice, while sound from a human point of view, seems harsh. He returns to the subject of friendship.

1. Comment on Sirach's attitude to the sinner (verses 4-7). Is this the last word on the subject? Is there *ANY* sense in which it can be taken as a rule for Christians? See verse 6 for Sirach's reasoning.
2. Verses 8-18. What are the characteristics of false friends? Are we ever in this category? If so, what can we do about it?

SIRACH 13

Practical advice on social mixing and its pitfalls.

1. What advice does Sirach give to those who associate with the rich? Is it applicable today when dealing with 'big business'? Does Jesus give any such advice in his parables? Compare Luke 14:8-10. What difference is there?
2. How is verse 24 a commentary on what goes before? What attitude should a Christian have? Do I ever fall into the behaviour described in verses 21-23?

SIRACH 14

This chapter shows the influence of earlier Wisdom writers.

1. Compare Sirach's Beatitudes (verses 1-2) with a) those of the other Wisdom books (Psalm 1:1; 32:1-2; 41:1; 119:1; 128:1) and b) New Testament (Matthew 5:1-12 and Luke 6:20-22). Make a list of all these Beatitudes, and prayerfully ponder which ones I need most at the present time.
2. Compare verses 11-19 with Ecclesiastes 2:24 ff.; 3:19; 9:5-10. In what way does Sirach improve on the earlier thinker?
3. Trace the ways in which the sage pursues wisdom (verses 20-27). What is his reward? How does New Testament develop this theme?

SIRACH 15

The scribe was a privileged person because of his study of the Law. Sirach's doctrine of free will.

1. Consider Sirach's eulogy of the scribe (verses 1-10). What equivalent person would be honoured in the Church today? Sirach equates Wisdom with the Law. How does New Testament go beyond this?
2. In what way is Sirach's teaching on free will (verses 1-20) a theological advance on much of Old Testament? cf. especially Exodus 10:1; Samuel 24:1 etc.

SIRACH 16

For scripture references in this chapter, see Numbers 16 for verses 6; Genesis 6:1-7 for verse 7; Genesis 19 for verse 8; Exodus 12:37 for verse 10. Verse 22 refers not to the Mosaic covenant but to the 'covenant with death', i.e. the date fixed for one's death.

1. Show how Sirach develops his argument concerning the justice of God, and individual responsibility for sin from scripture (verses 1-23). Can you add examples from your own experience?
2. How is nature an image of God's wisdom? Compare and contrast verses 26-30 with Genesis 1:16, 11-12, 24 ff. What note does Sirach add to the creation story?

SIRACH 17

Sirach's account of Creation.

1. Verses 1-14. What elements in the Genesis story of the creation of man does Sirach emphasise? What does he add? See especially verses 6-7. How does he interpret and summarise the Sinai experience?
2. Verses 15-32. What hope is offered by Sirach to repentant sinners?

SIRACH 18

The greatness of God is contrasted with human insignificance.

1. Verses 1-14. How does Sirach emphasise man's insignificance? What conclusion does he draw from this with regard to God's mercy?
2. Verses 15-33. Draw out the advice that Sirach gives in this section. What is meant by 'days of sin'? Which piece of advice do I most need at this time?

SIRACH 19

Like all the Wisdom writers, Sirach emphasises the importance of thoughtful speech.

1. Verses 1-17. What, according to the writer, is the right balance to be struck in conversation? On what principle should we speak?
2. Verses 20-30. Do you agree with Sirach's comments about true wisdom and spurious cleverness? Can you find any examples? Which do we value most today?

SIRACH 20

The subject is continued with examples from life.

1. Characterise the different people mentioned: a) the garrulous person; b) the man of few words; c) the tactless person. Which one(s) am I?
2. Compare Proverbs 10:19 and 17:27-28 with verses 5-7. Are they all making the same point? Or does Sirach improve on the earlier sages?

SIRACH 21

Proverbs concerned with many different aspects of life. The characters of the fool, the gossip and the sage reflect the Book of Proverbs.

1. Verses 1-10. What advice does Sirach give to sinners? Do you find any trace of a doctrine of retribution after death?
2. What further characteristics of the fool are noted in verses 11-28? What do you think of Sirach's comments on education? See verses 19-20.

3. Verse 27. Compare NJB translation: *SATAN* with RSV: *THE ADVERSARY*. What do you think this verse adds to our understanding of the nature of evil? Is there a 'personal devil'?

SIRACH 22

More maxims from the Wisdom school: the wise man, the fool, the sluggard. Advice on friendship.

1. Compare Sirach's comments on the sluggard (verses 1-2) with the character who frequently appears in Proverbs (eg Proverbs 15:19; 19:15, 24; 20:4 etc).
2. What do you think of Sirach's strictures on the upbringing of children?
3. Do you agree with Sirach's views on relationships with friends (verses 21-22)? Do you find it difficult or easy to forgive injuries?

SIRACH 23

Various faults are described: careless speech, bad language, lust. This last leads on to the favourite 'sinner' of the Book of Proverbs — the adulteress.

1. What are the graces that Sirach asks for in his prayer? With what two unruly instincts is he dealing?
2. Verses 7-15. What kinds of sinful speech are mentioned? List them. Do we nowadays take bad language too lightly? Why is Sirach so severe on it?
3. Verses 16-27. What three kinds of sex sins are catalogued? How relevant is this section for us today? Note the shrewdness of the comment in verse 16c. Have any such examples come to light recently? On what aspects of adultery does the author insist? Are there other aspects?

SIRACH 24

Sirach's great poem on Wisdom.

1. Trace the various aspects of Wisdom portrayed in this chapter, from creation (verse 3), through the Exodus (verse 4) to the promised land (verse 8). Apply these verses a) to the Holy Spirit, and b) to the incarnation of Christ.
2. Sirach identifies Wisdom with the Law (verse 23). What is a) the truth, and b) the limitation of this identification?

SIRACH 25

Various proverbs, including some fierce misogynism.

1. What advice for the elderly do we find in this chapter? Do we pay sufficient attention to the wisdom of age in our culture? Why does the Wisdom school take it for granted? In what areas would YOU consult an old person?
2. What shrewd comments do you find in verses 1-2 (cf. 26:28)? Give examples from your own observation.
3. Draw out the images of an unhappy household in these verses (13-26). Why is only the wife blamed? Re-write some of the proverbs with an 'evil husband' as the centre-piece. What does Paul have to say about verse 24? (cf. Romans 5:12 and 2 Corinthians 11:3).

SIRACH 26

The subject continued:

1. List the qualities of a good wife, according to the author. If you are a woman, do you find them patronising or inspiring or deflating? If a man, do you agree with Sirach?
2. What faults in a wife are particularly to be detested, according to Sirach? If you could add to the chapter, what would you say of a "good husband"?

SIRACH 27

The use of speech and language.

1. What advice does the writer give concerning business transactions? Consider verses 1-3, 22-29 in the light of modern business 'ethics'.
2. What faults are listed and warned against in this chapter? Examine your own conduct against verses 8, 16-21, 23.

SIRACH 28

The same subject continued.

1. Read verses 1-6 as a commentary on 'forgive us our trespasses as we forgive those who trespass against us' (Matthew 5:12). What motive does Sirach suggest for forgiving one's enemies?
2. List the examples of trouble which an evil tongue can bring on. Compare James 3:5-6.

SIRACH 29

Some sensible remarks about money matters; and advice to guests.

1. What value does Sirach attach to lending money to a neighbour? What are its perils? cf. Matthew 6:19-21 for an obvious echo of this chapter.
2. Are we content with the essentials for life listed in verse 21? Or do we want more? How much more? Do we fall into the trap described so vividly in verses 24-28 of cadging from others? Are we aware of the rights of the poor? (verse 21)? What should Christians do about social evils?

SIRACH 30

Sirach is as severe on children as he is on women.

1. Do you agree with Sirach's views on the upbringing of children? What reasons would you give for or against punishment? Can you think of any examples of 'spoilt children' who have disappointed their parents as described in verses 8-9?
2. What advice does Sirach give on how to keep healthy?

SIRACH 31

Social etiquette is dealt with at some length.

1. In what way is Sirach's teaching on wealth echoed by Christ? Does he allow for a rich man to be just? See verse 8.
2. Draw out a) the moral virtues and b) the good manners in Sirach's teaching on table etiquette (verses 12-24). Compare with Proverbs 23.
3. What advice does the author give concerning the use and abuse of wine?

SIRACH 32

A master of the feast was chosen to order wine, place guests at table, etc. This was a Greek custom, introduced into Palestine. Sirach does not condemn it. He merely urges good manners.

1. Verses 1-13. Draw up a list of hints for behaviour at formal dinner parties. What insight does Sirach give into the customs of his time? Can we apply his rules to such occasions today?
2. What advice does Sirach give for those who sincerely seek Wisdom (verses 14-24)? Can I choose a verse that is especially for me?

SIRACH 33

Various maxims.

1. Verses 1-18. What do you think of Sirach's analogy between the differing festivals and 'ordinary days', and human inequalities? What conclusion does he draw?
2. Verses 19-31. Slavery was taken for granted in Sirach's day. Does the slave have any protection by law? cf. verses 30-31. Does Sirach express any sense of a slave's humanity and rights?

SIRACH 34

Sirach, like most of the Wisdom teachers, scorned dreams as source of knowledge, though he makes one exception (verse 6).

1. What do you think of his comments, especially verse 3? Has modern psychology and psychoanalysis anything to add? What about the dreams in Genesis, Daniel and Matthew? Should we, normally, follow Sirach's advice? (verse 8).
2. What are the pre-requisites for a sacrifice pleasing to God? Compare Sirach's teaching with Amos' (Amos 5:21-24) and with Christ's (Matthew 9:13 and 12:7).

SIRACH 35

The great prophetic insight that ritual sacrifices are worth less without a true change of heart is echoed by Sirach.

1. Comment on verses 1-2. How does this apply to the Christian life?
2. Draw out examples of God's justice. What dispositions make our prayer acceptable to God?

SIRACH 36

Sirach's prayer for Israel. His advice concerning marriage.

1. What is the chief burden of Sirach's prayer (verses 1-17)? Can we make it a prayer for the unity of the Church? Note the Messianic reference (verses 8).
2. What are the advantages of marriage for a man? Do you agree with Sirach's conclusions (verse 26)?

SIRACH 37

Sirach is once more on his theme of friendship.

1. What examples of 'hidden agenda' are there in the list of advisers? What, in the end, is the best counsel? Do I give honest counsel according to the criteria in verses 7-15?
2. Compare the advice on moderate eating with Proverbs 25:16.

SIRACH 38

Many Jews considered it a lack of faith in God to consult a doctor (2 Chronicles 16:12). Sirach corrects this view.

1. In what, according to Sirach, does medicine consist? Compare verses 9-14 with James 5:13-16. What dimension is added by the New Testament writer? Do we observe these rules if we fall ill?
2. What do you think of Sirach's advice to mourners? In what spirit should we lament the departed? Are we in danger of forgetting this nowadays?
3. List the craftsmen and tradesmen given by Sirach. In what does their contribution consist? Do you agree with his conclusions in 33-34? Are you consoled by his final remark?

SIRACH 39

Sirach's eulogy of the scribe. Hymn in praise of God's creative activity.

1. What inspiration can we draw from the eulogy of the scribe? Note his various sources o wisdom. Who would be today's 'scribes'?
2. What theological mystery is the subject of verses 12-35? How does Sirach interpret Genesis 1 Is his conclusion pessimistic or optimistic?

SIRACH 40

Misery, according to Sirach, is caused by sin.

1. Verses 1-11. Trace the influence of Genesis 3:17 on this section. What is Sirach's main answer to the problem of human suffering?
2. Verses 12-27. With which of the comparisons do you most agree?
3. What arguments does Sirach use to discourage begging?

SIRACH 41

Death, and the fate of the wicked.

1. Verses 1-4. Contrast the two different attitudes to death. What are your own feelings about your own death?
2. What, according to Sirach, is the worst punishment of the wicked? Does the writer show any signs of believing in life after death?
3. What examples do you find in this chapter of behaviour of which one should properly be ashamed? Are the examples concerned with morality or with etiquette?

SIRACH 42:1-14

The collection of proverbs is completed with some on Sirach's favourite worry: women!

1. Verses 1-8. In what ways does Sirach show that he values commonsense above human respect?
2. Verses 9-14. What signs are there that a father has a *GENUINE* concern for his daughter? But cf. verse 11. Then discuss the section in terms of a son, and of men, from a woman's point of view.
   Note: A hymn of praise of creation begins at verse 15.
3. What is said in verses 15-25 a) of the stars - 'the signs of the times' -, b) of the word of God, and c) of God's foreknowledge? What is meant by verse 18?

SIRACH 43

The marvels of God's creation.

1. Which of God's attributes are reflected in his creation? What is Sirach's doctrine of creation? See especially verses 27-29.
2. What marvels are noted in this chapter? Do you think that modern science has increased man's sense of wonder or diminished it?

SIRACH 44

God's glory is proclaimed in the history of the Jewish people. The famous or illustrious men of verse 1 are literally 'men of hesed' - men of piety and loyalty to the Torah - hence the Hasidim (1 Maccabees. 2:42).

1. What classes of men are listed in verses 3-6? Do they in any way correspond to the books of the Bible?
2. In what way is Enoch presented as an inspiration? What is meant by 'repentance' in verse 16? Compare Genesis 5:24 and Hebrews 11:5.
3. Wisdom 10:4 characterises Noah as "righteous". Genesis 6:8 says that 'he found favour in the eyes of the Lord'. How does Sirach expand this?
4. What aspects of the Genesis accounts of Abraham, Isaac and Jacob are selected by Sirach for comment? What are his chief preoccupations with regard to the patriarchs?

SIRACH 45

Moses, Aaron and Phinias.

1. What aspect of Moses' leadership is emphasised by Sirach? See especially verse 5. How does he exemplify Sirach's doctrine of Wisdom?
2. Check out the number of times the following words appear in this chapter: covenant, priesthood, atonement, sanctuary. What does this indicate concerning Sirach's purpose and interests?
3. Look up the story of Phineas in Numbers 25. Compare Sirach's account with your own impression of the original story. How do you explain the difference?

SIRACH 46

Joshua, Caleb, Samuel.

1. What new title (new in Sirach) is given to God in this chapter? Note when it appears and when it recurs. What titles have been previously used?
2. How, according to Sirach, did Joshua exemplify his name?
3. What aspect of Samuel's mission is brought out by Sirach? Is the same aspect emphasised in 1 Samuel? What words recur in verses 13-20?

SIRACH 47

The two poems on David and Solomon are in the style of the poems in Maccabees.

1. What interpretation does Sirach put on David's early career? What aspect of his achievement does he bring out?
2. How far is Solomon an example of Sirach's thesis that the fear of the Lord is the basis of Wisdom?

SIRACH 48

Verse 11 either means that those who die in the love of God will see Elijah (i.e., will survive death); or simply that Elijah saw him. The text is uncertain.

1. Why does Sirach emphasise the fierceness of Elijah's mission? What lesson is he seeking to teach his readers?
2. Can you find any allusions to immortality in this chapter? See especially verses 11, 13-14 and 24-25. What kind of immortality is suggested?
3. Look at Malachi 4:5-6 and Luke 1:17 and compare verses 1-11. What did New Testament make of these passages?
4. Why is Hezekiah selected by Sirach from the Books of Kings? Which of his achievements does he praise?

SIRACH 49

Josiah, the exile, the return.

1. Sirach was not the only writer to reflect the tradition that Josiah left a fragrant memory. Loo up Zechariah 12:10-11. What warrant is there in 2 Kings 22-23 for such a eulogy? And c Jeremiah 23:10, 15-16.
2. Sirach sums up the whole of history in verses 14-16. Compare verses 8-13. What does h emphasise?
3. Make a list of the books of Old Testament explicitly or implicitly referred to by Sirach. Whic ones are omitted?

SIRACH 50

Simon the high priest is a forgotten figure, but Sirach sees him as the summit of Jewish history!

1. How is Simon the heir to those mentioned in 49:8-13?
2. Compare verses 20-21 with Luke 24:50-53. In what ways is Simon a fore-runner of Jesus? What was Luke conveying to his readers by this echo?

SIRACH 51

This chapter seems to have been added to the work, clearly concluded at 50:27-29. It contains a hymn of praise and thanksgiving, and a poem on Sirach's quest for wisdom.

1. Verses 1-12. For what is the psalmist giving thanks? Read the prayer as a Christian prayer of thanksgiving for salvation (see verse 10).
2. The final verses describe the author's search for and devotion to Wisdom. What encouragement is given to seekers? What use can a Christian make of this poem?

AN INTRODUCTION
TO
BARUCH

In what book of the Bible are cats mentioned? — Baruch 6:22

Who was Baruch? — The son of Neriah.

And who was he? — The father of Baruch.

That is, indeed, all that many of us know about this book, which is a late one, probably from the middle of the first century BC, and in Greek, though there may have been a Hebrew original. It is ascribed to Baruch, Jeremiah's secretary, but is clearly a late composition - an argument against idolatry. It seems to refer to parts of Isaiah 44 and to Jeremiah 10, and is alluded to, apparently, in 2 Maccabees 2:1-3. It is a good example of how the lessons of scripture can be retold to each successive generation, and it gives an insight into the lives of the Jewish communities of the Diaspora - their prayer life, observance of the Law, Messianic hope, contact with Jerusalem.

Its doctrine of Wisdom echoes that of Sirach, it is to be found in God's gift of the Law (4:1). The commandments (3:9) may be those of Wisdom (Proverbs 2:1) as well as those of the Law. The question in 3:10 (why are the Israelites in exile in a foreign land?) is answered in 3:12 - because they have 'forsaken the fountain of wisdom'. And Wisdom is defined as 'the book of the commandments of God, and the law that endures forever' (4:1). How is it to be attained? By repentance (4:2). The wise man is therefore he who turns back to God and walks 'toward the shining of her light' (4:2). God's creation, SIGN of the mystery of his Wisdom, is celebrated in poetry (3:15-37) that echoes Job 28. This short book deserves to be better known.

Structure of the Book of Baruch

Prayer of Baruch	–	1:1 - 3:8
Wisdom Poems	–	3:9 - 4:4
Prophetic discourse I	–	4:5-29
Prophetic discourse II	–	4:30 - 5:9
Letter of Jeremiah	–	6:1-72

BARUCH 1

1. It is clear that this book is not aiming at historical accuracy. Assuming that it was composed during the first century BC, what insight does this chapter offer into the life of the dispersed Jewish communities? See especially verses 5-6,14.
2. What aspects of Jewish history are brought out? Of what sin are their ancestors especially accused?

BARUCH 2

1. What two reasons are put forward in the plea to God to save Israel 'for thy own sake'? See verses 15 and 17. What kind of people are referred to in verse 18? See Zephaniah 2:3.
2. What promise is meant? (verses 30-32). cf. Jeremiah 31:31-33.

BARUCH 3

The Wisdom Poem begins at verse 9.

1. What is meant by verse 3? Compare Psalm 102:12-13. Can we make this prayer our own, for the Church, or for our nation? For what would we be praying in each case?
2. What is the author's doctrine of suffering, punishment and purification (verses 2-8)? Do we note its fulfillment in the events of our century, or do we complain like spoilt children when things go wrong?
3. Verses 9-14. What are the 'commandments of life'? What title is given to God (verse 12) and what are his attributes (verse 14)?
4. Verses 15-31. The writer lists various sources of Wisdom (rulers, Canaanites, Edomites, Arabs, story-tellers) and none had found her. Make a similar list of twentieth century 'sages'.
5. God, the source of Wisdom communicates through his creation. Comment on a Christian meaning of verse 37.

BARUCH 4

The first prophetic discourse begins at verse 5, when Jerusalem addresses the neighbouring towns and her own people in exile.

1. Verses 1-4. Israel's glory is the Law, in which is contained God's Wisdom. In what consists the glory of the Church? Is she ever in need of the warning contained in verse 3?
2. What titles are given to God in this chapter? Are any of them new ones?
3. Verses 5-29. What is the tone of this discourse? In what lies the prophet's hope? See verse 24. Can this be interpreted in a Messianic sense? How does it apply to me?
4. Verses 30-37. The second prophetic discourse describes at one level the return from Babylon to Jerusalem after the exile. What is its meaning at a deeper level? See especially verse 37.

BARUCH 5

1. Verse 4 contains the 'throne-names' of the holy city. Can they/should they be applied to the Church? What are the 'throne-names' of Jesus?
2. Read this chapter as applying to the destiny of the Church, the people of God. What strikes you particularly?
3. Note in chapters 4 and 5 the many references to or echoes of the prophetic books, evidently well known to the author. Identify as many as you can.

BARUCH 6
(The letter of Jeremiah).

1. What advice does the writer give to those obliged to live in pagan surroundings (verses 5-6)? Can this advice be adapted to our circumstances?
2. What does the writer say a) about the helplessness and uselessness of idols, and b) about the morals of the priests who serve them? See verses 10-11,28,43.
3. What, by implication, are the powers and characteristics of the true God?

AN INTRODUCTION TO 1 MACCABEES

This book (and also 2 Maccabees) brings us into a very different world from that of Kings or Chronicles. It was composed about the year 100 BC by a Palestinian Jew, translating a lost Hebrew original. It belongs therefore to the Hellenistic period when the Greeks had succeeded the Persians as the great world power. After Alexander the Great's death in 323 BC, his vast empire was partitioned among his generals. Seleucus ruled Syria and Mesopotamia. Ptolemy ruled Egypt. Palestine was caught in a struggle between Seleucid Syria and Ptolemaic Egypt.

Greek or 'Hellenistic' culture spread throughout the empire, bringing gymnasia, theatres, race-tracks, as well as the Greek language. Greek speaking Jews at Alexandria (Egypt) began the task of translating the Bible into Greek (the Septuagint, which is almost invariably the version quoted in New Testament).

From soon after the death of Alexander until 200 BC Judah was ruled from Egypt and during this time Hellenisation spread apace, as many of the upper classes were attracted to it.

Then in 223 BC, Antiochus III came to the throne in Antioch (Syria - Seleucid). In 198 BC he defeated Ptolemaic Egypt, and thus brought Palestine under Seleucid control. He was a fanatical Hellenist, as were his successors, especially Antiochus IV (Epiphanes) who claimed to be a manifestation of the god Zeus, whose cult he imposed on all his peoples, including the Jews. (cf Daniel 11:21 ff). In 168 he desecrated the Temple by setting up an altar to Zeus, and by offering swine there (1 Maccabees 1:64).

The Jews led a revolt, sparked off by a village priest in Modein, a few miles from Jerusalem. His name was Mattathias (1 Maccabees 2:27), and it was his son Judas who carried on the fight after his father's death in 166 BC. He was nicknamed 'Maccabaeus' which probably means 'hammer'. In 165 Judas defeated Antiochus' general Gorgias (1 Maccabees 4) and demanded a peace treaty. In December 165 the altar of the Temple was rebuilt and Jewish worship restored. This event is commemorated annually at the Dedication (Hanukkah) festival (1 Maccabees 4:36-61). Thus began the great Maccabean wars, which lasted until 134 BC. 1 Maccabees tells the story of this revolt. It is written in the style of the period - lofty, enthusiastic. Its theology emphasises faith in God (referred to as 'Heaven') and in the Law.

1 MACCABEES 1

The tribute collector or 'Mysarch' (verse 29) was Apollonius (2 Maccabees 5:24).

1. What were the temptations of Jews during the Hellenistic period? Do they in any way correspond to temptations Christians experience nowadays? What do you think of the reasoning referred to in verse 11?
2. List the offences against Judaism contained in the king's decree. How were Jews punished who refused to break God's Law?

1 MACCABEES 2

Mattathias' name means Gift of God. His sons' nicknames mean: fortunate (John), burning (Simon), chosen by God, or the hammerer (Judas), alert (Eleazar), favoured (Jonathan).

1. What incident led to the outbreak of religious war?
2. Was the refusal to fight on the sabbath (verses 29-38) martyrdom or fanaticism in your view? What conclusion did Mattathias draw?

3. Draw out the scriptural references in Mattathias' testament (verses 49-70). What aspects of sacred history does he emphasise? Note especially his stress on pious *DEEDS* (eg. verses 51,52,55 etc). Is this balanced by a corresponding mention of faith or of God's grace?

1 MACCABEES 3

Josephus says Apollonius was governor and military commander of Samaria. Judas Maccabaeus, 166-160 BC.

1. 'Judas took the sword of Apollonius' (verse 12). Of what Old Testament incident does this remind us? In what other ways does the writer build up a picture of Judas as an Old Testament hero?
2. What were Antiochus' intentions towards Judah (verses 35-36)? What preparations did Judas make for battle? How did he discover God's guidance? Why did the Israelites assemble at Mizpah?
3. Judas stands in poverty before God (verses 50-53). Can we take example from his prayer in adversity? What other signs of faith does Judas show?

1 MACCABEES 4

The battle of Emmaus. The purification and re-dedication of the Temple.

1. Study Judas' prayers before battle (verse 10,30-32). What scripture references does he make?
2. Follow the campaigns of Gorgias (verses 1-25) and of Lysias (verses 28-35) on a map. What were their aims? Why were they defeated?
3. The altar had been desecrated (1:54,59) because an altar to Zeus had been built onto it. How was it cleansed? What is the significance of the reference to a prophet (verse 46)? Mark the details of purification and re-dedication of the Temple (verses 36-61). How are we purified of sin, and re-dedicated to God?

1 MACCABEES 5

Idumea is the Greek name for Edom, country of Esau. The 'sons of Baean' (verse 4) were probably nomadic bandits.

1. Why were the surrounding peoples (verse 1) affronted at the restoration of the sanctuary? What explains similar reactions nowadays?
2. In what territories did Judas conduct campaigns in this chapter? Of which Old Testament hero does he remind you?

1 MACCABEES 6

Antiochus V Eupator was only nine years old at his accession. Philip (verse 14) was regent, and Lysias, who had been the king's tutor for the past two years, was governor of Palestine. The citadel (verses 18 and 24) was in Jerusalem, opposite the Temple.

1. What deed especially lay on Antiochus IV's conscience as he lay on his deathbed?
2. What signs are there during these campaigns of God's Providence? See, for example, verses 48-54,56. Why did Lysias make peace with the Jews? Did this peace give them freedom?

1 MACCABEES 7

Demetrius, by a coup d'etat, seized the throne in 161 BC.

1. Verses 1-20. What lesson may we learn from these verses concerning putting our trust in time-servers?
2. Verses 20-25. What evidence is there that Alcimus was a Helleniser?
3. Look up 3:38 ff. for Nicanor. What reason had he for hating and distrusting Israel (verse 26)?

4. Show the power of prayer in shaping these events. What Old Testament example did Judas evoke (verse 41)?

1 MACCABEES 8

In praise of the Romans. Like other great powers (Russia, America ...) the Romans sought to de-stabilise their enemies by supporting rebels *(Contras, freedom-fighters...)*.

1. This chapter explains the origins of Roman interest in Palestine. What would the prophets have advised about such an alliance between Rome and Israel? From your reading of New Testament do you think the Romans were to justify Judas' high opinion of them?
2. What was the reason for the appeal to Rome? See verses 31-32.

1 MACCABEES 9

The death of Judas Maccabaeus. The adventures of Jonathan Maccabaeus, 160-143 BC.

1. Verses 1-22. Trace the stages by which Judas' army became demoralised. Does Judas show faith or stoicism? Compare his dirge (verse 21) with that for Saul (2 Samuel 1:27). Why was he called *SAVIOUR* or *JUDGE*?
2. Verses 23-49. To what does the author seem to ascribe Jonathan's falling into the ambush set by Bacchides' men? See verse 43. Are there any other signs in the narrative of Divine Providence at work?
3. Verses 50-57. What was the sin of the high priest Alcimus? What was his punishment?
4. Verses 58-73. In what ways is Jonathan Maccabaeus described as a *JUDGE* in Israel?

1 MACCABEES 10

Alexander Epiphanes claimed to be a son of Antiochus IV. Onias IV, heir to the last legitimate high priest Onias III, was in exile in Egypt. Jonathan Maccabaeus came of a priestly family (2:1).

1. What terms did Alexander Epiphanes offer Jonathan? What terms did King Demetrius offer? Which did Jonathan accept, and why?
2. Who was Demetrius (verse 67) and why did he go to war with Alexander? What were the tactics of Jonathan that finally defeated Demetrius in Palestine?
3. What, in your view, is likely to be the outcome for church leaders if they take sides in political power struggles? Are there any occasions when the Church should intervene?

1 MACCABEES 11

Jonathan and Demetrius II.

1. What signs are there of Ptolemy (the king of Egypt)'s treachery against Alexander? What was the outcome for both of them?
2. What leads us to the conclusion that Jonathan Maccabaeus had a great personality? How did God use him?
3. What led to Demetrius II's downfall? What do you think of Jonathan's attitude through all these events? Do you find anything to inspire you?

1 MACCABEES 12

Jonathan's great career - and his downfall.

1. What are the sources of Jewish hope, according to Jonathan? See verses 9,15.
2. What is meant by verse 21? Are we meant to take it literally?

3. What signs are there that Jonathan is beginning to learn from his mistakes? See verses 26-27. What have I learnt from my mistakes when engaged in spiritual warfare? See verses 35-38.
4. What led to Jonathan's downfall? Was it inevitable?

1 MACCABEES 13

Simon Maccabaeus, 143-134 BC.

1. What arguments did Simon Maccabaeus use to the people of Jerusalem? Do you think he was right to send hostages to Trypho? What were his motives (verse 17)?
2. In what way was Simon a more radical high priest than Jonathan?

1 MACCABEES 14

Simon's achievements.

1. List Simon's achievements a) in the religious, and b) in the political, spheres.
2. On which of these achievements did the Jews lay emphasis? See verses 35-37. What were his duties as high priest and as governor of the Jews (verses 41-49)?

1 MACCABEES 15

Antiochus VII (verse 1) was the son of Demetrius I (see 10:50) and the brother of Demetrius II.

1. How did Antiochus VII woo the Jews?
2. What was the secret of Simon's success? See verses 15 ff.

1 MACCABEES 16

John (verse 1) is Simon's son - John Hyrcanus, who succeeded his father in 134 BC.

1. In what ways was John's generalship reminiscent of Jonathan's?
2. What echoes of the Books of Kings do you find in this chapter? What is the purpose of the whole book? Does it serve this purpose today?

AN INTRODUCTION TO 2 MACCABEES

This book is not a continuation of 1 Maccabees. It covers roughly the period between the end of the reign of Seleucus IV, the father of Antiochus IV Epiphanes, and the defeat of Nicanor by Judas Maccabaeus - about fifteen years, corresponding to 1 Maccabees 1-7. It differs considerably in style, being rhetorical, turgid, full of signs and wonders. It was written in Egypt about 124 BC, so is earlier than 1 Maccabees. Its purpose is instruction and edification, placing more emphasis than 1 Maccabees on the importance of the Temple, and on doctrines dear to the Pharisees, eg. the resurrection of the just (7:9; 14:46). The book is arranged round the theme of the Temple: the first part ends with the death of Antiochus IV Epiphanes who defiled the Temple (4:1 - 10:8); the second part (10:9 - 15:36) ends with the death of Nicanor, another persecutor.

The book affirms the resurrection of the just, punishment in an after-life (6:26), the possibility of prayers for the dead (12:38, 41-46), the efficacy of martyrdom (6:18 - 7:41), the intercession of the saints (15:12-16). It is important therefore as a witness to Jewish beliefs in these doctrines during the second century BC.

2 MACCABEES 1

An interesting piece of evidence that Jews in Egypt and in Jerusalem were in communication with each other. Letter I was written in 124 BC; Letter II in 164 BC. Aristobulus (verse 10) was a Jewish philosopher of Alexandria. "The king" (verse 11) is Antiochus IV Epiphanes.

1. Verses 1-9. What evidence is there in this letter that the Jewish community in Egypt worshipped God according to the Law? What was the feast they were invited to celebrate? Compare verse 2 with Leviticus 26:44. What consolation is there for Jewish exiles?
2. Verses 10-17. The author gives a popular account of Antiochus' death (cf. 1 Maccabees 6 and 2 Maccabees 9 for other versions). What is the moral to be drawn from the story? (NB. Nanaea was the goddess Artemis).
3. Verses 18-36. Sort out the natural origin of this story - the discovery of a pool of crude petroleum - from the references to Nehemiah and the sacred fire. What is the point of the story?

2 MACCABEES 2

The second letter continues until verse 18. Jeremiah was one of the most venerated figures among the Jews after the exile.

1. Verses 1-18. How do the writers of the Letter seek to convey the continuity of Temple worship with its origins? Note the offer of books to the Egyptian Jews. How does the Christian Church preserve and emphasise its roots in the Bible and in the apostolic community? For what reason?
2. Make a summary of the writer's aims as expressed in verses 19-23. What were the difficulties of his task?

2 MACCABEES 3

Onias III (verse 1) was the son of the high priest (Sirach 50:1-21) who in turn was the son of Onias II. They were descendants of Joshua (Nehemiah 12:10-11); Seleucus (verse 3) was elder brother to Antiochus IV and father of Demetrius I.

1. To what use was the temple wealth put a) in the mind of Apollonius, and b) according to the high priest? Who was the real instigator of the attack on the temple treasury?
2. What title is given to God (verse 24)? What does it mean?
3. What was the meaning of Heliodorus' vision?

2 MACCABEES 4

For Hellenising practices, cf. 1 Maccabees 1:11-15. To 'wear the Greek hat' (verse 12) meant to take part in gymnastics under the protection of the god Hermes.

1. What were the principal features of the Hellenisation of Jerusalem?
2. Mark the stages in the decline of the priesthood, from Onias, to Jason, Joshua (verse 7), to Menelaus (verses 23 ff). What caused this rapid fall in standards?
3. Look up Daniel 9:25 ff. and Daniel 11:22 for a prophetic view of Onias. What was the reaction of the people to his murder? See verse 35.

2 MACCABEES 5

'The city' - verse 2 - refers to Jerusalem.

1. What was the meaning of the omen in the sky?
2. What moral does the writer draw from Jason's end? Is it true to life?
3. What are the theological explanations suggested for the pillage of the Temple? See verses 15-20.
4. What does the author emphasise in his reference to Judas Maccabaeus (verse 27)?

2 MACCABEES 6

The year is 167 BC. The great persecution of the Jews.

1. What details are given concerning the enforced programme of Hellenisation? (Verses 1-11).
2. Verses 12-17. What moral does the author draw from the evils he is relating?
3. What new religious element is present in the story of Eleazar?

2 MACCABEES 7

The martyrdom of the seven brothers and their mother.

1. Draw out the teaching in this chapter on the resurrection of the just.
2. What does the mother say about creation? See verses 23,28. Is there an advance on Genesis 1?
3. What did the martyrs believe concerning their death for and on behalf of the nation? In what ways are they types of Christ?

2 MACCABEES 8

The end of the persecution and the vindication of the Jews.

1. What, according to the author, is the first result of the death of the martyrs?
2. List the occasions when the people 'besought the Lord'. Find other examples of faith and trust in God, and of pious observance of the Law.
3. Compare verses 14, 28-30 with Acts 2:44,45. What Old Testament examples does Judas evoke?
4. How does the author explain theologically the events of this chapter? See verse 36.

2 MACCABEES 9

The death of Antiochus Epiphanes is described in detail.

1. Compare the account of Antiochus' sufferings with 1 Maccabees 6:1-16, and cf. Acts 12:23. Was his repentance genuine? Did the writer believe in it?
2. Comparing verses 19-27 with 28-29, in what state of mind does Antiochus seem to have been at his death?

2 MACCABEES 10

The purification of the Temple. Jewish wars with their neighbours.

1. Compare verses 1-8 with the Introductory Letters in chapter 1. In what spirit was the Temple purified? See verse 4. When is the new fire (verse 3) used in the Christian liturgy? What does it signify?
2. List the occasions when the author mentions prayer before battle. What did Judas' heavenly bodyguard symbolise?

2 MACCABEES 11

Jewish victory over Lysias.

1. The familiar pattern of penance, prayer, angelic assistance and victory leads to a negotiated peace. What are its terms? Do we take seriously the necessity for prayer and penance in our own spiritual combat? cf. Ephes 6:10f.
2. What concessions did the king make to the Jews?

2 MACCABEES 12

This is an important chapter theologically. It reveals the thinking of second century Judaism on 'the last things'.

1. What evidence of persecution of the Jews by neighbouring peoples have we in this chapter? How does the author depict Judas as a 'judge' of old? See especially verses 15,38.
2. What titles are accorded to God in this chapter?
3. What was the meaning of Judas' sacrifice for the dead (verses 39-45)?
4. Does the author believe in the efficacy of prayer for the dead? Does he believe only in the resurrection of the just? What bearing has this incident and the author's comments on the Catholic doctrine of purgatory?

2 MACCABEES 13

The death of Menelaus, which marks the beginning of Hasmonaean power in Judea.

1. What aspect of Menelaus' death does the author underline?
2. This chapter gives another example of the power of prayer (verses 9-17). What was the outcome? What is the significance of sunrise? (verse 17).

2 MACCABEES 14

The activities of Alcimus, the relations between Nicanor, the commander of Demetrius' army, and Judas.

1. Compare what is said of Alcimus in 1 Maccabees 7 with his activities as described in this chapter.
2. What impression have you formed of the relations between Judas and Nicanor?
3. Suicide is rare in the Bible. What view did the author take of the death of Razis? What reaction did *you* have to the story?

2 MACCABEES 15

The defeat of Nicanor by Judas Maccabaeus.

1. Verses 1-5. How does the writer make it clear that the forthcoming battle will be between God and the forces of evil?
2. How did Judas prepare his troops for battle? What inspiration did he put before them?
3. Onias represented the priesthood and the Law, Jeremiah the prophets. Of what New Testament scene does this vision remind you? What does the author believe a) concerning the afterlife, b) concerning the saints' intercession?
4. What priorities did the combatants have? (cf. verses 17-18 with Luke 14:25-27).

NEW
TESTAMENT

THE SIGN OF Jonah
UNLESS A MAN IS BORN THROUGH WATER + THE SPIRIT HE CANNOT ENTER THE KINGDOM OF GOD
JOHN 3: VI.
THE WATER BEFORE + THE WATER AFTER FOR NOW + EVER FLOWING FOLLOW EACH OTHER
ANON.

AN INTRODUCTION TO THE GOSPEL OF MATTHEW

'Matthew, Mark, Luke and John,
Bless the bed that I lie on'

We are accustomed to thinking of the four evangelists as being figures fairly well known to us from the New Testament itself. We think of Matthew, the reformed tax collector, and John the beloved disciple as being eye witnesses of the events they describe, Mark as the interpreter of Peter, and Luke as the companion of Paul.

This may be largely so, but a careful reading of Matthew's gospel at least should give us pause. It is very carefully constructed, full of quotations from scripture in good Greek. Can it really be the work of the man described in Matthew 9:9 "a man named Matthew sitting at the tax office"? The internal evidence surely points to the author as a scribe - a man very well acquainted with scripture (by which, of course is meant the Old Testament) and capable of arranging his material according to his own scheme. That he used sources, written as well as oral, is not in dispute. Papias says that 'Matthew collected the sayings in the Hebrew language and that each one translated them as best he could'. Does this mean that the evangelist used some material ascribed to the apostle Matthew as the foundation for his gospel which he wrote in Greek? Many think he wrote later than Mark, but it is less certain whether he USED Mark.

After the introductory chapters 1 - 2, the gospel can be seen to be divided into five discourses, sandwiched between blocks of narrative: chapters 1-2 - infancy narrative; 3-4 - narrative section; 5-7: Sermon on the Mount; 8-9 - nine miracles; 10: Instruction for the Apostles; 11-12 - narrative section; 13: the Parables; 13:53 - 17: narrative section; 18: The Church; 19-23 - narrative section and attack on the pharisees; 24: Apocalyptic discourse; 25: narrative section; 26-27 - Passion Narrative; 28: Resurrection Narrative.

We have concentrated in the study on Matthew's use of Old Testament themes to express his faith in Jesus the Messiah.

It is difficult to date this gospel, but most scholars believe it was composed after the destruction of the Temple in AD 70, perhaps in Syria.

MATTHEW 1

Matthew's Prologue consists of a genealogy of Christ, followed by his version of the story of the virgin-birth.

1. What is the primary purpose of the placing of this genealogy at the beginning of the gospel? See verses 1 and 17.
2. Look up Tamar (Genesis 38), Rahab (Joshua 2), Ruth (Ruth 4:18-22), the wife of Uriah (2 Samuel 11). Why do you think these four women have been introduced into Jesus' genealogy? What have they in common?
3. What task is laid on Joseph (verses 20-21)?
4. Compare verse 23 with Isaiah 7:14. What features of the prophecy is Matthew emphasising?

MATTHEW 2

By careful use of scripture, Matthew reveals Jesus as the new Moses.

1. Where in Old Testament do we meet Magi? See, for example, Exodus 7:11, 22; 8:18, etc and Daniel 2:2, etc. In these Old Testament stories the magicians were always worsted. What point is Matthew making here?
2. Compare verse 6 with Micah 5:2, and verses 2, 7, 9 and 10 with Numbers 24:17. Should Herod and the Jewish leaders have recognised the Messiah from the Magi's information and from their own knowledge of scripture? Do we ever ignore the truth?
3. Compare the infancy of Jesus as recorded in this chapter with that of the infant Moses (Exodus 1-2). Is Matthew making a point?

MATTHEW 3

The gospel as received from tradition now begins - with the fore-runner, John the Baptist, and the baptism of Jesus, who is revealed as Messiah.

1. John the Baptist quotes Isaiah 40:3 (verse 3). What would this have conveyed to his hearers? What does it convey to us?
2. Matthew is concerned to underline that John the Baptist is the new Elijah. With verse 4 cf. 2 Kings 1:8, and cf. Matthew 11:14 and 17:10-13. What was a) Elijah's task in his lifetime (cf. 1 Kings 17-20) and b) after his death cf. Malachi 4:5-6)?
3. Why did Jesus allow himself to be baptised by John (verse 15)? How does it fulfil "all righteousness", i.e. the Law? How is the Trinity revealed in these verses?

MATTHEW 4

The first narrative section: Jesus in the wilderness, the call of disciples, Messianic miracles.

1. Verses 1-11. What temptations of the Israelites in the desert were undergone by Jesus? With verse 2 compare Exodus 16; with verse 6 compare Numbers 14:39-45 and with verse 9 compare Exodus 32. What is Jesus' response to each test?
2. What significance does Matthew attach to Jesus' return to Galilee from Judea? (verse 13). Read Isaiah 9:1-2 to set his quotation in context. From this use of scripture what conclusion is to be drawn?
3. Verses 23-25. Comparing these verses with Isaiah 35:5-6 how do we know that the Messianic age has begun?

MATTHEW 5

As the Law was given to Moses on Mount Sinai, so Jesus the new Moses gives the New Law from a mountain.

1. Verses 3-12. With verses 3 and 5 compare Zephaniah 2:3, 3:12; with verse 4 compare Isaiah 61:2; with verse 6 compare Isaiah 55:1-2. What teachings of the prophets is Jesus emphasising?
2. Verses 13-37. How does Jesus now go beyond the interpretation of the Law given by the scribes and pharisees with regard to the commandments?
3. Verses 38-48. How great a change is needed in our attitudes to obey these injunctions? What is the highest point reached?

MATTHEW 6

Prayer, fasting and almsgiving were the traditional Jewish pious practices.

1. Verses 1-18. What would be our form of temptation to ostentation and hypocrisy in prayer, fasting and almsgiving?
2. List the advice Jesus gives on prayer. What particular clause of the Our Father is reiterated? Why?

3. Verses 19-24. What advice does Jesus give to the rich? Examine yourself on verse 21.
4. Verses 25-34. Why is anxiety wrong? Note the number of times it is mentioned. Should we take these words literally? How should we handle anxiety?

MATTHEW 7

The last section of the Sermon on the Mount lays the foundations of the kingdom.

1. What does Jesus teach in this chapter about discernment and sound judgement? Why are we to refrain from judging the motives of others?
2. How are we to distinguish false from true prophets? What do Jesus' words add to Old Testament rules (Deuteronomy 13:1-5)?
3. What is the importance of the teaching in verses 21-23? How do we do "the will of my Father"? What is the twentieth century counterpart to the activities described in verse 22?
4. Compare verses 24-27 with Ezekiel 13:10-14. What is the lesson of each parable?

MATTHEW 8-9

The Sermon on the Mount is followed by nine acts of power, in three groups of three each.

MATTHEW 8

Five acts of power inaugurate the Messianic era: the cleansing of a leper, the healing of the Centurion's servant, the healing of Simon's mother-in-law, the calming of the storm and the exorcism of the demoniacs.

1. Look up the requirements for the cleansing of leprosy in Leviticus 14:1-20.
2. Matthew quotes Isaiah 53:4 in relation to Jesus' healing miracles. What does he intend to convey by this? See verse 17.
3. Compare verses 19-22 with 1 Kings 19:20-21. What are the demands of true discipleship?
4. Compare the cleansing of the leper and the healing of the centurion's servant on the one hand, with the calming of the storm on the other. What is the lesson Jesus is teaching? See especially verses 10 and 26.
5. Compare verses 23-27 with Psalm 106:9 and Jonah 1:4-6. Are the resemblances more than merely verbal?

MATTHEW 9

Four more acts of power: the healing of the paralytic; the cure of the woman with an issue of blood; the raising of Jairus' daughter; and the healing of the blind men and the dumb demoniac (these last four bracketed together in twos).

1. What is the essential teaching conveyed by verses 1-8? Compare 8:28-34.
2. Read Hosea 6:6 quoted by Jesus in its context in Hosea's teaching, and compare with Matthew 9:13. What is Jesus bringing to our attention?
3. The blind men (verse 27) give Jesus a Messianic title. How is the coming of the Messiah inaugurated in this chapter? See especially verses 2, 9, 15-17, 25, 30, 33.
4. What new note is struck in this chapter, pointing to an underlying, but growing opposition to the kingdom?

MATTHEW 10

The second discourse - instruction of the apostles.

1. The gospel was to be preached first to the Jews (verse 6) who are visited by their chosen Messiah (verse 23). What advice does Jesus give to his disciples a) in case of rejection of his message b) in time of persecution?
2. What are the qualities needed for discipleship? See especially verses 24, 26, 28, 37-39?

MATTHEW 11

A new theme is introduced: the unbelief of Israel. John bears witness from prison, and the Israelite towns are warned by Jesus.

1. What kind of Messiah was John the Baptist expecting? See 3:8,10,12. Look up Isaiah 26:19, 29:18, 35:5 ff. and compare with Jesus' reply (verses 4-5).
2. Examine Jesus' prophetic role in verses 16-24. Tyre, Sidon and Sodom were condemned in Old Testament for their pride and evil deeds. In what way does Jesus characterise his contemporaries?
3. Compare Jesus' words at verse 19, and at verses 25-30 with Proverbs 8:22-36, Wisdom 8:3-4; 9:9-18; Sirach 24:3-9, 19-20. In what way does Jesus claim to be a Wisdom teacher here?

MATTHEW 12

A series of conflict stories begins: the disciples are criticised for breaking the sabbath; the man with a withered arm is healed on the sabbath; Jesus is accused of sorcery; his family try to intervene.

1. Verses 1-14. What is the essence of Jesus' teaching concerning the sabbath? Does he overturn the Law? Do his scriptural references (2 Samuel 21:2-7 and Hosea 6:6) clarify the situation? What was the effect on the pharisees?
2. What interpretation does Matthew put (verses 15-21) on the Servant Song he quotes (Isaiah 42:1-4)? Does the context in the gospel further explain it?
3. What is the sin against the Holy Spirit which, Jesus says, can never be forgiven? How does this terrifying assertion square with the general teaching that God will forgive all sins?
4. In what way does Jesus hint at his resurrection in verses 38-40? What warning does he give in verses 43-45?

MATTHEW 13

The great parabolic discourse. The theme of little faith is introduced.

1. Matthew once more quotes Isaiah (6:9-10) at the beginning of the parabolic discourse. What warning is he seeking to convey? cf. 11:16-19, 20-24; 12:7, 14, 24-32, 34, 39, 45.
2. Verses 24-30. What is the teaching of this parable, found only in Matthew? Does it throw any light on life after death?
3. Look up Ezekiel 17:22-24. The people would have known this parable. What similarities are there with that of the mustard seed (verses 31-32) and what differences? What is the teaching Jesus is giving in verses 31-33?
4. Examine verses 51-52 in the light of our knowledge of Old Testament. Can we build on what is old? Or have we neglected the foundations on which Jesus built? What should be done about this?
5. Verses 53-58. Examine your life: are there graces that you have missed because of unbelief?

MATTHEW 14

'he death of John the Baptist; the feeding of the five thousand; Jesus' walking on the sea; 'eter's 'little faith'.

. What is the difference between the Baptist's faithfulness and Herod's keeping his promise?

'. Compare verses 13-21 with 2 Kings 4:42-44. Did Jesus make a further point than that indicated in 2 Kings 4:44? What was it?

'. Verses 22-33. This is the first of three episodes, unique to Matthew, that concern Peter. How is he characterised? See verse 31 and cf. 16:8.

MATTHEW 15

Another conflict story; a Gentile woman's faith; the feeding of the Gentile four thousand.

1. Verses 1-20. How does Jesus use scripture to deepen the understanding of his hearers of the real dimensions of the moral law? Has the Church ever been guilty of placing her own tradition above the word of God (verse 6)? Give examples.
2. How are the unbelief of Israel (chapters 11,12 and 13:58), the little faith of the disciples (14:31 and 16:8) contrasted with the faith of a Gentile in this chapter?
3. Compare verses 32-39 with 14:13-21. What are a) the similarities and b) the differences? Why do you think Matthew included both accounts?

MATTHEW 16

Further conflict with the Pharisees and Sadducees; Peter at Caesarea Philippi; Jesus foretells his passion.

1. Jesus compares the teaching of the pharisees and sadducees to leaven which, while fermenting dough, can also make it go bad. Can you think of any false doctrines or attitudes, current today, that we should be on our guard against?
2. Verses 13-23. This is the second of the episodes concerning Peter. On verse 18 the Catholic Church has largely based the claims of Peter's successors to the primacy and supremacy of the see of Rome. a) How are we to understand what is said of Peter and of the Church in verses 17-19 and b) do you think the Church should take more seriously the rebuke to Peter in verse 23?
3. Compare the "must" of verse 21 with verses 24-25. Have we really glimpsed the cost of discipleship? Examine the consequences for your own life.

MATTHEW 17

The story of the transfiguration; the healing of the epileptic boy; the Temple poll tax.

1. In the story of the transfiguration why were Moses and Elijah also present? What is the significance of the bright cloud? cf. Exodus 13:22, 19:16, 34:29.
2. What does Jesus say about faith in prayer in this chapter?
3. Verses 24-27. This is the third episode concerning Peter that is found only in Matthew. What is its significance?

MATTHEW 18

This is the fourth discourse - on the Church.

1. List the kind of people who belong to the Kingdom. What qualities must they have?
2. Notice the context of the parable of the lost sheep, and compare with Luke 15.
3. What teaching is contained in this discourse a) on fellowship and b) on forgiveness?

MATTHEW 19

Jesus' Galilean ministry is now ended, and he begins to teach in Judea.

1. Compare Matthew's account of Jesus' teaching on divorce (verses 3-12) with that in Mark 10:1-12 What differences or modifications do you find? Do verses 11-12 refer to celibacy or to marriage?
2. Consider Jesus' teaching on riches and possessions. Why does he see them as a burden and an obstacle rather than a reward?
3. In what sense will the apostles be heirs to the patriarchs (verse 28)? and cf. Daniel 7:22. What is Jesus seeking to convey in verses 28-29?

MATTHEW 20

The parable of the labourers in the vineyard is unique to Matthew.

1. Verses 1-16. What is your instinctive response to this parable? What is its meaning a) for the Jews of Jesus' own time, b) for the Church today?
2. What is meant by 'the cup that I am to drink' (verse 22)? cf. Isaiah 51:17.

MATTHEW 21

21:1 - 22:10 represent Christ's final warning to Israel.

1. Look up Isaiah 62:11 and Zechariah 9:9-10. What is Jesus teaching by his acted parable?
2. What was Jesus condemning in his cleansing of the Temple and his cursing of the barren fig tree? If he came to our church would he find things to condemn? What should be our response?
3. What is the teaching a) for the Jews of Jesus' time and b) for us, of the two parables (verses 28-32 and 33-40)?

MATTHEW 22

In verses 1-14 Matthew has combined two parables. cf. Luke 14:16-24.

1. In verses 1-14 what are we taught about the pattern of Jesus' ministry? Who were the original invited guests? Who replaces them? What is the significance of the wedding garment? cf. Zechariah 3:1-5.
2. Look up Deuteronomy 25:5-10 and Ruth 4 for the background to the sadducees' question to Jesus (verses 25-33). Were they sincere in their question?

MATTHEW 23

The sevenfold indictment of the scribes and pharisees is addressed to the crowds and to the disciples. From now on, Jesus' warnings are largely addressed to his disciples.

1. Verses 1-12. How far can these verses be said to apply to the Church? What are a) the duties of all members, and b) the dangers to those in authority?
2. Gather the parts of the indictment (verses 13-36) that apply to those in authority in the Church today. Consider especially verses 13,23-24,28,29-30. Where is my place in all this?
3. Compare verses 37-39 with Jeremiah 7. Why was judgement on Jerusalem inevitable? Are there any signs of God's judgment on the contemporary Church? Am I doing anything about it?

MATTHEW 24

The apocalyptic or eschatological discourse.

1. What are the signs of the beginning 'of the birth-pangs'? Do they occur in every age or are they special to the last days?

[illegible]. In verse 15 Jesus refers back to the prophecy of Daniel (9:27; 11:31) which in its turn referred to the statue of Zeus set up in Jerusalem by Antiochus IV Epiphanes (1 Maccabees 1:54). What abominations have occurred in our century?

3. What are the signs of Christ's second coming? Compare Zechariah 12:10-12 and Daniel 7:13-14. How would the disciples have interpreted these prophecies? Does the resurrection of Christ in any way change our perspective?

4. What is the warning contained in the reference to the Flood? See Genesis 7:11-23. What is Jesus saying to US in this chapter?

MATTHEW 25

To understand the parable of the ten virgins it is necessary to remember the marriage customs of Jesus' time. The bride processed from her home to the home of the bridegroom, and this solemn taking of the bride from her father's house to his own by the bridegroom was the symbolic act of marriage. The bride's female attendants seem to have gone to meet the bridegroom and his party to accompany them to the house of the bride. These ceremonies were held at night, so torches and lamps were needed. The closing and barring of the house (cf.Luke 11:7) was not a simple task, and the door was only reopened in case of emergency. Those late could not expect to be admitted.

1. Verses 1-13. What is the point of this parable? Compare Matthew 7:21-23. In what did the foolish virgins fail?
2. Verses 14-30. What talents have you? Do you use them fully in God's service?
3. Verses 31-46. Does this parable mean that we shall be judged according to our works? cf. 10:32-33. What could feeding the hungry, etc. also mean?

MATTHEW 26-27

The Passion Narrative now begins, largely based on Mark, with some typical Matthean additions.

MATTHEW 26

Jesus at Bethany; the preparations for the Supper; the Last Supper; the agony in the garden; Jesus' arrest; Peter's denial; the trial before Caiaphas.

1. What is the significance of the action of the unknown woman in anointing Jesus' *HEAD*? cf. Leviticus 8:12; 1 Kings 1:39 and Psalm 133:2. To what central act of Jesus did it point? See verse 12.
2. Follow Judas' activities as described by Matthew. cf. 26:14-16, 20-25, 47-50; 27:3-5. Does he give any explanation of Judas' conduct?
3. At the Last Supper what does Jesus' reference to the covenant (verse 28) mean? What is the connection with Exodus 24:6-8 and with Jeremiah 31:31-34? How are our sins forgiven through the shedding of Jesus' blood?
4. Consider the use of the Old Testament in this chapter. cf. verse 23 with Psalm 41:9; verse 15 with Zechariah 11:12; verse 31 with Zechariah 13:7; verse 39 with Isaiah 51:17; verse 56 with Isaiah 53; verse 64 with Daniel 7:13.

MATTHEW 27

The trial before Pilate; the death of Judas; Jesus' scourging, crucifixion and death.

1. Consider the intervention of strangers to Jesus in this chapter (Pilate, his wife, Simon of Cyrene). How do they compare a) with the Jewish authorities and b) with the apostles?
2. What is the significance of the part played by the disciples mentioned in verses 55-61?

3. Read Psalm 22 and compare it with this chapter. What direct or indirect references does Matthew make to this psalm?
4. What is the significance of verses 51-53?

MATTHEW 28

Jesus' resurrection. He appears first to the women disciples, (attested in all four gospels) and to the eleven apostles.

1. What was the response of Jesus' disciples to the resurrection? Note verses 8,10,17. What was the response of his enemies? See verses 27:63-66; 28:11-15.
2. What authority has Jesus given to his church? On what is this authority based? What impression has Matthew sought to give of the kind of people to whom this power was entrusted? How should we therefore see the Church of our own day?

AN INTRODUCTION TO THE GOSPEL OF MARK

If we can imagine ourselves about the year AD 65, aware that the generation of those who knew Jesus in the flesh was dying out, how would we set about gathering materials to write about what we now call a gospel? There seem to have been very early attempts to list Jesus' sayings, and there must have been preserved in the Church at least in Palestine a collection of them. They were not, however, known by Paul. There would be anecdotes perhaps attached to the sayings, there would be memories of Jesus' parables particularly among those who had first heard them or who were using them in sermons, and there would, of course, be the stories of those who had been cured, or whose parents or relatives had been cured. It is also fairly certain that a narrative of the Passion was already put together at that date in Jerusalem, and, perhaps, connected with the places where Jesus had suffered.

Who was Mark? Tradition believes he was John Mark (Acts 12:12, etc.) whose mother owned the house where the last supper was held, and which was certainly used as a gathering place for the first Christians, and who was the cousin or nephew of Barnabas. It is possible that he was the young man of Mark 14:51-52, and the companion of Paul (Philemon 24) and of Peter (1 Peter 5:13). He is traditionally believed to have used Peter's reminiscences in writing his gospel.

It was probably written before the fall of Jerusalem, around the time of Peter's death (AD 64) in Rome. It is in Greek, less polished than Matthew's or Luke's and, while in many ways the simplest of the four gospels (as it is certainly the shortest) it contains many vivid details that seem to point to an eye witness account.

In this study we have concentrated on the narrative sections, often the most detailed of all the synoptics.

MARK 1

Mark, without preliminaries, launches straight into the story received from tradition - the ministry of the Baptist, the baptism of Jesus, his mission, his earliest disciples, and his first miracles.

1. Compare Mark's short preface (verse 1) with Matthew 1, Luke 1-2 and John 1. Is his a summary of theirs, or does he go further?
2. How does Mark describe John's baptism (verse 4)? Compare verse 8 and cf. Acts 19:1-6.
3. Verses 12-13. Mark's account of Jesus in the wilderness is quite distinct from Matthew's or Luke's. What is the significance of the beasts and of the angels? cf. Isaiah 11:1-9.
4. How does Jesus begin his ministry? Notice the frequency of the word 'immediately' and the verbs like 'rebuked' (verse 25), 'took her by the hand and lifted her up' (verse 31), 'healed' and 'cast out' (verse 34). What impression does this give us of Jesus?
5. What accounts for a) the reaction of the possessed man and b) the faith of the leper?

MARK 2

A series of conflict stories - involving the Jewish leaders.

1. What aspects of Jesus' behaviour at once caused conflict with the authorities? (See verses 9,11,15,17,28). What did he seek to bring out?
2. Who were those attracted to Jesus? (See also chapter 1). What led them to him?

MARK 3

The fourth conflict story is followed by a section concentrating on the training of the twelve apostles; the final conflict story concerns Jesus' family.

1. Pick out the strong expressions of feeling in this chapter (eg. verses 5,21,28-30). Is it just Mark's style (or perhaps Peter's), or do you think it tells us something about Jesus himself?
2. What evidence is there in this chapter that Jesus' family were not in sympathy with him at this stage? See also 6:1-6 and John 7:5. What significance does this have?

MARK 4

Mark's version of the parabolic discourse; the calming of the storm.

1. What does the parable of the sower teach concerning the different responses to Jesus' teaching, and the different types of listener? Can we find ourselves in this parable?
2. Verses 26-29 are peculiar to Mark. What is its meaning? How can we emulate the patience of the farmer? What is Mark's explanation for Jesus' use of parables (verses 33-34)?
3. Verses 35-42. What is the special significance of this miracle? Why did it impress the disciples more than his healings and exorcisms? What is its significance for us today?

MARK 5

The cure of the demoniac; of the woman with the issue of blood; the raising of Jairus' daughter.

1. Verses 1-20. This disconcerting story appears in all three synoptic gospels. What is its meaning? Should we take it literally, or psychologically, or is there a natural explanation? How do you react to the fate of the pigs?
2. Verses 21-43. What taboos did Jesus challenge in these two episodes? Look up Leviticus 15:19-27 and 21:2-4. What quality did Jairus and the woman have in common? How did this free them to follow Jesus? What are the taboos that bind me?

MARK 6

Jesus' return to Nazareth; the mission of the Twelve; the beheading of John the Baptist; the feeding of the five thousand; Jesus walks on the water.

1. What are the powers bestowed on the apostles? (verses 7,12-13). Contrast Jesus' instructions (verses 8-11) with Matthew 10:7-14. How do you account for the differences? Which of these instructions are for all time?
2. What was the character of Herod? See also Luke 9:7-9; 13:31 and 23:6-12.
3. What do we learn from verses 30-44 a) about openness to the needs of others and b) trust in Providence?
4. How does Mark describe the apostles (verse 52)? What other evidence of incomprehension do you find in this gospel? How far do we see ourselves in this 'mirror'?

MARK 7

Jesus' attack on the legalism of the Pharisees; the healing of the Syro-Phoenician woman's daughter; the cure of a deaf-mute.

1. Verses 1-23. a) What were the faults with which the scribes and pharisees charge Jesus? b) What were the details of his retort (verses 6-13)? c) What is the meaning of the parable (verse 15)? d) What equivalent faults beset the Church today? Are we aware of them?
2. Verses 24-37. Jesus works two miracles in Gentile country. Contrast the attitude of the woman (verses 25 ff.) and of the friends of the deaf mute (verse 32) with that of the religious authorities. What is the significance of this contrast? Can it be paralleled in our experience?

MARK 8

The feeding of the four thousand; the 'leaven of the Pharisees'; the cure of a blind man; Caesarea Philippi; Jesus predicts his passion.

1. List the occasions when the faith of the disciples and of the religious leaders is lacking.
2. Compare the two miracles (7:31-37 and 8:22-26). What can we learn from them about the cost and the patience needed in leading people to the gospel?
3. List the details in Jesus' foretelling of his passion (verse 31). What response is required of a disciple?

MARK 9

The transfiguration of Christ; the cure of the epileptic boy; discourse to the Twelve.

1. Jesus briefly manifests himself as the Messiah. Compare 9:2-8 with Daniel 10:5-10. Note that the same disciples were present at the raising of Jairus' daughter (5:37). On what other occasion were these three witnesses? cf. also Galatians 2:9.
2. Contrast the attitude of the father of the epileptic boy (verses 17-24) with that of the Gentiles in chapter 7. What do we learn however, about progress in faith from this man?
3. Compare Jesus' second prediction of his passion (verse 31) with his first (8:31). What response did it receive from his disciples?
4. Consider Jesus' teaching on discipleship (verse 35-50). Examine ourselves on each point - a) quality of childlike dependence on God, b) openness to outsiders, c) alertness to detect and to avoid occasions of sin, d) fervour and zeal.

MARK 10

Jesus' teaching on divorce, children, the danger of riches. The disciples' petition; the cure of Bartimaeus.

1. How is the teaching of 9:36 reinforced in verses 13-16?
2. What do we learn in these chapters of the impact Jesus had on his followers? See especially 9:3, 10:24,26,32,41. Is Peter speaking here?
3. Compare Jesus' third prediction of his passion with 8:31 and 9:31. What further details does he add?
4. Verses 35-45. Matthew 20:20-23 says the sons of Zebedee made this request through their mother. Which do you think is the more likely account, Matthew's or Mark's? Why?
5. What were the steps Bartimaeus took to regain his sight? What can we learn from him?

MARK 11

Holy Week begins: Palm Sunday; the cleansing of the Temple (Monday); the fig tree and Jesus' challenge to the Jewish leaders (Tuesday).

1. What is the meaning of the cry of the crowds (verses 9-10)? What did it mean a) to them, b) to us?
2. In what way does the fig tree signify the Jewish nation (verses 12-14, 20-21)? Could it also signify a given generation of Christians? What is the teaching concerning prayer? cf. Verses 15-19 and 22-25.
3. Can we, do we put God to the test? Consider verses 27-33.

MARK 12

Parable of the vineyard; paying taxes to Caesar; the greatest commandment; the widow's mite. (All these conflict stories are artificially within Tuesday).

1. Notice the gradually increasing ferocity of the tenants to the servants (verses 3,4,5,8). What does this warn us about allowing evil habits to take hold of us? What was the reaction of Jesus' hearers to the parable? What does it tell us of them?

2. What principle is contained in verse 17? Is it of universal application?
3. Do we learn anything of the afterlife in Jesus' teaching (verses 24-27)?
4. Compare verses 38-40 with verses 41-44. What is the evangelist teaching by the insertion of this saying at this point? and cf. Matthew 23:5-7.

MARK 13

In Mark's version of this discourse the prophecy is concerned only with the destruction of Jerusalem. (See verse 4 and cf. Matthew 24:3).

1. What spiritual dangers does Christ warn his disciples about (verses 5-8)? At times of crisis what kind of things lead me astray? What kind of 'wars' take place within me?
2. What advice does Jesus give about giving testimony or speaking in dangerous situations? Do we worry unnecessarily, or do we pray and 'say whatever is given in that hour'?
3. Jesus mentions the fig tree again (verse 28) and warns his disciples of the coming crisis. What warning is contained for us in verses 28-37?

MARK 14

The anointing at Bethany; Judas betrays Jesus (Wednesday); the Last Supper; the agony in the garden; Jesus' arrest; Jesus' trial before Caiaphas; Peter's denial (Thursday).

1. Verses 1-11. Consider the contrast between the action of the woman, anointing Jesus, and Judas selling him. How does this demonstrate the truth of Luke 2:35 and of Mark 13:12? What were the motives behind these different actions?
2. At the Passover meal, the head of the family says ' This is the bread of affliction which our fathers ate in the land of affliction'. What dimension did Jesus add when he said 'This is my body'?
3. Note the reactions of the disciples in this chapter. See verses 4-5,10,19,29-31,40,50. Has Mark in any way prepared us for their collapse?
4. What do we learn of Jesus' feelings? See verses 6,18,21,25,27-32,33-42.
5. Trace the accusation concerning the Temple that was made at Jesus' trial. See verses 57-58, 13:2, John 2:19, Acts 6:14. What had Jesus said?
6. Did Jesus state that he was the Messiah? What does the action of the high priest (verse 63) and his accusation (verse 64) lead us to think?
7. Compare Peter's conduct with that of Judas. Why was one eventually saved and not, apparently (verse 21) the other?

MARK 15

The events of Good Friday: Jesus before Pilate, his scourging, crowning with thorns, crucifixion, death and burial.

1. What were the mistakes made by Pilate? What do they tell us about him? Are we ever guilty of the same kind of actions?
2. Consider the silence of Jesus throughout these scenes, especially verses 5,16-20, 29-32. Was it the silence of meekness, of depression, of acceptance?
3. What do we learn about the women listed in verses 40-41? For Mary the mother of James and of Joseph cf. 6:3. Why are their names given and their presence noted at this juncture?
4. Why was Pilate surprised that Jesus was already dead (verse 44)? What does this indicate about Jesus?

MARK 16

Verses 9-20 (longer ending) were not written by Mark, but are accepted as inspired scripture. The resurrection narrative is cut short in Mark at verse 8.

1. What did the women see? Who spoke to them? Why were they so afraid?
2. Compare the list of apparitions in verses 9-14 with those recounted in the other gospels and in 1 Corinthians 15:5-7. How do you account for discrepancies?
3. What feature of the response of the disciples to Jesus' resurrection does the writer emphasise? See verses 8,10-11,13,14. Do we ever merit to be 'upbraided for our unbelief and hardness of heart'?
4. If we truly believe what is recorded at verse 19, do we accept the challenge of verses 15 and 20? Do we believe that we have the powers described in verses 17-18?

AN INTRODUCTION
TO
THE GOSPEL OF LUKE

If one could imagine the Bible without St Luke's gospel, one would realise how very much the Christian world owes him. No shepherds, no manger, no crib, none of the Christmas story except the Wise Men - in fact none of the 'Joyful Mysteries of the Rosary'! We would know very little of Mary (she is silent in Matthew's and Mark's gospels, and utters one sentence in John's), no Good Samaritan, no Prodigal Son or Repentant Thief - no Magnificat, no Benedictus or Nunc Dimittis.

Tradition is unanimous in ascribing the Third Gospel to Luke, who is mentioned three times in Paul's letters. He is described in Colossians 4:14 as 'the beloved physician'; he is listed with Mark in Philemon 24; and in 2 Timothy 4:11, the aging Paul writes most poignantly 'Luke alone is with me'. He is in each case mentioned as being beside the imprisoned Paul. The gospel is stamped with his own personality, his sensitivity, his gift for narrative, his concern for the poor, his interest in women, in non-Jews (he was a Gentile convert himself), his respect for the apostles - he often omits unflattering comments on their obtuseness found in Mark.

His Greek is excellent, though his respect for his sources means that he incorporates some of their Aramaic flavour. The date of his gospel is perhaps AD 80 or a little after.

In studying this gospel we have concentrated our attention on the sections peculiar to Luke, or, where one can compare his version with Mark's, on his particular rendering or emphasis.

LUKE 1

Luke's infancy narrative is different from Matthew's, though also telling of the virgin birth of Jesus. Prologue; annunciation to Zechariah; annunciation to Mary; visit of Mary to Elizabeth; birth of John the Baptist.

1. What credentials does Luke present for writing his gospel? What kind of witnesses does he assemble in verses 1-4? Who was Luke? Look up Colossians 4:10-14 2 Timothy 4:11.
2. Compare verses 5-23 with Daniel 9:20-27. Draw out the similarities of time and place and message. In what ways are the two passages both 'good news'? In what essentials do they differ?
3. What was the mission assigned to John the Baptist?
4. Compare Zechariah's and Mary's response a) to the angel and b) to his message.
5. Draw out all that Gabriel tells Mary about her son (verses 31-33). What Old Testament influences lie behind Luke's account?
6. What is the virtue Elizabeth praises in Mary? cf. also verse 38.
7. Compare the Song of Mary (verses 46-55) with the Song of Zechariah (verses 68-79). What do we learn a) about the character of God and b) of the promises made to Israel?

LUKE 2

Birth of Christ; presentation of Jesus in the Temple; Jesus in the Temple as a boy.

1. What is the most significant aspect of the circumstances surrounding Jesus' birth and his first worshippers that is brought out by Luke? Contrast Matthew 2.
2. Note carefully verses 19 and 51. Why do you think these verses are there? What do they indicate about Luke's sources for this chapter?
3. In what ways does Luke emphasise that Jesus was a Jew?

4. Draw out all the references to the Holy Spirit in these chapters. To what especially does Luke attribute his influence?
5. Look carefully at verses 25 and 38. What would Simeon and Anna have understood by the 'consolation of Israel' and the 'redemption of Jerusalem'? In what way is Mary implicated? (verses 34-35).
6. Between verses 40 and 52 there is one incident, the only recorded event in Jesus' childhood. How does it illustrate these two statements? In what way is it somewhat disconcerting? What did it mean for Luke?

LUKE 3

The teaching of John the Baptist; Jesus' baptism; genealogy of Christ the son of Adam.

1. Consider carefully John the Baptist's sermon (verses 7-17). Note its connection with verse 6. Salvation is open to all. How should we apply John's teaching to our own lives? See the consequences of John's honesty and fearlessness (verses 18-20).
2. How does Luke describe Jesus' baptism? What significant detail does he add to Mark 1:9-11?
3. Luke's genealogy is very different from Matthew's. Compare the two (cf. Matthew 1:1-17). What is the reason for the apparent discrepancies, bearing in mind that all biblical genealogies have a theological rather than a historical purpose?

LUKE 4

The temptation of Jesus in the wilderness; his rejection at Nazareth. Early miracles taken from Mark; exorcisms and healings.

1. Verses 1-13. Consider in each case Jesus' response to the temptations. What does this teach us about the use of scripture in our lives? Do WE search the Bible for guidance in times of crisis or temptation?
2. Compare verse 3 with John 6:26-34; verses 5-7 with John 6:15 and verse 9 with John 7:1-4. What does this comparison teach us about a) the humanity of Jesus and b) the real meaning of Luke 4:1-13?
3. Verses 16-30. Look up the scripture texts that Jesus used in the synagogue: Isaiah 61:1-2; 1 Kings 17:1-16, 18:1; 2 Kings 5:1-14. What was the response of his audience a) initially, b) as his intentions became clearer, c) at the climax? What affected them particularly?
4. Verses 31-44. Luke takes a section from Mark (1:21-39). In what ways does he modify it?

LUKE 5

The call of Simon; cure of a leper and of a paralytic; call of Levi.

1. Verses 1-11. Trace the development of Simon's response to Jesus.
2. Jesus sees into the hearts of his listeners and answers their unspoken questions (verse 22 and cf. 4:23 and 6:8). He finds unbelief in their hearts. What does he find in mine?
3. Compare verses 34-39 with Mark 2:18-22. What significant addition does Luke make? Is the remark often true of human nature?

LUKE 6

Two conflict stories from Mark; the selection of the twelve apostles; the sermon on the plain.

1. Trace the growth of opposition to Jesus from the religious leaders thus far. Do we ever allow ourselves to grow in hardness of heart? In what areas?
2. How did Jesus prepare for his selection of apostles? Why did he choose twelve?
3. Compare the four beatitudes (verses 20-23) with the four woes (verses 24-26). When and in what form will the reverse come? cf. 16:25.

4. What is the character of God our father as described by Jesus? What is the character of the true disciple?
5. Consider verse 45. Is there 'good treasure' in my heart? If not, how can I be healed? See verses 46-48.

LUKE 7

The healing of the centurion's servant; the raising of the young man of Nain; Jesus and the Baptist; the sinful woman.

1. Notice the stages by which the centurion approached Jesus: elders (verse 3), friends (verse 6). Are we justified in seeking the prayers of the saints and of our friends when we approach God?
2. Find miracles in Luke's gospel to match each of those listed by Jesus in verse 22. What was the doubt in John the Baptist's mind? cf. 3:16,17.
3. Note verse 29. How does it prepare the way for the incident in verses 36-50?
4. Contrast the interior attitude of the woman with that of the pharisee. How do they illustrate Jesus' parable in 6:45? Are we ever guilty of behaving like the pharisee?

LUKE 8

After a long section of material from an independent source, Luke now takes up Mark's narrative once more, with the parable of the sower; the storm on the lake; the cure of the demoniac; the healing of the woman with an issue of blood; the raising of Jairus' daughter.

1. Luke gives an insight into the financing of Jesus' mission (verses 2-3). cf. 1 Corinthians 9:4-5. What else do we know of the ministry of the women disciples?
2. Verses 19-21. What interpretation does Luke put on this episode? cf. Mark 3:31-35.
3. Verses 26-39. Compare Mark 5:1-20. By what touches does Luke soften the story and make it clear that the man became a disciple?
4. What do the stories of verses 41-56 tell us of the growth of faith and of its importance? How can our faith be increased?

LUKE 9

Luke's independent account of the feeding of the five thousand is followed by a long section taken once more from Mark, but with the material in Mark 6:45 - 8:26 omitted. Luke takes up the Marcan narrative with the events at Caesarea Philippi; the Transfiguration; the cure of the epileptic boy.

1. Luke knows more of Herod Antipas than do the other evangelists. cf. 8:3; 23:6-12; Acts 13:1. What do we learn of Herod in this chapter? Is it in character with the other synoptics?
2. What does the story of the multiplication of the loaves convey to you? What did it mean a) for the disciples, b) for the crowds? What truth was Luke emphasising? cf. verses 11,16.
3. Verses 18-27. Trace the connection between the three sections; 18-20, 21-22, 23-27. What do we learn of the meaning of the gospel and of true discipleship?
4. Verses 28-36. Matthew sees the Transfiguration as the manifestation of a new and greater Moses, Mark as the revelation of the Messiah as the crown of the Law and Prophets. What is it for Luke? See especially verses 28-29,31. Note from whose point of view it is described. cf. verse 32 with 22:45.
5. Verses 37-48. What points are underlined by Luke in this section? See verses 43b-45.
6. Verses 49-62. What characteristics of James and John do we find in this section? How would you characterise the three would-be disciples? Contrast Jesus' own attitude (verse 51).

LUKE 10

Here begins (from 9:51) a long section which is largely peculiar to Luke. It is in the form of a travel narrative and runs to 19:44. Mission of the seventy; the greatest commandment; the parable of the good Samaritan; Martha and Mary.

1. Luke gives two mission discourses, one to the twelve (9:1-5) and one to the seventy (10:1-12). Compare and contrast the two. What report did the seventy make?
2. Verses 21-24. What caused this outburst of joy on the part of Jesus? What do these verses reveal to us of Jesus' life with the Father? and cf. 9:28-36.
3. How does the parable of the good Samaritan illustrate Jesus' discussion with the lawyer (verse 25)? How do the details in the parable (verses 31-32,34,35) help us to understand God's law of love?
4. Verses 38-42. Read this story as a parable of discipleship. How do the two sisters complement each other? cf. verses 40 and 39. Jesus commends Mary, but what is the place of service in the Church?

LUKE 11

The Lord's Prayer; the sign of Jonah; woe to the Pharisees and Lawyers.

1. Verses 1-13. How does Luke emphasise one clause of the Our Father? cf. Matthew 6: 14,15. Compare Matthew 7:7-11 with Luke 11:9-13. In what significant detail do they differ?
2. Compare the attitudes of Jesus' audience: see verses 14-16, 27,29. How does Jesus react to them? What are the equivalent attitudes today?
3. Verses 33-36. Compare these verses with Proverbs 13:9; 20:27; and Psalm 119:105. What is the teaching in each one? How does one idea lead to another through the associations of a lamp?
4. Verses 37-54. Make a list of the faults of which Jesus accuses a) the pharisees and b) the lawyers. How are his accusations confirmed in verses 53-54? Has the modern Church anything to examine itself over in the light of Jesus' words? What is the impression we have of Jesus?

LUKE 12

Parable of the rich fool; necessity of being on the watch; the faithful servants.

1. Verses 1-12. What qualities do we need before we can attain this openness and fearlessness? What, basically, hinders us?
2. Verses 13-21. Compare this passage with Sirach 11:14-20. What are a) the similarities and b) the differences in the moral of each?
3. Verses 22-34. What programme for our lives is contained in these verses? Do we take them seriously? Do we at least tithe our income?
4. Verses 35-48. What warning is contained a) for the disciples and b) for Peter and the other apostles (therefore for Church authorities)?
5. Verses 49-59. What is meant by the fire of verse 49? Compare verse 50 with verses 51 and 53. Can division and dissension ever be purifying? Apply this to our own situation.

LUKE 13

The parable of the barren fig tree; the healing of the infirm woman; the narrow door; lament for Jerusalem.

1. What is the connection between sin and calamity? See verses 1-5 and John 9:3. What advance does Jesus' teaching show on Old Testament? What connection is there between verses 1-5 and the parable in verses 6-9?
2. Verses 10-17. What is wrong with the attitude of the ruler of the synagogue? Note the reaction of the crowd (verse 17). What situation does the woman's condition symbolise?

3. Verses 23-30. What warning is contained in these verses a) to the Jews of Jesus' time, b) to members of the Church today? cf. Matthew 7:13-14, 21-23.
4. Verses 31-35. What do we learn of Jesus' own feelings in this passage?

LUKE 14

Healing on the sabbath; parables of the supper and of the tower.

1. Verses 7-11. Compare this parable with Proverbs 25:6-7. What moral does Jesus draw?
2. Verses 12-24. What were the categories of people invited to the banquet? How does Jesus' gospel fulfil the prophets? cf. Zephaniah 3:19; Isaiah 35:5-6.
3. Jesus' teaching is stern (verse 26). What does he say about forethought? Are we inclined to take on more than we are prepared to see through? What is the remedy for the disciple who has lost fervour (verses 34-35)?

LUKE 15

Parables of the lost sheep, the lost groat and of the prodigal son.

1. What do these three parables have in common? Note the similar structure of the first two. What do we learn about God from them all?
2. Consider the characters of the younger son (verses 13,15-18), of the father (verses 20,22-24,28b-32), of the elder son (verses 25-30). With which do you have the most sympathy? Why?

LUKE 16

Parable of the unjust steward, and of the rich man and Lazarus.

1. Verses 1-9. What are your feelings on reading and considering this parable? Does it seem baffling? What kind of man is the steward? How would you characterise him? Why does Jesus call him 'shrewd' (verse 8)? Is this praise? If so, in what sense? In your view, does the outlook of the Book of Proverbs throw any light on the understanding of this parable?
2. What is the meaning of verses 8-9? Do you agree with verse 8b?
3. Luke probably added verses 10-13 to the parable because they refer to money. What , in fact, is their teaching?
4. Verses 19-31. For what was the rich man punished? Can we apply this parable to our own life situation? Is there any hope for the rich man? cf. verses 29 and 18:27. What kind of man is revealed in verses 20 and 24? What does he think of Lazarus?

LUKE 17

Teaching on the kingdom; cure of the ten lepers; the days of the Son of man.

1. Verses 1-10. What advice is given to the disciples in these verses? Which do we need especially at this time?
2. Verses 11-19. This is the only occasion when Jesus comments on ingratitude. What other aspects are emphasised? cf. 10:19 and 33.
3. Verses 20-37. How is the teaching of verses 22-37 summed up in verses 20-21? In what sense is the kingdom of God always in the midst of us? In what sense has it not yet arrived? What should we learn from the contemporaries of Noah and Lot?

LUKE 18

The parables of the unjust judge, and of the pharisee and of the publican. The rich young man; the healing of a blind man.

1. How does the parable of verses 2-8 illustrate verse 1; and that of verses 10-14 illustrate verse 9? Learn verses 7-8 by heart and draw courage from them in times of trial.
2. Notice that the pharisee is not actually praying (verse 11). Are we ever tempted to remain locked up in ourselves when ostensibly at prayer? Into what trap did the pharisee fall (verse 12)? In what consists the prayer of the tax collector?
3. Luke now uses Mark for the first time since 9:50 (verses 15 ff.). What small changes does he make? cf. Mark 10:13-34. Which bears the mark of an eye witness?

LUKE 19

Zaccheus; the parable of the pounds; Palm Sunday; the cleansing of the Temple.

1. Compare and contrast the two men at 18:35 and at 19:2 in their circumstances, their need, their attitude to Jesus and their reward. What have the two in common in their outward situation?
2. Verses 11-27. Compare and contrast this parable with that of the talents (Matthew 25:14-30). What is the significance of Luke's introduction (verse 11)?
3. Verses 28-40. What made the multitude rejoice as Jesus entered Jerusalem? Compare verse 38 with 2:13-14. Why does Luke remind us of the Nativity at this juncture?
4. Verses 41-48. What is Jesus foretelling for Jerusalem? What was the 'visitation' they did not recognise? cf. verses 47-48 and 6:11; 11:15, 53-54.

LUKE 20

Conflict with the Temple authorities: parable of the vineyard; tribute to Caesar; the resurrection query.

1. How does Luke record the increasing opposition to Jesus from the authorities?
2. How would you characterise Jesus' attitude to his enemies in this chapter?

LUKE 21

The widow's mite; the apocalyptic discourse.

1. Compare verse 15 with Mark 13:11 and Matthew 10:20. What is the significance of Jesus being assigned by Luke the role which the other evangelists give to the Holy Spirit?
2. Does Jesus give any reason for the coming destruction of Jerusalem? cf. verse 23-24.
3. With what spirit should Christians look forward to the second coming of Christ? See verses 26-28 and 34-36. Examine your attitude in the light of these verses.

LUKE 22

Luke's Passion Narrative shows many divergences from Mark's, and in some ways anticipates John's.

1. Verses 14-20. Luke, more clearly than Matthew or Mark, shows the development from Passover meal to institution of the Eucharist, cf. verses 15 and 19 (contrast 'eat this passover before I suffer' with 'This is my body'...); and verses 17-18 and verse 20. Study if you can the structure of the Jewish seder, which helps considerably to clarify this.
2. What final instructions does Jesus give his followers in verses 24-38? What had he to say especially to Peter, and through him, to the Church? How does he warn them all of his impending death? See verse 37.

3. Luke's account of the agony in the garden adds two very significant details, the sweat of blood and the appearance of the angel. What do they tell us about the humanness of Christ? Compare Mark 14:33-34. Why did Jesus shrink from the cross?
4. Trace the course of Peter's fall from verses 31-62. What caused his repentance? What warning for Church leaders is contained in this story?
5. What differences are there between Mark's account of Jesus' trial before the Sanhedrin (Mark 14:53-64) and Luke's (22:66-71)?

LUKE 23

Jesus' trials before Pilate and Herod; the way of the cross; the crucifixion, death and burial of Jesus.

1. Verses 1-5. What three accusations do the Jews make against Jesus? What basis did they have in the facts given by the evangelists? What leads Pilate to consider him innocent?
2. Verses 6-12. Only Luke gives this account. What does it tell us a) of Herod's deterioration since we last encountered him, b) of Jesus?
3. Consider Jesus' words on the way to Calvary and on the cross, as recorded by Luke. In what ways do they soften and humanise the picture given in Mark? What do they further teach us about Jesus?
4. Notice how Luke emphasises the witness of Joseph of Arimathea (verses 50-53) and of the women disciples (verses 49,55-56). How do these compare with the apostles?

LUKE 24

The resurrection narrative; the disciples on the way to Emmaus; the risen Christ appears to his disciples; the ascension of Jesus.

1. Luke collects several virtually unknown people as witnesses (cf. 23:49; 24:10,13). What is the importance of these testimonies?
2. Verses 13-35. Imagine the feelings of the two disciples as they walked to Emmaus. Trace the gradual change from verses 14-15, 16,21 through to 27,29,31-32. What is meant by the reference to the fulfilment of scripture?
3. Compare verse 30 with 9:16 and 22:19. What is Luke telling us? cf. verse 35.
4. What were the feelings of the apostles when Jesus appeared? Had they had any preparation? (verse 34). Yet what was their reaction? How did Jesus convince them? What was the commission Jesus gave them?
5. Note especially verses 48-49. Why were the disciples not yet ready to go forth and preach the gospel? Compare verses 50-51 with Sirach 50:20. Why did Luke end his gospel in Jerusalem? (See Matthew 28 and John 21).

AN INTRODUCTION
TO
THE GOSPEL OF JOHN

The fourth gospel is probably the most profound and the most beloved book in the whole Bible. It has provoked more study than any other, and yields its mysteries only to those who approach it in prayer and in reverence. Who was the author? Was he the disciple whom Jesus loved, and was that disciple John the son of Zebedee? Are the discourses of Jesus an authentic record? What plan does the gospel follow?

The author claims to have been an eye witness of the scene he records (1:14; 19:35) a claim not made by any other evangelist. In 21:24 he asserts his identity with the beloved disciple. He never mentions the son of Zebedee by name, and only, in fact refers to him once as such (21:2), and he calls the Baptist simply **John**. He concentrates most of his account on Jesus' ministry in Judea, barely mentioned in the synoptics, and most of his gospel, with some significant exceptions, uses material that is not in Matthew, Mark or Luke, though there are some interesting signs that he and Luke used a common source on some occasions, especially for the Passion Narrative eg. Luke has a rudimentary discourse at the Last Supper, Luke mentions Peter's visit to the tomb etc. Could a fisherman of Galilee have written this amazing work, revealing himself as one of the most profound theologians of all time?

Stranger things have happened. One thinks of the writings of illiterate or semi-illiterate women like Catherine of Sienna, Julian of Norwich or Margaret Mary Alacoque. The John who appears in the synoptics was probably very young (his nickname was 'son of thunder'!). A life-time of meditation on the mystery of Christ can be supposed, as the gospel as we have it probably dates from the end of the first century. We know that it contains many topographical details that point to a Palestinian and to a pre-AD 70 origin. With Paul, the author of the Fourth Gospel, whoever he was, ranks as one of the greatest, if not the greatest of the seminal theologians of Christianity.

Some scholars can discover evidence that there was originally a 'signs Source' - (2:11; 4:54); others note the reference to Jewish festivals - Passover (three times), Tabernacles, Dedication, possibly Pentecost. There are also signs that the narrative has been carefully constructed to introduce a discourse: chapter 4: the woman of Samaria; 5: the healing of a cripple; 6: the feeding of the five thousand - all followed by important discourses; the link between the story of the man born blind (9) with the blindness of the Jews (8-10), presupposing some dislocation of the text.

The study section will concentrate on the text as we have it, especially noting the resonances from the Old Testament.

JOHN 1

The prologue; the baptism of Jesus; his first disciples.

1. Verses 1-18. Why is Jesus called the Word? cf. Genesis 1:3 ff., Psalm 147:15, 18-19; Isaiah 55:10-11. What is Jesus' relation to God, as explained in this section?
2. Compare all that is said about the Word of God with Old Testament teaching on God's Wisdom cf. Proverbs 8:22-31; Sirach 24:1-22; Wisdom 7:22 - 8:1.
3. What is said of Jesus' relation to mankind? See verses 14-18. Note the use of words like 'grace', 'truth', 'glory', which will be keynotes in John's gospel.

4. Verses 19-28. Note that the question put to John the Baptist (verses 19-21) was, according to Matthew 16:13-15, put to his disciples by Jesus concerning himself. What does John declare of himself and of Jesus?
5. Verses 29-35. John's account of Jesus' baptism is from a different point of view to that of the synoptics What did John learn of Jesus? cf. verses 26-27 with verses 29 ff. What do WE know of Jesus?
6. What is meant by the expression 'Lamb of God' (verses 29,36)?
7. Verses 35-51. What was it that brought each of these disciples to Jesus? What do we learn of each one of them from Jesus' conversations with them? Make a list of the titles they give him. What does this indicate concerning the theological meaning of the text?

JOHN 2

The wedding at Cana; the cleansing of the Temple.

1. Verses 1-12. What part did Jesus' mother play in this incident? Why is she addressed as 'Woman'? cf. 19:26, Genesis 3:15 and Revelations 12:1.
2. In what sense is this miracle a sign? Is there any Eucharistic undertone? cf. Luke 22:17-18. What is the symbolism of a wedding?
3. Verses 13-25. What is symbolised by the cleansing of the Temple? Note John's comment on verse 20 (verses 21-22).
4. What indications are there that the faith of many so-called followers was weak? Is my faith dependent on signs and wonders?

JOHN 3

Discourse to Nicodemus; relations between Jesus' disciples and John's.

1. How far advanced was Nicodemus as a follower of Jesus? What was lacking to him? cf. 7:50.
2. What do you understand by being 'born anew'? cf. verses 5,8. Is it sufficient to have been baptised in infancy, been confirmed? What more is needed?
3. Why was it necessary for the Son of man to be "lifted up"? What does belief in him (verse 15) involve? Learn verse 16 by heart.
4. Verses 17-21. Can there be any salvation for those who have never heard of Jesus? Can they 'meet' him in any other way than through the Church's preaching? What do you think? cf. verses 17 and 21.
5. Verses 22-36. What do we learn of John the Baptist from this passage?
6. What does verse 34 mean? What claims are made for Christ in verses 30-36?

JOHN 4

The Samaritan woman; the healing of the ruler's son.

1. Verses 1-6. Compare Genesis 24:11; 29:2-12; Exodus 2:15-17. What did spring water symbolise in Old Testament?
2. Verses 7-15. What did Jesus mean by 'living water'? What did the woman understand by it?
3. Verses 16-26. What does this scene teach us about Jesus' non-judgmental acceptance of others? cf. also Matthew 9:10 and John 8:1-11. How did Jesus bring the woman to recognise and accept her need of salvation?
4. Verses 27-42. What does this section teach us about the necessity of evangelism?. Who are the 'Samaritans' in our world? Notice the stages of their progress in faith.
5. Verses 43-54. Compare the attitude of the Galileans (verse 45) with the official (verse 46) and with the Samaritans of verse 42. Reflect on the number of times in this chapter that belief is mentioned.

JOHN 5-10

These chapters are all centred round Jewish feasts (cf. 2:13). Chapter 5 is probably Pentecost; chapter 6 is Passover (verse 4); chapters 7-8 are Tabernacles (7:2 and 8:12); chapter 10 is Dedication (verse 22).

JOHN 5

The great conflict with the Jewish leaders now begins. The healing of the man by the pool of Bethsaida; discourse that follows.

1. Verses 1-18. Imagine the isolation and hopelessness of this man. In what way does Jesus challenge him? What charges are the Jews preparing against Jesus? a) Were they true? b) In Jewish terms how serious were they?
2. Verses 19-29. What hints does Jesus give a) of who he is, and b) of his resurrection?
3. Verses 30-47. Look up Sirach 48:1 (cf. verse 35) and Deuteronomy 5:23 (cf. verse 37) and Deuteronomy 31 for the Old Testament background to these verses. What does Jesus mean when he says (verses 39 and 46) that scripture speaks of him?

JOHN 6

As the miracle at Bethsaida in chapter 5 introduced a discourse, so in this chapter does the miracle of the multiplication of the loaves precede an important discourse that reveals the underlying meaning of the miracle.

1. Verses 1-15. Compare the account of this miracle with Mark's. cf. especially verses 2-5 with Mark 6:32-37. What emphasis does John's version put on it? What effect did the miracle have on the people?
2. Verses 25-34. What text does Jesus use? (See verse 31 cf. Exodus 16:4). How does he seek to lead them from the desert miracle to its deeper spiritual meaning?
3. Verses 35-47. Look at Jesus' second text (verse 45 - cf. Isaiah 54:13). How is the bread of the Eucharist our spiritual nourishment in a similar way to the bread of scripture?
4. Verses 48-56. Show how Jesus explores the mystery of the bread more deeply. What is meant by eating his body and drinking his blood?
5. Show how Jesus' hearers gradually moved away from him in their understanding, from verse 28 on. What is the reaction a) of the disciples and b) of the apostles?

JOHN 7

The feast of Tabernacles - Jesus' discourse.

1. What illustrations are found in these verses of the various opinions concerning Jesus? How many were checked by ignorance, prejudice or pride? Are these attitudes all prevalent today?
2. Verses 37-39. The Church's devotion to the Heart of Jesus is nourished by these lines, and by John 19:31-34 and 1 John 5:6 ff. What do they mean? What promise does Jesus make?
3. What action were the authorities taking concerning Jesus? How did they respond to Nicodemus?

JOHN 8

The woman taken in adultery. The feast of Tabernacles' discourse continued.

1. Verses 1-22. This passage is probably not originally part of John's gospel. It may have been introduced as an illustration of 8:15. Picture the scene: Jesus, the crowd, the scribes and pharisees - and the woman. Contrast Jesus' approach to that of the pharisees. Do WE ever fall into their trap? What excuses do we make when we do?

2. Verses 12-20. The scene is the feast of Tabernacles (7:2) when candles were lit in the Temple. Why does Jesus call himself the light of the world? Who were those among his audience who walked in darkness?
3. Verses 21-30. Contrast those who refused to recognise Jesus with those who believed. What warnings does Jesus give?
4. Verses 31-59. Trace the downward path of Jesus' antagonists: from false pride, to refusal to face the truth, to choice of evil, to attempted murder. What, on the contrary, is the path of those who accept Jesus' words and believe in him?

JOHN 9

The healing of the man born blind.

1. What light does Jesus cast on the mystery of innocent suffering? See verses 2-3 and compare and contrast Luke 13:1-5.
2. This miracle is an illustration of two sayings of Jesus, verses 5 and 39. Consider a) the beggar and b) the pharisees with regard to these two verses. What are our areas of spiritual blindness?

JOHN 10

The parables of the good shepherd; the feast of the Dedication discourse.

1. Verses 1-6. In what way does this parable refer to the attitude of the pharisees to the beggar of chapter 9? cf. verses 19-21.
2. Verses 7-10. How can Jesus be the "door of the sheep"? cf. 14:6. What are the privileges and blessings accorded to those who enter by that door? and cf. verses 28-29.
3. Verses 11-18. God himself is the good shepherd cf. Ezekiel 34:12. What does Jesus' claim mean? What references to his saving death do you find in this section?
4. Verses 22-42. What claims does Jesus make here? How do his hearers react?

JOHN 11

The raising of Lazarus.

1. Verses 1-16. Compare verse 4 with 9:3. Why did Jesus delay? Does verse 15 explain why God sometimes delays in answering prayer? What is the meaning of the parable in verses 9-10?
2. Verses 16-27. Compare Martha's profession of faith with Peter's (Matthew 16:16). What can we learn from Martha? Can she, like Peter, be called an apostle?
3. Verses 28-44. The word used in verse 33 translated in RSV as 'deeply moved in spirit' is used in three other places (Mark 1:43 and Matthew 9:30 - 'sternly charged them'; and Mark 14:5 - 'reproached'). Could it imply anger here? If so, in what sense?
4. What is the special significance of this miracle? Compare it with the other resurrection miracles in the synoptics (Mark 5:35-43 and Luke 7:11-17). What differences do you note?
5. Why did Jesus pray aloud before raising Lazarus? Why did he weep when he heard of his death if he knew he was going to raise him?
6. Verses 45-57. What were the varied effects of the miracle? Do we observe this same phenomenon in our times with regard to the Easter story? What enkindles and strengthens my faith?

JOHN 12

The anointing at Bethany; Palm Sunday; John's account of Jesus' agony.

1. Verses 1-11. What significant information does John supply, not given by any of the other evangelists (cf. Matthew 26:6-12; Mark 14:3-8)? What does it suggest about a possible motive for the betrayal of Jesus? Do we sufficiently heed scriptural warnings like Matthew 6:21?
2. Verses 12-19. In what ways does John stress the meaning of this event? See especially verses 16-19.
3. Verses 20-26. In what way did Jesus respond to the Greeks? cf. verse 21 with verses 25 and 26. Are we content just to 'see'? Or are we ready to follow Jesus until or even unto death (verse 24)? What is promised in verse 25?
4. Verses 27-36. John's account of Jesus' agony. What a) similarities and b) differences are there from the synoptic versions (Matthew 26: 38 ff.; Mark 14:33 ff.; Luke 22:40 ff.)? What aspect of Jesus' passion does John emphasise throughout?
5. What appeal does Jesus make to the Jewish nation in verses 31-36? Does this appeal still apply a) to the Church today, b) to the world, c) to me? Note the last sentence of verse 36.
6. Verses 37-50. John summarises the problem of unbelief. What different categories of unbelievers does he distinguish, and what are their motives? cf. verses 42-43. Under what judgment will they fall?
7. How do Jesus' words at verse 46 illustrate John's quotations from Isaiah in verses 38-41? Are WE convicted by these words?

JOHN 13

The washing of the feet of the disciples; the last supper discourse.

1. Verses 1-20. The washing of the feet is only recorded in John, and in his narrative it replaces the institution of the Eucharist. What is its meaning? Consider its use in the Maundy Thursday liturgy. How should it be expressed in the everyday life of the Church?
2. Verses 21-30. What further light does John throw on the causes of Judas' action? cf. 12:4-6.
3. Draw out Peter's various remarks in this chapter. What do we learn about him from them?

JOHN 14

Continuation of the discourse.

1. Verses 1-11. Consider these words as addressed to the Church throughout the ages. In what consists our hope, our security and our safeguard?
2. How is Philip's request for the manifestation of the Father answered? What are we to understand by the 'works' of the Father (verse 10)?
3. Verses 12-24. What do we learn a) of the Holy Spirit and b) of the divine indwelling?
4. Verses 25-31. The Holy Spirit (Advocate or Counsellor) will be the Teacher of the Church. What does this mean for the ongoing life of Christians as a group and as individuals?

JOHN 15

Continuation of the discourse.

1. Compare verse 1-6 with Isaiah 5:1-7 and with Ezekiel 19:10-14. What truths is Jesus conveying when he declares himself to be the true vine? What did the vine symbolise in the prophets?
2. What is the good fruit expected? How is it produced?
3. What is the new commandment that Jesus gives his disciples? See 13:34-35; 15:12-14. How is it new? In what way does Jesus build on Leviticus 19:18?

JOHN 16

Continuation of the discourse.

1. Verses 1-15. Of what sin will the Spirit convict the world? Of what righteousness? Of what judgment?
2. What continuing action will the Spirit have in the Church? Can it be incapsulated in an institution or an office?
3. Verses 16-33. Does 'a little while' refer to the time between Jesus' death and resurrection, or between the Ascension and Pentecost, or both?
4. What do we learn in verses 23-28 about prayer?
5. In what two opposing spheres do we live? See verse 33. What should be our prevailing temper?

JOHN 17

Jesus' priestly prayer of offering and intercession.

1. Verses 1-5. What glimpses do we have here of Jesus' interior life of prayer and intimacy with the Father? See especially verses 3 and 5.
2. Verses 6-19. Note what Jesus has already done for his disciples. What more does he ask for them? (Verses 11,15,17). How does Jesus consecrate himself for their sake?
3. Verses 20-26. What graces does Jesus ask for the Church, i.e. for those who believe in him through the 'word' of the disciples?

JOHN 18-19

John's Passion Narrative shows considerable divergences from the synoptics'.

JOHN 18

Jesus' arrest; his interrogation by Annas; Peter's denial; Jesus' trial by Pilate.

1. Verses 1-11. What differences can you find in John's account of Jesus' arrest from the parallel passages in the other gospels (Matthew 26:47-56; Mark 14:43-50; Luke 22:47-53)? What features of Jesus is he emphasising?
2. Verses 12-27. What questions did Annas ask Jesus? How did he respond? Compare Peter's rash bravery (verse 10) with his cowardice now. Are we capable of such uncertainty of mood and behaviour? What underlies our lack of self-knowledge?
3. Verses 28-40. Trace the attempts made by Pilate to save Jesus from death. How did the Jewish authorities react?

JOHN 19

Ecce homo; the crucifixion, death and burial of Jesus.

1. Verses 1-16. What led Pilate finally to capitulate? See verse 12. Compare Matthew 27:24-26, Mark 15:15, Luke 23:23.
2. Verses 17-22. All four gospels tell us that Jesus was crucified as King of the Jews. What was the significance of this a) for the Romans, b) for the Jews, c) for us?
3. Verses 23-24. Why does John emphasise the seamless tunic? cf. Leviticus 8:7; 21:10; Psalm 22:18.
4. Verses 25-27. Note the women by the cross - Jesus' mother, his aunt and Mary Magdalen. What is the significance of Jesus' words in verses 26-27? Are they limited to a historical record?
5. Verses 28-37. John is silent about the cry of desolation in Mark. He shows instead Jesus breathing forth the Spirit as he dies. Observe the theological points throughout this chapter, the references to

scripture and the final emphatic testimony to the Pierced One (verses 34-37). Check each Old Testament reference and ponder on the meaning of each with regard to John's theology.

6. Verses 38-42. What does John tell us about Joseph and Nicodemus? Trace the latter's growth in faith. See 3:1-15; 7:45-52.

JOHN 20

The tradition is clear that Mary Magdalen and the other women were the first to find the empty tomb. It is in all four gospels, but John records the testimony of the unnamed beloved disciple who had been at the cross (19:26).

1. Verses 1-18. What was the progress in faith of a) Mary Magdalen, b) Peter and c) the beloved disciple?
2. Compare the Matthew tradition (Matthew 28:9-10) with verses 11-18; and the Lucan tradition (Luke 24:12 margin) with verses 3-10. In what ways has John developed and 'theologised' these traditions?
3. Verses 19-23. What was the state of mind of the disciples when Jesus came? See verse 19. How does this square with verse 8? What commission did Jesus give them?
4. Verses 24-31. Why did John record this episode? cf. verse 29. Are we ever tempted to doubt like Thomas?

JOHN 21

An appendix to the gospel; a miraculous draught of fishes and the rehabilitation of Peter.

1. Verses 1-3. Notice the disciples listed. How does it agree/disagree with lists in the synoptics and in Acts (Matthew 10:2-4; Mark 3:16-19; Luke 6:14-16; Acts 1:13)?
2. Verses 4-14. Compare this scene with Luke 5:1-11, noting the similarities and the differences. Why did the disciples return to their fishing?
3. Verses 15-25. What is the significance of this scene? Why does Jesus call Peter Simon? Why does he commission him three times? What does the whole scene teach us concerning Jesus?
4. Compare what is said of Peter's future (verses 18-19) with the obscure reference to the beloved disciple (verses 21-23). 'What is that to you'? What message here for Church leaders? Does it indicate a whole area in God's dealings with mankind in which the Church has no part?
5. Check the occasions when the unnamed disciple gives testimony (19:35 and 20:24), and the references to the beloved disciple (13:23 ff; 20:2 ff.; 21:7). What are we to make of them?

BEHOLD YOUR MOTHER
THEY DEVOTED THEMSELVES TO PRAYER ... WITH MARY THE MOTHER OF JESUS
ACTS: I, 14.

AN INTRODUCTION
TO
THE BOOK OF ACTS OF THE APOSTLES

This book is unique in the New Testament, giving information concerning the early growth of the Church that we could only piece together in a fragmentary way if we had no more than Paul's letters and occasional references from secular historians to go on. The author is undoubtedly Luke. His prologue (1:1) refers to his gospel, and is addressed to the same Theophilus as his earlier work. However, though the book has been known as the Acts of the Apostles since the second century, it centres only on the two Apostles par excellence - Peter (1-12), and Paul (13-end).

From where did Luke get his materials? In the Prologue to the gospel he makes it clear that he has taken care to consult eye witnesses wherever possible (Luke 1:2). He was a careful writer, using his sources and editing skilfully. The first five chapters of Acts seem to draw on documents and oral traditions from the primitive Christian community in Jerusalem; he seems to have first hand knowledge of Peter's movements at that time, and also of Philip's (8:4-40); the early church at Antioch of which he may have been a member (cf. Western text of 11:28) could have supplied materials (6:1 - 8:3; 11:19-30; 13:1-3). His knowledge of Paul, though he shows no acquaintance with the letters (why should he, if they travelled together?) would have provided most of the rest of the book.

Acts is not a quarry of texts to justify later structures or sacramental practice in the Church; nor is it history or biography in the modern sense. It is a work of theology, designed to show that the first Christians preached the resurrection of Jesus the Christ, that they used scripture as well as eye witness accounts to teach this doctrine, that they lived a common life of prayer, sharing of goods and worship in Jerusalem, and that the Holy Spirit guided the apostles to extend their teaching outwards from Jerusalem to the ends of the earth.

The Book of Acts is full of good stories, from Peter knocking at Mary's house and being kept waiting by the servant, to Paul and Silas in prison during the earthquake in Philippi, to the famous description of the shipwreck. It is a book to be enjoyed.

ACTS 1

The ascension of Jesus; the replacement of Judas by Matthias.

1. Verses 1-11. What promises did Jesus make to the apostles before his Ascension? What commission did he give them? Compare the account of the ascension (verse 9) with a) Luke 24:51 and b) with that of Elijah (2 Kings 2).
2. Verses 12-26. What were the tasks to which the disciples devoted themselves in the days immediately following the ascension? Why did Judas have to be replaced? What are the criteria for apostleship (verses 21-22)? Compare Judas with Jesus' brothers (verse 14) cf. John 2:12; 7:3-5.

ACTS 2

The day of Pentecost; Peter's discourse; the life of the first Christians.

1. Verses 1-13. What is the meaning of the wind and the tongues of fire? cf. this section with Genesis 11:1-9.
2. Verses 14-36. Note Peter's use of Old Testament. What facts of Jesus' life and teaching does he see fulfilled in scripture? How should *we* use Old Testament?
3. Verses 37-47. What programme of life does Peter propose to his hearers? Is this still the basic Christian gospel? Why do you think it is sometimes lost sight of? Comment on verses 42-47. How much of this is part of our lives as Christians?

ACTS 3

The healing of the crippled man; Peter's second discourse.

1. The cure of this man (verse 2) is symbolic of the whole dynamics of conversion. Draw out the elements: need, necessity of faith, healing and salvation. In what ways does Peter use it as a model for his subsequent preaching?
2. What use does Peter make of scripture in verses 17-26? Look up Deuteronomy 18:15-16, Genesis 22:18.

ACTS 4

Peter's discourse to the Jewish rulers; imprisonment of Peter and John; their release; the prayers of the faithful.

1. What effects did the healing of the lame man have a) on the religious leaders b) on the apostles and c) on the people?
2. How does Peter make capital of the affair? What important principle does he state in verse 19? Is this principle always observed a) in the life of the Church, and b) in our own lives? Have there been any occasions when it has brought me into conflict with received religious authorities?
3. Analyse the prayer in verses 24-30. Note that they pray for 'boldness' (verse 29), and cf. especially verse 31. Do we pray in such terms when we feel under attack?
4. Examine the summary in verses 32-37. Are these ideals reflected in our church fellowship? If we think our parishes are too large and impersonal, what steps are we taking to remedy this?

ACTS 5

This disagreeable story probably reflects a prophetic interpretation of a sudden death. cf. 2 Kings 2:23-25.

1. What was the sin of Ananias and Sapphira? Compare their attitude and behaviour with that of Barnabas (4:36-37)
2. Pick out the verbs and adjectives in verses 17-33 that express the feelings of the religious authorities towards the apostles. Note the part played by the angel (verses 19-20) and by Gamaliel (verses 34-39). Do we seek God's guidance through people and events?
   For a further note about Gamaliel see 22:3

ACTS 6

Hellenists were Jews from outside Palestine who spoke Greek and used the Septuagint Bible; the Hebrews were Palestinian Jews who spoke Aramaic and used the Hebrew Bible. Members of both groups joined the Christians.

1. Is there any sense in which modern deacons could be said to derive from those mentioned in verse 3?
2. In what way are the accusations against Stephen (verses 11 and 13) similar to those brought against Jesus?

ACTS 7

Stephen's speech at his trial; his martyrdom.

1. In what way does Stephen a) seek to convince his hearers that land and temple are of lesser importance, b) point out that sacrifices were not encouraged by the prophets?
2. Show the ways in which Stephen presents Moses as a forerunner of Christ. What features does he stress? What reaction does it evoke from his audience?
3. Note the parallels between Stephen's death and Jesus'.

ACTS 8

Philip's mission to the Samaritans; Simon Magus; the conversion of the Ethiopian eunuch.

1. Observe how verses 1-4 lead in various themes of Acts. Identify them.
2. Trace the stages of Samaria's evangelisation (Luke 9:52-56, John 4, Acts 8:5 ff). Why did Peter and John have to go there?
3. What was the reason for Simon's fall into sin? What was lacking to his faith? What sin gets its name from this incident? Is it prevalent today?
4. What can we learn from Philip's method of evangelising? cf. his obedience to Spirit, his use of scripture.

ACTS 9:1-31

The conversion of Saul - first account. Peter's miracles at Lydda and Joppa.

1. What have we already learnt of Saul (see 7:58, 8:1-3)?
2. Compare the three accounts of his vision (verses 3-8; 22:6-11; 26:12-18), with regard to place, time and contents. What differences are there in detail?
3. Paul always claimed that he saw the risen Lord (cf. 1 Corinthians 15:8). What truth did he learn from Jesus that was to mark his whole teaching? See verses 4-5.
4. What special mission was to be Paul's?

ACTS 9:32-43

1. Look up Lydda and Joppa on a map. What evidence is there of the growth of Christianity in this area?
2. Tabitha is described as a 'disciple' (verse 36). Note carefully as you read Acts the important part played by women disciples. How did Tabitha exercise her ministry?

ACTS 10

The conversion of Cornelius. Peter's discourse on the occasion.

1. Verses 1-8. What were the virtues of Cornelius? What is meant by verse 4? cf. Leviticus 2:2 and Tobit 12:12.
2. Verses 9-16. What important lesson was being taught to Peter? Why did he have to be told three times? What shows us that Peter took it to heart? cf. verse 28-29 but cf. Galatians 2:11-12; and verses 34-35.
3. Verses 17-48. What events in the life of Jesus does Peter bring out in his sermon?
4. What conclusions should be drawn from verse 47? Do you think the Church has exhausted its possible application to our present situation with regard to inter Communion among Christians?

ACTS 11

The circumcision party was a conservative group (cf. Galatians 2:12) who insisted that all Gentile converts should be circumcised and observe the Law of Moses.

1. What most impressed the Jewish Christians from Peter's account?
2. Antioch in Syria was the third largest city in the Roman empire. What features of Christian life there are recorded?
3. Check out what you know of Barnabas (verses 22-26, 30 and 4:36).

ACTS 12

Peter appears for the last time in this chapter, except for Acts 15. He went to 'another place' (verse 17). According to tradition this was Antioch. He later went to Rome.

1. Check out all we know of James the brother of John (cf. Mark 1:19; 3:17; 5:37; 9:2; 10:35; 14:33; Luke 9:54). What was his nickname? What special privileges did he have?
2. How did the Christian community react to the news of Peter's arrest? See verses 5,12. What does this teach us about fellowship?
3. What do we learn of the character of Herod Agrippa I? What lesson has his sudden death for us all?

ACTS 13

Look up Paul's first journey from Antioch to Cyprus to Perga in Pamphilia, to Antioch in Pisidia, Iconium, Lystra, Derbe and back to Antioch.

1. Note the way in which the church in Antioch was governed, by 'prophets and teachers' (verse 1). How did they seek guidance? Does such a form of church government exist anywhere today?
2. Verses 5-12. Compare Paul's confrontation with Elymas with that of Peter with Simon Magus (8:9-24). What is the significance of these encounters?
3. Check out all you know of John Mark, Barnabas' cousin. cf. 12:12; 12:25; 13:5; 13; 15:37,39. What impression do you form of him? He is reputedly the author of Mark's gospel and Peter's interpreter. cf. 1 Peter 5:13. He was later reconciled with Paul (Col. 4:10; Philemon 24; 2 Timothy 4:11). What encouragement does this give us?
4. Paul always started his ministry in the synagogue. What emphases does he make in his account of Jesus of Nazareth? Note the structure: history; Messianic claim for Jesus; Pauline doctrine of justification by faith; warnings based on the prophets. Compare this structure with Acts 2:14-40.
5. What effects did Paul's preaching have (see verses 42-47)? How did Paul and Barnabas take Jesus' advice (Luke 10:10-11)?

ACTS 14

A miracle at Lystra. Return to Antioch of Paul and his companions; end of the first missionary journey.

1. Verses 1-7. Note the response to the gospel: faith, divisions, opposition. In what ways have you experienced this pattern?
2. Verses 8-18. Compare the healing of the cripple at Lystra with that of the beggar in Jerusalem (Acts 3). Are they also to be compared in their outcome?
3. Note carefully Paul's address to a totally pagan audience (verses 5-17). Would similar arguments be used today?
4. Paul and Barnabas returned to Antioch by the same route (verses 21-26). In what way did they organise and build up the churches they had founded?

ACTS 15

Two controversies are combined in this chapter: 1) the question of obliging Gentile converts to observe the Law of Moses; 2) social relations between Christians from Jewish and from pagan backgrounds.

1. Compare this chapter with Paul's own account in Galatians 2. The point at issue in verses 1-2 is: on what terms can Gentiles be saved? What is a) the reply of the Judaisers (verses 1,5); b) Paul's (verses 2-4); c) Peter's (verses 7-11)?
2. What do you think is the answer? Write down what, in your view, is necessary for salvation.

3. Look up James, the 'brother of the Lord' (Matthew 13:55; Mark 6:3; Acts 12:17; 15:13,21; 21:18; Galatians 1:19; 2:9,12). Note his importance and influence in Jerusalem. What was his suggested solution to the social differences between Jewish and Gentile converts? Can we impose cultural patterns on young churches? How do we distinguish between essentials of the faith and non-essentials?
4. Who is the guide through all these controversies? cf. verses 8-10, 12, 16-18, 28.

ACTS 16

Paul's second journey begins: from Antioch through Syria and Cilicia to Derbe and Lystra across into Macedonia and Achaia, back to Ephesus and thence to Jerusalem.

1. Look up Timothy, one of Paul's most faithful companions: 16:1-3; 17:14-15; 18:5; 19:22; 20:4; Romans 16:21; 1 Corinthians 4:17; 16:10; 2 Corinthians 1:1,19, etc. Notice that Paul had Timothy circumcised. Why?
2. By what means was Paul guided at this time? cf. verses 6,7,9-10. Look up the route on a map. Have we experience in our own lives of God's remarkable intervention? Where was the great development of early Christianity to occur?
3. Notice the importance of women disciples in the growth of the early church. With verses 14 ff. cf. 12:12, 13:50; 17:4,12,34; 18:2,26. What evidence have we here that Lydia was truly converted?
4. Note that Luke has now joined Paul (verses 10,11 etc). Look up Col. 4:14, 2 Timothy 4:11 and Philemon 24 for references to him.
5. Verses 16-24. What was the origin of the persecution of Paul and Silas? In what way was it different from the earlier forms of opposition to the gospels?
6. Verses 25-40. What caused the jailer to come to conversion? What did he have to affirm in order to receive baptism? Note that both Lydia and the jailer brought their households for baptism too. Would this have included children?

ACTS 17

Paul's mission to Thessalonica, Beroea and Athens. His speech in the Areopagus.

1. Compare and contrast Paul's mission to the Thessalonians and to the citizens of Beroea. What are a) the similarities and b) the differences? Do we follow the example of the Jews of Beroea? See verse 11.
2. Study Paul's sermon in Athens. Note a) its starting point, b) its emphasis on Greek philosophy and literature, c) its message. Why did Paul largely fail in Athens? See especially verses 18-21, 31.

ACTS 18

Paul in Corinth. From here he wrote to the Thessalonians (1 and 2). We are in AD 50-52.

1. What information do we receive here concerning a) the dating of these events (verse 2) and b) the financing of Paul's mission (verse 3)?
2. What encouragement did Paul receive in Corinth amidst so many trials?
3. Note the stages in Paul's ministry (verses 4,7 and 12). Note how each difficulty brought fresh graces. Do we too experience this in our Christian lives? If not, is there anything in our attitude that accounts for it?

ACTS 19

Paul in Ephesus. Riot there.

1. Do verses 1-7 give us an understanding a) concerning Apollos' Christianity, b) our own? Does this section refer to what we call the sacrament of confirmation or is it 'baptism in the Spirit' or both?

2. What were a) the difficulties and b) the great blessings of Paul's Ephesian ministry? How does it differ from other missions described in Acts?
3. How was Paul guided in his planning? See verses 21,22 and cf. 16:6-10). Do we seek God in prayer before making decisions or do we allow ourselves to drift?
4. Consider the lively account of the riot at Ephesus. What was its origin? Are business interests ever threatened in your experience by the preaching of the gospel? What would be a modern counterpart to this story?

ACTS 20

Paul at Troas. His farewell to the Ephesians.

1. Notice the list of Paul's companions, fruit of his missionary activity: several of them are mentioned in his letters (Sopater - Romans 16:21; Tychicus - Col. 4:7; 2 Timothy 4:12; Trophimus, an Ephesian - 2 Timothy 4:20). When does Luke rejoin them?
2. Verses 7-12. Read this story as a good illustration of a very early Eucharist, with service of the Word (verses 7,9) and of the Eucharist (verses 7,11). When was it held?
3. Verses 13-38. What are the virtues that Paul cites as good pastoral care? See especially verses 28,31,35. What portrait does Paul paint of himself in this farewell discourse? (Or rather, since Luke composed it - how does Luke portray him?).
4. Consider the scene in verses 36-38 and cf. 21:4-6. Is there this same love in our Christian communities? If not, what should we do about it?

ACTS 21

Paul on his way to Jerusalem. His reception by the church there. His arrest. (AD 58).

1. Look up what you can find in Acts about the prophets mentioned (11:27-28; 13:1; 15:32; 21:9-10). What do you know of a) Agabus and b) Philip the evangelist?
2. Compare the warnings to Paul with Jesus' predictions of his crucifixion.
3. What role does James play in welcoming and warning Paul? What practical proposal does he make? What do you understand by it?
4. Consider verse 21, and reflect how soon that strong Jewish influence faded from the Church, while the message spread among the Gentiles. Is this happening today to the Western church with its resources, its learning, its wealth? Which are the growing churches? What should we learn from this?
5. Verses 27-40. What are the parallels between the accusations made and the treatment meted out to Jesus and to Paul? Consider also how similar accusations (verse 28) were made against Stephen. What accusations are made today against Jesus' disciples in many lands?

ACTS 22

Second account of Paul's conversion.

1. What new do we learn of Paul from his address?
2. Draw out the phrases where Paul, speaking to Jews, emphasises the Jewish aspects of his testimony.

ACTS 23

Paul's trial before the Sanhedrin. His imprisonment at Caesarea.

1. How did Paul manage to divide his judges among themselves? How did God use this event to bring Paul even further on his journeying?
2. How did God send deliverance to Paul in this case? How did the Roman authorities view Paul?

ACTS 24

Paul in prison in Caesara under Felix.

1. What charges were brought against Paul? What proofs were offered? What did he say in his own defence?
2. Compare Felix with Herod Antipas in his attitude to John the Baptist. See verses 23-26. cf. Mark 6:14-28.

ACTS 25

Festus takes action over Paul (AD 60) who appeals to Caesar.

1. Compare Felix with Festus. What evidence is there that Festus behaved fairly with regard to Paul? But what was his great failing? Is there any excuse for him?
2. Why did Paul appeal to Caesar?

ACTS 26

Third account of Paul's conversion.

1. Compare Acts 9 and 22 with this address. What aspects did Paul emphasise for this particular audience? What was the real issue at stake? (See verses 6-8 and 13-15).
2. Look at verses 16-18 and compare the language with that of Old Testament prophets, eg. Jeremiah 1; Ezekiel 2:1,3; Isaiah 9; and 42:7,16. What was the reaction of Festus and of Agrippa?

ACTS 27

Paul's journey by sea to Rome. The shipwreck at Malta.

1. Follow Paul's journey on a map. What marks of God's favour did he receive in the course of it? What various forms did these marks take?
2. Why was Paul's advice disregarded at first, but heeded later? Contrast Paul's calm and leadership (verses 22 ff. and 33-36) with the panic reactions of the sailors (verses 30-31) and of the soldiers (verses 42,43). What accounts for this? cf. also Paul's bearing in chapters 22 and 26.

ACTS 28

The journey from Malta to Rome. His life in Rome under military guard (AD 61-63).

1. Observe the reactions of the Maltese to Paul's sangfroid over the viper. How was their respect for him justified?
2. Notice that there were already Christians in Rome and its environs (verses 14,15) to whom Paul's letter to the Romans of three or four years before had been written. How did they welcome Paul and his companions?
3. What approach did Paul make to the Roman Jews? What success did he have with them? See verses 24-28. What is the significance of the quotation from Isaiah? cf. John 12:40 and Matthew 13:14-15.
4. The book ends without any information concerning the outcome of Paul's appeal to Caesar, nor his subsequent fate. cf. 12:17. Why do you think Acts ends where it does? What is the significance of verse 31? cf. 1:8.

AN INTRODUCTION
TO
THE LETTER TO THE ROMANS

Question: What is salvation?
Answers:

(1) Not everyone who says to me, Lord, Lord, shall enter the kingdom of heaven, but he who does the will of my Father who is in heaven (Matthew 7:21).

(2) The time is fulfilled, and the kingdom of God is at hand; repent, and believe in the gospel (Mark 1:15).

(3) Truly, I say to you, today you will be with me in paradise (Luke 23:43).

(4) I am the way, and the truth, and the life; no one comes to the Father but by me (John 14:6).

(5) You see that a man is justified by works and not by faith alone (James 2:24).

(6) As the outcome of your faith you obtain the salvation of your souls (1 Peter 1:9).

(7) He who says he abides in him ought to walk in the same way in which he walked (1 John 2:6).

All these answers have been given, by different New Testament voices. Paul's answer in the letter is that salvation depends, not on observance of the Law, but on the free gift of God's grace in Christ Jesus.

It sometimes comes as a surprise to us, to realise and to remember that Paul's letters were written before any of the gospels, and that he was probably never acquainted with any of them. His earliest letters, to the Thessalonians, were written about AD 50, and the letters to the Galatians and to the Romans probably during the winter 57-58. In Romans he deals with the problem of whether the Christian gospel is open to those who have never been Jews, who have never known the Law as given to Moses, (chapters 2-7); his conclusion that the Christian life is the life of the Holy Spirit in the believer (chapter 8) is the climax of the first part of the letter.

The second great question, one that caused great perplexity among his fellow Jews,was why the chosen people seemed to have rejected their promised Messiah. Paul points out that to Gentiles the Jewish refusal has led to their adoption instead, but that in the end the natural olive branches will be grafted back (chapter 9-11) and 'so all Israel will be saved' (11:26). The last part of the letter (chapters 12-15) deals with practical aspects of Christian living.

ROMANS 1

Introduction. The terrible state of the Gentile world.

1. The letter was written from Corinth in the winter of AD 57–8. Re-read Acts 20:2-3 for the setting of the letter and Romans 16:1 for its bearer.
2. Look carefully at the credal formula with which the letter opens (verses 2-4) and list the articles of doctrine contained in them.
3. What does Paul say about himself? See verses 1, 5, 9-16. In what circumstances did he eventually come to Rome?
4. How does Paul sum up the gospel that he preaches? See verses 16-17. How would you sum up what the good news is for you?
5. Verses 18-23. How can everyone know God in some measure? What *can* be known about him? (verse 20). What has led to the futility of idolatry? Is our generation guilty of the same futility and foolishness?
6. Verses 24-27. How does idolatry lead to sexual immorality and perversion?
7. Verses 28-32. What other sins come in its train?

. Notice how, in verses 24,26,28 Paul says 'God gave them up'... How is this the working out of God's wrath (verse 18)? Can we see it at work in our day?

ROMANS 2

The Jews are also guilty, because they count on the Law and circumcision to save them.

. Verses 1-11. How does Paul show a) that no one should be complacent and judge others, and b) that God will 'render to every man according to his works'? How does this square with justification by faith?

3. Verses 12-16. How will Gentiles (ie. those who do not know the Law) be judged? How does this apply to those who have never been evangelised?

3. Verses 17-29. In what way does Paul's teaching in this section apply to 'respectable church goers' today? How does it agree with Jesus' teaching on the dangers of hypocrisy? cf. Matthew 6:1-6 and 23:13 ff.

ROMANS 3

All are under judgment. Necessity for faith in God's grace.

1. What words does Paul use to describe scripture (verses 2 and 19)? What advantage does the Jew have? In verses 1-8 he answers four objections. What are the objections and what are his answers?
2. Verses 9-20. Paul quotes Old Testament to describe man's predicament. What is his conclusion? See verses 19-20. Would Jesus have said anything different? cf. Matthew 15:1-20.
3. Verses 21-30. What does Paul mean by saying a) that we fall short of the glory of God (ie. the presence of God indwelling) and b) that all his grace is a gift? What form supremely does this gift take? See verses 24-26.
4. What follows therefore? In what sense does Paul uphold the Law?

ROMANS 4

The references to Abraham in verses 1,12 and 16-22 mark the stages in the argument.

1. Look up 1 Maccabees 2:52, Wisdom 10:5, Sirach 44:20 ff. for the late Old Testament doctrine of justification by works. How does Paul interpret the justification of Abraham? See verses 3,7,8. Can we *earn* salvation?
2. How is the argument carried on in verses 11-12 to include the Gentiles? How can the Law bring 'wrath'? How is the timing of Abraham's justification of vital importance to the issue of the admission of the Gentiles?
3. Verses 16-25. Note a) the reference to God's creative and redemptive acts in verse 17. How does this prepare us for the reference to Christ's resurrection in verse 25? b) What aspects of Abraham's faith are now emphasised? (verses 18-22). c) How is Abraham's faith applied to us, his descendants? (verses 23-25)

ROMANS 5

The relationship between faith and salvation. Sin and death from Adam; grace and life from Jesus Christ.

1. What are the blessings of salvation? What, for Christians, is the value of suffering?
2. What are the two supreme ways in which God's love is shown to us?
3. What does Paul teach about 'original sin'? See Genesis 3:16-24 and Wisdom 2:24.
4. In what sense is Christ a 'second Adam', and in what sense does he reverse Adam's deed? See verses 14-21.

ROMANS 6

Baptism by which we die to sin in ourselves and rise to life in Christ.

1. Verses 1-6. Consider this theology of baptism, a dying in Christ to our sins and a rising with him to newness of life. Does our baptismal liturgy emphasise this sufficiently? Does the popular approach to 'christening' a child show any understanding of its import? Can you suggest a more theological approach to this important sacrament?
2. What are the consequences of baptism? See verses 5-11. How should we live this out? See verses 12-13. How is purity of mind and body an important Christian virtue? How can we be freed from impurity and all other kinds of bondage to sin (verses 22-23)?

ROMANS 7

Paul paints the human struggle against sin in human terms.

1. In his example from marriage, Paul says the death of a husband frees his wife to marry again. In the case of the Christian, whose death frees him from bondage to the Law? And who is the new spouse? What are the fruits of this new union, in contrast with those of the old one? See verses 5-6.
2. Paul describes a human situation: the arousal of passion by the very prohibition of the Law (verse 7), our incapability in face of our own corrupt sinful nature (verses 14-17), the clearness of our knowledge of what we should do contrasted with the strength of our passions (verses 15,22), the whole struggle summed up vividly in verses 19-23. Do we find that this describes our own experiences?

ROMANS 8

The life of the Christian in the glory of God in the Spirit. This chapter is a commentary both on Genesis 1 and on Ecclesiastes 1.

1. 7:25 gave Paul's answer to the terrible struggle in sinful mankind. How does he develop this idea in verses 1-4? How is it that Christ has freed us?
2. Verses 5-17. What are the characteristics of those who live according to the flesh? Contrast those who live according to the Spirit.
3. What does it mean to be children of God? How does the Spirit act in us? See verses 15-17.
4. Verses 18-25. These verses are Paul's commentary on Ecclesiastes 1:2 - the word 'futility' is the 'vanity of vanities' of the Preacher. Re-read the first chapter of Ecclesiastes with this in mind, and also Genesis 3. What does Paul add to the Old Testament insights?
5. What does Paul say about Christian prayer in this chapter? How does he complete the traditional themes of conditions for prayer, its efficacy, etc.? See verses 15-17, 26-27.
6. What are the four great blessings accorded by God to those who are reborn in Christ? See verses 28-30.

ROMANS 9-11.

The case of Israel.

ROMANS 9

Israel, God's chosen people. Their reluctance to accept salvation in Christ.

1. Verse 1-5. Consider the great privileges of God's chosen people. Which of these have been inherited by Christians?
2. Verses 6-18. What conclusions does Paul draw from his study of the scriptures? How has God kept his promises? What principles of election does Paul find in the stories of Isaac and of Jacob? How does he interpret the story of Pharaoh?

. If you are ready with an objection (verse 19) what answer does Paul suggest? How does he interpret the text chosen to illustrate this (verses 25-33)? Are you encouraged or disheartened by this chapter? Read on.

ROMANS 10

The subject continued. Why did Israel not respond to the gospel?

1. This is quite a tough chapter! Begin by reading the requisite Old Testament texts: Leviticus 18:5 (see verse 5). How does Paul summarise this in verses 1-4? How is man said to live by keeping the Law? Why, according to Paul, is this unenlightened? (verse 2). What IS the righteousness that comes from God if not the law? see verse 4. Are there Christians who make the same mistake - of trusting in the fulfilment of their obligations, rather than in the grace of God?
2. Now read Deuteronomy 30:11-14. What is meant by "the word is very near to you"? What does Paul read into this (verses 6-8)? How did Jesus sum up the Law? (See Mark 12:29-30). What confession of faith is Paul quoting (verses 9-10).? How does he sum up his argument (verses 12-13)?
3. Verses 14-17. What is the gospel that the Jews, according to Paul, have neglected? How is it to be brought to them?
4. Verses 18-21. What does Paul say about the warnings of the prophets to the people of Israel? How does he interpret them?

ROMANS 11

Paul makes it clear that Israel remains 'chosen' and will be saved - their slowness leaves time for the Gentiles to come to Christ.

1. Verses 1-6. How does Paul use scripture here to back up this argument - that God has not abandoned his chosen people, now represented by a remnant who follow Christ?
2. Verses 7-12. To what unexpected result has the unbelief of Israel led?
3. Verses 13-24. How does Paul show through the parable of the olive a) that the Gentiles have nothing to boast of and b) that the Jews will eventually be saved too?
4. Verses 25-36. What is God's ultimate purpose for Israel as revealed in the prophets? How had God shown his mercy to the Gentiles?

ROMANS 12

The new Temple - the people of God.

1. Verses 1-13. What is meant by a) your bodies (verse 1) and b) one body (verses 4 and 5)?
2. What gifts of "the body" are singled out for mention in verses 6-8? Compare them with the lists in 1 Corinthians 12:8-10, 28-30 and 2 Peter 1:5-7.
3. How is charity to be exercised a) towards the Christian community and b) towards everyone else?

ROMANS 13

The essentials for Christian living.

1. What principles for civil duties and obligations does Paul lay down in this chapter? Are there occasions when authority is unlawful, or makes unlawful demands? cf. Acts 5:29 and Matthew 22:21.
2. How does Paul amplify the Old Testament injunctions to love the neighbour? Who is the neighbour for a Christian? cf. Luke 10:30-37.
3. What does Paul mean by the "hour" (verse 11)? How does he agree with John 13:1?

ROMANS 14

Paul's concern for those of weak faith - they must not be scandalised, but given time to grow.

1. What principles should guide Christians in their attitude to each other's differences of approach to non-essentials? What examples of scruples does Paul give? See verses 2, 5. How can these principles be applied to inter-Church dialogue and relations?
2. How does Paul echo Christ's teaching on judging others and on giving scandal? Compare verses 10-13 with Matthew 7:1 and 18:6.

ROMANS 15

The subject continued. Paul gives his readers some details concerning his own ministry, and relates his plans.

1. What sources of help and encouragement for our Christian living are suggested in verses 3-5?
2. Why, according to Paul, did Jesus confine his ministry during his life-time to the Jews? See verse 8. Did he also welcome Gentiles (verses 7 and 9). What interpretation does Paul put on the scripture he quotes (verses 9-12) with regard to the evangelisation of the Gentiles?
3. Verses 14-33. What does Paul tell us a) of his reason for writing to the Romans b) of the scope of his journeys and c) of his reason for going to Jerusalem? See Acts 19:21; 24:17.
4. Why did Paul set so much store by the collection for Jerusalem (verses 26-27)? Does this apply to church collections? In what other ways should we support each other financially?
5. In what terms does Paul ask his readers for their prayers? See verses 30-33.

ROMANS 16

Some scholars believe that this chapter was not part of the original letter to the Christians of Rome, but a separate note for the church at Ephesus, as most of the names listed seem to be Greek, and connected with the churches in Asia Minor.

1. What do we learn of Phoebe from verses 1-2? Look up Cenchrae on a map.
2. Look up Acts 18:2 ff. for Prisca and Aquila; Mark 15:21 for Rufus. Note the number of women mentioned (at least nine). What does this indicate about the position of women among the earliest Christians?
3. Note the references in verses 1-16 a) to diligence and zeal, and b) to suffering borne for Christ. Note the comment in verse 16 - All the churches...
4. What does the reference to those who 'create dissensions' mean? See verses 17-18.
5. How is God described in verses 25,27? What is the mystery hidden in prophecy but now revealed?

AN INTRODUCTION TO THE LETTERS TO THE CORINTHIANS

Corinth was one of the great cities of the Greek world, famous for its libraries, its commerce, and also for its immorality. Paul was there from AD 50 to 52, and most of his converts there came from among the very poor (1 Corinthians 1:26-28). It would seem that Paul, after leaving Corinth, wrote at least four letters to that church. In 1 Corinthians 5:9-13 he refers to a letter which has not survived, though it is possible that a fragment of this 'first letter' appears in what is now 2 Corinthians 6:14 - 7:1, a passage which seems to have been interpolated from an alien context. The canonical First Letter (1 Corinthians) was written from Ephesus at Easter 57. Shortly afterwards, a crisis developed, and Paul was forced to pay a brief and painful visit there (2 Corinthians 1:23 - 2:1; 12:14; 13:1-2). While there, he promised another and longer visit (2 Corinthians 1:15-16) which he was never able to undertake. He sent another disciple to whom he delegated his authority, but this provoked a further crisis. Paul, still unable to come, wrote a 'severe letter' which *may* be 2 Corinthians 10-13. This letter had the desired effect (2 Corinthians 7:8-13), and Paul wrote from Macedonia towards the end of AD 57 a fourth letter, our 2 Corinthians 1-8 with chapter 9 added by a later editor from perhaps a fifth letter.

AN INTRODUCTION
TO
1 CORINTHIANS

This letter largely deals with practical problems that had arisen in this tumultuous community (it was still quarrelsome at the end of the first century when Clement wrote from Rome to try to settle differences there). While Paul was at Ephesus (AD 54-57) cf. Acts 19:1-20:1), a delegation from Corinth arrived to put certain problems to Paul (1 Corinthians 16:7) and as he had also heard from Chloe's people (1 Corinthians 1:11) that trouble had broken out, he wrote the letter we know as 1 Corinthians. He deals first with the quarrels and scandals that were disturbing the community there (1-6), and the abuses in public worship (11); and he answers certain questions brought by the delegation: what is the value relatively of marriage and of celibacy (7); what should be the attitude of Christians to meat that had been offered to idols (8-10); the value of the charisms (12-14); the resurrection of the dead (15).

In this very practical letter, while some parts of it are clearly related to its particular situation (the position of women in Corinth, slavery, the belief, shared by Paul, that the return of Christ was imminent - 7:17-24), he lays down very important principles for Christian marriage, chosen virginity, relations between Christians and pagans, the conduct of church worship and the use and place of the charisms, and, above all, this letter contains the earliest written account of the last supper (11:23-34) and a very early list of witnesses to the Resurrection (15:3-9).

1 CORINTHIANS 1

After the usual introduction, Paul turns to the problem of divisions in the church at Corinth: rivalries between different groups, claiming authority from different evangelists.

1. Read Acts 18:1-18 for the background to Paul's Corinthian ministry. Note that a Sosthenes is mentioned as ruler of the synagogue at Corinth (Acts 18:17). What is the occasion for the letter? See verses 10-17. What would the four factions represent? For Apollos see Acts 18:24 ff.). What encouragement is there in this chapter for those who strive for Christian Unity? See verse 2.
2. Verses 17-31. What does Paul mean by 'wisdom'? Compare Isaiah 29:13-14.
3. In what way is the message of the cross 'folly' to Gentiles and a 'stumbling block' to Jews? Can this be said to be still true today?

1 CORINTHIANS 2

Paul tries to get to the root of the Christian message - not staying at the level of surface rivalries.

1. Verses 1-5. Compare what Paul says of himself and of his own preaching with his description of his Corinthian converts (1:26-31). What does this tell us about God's choice? Compare Jesus' calling of his apostles.
2. What is the 'secret and hidden wisdom of God' (verse 7) of which Paul speaks? How is it to be possessed and by whom understood?
3. Draw out Paul's references to the work of the Holy Spirit.

1 CORINTHIANS 3

The place of preaching in the churches.

1. What is meant, in Paul's vocabulary, by the 'unspiritual man' (2:14) or the 'men of the flesh' (3:1)? Do we often experience this distinction? How do 'unspiritual' persons react to the things of God? In what situation, according to Paul, were most of the Corinthian converts?

2. What is the work of a Christian preacher (verses 5-23)? What is his place in God's scheme? What is meant by the parable of the builder?
3. Verse 15b was used in the catechism as a proof text of Purgatory. Do you think Paul meant this, or what did he mean?
4. Verses 16-17. These two verses contain a doctrine of enormous importance. Paul sees the Jewish temple as replaced by the people of God, indwelt by God's Spirit. Meditate on the implications of these two verses for our understanding of the Church, and of ourselves as members of the Church.
5. How does Paul sum up his argument (verses 18-23)? Look up Job 5:13 and Psalm 94:11. How do these texts enlighten us as to his meaning?

1 CORINTHIANS 4

The ministry of an apostle - one sent with a message from God.

1. What has Paul to say about the ministry of an apostle? Why are men's judgments of so little value? What picture does he give of the Corinthians?
2. How does Paul express his love of his converts? Whose example are they to follow?

1 CORINTHIANS 5

Having roundly scolded the Corinthians for their factions, Paul now lists two further sources of scandal: a case of incest (chapter 5) and litigation in pagan courts (chapter 6).

1. Incest was common in Corinth, but forbidden to Jews by Leviticus 18:8 and to Christians (Acts 15:20). What penalty does Paul impose? Why should excommunication (handing over to Satan) eventually 'save his spirit'?
2. Why is an immoral brother more dangerous to the Christian community than all the immorality of non-Christians? What is the meaning of the parable in verses 6-8?
3. What elements in this chapter are of universal importance? How can they be applied to our situation nowadays?

1 CORINTHIANS 6

Paul scolds the Corinthians for resorting to pagan law courts to settle their disputes between Christians. The evils of sexual immorality.

1. Verses 1-11. What do we learn from this section about the evils and scandal of Christians taking each other to court? Are we sufficiently aware of the scandal caused nowadays by Christian disunity? What line should be drawn between loyal dissent and factiousness? See verse 5,7.
2. Verses 12-20. What reasons does Paul give for urging the sinfulness of sexual immorality? What is the most cogent reason for Christians? How can we 'glorify God in our body'? How should one train the young in purity of mind, heart and body?

1 CORINTHIANS 7-14

Answers to various questions

1 CORINTHIANS 7

Marriage and celibacy. Paul is thinking in terms of a very brief interlude before the second coming of Christ.

1. Verses 1-11. What is Paul's teaching concerning Christian marriage? How does it show an advance on Old Testament teaching? See, eg. Deuteronomy 22:13-29.
2. Verses 12-16. This section concerns the so-called Pauline Privilege. What relevance does it have for our time? Note, it is not a question of marriage between Christians of different denominations, but of marriage between Christians and unbelievers.

3. Verses 17-24. What is the principle laid down in verse 17? Is it universally applicable, or only for times of crisis?
4. Verses 25-35. Why did Paul remain unmarried? How has his advice traditionally been taken in the Church? Is there a place for the single state in other than the recognised forms of consecrated religious life?
5. Verses 36-40. What advice is given to engaged couples and to widows?

1 CORINTHIANS 8

Food offered to the gods was later sold in the open market. Christians were faced with the problem of whether they should eat it or not.

1. What principles does Paul lay down concerning this question? a) Is knowledge that idols are 'nothing' sufficient reason for eating meat that has been offered to them? b) What about scandal to the weak?
2. How can this principle be applied, for example, to social relations between Christians of different denominations who have varying attitudes to such things as alcohol, cards, contraceptives, etc?

1 CORINTHIANS 9

Paul uses his own example to instruct the Corinthians.

1. What is the basic principle which should guide all our freedom? See verses 12b and 8:3.
2. What do we learn concerning Paul's personal behaviour? How was his mission supported? See verses 6,15.
3. What rights, according to Paul, does a Christian worker have? Do we always respect these rights in our ministers?

1 CORINTHIANS 10

Paul now takes examples from Israel's history, to show that even the strong, if they become arrogant, can be 'disqualified' (cf. 9:27).

1. Verses 1-5. What experiences did the Israelites have and how do these events foreshadow the Christian experience?
2. Verses 6-13. What sins did the Israelites commit in the wilderness? How can we learn from them?
3. How does Paul compare the Eucharist with a) the sacrificial meals of the Israelites (verses 16-18) and b) contrast it with pagan sacrifices (verses 19-22)?
4. What practical solutions does he offer for the question of idol-meat?

1 CORINTHIANS 11

This chapter deals with two aspects of decorum in worship: verses 1-16 refer to women's dress; verses 17-34 to the Lord's Supper.

1. Verses 1-16. Much of this section reflects customs long out of use, but what important principle is stated in verses 11-12? Paul states that a woman must appear as a WOMAN by the way she dresses her hair (verse 10). Can this therefore be interpreted as a revaluing of woman's place in the Church? cf. Galatians 3:28.
2. Verses 17-22. What was wrong with the Corinthians' celebration of the agape or love feast? What principle of unity had they forgotten?
3. Verses 23-34. What does Paul teach concerning the Eucharist? Compare verses 23-25 with Luke 22:19-20. What does verse 26 mean? Does he mean in verse 29 that the 'body'is the real presence of Christ in the Eucharist, or the presence of Christ in the Church (the body of Christ) or both?

1 CORINTHIANS 12

The spiritual gifts or 'charisms'. This chapter was much neglected in the Church until recent times. Chapters 12-14 deal with the charisms of the Spirit.

1. List the different gifts received from the Spirit. Have we experienced any of them?
2. How does the analogy of the Church as a body clarify Paul's teaching a) on the charisms and b) on the unity of Christians?

1 CORINTHIANS 13

Paul's famous hymn to Charity.

1. Why is love so much more important than any other gift? The word Paul uses for love is *AGAPE*, in Latin *CARITAS*. Is English impoverished by our using one word? Could you suggest another word, less debased by popular misuse?
2. List the ways in which Paul describes love. How does Jesus' life illustrate them? Are any or some of them lacking in me?

1 CORINTHIANS 14

The gift of prophecy does not mean the power to foretell the future, but to explain scripture, and to read the signs of the times.

1. Draw out Paul's teaching on the gift of tongues. What is its place in prayer? Why is prophecy to be preferred?
2. What rules does Paul lay down for prayer meetings? Are they all applicable today? See especially verse 40.

1 CORINTHIANS 15

Some Corinthians rejected the doctrine of the resurrection of the dead (verse 12). The Greeks found it a difficult idea to swallow (cf. Acts 17:18,32).

1. Verses 1-11. What was the gospel, according to Paul? How does his list of witnesses to Jesus' resurrection tally with the gospel accounts?
2. Verses 12-34. What follows from a denial of the resurrection? What are the final consequences of Christ's resurrection?
3. Verses 35-50. What is the analogy between Adam and Christ? cf. also verse 22.
4. Verses 51-58. What will take place when Christ comes again? In what way should a Christian live, in view of his faith in Christ's return?

1 CORINTHIANS 16

Final instructions and greetings.

1. What practical arrangements does Paul make for the collection? Why was he so keen about it?
2. What commands does he give the Corinthians in verses 13-14? Why were they especially important for that particular church? Are they especially important for me? Learn these verses by heart.

AN INTRODUCTION TO 2 CORINTHIANS

CHAPTERS 1-9

This letter contains some of the most characteristically Pauline passages, revealing the depth of his theology, and the warmth of his temperament. He is seen as a very affectionate, feeling man, hurt by misunderstanding and deeply involved in his converts at Corinth. Chapters 3-6, where he speaks of his experiences as an apostle, compares the old and new covenants, and states his belief in heaven with Christ, are among the greatest in the whole Bible. In chapters 8-9 he gives a theological basis for the church collection - it is a sign of unity among Christians, a sign of faith in God who will certainly reward the cheerful and generous giver.

CHAPTERS 10-13

Some scholars believe these chapters to be part of the severe letter. There is certainly a marked change in tone. They are what is described by the New Jerusalem Bible as Paul's Apologia, in which he lays bare his feelings and catalogues his sufferings, while still repeatedly declaring his love for the unruly Corinthians. Nowhere does Paul seem more himself, yet so Christ-like; so human, yet so saintly.

2 CORINTHIANS 1

Greetings and details of Paul's plans.

1. Consider the formal greeting (verses 1-2). How does Paul describe himself? Compare with Romans 1:1 and 1 Corinthians 1:1.
2. How does Paul refer to his sufferings and to those of his converts? See verses 4-7. What great advantage has Christianity over most of the world religions in its attitude to suffering?
3. What do we learn about Paul in this chapter?

2 CORINTHIANS 2

It is possible that the man referred to in verses 6-7 is the offender of 1 Corinthians 5:1.

1. What can we learn from verses 1-7 concerning discipline and its purpose and effects? Are we ever inclined to vindictiveness against severe offenders? What is our attitude towards those in our community who 'give scandal'? See verse 7.
2. Does Paul promise success in every case and at all times to those who preach the gospel?

2 CORINTHIANS 3

This is one of the most important chapters in the Bible. It is not easy reading, because it requires knowledge of the Old Testament to understand the argument - that the giving of the old Law on Sinai has been superceded by the gift of the Holy Spirit who dwells in us, changes our hearts, and gives us the power to keep the Law - makes us pleasing to God, and able to grow like him.

1. Read Exodus 33-34, especially 33:18-23 and 34:29-35 for the Old Testament background to this important chapter.
2. What contrast does Paul make between the old and the new covenants? List the ways in which the new is superior to the old.
3. Meditate on verse 18, learn it by heart, and apply it to one's life of prayer.

2 CORINTHIANS 4

The subject continued. Paul's own experience as an apostle.

1. Are there aspects of the gospel, revealed to us, which we resist and try to hide from ourselves, because we cannot face the implications? What does Paul suggest? see especially verse 6.
2. Why is the treasure (verse 60) in earthen vessels? How does Paul describe his own ministry? Can any of this find a resonance in our own experience?
3. What is awaiting the faithful disciple?

2 CORINTHIANS 5

This is one of the few sections in scripture that treats of life after death.

1. What awaits the Christian at death? How is the gift of the Spirit a guarantee that we shall have a life with God? On what are we to be judged at death?
2. Verses 11-21. In what sense can we all be said to have died (verse 14)? What effect has Christ's dying had (verse 15)? See verse 21.
3. What is meant by saying that those who are "in Christ" are a 'new creation'? See verses 18-19.

2 CORINTHIANS 6

It is possible that 6:14 - 7:1 are part of an earlier letter. They are out of place here. Notice 6:13 and 7:2.

1. How does Paul describe the life of an apostle? What is the final impression: positive or negative?
2. Verses 14 - 7:1. Paul warns against the danger of infiltration by paganism. What scripture does he use to support his argument? How do we apply these principles to the problem of a) inculturation and b) relationships with a secularised world?

2 CORINTHIANS 7

Paul's relations with the Corinthian Christians.

1. Verses 6:11-13, 7:2-7. What do we learn here of the generosity of Paul's heart and his great love for his converts?
2. Titus, Paul's envoy, had returned from Corinth with a good account of the church's attitude. How does Paul show that these crises can be for everyone's good if occasion is taken to learn from them? Have you any examples from your own experience?

2 CORINTHIANS 8

For this collection, cf. 1 Corinthians 16:1.

1. In what condition was the Macedonian church at this time? See verses 1-6. What was their spiritual state? How can they be an example for us all?
2. What arguments does Paul use to encourage generosity in giving aid? (verses 7-15). How can we be inspired by these arguments to help the needy at home and abroad?
3. What qualities does Paul commend in Titus and the other two workers mentioned in verses 16-24? (Traditionally, verse 18 has been thought to refer to Luke).

2 CORINTHIANS 9

This chapter is probably an independent note addressed to the Corinthians on the subject of the Collection at some other date, placed here by an editor.

1. Is there any hint that Paul was uncertain of the Corinthians's generosity in giving aid? See verses 1-5.
2. What further arguments does Paul use to urge the Corinthians?

2 CORINTHIANS 10-13

It is possible that these chapters form part of the 'severe letter' (2 Corinthians 2:3 ff.) They were certainly written in a very different mood from chapter 9.

2 CORINTHIANS 10

Paul seems to be responding to sarcastic accusations from some church members.

1. What accusations did the disaffected group make against Paul?
2. How did he deal with these accusations? Have we sometimes not only the right but the duty to refute false accusations? On what principles?
3. What claims does Paul make for himself?

2 CORINTHIANS 11

We do not know what the intruding preachers were teaching in Corinth, but possibly verse 4 provides a clue: did they concentrate more on the historical Jesus and less on the risen Lord?

1. Verses 1-15. What, apart from their doctrine, made these other teachers unacceptable to Paul? In what way did their attitude to the people differ from his?
2. Why is Paul driven to talk about himself? What do we learn new about him? Which of his adventures are recorded in Acts?

2 CORINTHIANS 12

We are indebted to the unruly, uncharitable, selfish Corinthians, since their behaviour provoked this outburst, and tells us so much of Paul's intimate life with God.

1. How does Paul describe his mystical experiences? What sort of fruit did these experiences have in his life and in his teaching?
2. Why did he receive the 'thorn' in the flesh (verse 7)? What lessons did it teach him? Have I such a 'thorn'? Do I let it teach me?
3. What was most Christ-like about Paul's attitude to his converts? How does his love for them underly all the hurt he felt at their suspicion, superficiality and ingratitude? Do we *LOVE* our fellow Christians as Paul did?
4. What were his greatest anxieties about the church at Corinth? See verses 20-21.

2 CORINTHIANS 13

After a sad conclusion to the body of the letter, Paul ends in charity, and with an important doxology.

1. Verses 1-6. When and in what circumstances does Paul intend to hold a judicial enquiry? Are there occasions when love demands severity?
2. Verses 7-10. Notice the depth of Paul's disinterested love. He only wants the real good of his converts, even at the expense of his own humiliation. To what truth is he referring in verse 8?
3. Examine carefully the concluding exhortation and prayer (verses 11-14). How does verse 11 sum up the whole letter? How does verse 14 give us teaching on the Trinity?

AN INTRODUCTION
TO
THE LETTER TO THE GALATIANS

In this letter Paul is at his most explosive. With hardly an introductory formula (cf. Galatians 1:1-5 with his other letters), he launches into the attack. 'I am astonished that you are so quickly deserting him who called you in the grace of Christ' and turning to a different gospel (1:6)), and in chapter 3 he calls them 'foolish Galatians' (3:1). What had happened? Who, in any case, were the Galatians?

It seems they were the people of North Galatia (see Acts 16:6 and 18:23), a Celtic people in Arabia, between Bythinia to the north, Cappadocia to the east and Phrygia to the west. What had provoked Paul's letter? 'Some who trouble you and want to pervert the gospel of Christ' (1:7) had queried Paul's authority as an apostle, apparently on the grounds that he was not one of those who had known Christ personally. They claimed that his teaching was unsound, presumably because he appeared to neglect the Law of Moses. They further had accused him of opportunism for having permitted circumcision (5:11) and of watering down the gospel to make it easier for Gentiles. All this had unsettled the Galatians, insecure as new converts, and probably anxious to measure up to the seemingly stricter demands of these Judaizers.

Paul wrote this strong letter, in fact, to reassure them. He shows deep affection for them, and seems to have memories of their kind treatment of himself during an illness (4:12-15). He gives a lively account of his confrontation with Peter at Antioch over the question of table fellowship. The last two chapters of Galatians are among the most important that Paul ever wrote.

The letter was probably written about AD 57.

GALATIANS 1

Paul goes straight to the point, after the briefest of preliminaries. To defend his teaching, he launches into an apologia.

1. Verses 1-10. Compare this opening with Romans 1:1-15 or with 1 Corinthians 1:1-9 or any other of Paul's letters. What differences do you find?
2. What does Paul say in these verses a) about God; b) about Christ; c) about himself; d) about the gospel.?
3. Verses 11-24. What information does Paul give concerning his conversion and early career as a Christian? What is he emphasising? Who were Cephas (verse 18) and James (verse 19)?

GALATIANS 2

This chapter contains interesting biographical material concerning Peter and Paul.

1. Verses 1-10. Why did Paul go to Jerusalem? Whom did he meet there, and what was the outcome? What was the real issue at stake? (See verse 3). Who were the false brethren who spied out the freedom of Paul and his converts?
2. Verses 11-21. Why was Paul obliged to oppose Cephas? Note the scenario: Paul and Barnabas and their Gentile converts welcoming Cephas and all sharing a meal; then a group of Jewish Christians arriving from Jerusalem, and Cephas out of human respect (verse 12) eating apart with them, and dragging Barnabas in too! What lay behind all this? See especially verses 16,20.
3. What may we learn from this chapter concerning the principles governing Christian communities, unity of churches and co-operation with authorities, and honest, loyal dissent?

GALATIANS 3

Paul wrestles with the question of the Law and its inefficacy for our salvation. He invokes the example of Abraham, as one who was justified before ever the Law was given.

1. Verses 1-5. The immediate problem seems to be that the Galatian converts have been told they must be circumcised (verse 3). What is the experience of the Spirit that Paul is appealing to? How can we apply this situation to our own church life?
2. Verses 6-9. In what sense can Christians be said to be children of Abraham?
3. Verses 10-14. How does Christ's death free us from bondage to the Law and to sin?
4. Verses 15.29. What does Paul mean by the promise to Abraham coming before the Law? What was the purpose of the Law? (verse 19). Can it, of itself, create the dispositions necessary for obedience to it? (verse 21).
5. What did Christ's coming mean?
6. Consider verses 28-29 in detail, working out the implications for the people of God. If each clause was taken seriously, what changes would this entail in the life of the Church and of the world?

GALATIANS 4

Paul uses the examples of the difference between a minor still under tutelage contrasted with an adult legatee, and that of a slave and a free born son, to teach the difference between the soul in bondage to the Law and the Christian freed by his adoption as a child of Christ.

1. Verses 1-7-. What is meant by the comparison with an heir to a property? What event made us 'come of age'?
2. Make a list of all the blessings that Christ's redeeming death has bought for us (3:26 - 4:7).
3. What kind of religious belief and practice is described in verses 8-11? In its context it evidently means that the Galatian Christians, though of Gentile origin, were trying to keep the whole Jewish law. What kind of temptations recur through the ages to seek security in legalism and pious practices? How do we know if we are really free?
4. Verses 12-31. Paul uses Genesis 16 as an allegory. Work it out with regard to Paul's argument. Is this a perennial problem in the Church? Can you think of any other occasions when the faithful have behaved like children of the slave woman instead of children of the promise?

GALATIANS 5

The consequences of Christian freedom: a new life of faith in love contrasted with the bondage of a sinner. The fruit of the Spirit.

1. Verses 1-12. What results for the Galatians would come from accepting circumcision? See verses 2, 3, 4. What does it mean to wait by faith for the hope of righteousness 'through the Spirit' (verse 5)?
2. Verses 12-15. What abuses of freedom are mentioned in these verses?
3. Verses 16-21. What does Paul mean by 'the flesh'? Notice that the list of sins in verses 19-21 includes other than sexual sins. List the sins in the order of the Ten Commandments.
4. Verses 22-26. Those who live by and walk in the Spirit produce a harvest. What is this harvest? Does it mean that we ATTAIN these virtues by practice, or do they grow naturally from the indwelling Spirit within us? Why is this harvest not always abundant?

GALATIANS 6

Concluding advice. Paul's impatience and anger have dissipated, and he ends his Letter in charity and peace.

1. Verses 1-6. List the items of advice that Paul gives for relations between people. What should be our attitude a) to ourselves and b) to each other? What hint is given in verse 6? Do we always observe it?
2. Verses 7-18. What is the core of Paul's teaching? Note especially verses 14-15. Who is now the Israel of God?

AN INTRODUCTION
TO
THE LETTER TO THE EPHESIANS

I appeal to you for my child, Onesimus,
whose father I have become in my imprisonment
(Philemon 10).

There are a few scholars who have suggested that the author of this letter was Onesimus, who was Bishop of Ephesus towards the end of the first century. This may seem preposterous, but, in fact there are quite a few difficulties about the Pauline authorship of this letter, and also about its destination. The title 'To the Ephesians' was not on the original text, there are hints that the writer does not know his audience personally (1:15; 3:1-2; 4:21), and the writer speaks as if someone other than himself founded the church there (2:20; 3:5), an 'apostle', seeming to infer that he does not rank as such himself. The style of the letter is not like Paul's, and there are some puzzles. For example, Paul in Colossians 1:26 uses the word 'mystery' to mean the mystery of Christ's hidden presence in the church; but in Ephesians 1:9 and 3:4 it is used to mean the revelation of God's plan to reconcile Jews and Gentiles in Christ.

The image of the church in Ephesians is more universal than in Paul's letters, where the emphasis is on the local community; in Ephesians one gets more the sense of a later generation looking back to the time of the founders (2:20; 3:5). It is perhaps the case of a late first century Christian editing Paul's letters, and introducing them with a summary of his own, based largely on Colossians, but developed, because the church had moved on and acquired a somewhat different perspective.

It does not, of course, matter at all whether Paul or some other writer was responsible for this very great epistle, bringing together as it does the great themes of the new humanity in Christ, the Church as Christ's body, and the vision of the pleroma - the oneness of all things in Him.

EPHESIANS 1

1. In this great hymn are listed six spiritual blessings 'in the heavenly places' (verse 3). Can you pick them out?
2. Take verses 16-23 as an example of Christian prayer. What are a) the graces and b) the spiritual truths that the writer prays for on behalf of his readers? Do we pray enough for the spiritual welfare of others, or do we concentrate on material blessings in our petitions for them?
3. What do we learn concerning Christ in this chapter? See especially verses 20-23.
4. What do we learn concerning a) the Father and b) the Holy Spirit?

EPHESIANS 2

1. Verses 1-10. Contrast man's state before and after his redemption in Christ. What characteristics especially of fallen man are described in verses 1-3? God's initiative is emphasised. What part do we play (verse 8)?
2. Verses 11-22. Compare the situation of Jews and Gentiles before Christ's death on the cross (verses 11-12). What has Christ's death meant for them both? What is the resulting situation?

EPHESIANS 3

1. Verses 1-13. What occasion is referred to in verse 3? What is the 'mystery of Christ' which was revealed in the New Testament? What was Paul's mission? (verse 8).

Verses 14-21. What are the graces the writer prays for on behalf of his readers? In what way does his prayer offer a reflection on the virtues of faith, hope and charity?

EPHESIANS 4

1. Verses 1-6. What threat to Christian unity is shadowed in the exhortation to lowliness, meekness, patience and forebearance? What principle of unity is invoked in verses 4-6?
2. Verses 7-13. What are the gifts listed that come to us as a result of Christ's ascension? What is their purpose? (verse 12). Does the Church make full use of these gifts in her members? Do we *expect* to receive such gifts in our community?
3. Verses 14-16. What kinds of false or unorthodox teaching threatens the unity of Christians today? See verses 15-16.
4. Verses 17-32. In what ways does the writer's description of the Gentile world of his time (verses 17-19) apply to the secular world of today? What are the principles that should govern the life of Christians? What things should we put away? (verses 25 ff.). Notice the reason given each time.
5. Note all the references in this epistle to honesty and plain speaking between Christians. What virtue must always accompany and inspire 'speaking the truth'?

EPHESIANS 5

1. Consider verses 3-17, in the light of the present day and draw out a) the teaching on sexual morality, pornography, etc. and b) the duty of Christians to throw light on a confused and despairing generation.
2. What does the writer say a) about Christian marriage and b) the Church, in this passage? How does one throw light on the other? Compare this teaching on marriage with 1 Corinthians 7.

EPHESIANS 6

1. How is advice to parents and to children balanced? Are both parts of the section equally observed?
2. Slavery should have no part in a Christian society - the writer was a man of his time - but is there any aspect of the advice given in verses 5-9 which could apply to modern industrial relations?
3. How does the writer interpret the Old Testament doctrine of holy warfare in the spiritual combat? What are the virtues with which we must arm ourselves? What above all should we never cease to do (verses 18-19)?

AN INTRODUCTION
TO
THE LETTER TO THE PHILIPPIANS

It was at Philippi that Paul established his first European church about 50 AD in the home of Lydia (Acts 16:14). Philippi was a Roman colony, though there were many Greeks in the town and some Jews, though these did not have a synagogue but met by the riverside (Acts 16:13). Paul apparently only went there once, when he founded the church, but the Philippians twice sent him money when he was in Thessalonica (Philippians 4:16), and again when he was in prison (4:18) by Epaphroditus, who, however, fell ill while he was visiting Paul (2:36). Paul writes to thank them for their generosity, to give news of Epaphroditus and to warn them against the Judaisers (3:2) who were in the area.

The letter was probably written from Ephesus while Paul was in prison, about 56 or 57. The references to Caesar's household (4:22) and to the praetorian guard (1:13) could apply to Ephesus, and we know he suffered there severely (1 Corinthians 15:30-32; 2 Corinthians 1:8-10). Paul had a special love for the Philippians, and this letter is full of affection for them. Their only problems seem to have been a certain friction between two ladies (4:2) and a vaguer threat from Judaisers.

PHILIPPIANS 1

Introduction. Paul gives an outline of his own situation - prison.

1. Look up Acts 16:12-40. Note that Philippi, a Roman city in Macedonia, was the first European church that Paul founded.
2. Compare the greeting to bishops and deacons (verse 1) with the greetings in the other letters. Would Philippi have had a bishop and deacons in our modern sense? What other words could be used to translate these terms?
3. Verses 3-7. What gave Paul joy in writing to the Philippians? What made him so sure they were on the road to salvation?
4. Verses 8-11. What special graces did Paul pray would be granted to them? Do we pray thus for our Christian friends?
5. What does Paul say about a) his faith in and b) his desire for heaven? Why does he think he will not die yet?
6. How does he refer to his imprisonment? Can we be equally positive about any trials we may have to bear?

PHILIPPIANS 2

He exhorts them to unity and humility, and quotes an ancient Christian hymn. He describes the mission of Timothy and Epaphroditus.

1. Verses 1-4. What virtue is especially emphasised here? Is there any sign in this letter that the Philippian Christian community was divided? See 1:1,4,7,8, etc. where 'all' is repeated and repeated.
2. Verses 5-11. This is an early Christian hymn, quoted by Paul. How is Christ contrasted with Adam and compared with the 'servant' and with the son of man in Daniel (Daniel 7:13)?
3. Verses 12-18. What advice is here given? How can we 'hold fast the word of life'?
4. Verses 19-30. What qualities did Timothy and Epaphroditus have as co-workers with Paul? How do we measure up to their standards?

PHILIPPIANS 3

The way of Christian salvation. Paul offers his own example and experience.

1. What is meant by 'we are the true circumcision' (verse 3)? Look up Jeremiah 9:26. What are the essential characteristics of Christ's disciples? In what sense are we tempted to rely 'on the flesh'?
2. Paul lists the human and religious reasons that should give him confidence 'in the flesh' (verses 4-6). What are the reasons that give us that same 'confidence'? Do we rely on them, or do we count them all as loss for the sake of Christ?
3. Verses 7-11. How does Paul express and sum up what his following of Christ means to him? How does he 'know Christ'? How do we know him? (Verses 10,11).
4. Verses 12-21. What is the end to which all Paul's striving is leading? What is the one thing (verse 19) which can prevent us attaining that goal? Do we take this warning seriously enough?

PHILIPPIANS 4

He refers to individuals in the church, thanks them all for their love and support and concludes with a blessing.

1. Verses 1-9. What glimpses do we get in these verses of church life in Philippi? What virtues does Paul especially emphasise? Is our church life guided by these principles?
2. Do we share Paul's outlook on life as described in verses 11-13? If not, how do we attain it?
3. Draw out all the teaching in this letter about Christian giving and sharing.

AN INTRODUCTION
TO
THE LETTER TO THE COLOSSIANS

Colossae was in Asia Minor about 110 miles east of Ephesus, an important textile centre. The church there was not founded by Paul (2:1), but by Epaphras (1:6-7) perhaps himself a convert of Paul, to whom he had reported some dangerous tendencies in local teachers (2:8, 16-23), a hotch-potch of early Gnosticism and Jewish practice.

It is interesting to remark how persistent have been such tendencies in Christianity at least in popular folk religion. One thinks of the excesses of mariolatry and of the worship of angels and of saints in some countries (cf. 2:8); of the medieval devotion to ascetic practices, sometimes of a highly exaggerated sort (cf. 2:16-18).

The letter shows an interesting development (further emphasised in Ephesians) on 1 Corinthians 7, where Paul wrote as if there was no need to prepare for the future, as the second coming of Christ was imminent. By the time he wrote to the Colossians, the Christian community was beginning to see the need for laying the foundations for the future - for raising children and educating them in the faith, for developing a theology of marriage and of social relationships.

Paul was in prison, probably in Rome under house arrest (Acts 28:16-31). This would date the letter to AD 61-3, which probably explains the advanced Christology of Colossians.

COLOSSIANS 1

Paul's prayer for his readers. The great Christological poem. The reconciliation of the Gentile Colossians with God in Christ.

1. Verses 1-14. What are the graces the Colossians have received when they accepted the gospel? See verses 4-5. What does Paul especially ask for them in his prayer (verses 9-12)? Make this prayer our own - for ourselves and for each other.
2. Verses 15-20. Compare this poem with John 1:1-14 and with Proverbs 8:22-31. What is said concerning Christ's pre-existence, his relation to creation, and to the church?
3. Verses 21-29. What was the state of the Colossians before their conversion? What accounts, in many people nowadays too, for this situation of estrangement and of hostility (see verse 21)? How have the Colossians been reconciled to God? How is our generation to be reconciled?
4. What are the conditions necessary for perseverance in the faith?
5. What was Paul's attitude to his suffering? See especially verse 29. Do WE count on the energy Christ 'mightily inspires within us' for his service, or do we trust in our own strength?

COLOSSIANS 2

Paul warns them against errors: false asceticism, angel worship.

1. Verses 1-5. What is the mystery of which Paul writes?
2. Verses 6-15. What has Christ done for us? Make a list of each aspect of our redemption and its effects.
3. Verses 16-23. Paul is attacking some (Jewish? Gnostic?) teachers who would emphasise non-essentials. Are we Christians ever in danger of making the same mistake? Give some examples either from this chapter or from your own observation and experience.

COLOSSIANS 3

Rules for Christian behaviour. Family morality.

1. Verses 1-17. If we have been 'raised with Christ', how should we live? What should we avoid doing? What virtues, above all, should mark our way of living?
2. Compare verses 18-25 with Ephesians 5:22 - 6:9.

COLOSSIANS 4

Advice on prayer. News of other evangelists. Final greetings.

1. What advice does Paul give a) about prayer and b) about relations with non-Christians? Can I learn from verses 3,4,12 how to pray for others?
2. Find out all you can about the people mentioned in this chapter: Tychicus in Acts 20:4; Titus 3:12; Onesimus in Philemon; Aristarchus in Acts 19:29; Epaphras in Colossians 1:7; Demas in Philemon and in 2 Timothy 44:10; Archippus (probably a son of Philemon) in Philemon 2.

AN INTRODUCTION
TO
1 and 2 THESSALONIANS

How many of us realise, when we come to the 29th Sunday of the Year and turn to the Second Reading (1 Thessalonians 1:1-5) that we are actually reading the very first words of what we now call the New Testament! Paul's letters to his converts of Thessalonica were written in AD 50. No earlier letter is known, the gospels, of course, were not yet written, and though some believe that the Letter of James dates from 49, most scholars date it in the sixties. Paul, of course, had no idea that he was making history. He just sat down and wrote, in some concern, to a church newly converted, now suffering persecution, and with some gaps in the instruction he had been able to give during the short time he had been there (Acts 17:1-10,13).

Thessalonica was an important seaport in Northern Greece, cosmopolitan, like many ports, with a large Jewish population. Paul, Silvanus and Timothy arrived there in AD 50, having been arrested and imprisoned in Philippi and then expelled from there (Acts 16). In Thessalonica, Paul preached in the synagogue and made converts especially among the "devout Greeks" and not a few leading women (Acts 17:4). They had to leave the synagogue, and the church met in the house of a certain Jason (Acts 17:5), but the Jews attacked the house, and in the uproar Paul and Silas were obliged to leave.

Paul wrote 1 Thessalonians probably from Corinth. It is a gentle letter, assuring them of his love and affection, and giving further instruction especially concerning the resurrection of the dead and the second coming of Christ. 2 Thessalonians was written a few months later. Paul has had disturbing news. Not only is persecution continuing, but some enthusiasts were declaring that the Day of the Lord had already come (2 Thessalonians 2:2). The apostle writes to reassure them, and to encourage steady work.

The most important teaching in these letters is their eschatology - the doctrine that Christ will come at the end of all things to judge the living and the dead. In 2 Thessalonians Paul teaches that before the event takes place, there will be apostasy on a large scale, and an anti-Christ, an agent of Satan, will try to undo the work of Christ. Satan is always active, but the anti-Christ cannot appear yet because something or someone (2 Thessalonians 2:6-7) is preventing it. When he does appear Christ will come and destroy him. Late New Testament books deal with other aspects of eschatology (Matthew 24 and par., 2 Peter 3, Revelation) but Paul has laid the foundations in these letters.

1 THESSALONIANS 1

Read Acts 17:1-10, 13 for the background. Notice how short a time Paul had spent in Thessalonica. Introduction and praise of the Thessalonion Christians.

1. What qualities are especially commended in this church?
2. What do we know of the 'affliction' (verse 6) in which the Thessalonions received the gospel? See Acts 17.
3. How did they spread the gospel themselves?
4. Paul gives a short summary of his teaching (verses 9-10). What are the main points?

1 THESSALONIANS 2

Paul's motives in preaching to them. His commendation of their faith and courage. His concern for them.

1. Check with Acts 16:19-40 for the events at Philippi (verse 2). What are the qualities of an apostle mentioned in 1-12?
2. How did the Thessalonions respond? (verses 13-16). What sufferings befell them?

1 THESSALONIANS 3

His relief at hearing news of them from Timothy.

1. What especially shows Paul's love and concern for the Thessalonians? What did he ask for in prayer for them? Why do you think he was concerned to supply anything lacking in their instruction?
2. What virtue does he emphasise above all?

1 THESSALONIANS 4

He exhorts them to holiness, purity and charity. His doctrine of the resurrection of the dead.

1. In what way should Christians live? What sins especially should they avoid and why? What are their characteristic virtues?
2. Verses 13-18. What does Paul teach here concerning the Lord's second coming?

1 THESSALONIANS 5

How Christians should be always ready and on the watch for Jesus' return. Final greetings.

1. Verses 1-11. Check the echoes from the gospels in these verses. What did Christ say a) about the timing of the Day of the Lord and b) about the preparations needed? How does Paul exhort the Thessalonians to be watchful?
2. Make a list of the advice given in this chapter. Note especially verses 17, 19-21. How do we apply this?

2 THESSALONIANS 1

More instruction on the return of Christ and the judgment.

1. How does Paul console his converts in their sufferings and hardships? How does he describe the Day of the Lord?
2. What graces does he pray for for them?

2 THESSALONIANS 2

How to tell the signs of the Lord's coming. Paul emphasises that 'the end is not yet'. We must watch and persevere to the end.

1. Much of what Paul says in this chapter is based on his oral teaching to his original readers. What is his main point in verse 2?
2. What does he say a) about the rebellion and b) about the man of lawlessness? How do we understand this rebellion? Has it occurred once and for all, does it recur, or is it still to come? What is meant by the man of lawlessness? cf. Daniel 11:36.
3. Notice the numerous references to deceit in this passage (verses 2,3,9,10,11,12). Is it a coincidence that Jesus calls Satan the father of lies (John 8:44)?
4. Verses 13-15. God took the initiative in our salvation. What is involved in this? How must we play our part?
5. What four prayers does Paul make for his converts?

2 THESSALONIANS 3

Patience and hard work are emphasised, and attention to humdrum duties.

1. Paul asks for their prayers. What do verses 1-4 tell us about his circumstances at the time of writing?
2. What has Paul to say about the necessity of hard, daily work? How did he set them an example? What advice, based on this text, would you give to a person made redundant at his place of employment?
3. Suppose that these two letters were the only New Testament writings that had been preserved and that the whole Christian gospel had been relayed entirely by oral tradition. Go through 1 and 2 Thessalonians, making a list of all the points of doctrine contained in them. Then make a further list of the essential Christian doctrines omitted. Compare the two lists.

AN INTRODUCTION
TO
THE SO-CALLED PASTORAL EPISTLES
(1 and 2 TIMOTHY and TITUS)

These three letters, which contain some Pauline material, especially 2 Timothy, were probably composed by a disciple of Paul, about the year 80. The reasons why they are not nowadays ascribed to Paul are as follows: there is little reference to the great Pauline preoccupations - the cross, the Body of Christ; there is no argument, just condemnation of false teaching; the style is dull and rather flat. The structures of church government seem to have advanced, and the whole atmosphere is that of a second generation Christianity, grappling with mundane problems of day to day organisation, and authoritarian in its attitude to erroneous doctrine.

1 TIMOTHY

I must confess that this is not my favourite epistle, and it has been responsible, together with 1 Corinthians 11:3-16, for the charge of anti-feminism, directed against Paul. I do not believe he was in fact responsible for much of this letter, but find its tone distasteful with regard to women, especially 2:11-15. However, it is possible that verse 15 means 'women will be saved through the birth of the Child' (RSV mgn) which puts a different complexion on the matter, reversing Genesis 3:16 and confirming Genesis 3:15. And there is an interesting reference to women deacons (3:11) and to the enrolment of widows (5:9 ff), pointing to structures that did not exclude women as totally as 2:11 would imply.

The letter abounds in good, sound sense and practical advice. It is a good blue-print for all bishops, parish priests and other church leaders.

1 TIMOTHY 1

Problems of false teaching. The Law is for evil-doers, not for those on the way to salvation.

1. What false teaching is attacked by the author? Are there still sects which misuse scripture or engage in idle speculation (verses 4,6)?
2. Verses 8-15. How does the author indicate the limitations of the law? cf. verse 9 with Romans 7:7, 12-14. What is the 'gospel of the blessed God'?
3. Note the number of occasions in which faith is mentioned. Why is it linked several times with conscience?

1 TIMOTHY 2

Intercessory prayer enjoined on the churches. Women to remain silent and dress suitably.

1. Draw out the theological truths contained in verses 1-7.
2. Why does the author enjoin prayer for the king and those in authority? See verses 2 and 4. What benefits are asked for? Do we pray for our political leaders, or do we merely criticise them?
3. What situation is the author reflecting in verses 9-15? Compare Galatians 3:28. Why this change in attitude? Is verse 14 a fair interpretation of Genesis 3? Are women basically inferior to men? cf. John 11:24-27; 20:18 etc. and 1 Timothy 3:11.

1 TIMOTHY 3

The qualities necessary in a bishop or deacon. The mystery of the church.

1. Verses 1-7. What qualities are required in a bishop (elder)?

2. Verses 8-13. What qualities are required in a deacon or in a deaconess (verse 22)? Compare the two lists, and note the emphases. What is missing in these verses?
3. What is meant by the description of the church in verse 15?
4. Take each clause in the fragment of the hymn (verse 16) and explain it.

1 TIMOTHY 4

Rejection of marriage was one of the hall-marks of Gnosticism.

1. Verses 1-5. What heresies are detailed in these verses? What does the author say concerning a) marriage (see verse 4 and 2:15) and b) food? How should we put this teaching into practice?
2. What advice is given to a young minister of the gospel? Is enough emphasis placed on this duty in the training of priests and ministers?

1 TIMOTHY 5

Concerning widows and elders.

1. There are three categories of widows mentioned. Distinguish the three.
2. What qualities are essential for a consecrated widow? Do you think the Order of Widows should be revived in the Church? What would be the advantages?

1 TIMOTHY 6

The duties of slaves. The problem of false teaching. Timothy is urged to draw strength from his ordination to the service of the Church. The duties of wealthy Christians.

1. What characteristics of false teachers are given in verses 3-5,20,21? What positive advice is given in verses 11-14? Make these two sections into an examination of conscience.
2. What is said about a) the dangers and b) the right use of money? What theology should lie behind our attitude to riches? Compare verses 6-8 with Proverbs 30:8-9.
3. Summarise the doctrinal points in this chapter. See verses 13-16.

2 TIMOTHY

This letter seems to incorporate genuine Pauline fragments (cf. 1:15-18; 4:9-17,19-20). If it was put together by a disciple of Paul, as seems likely, he was perhaps someone who had been close to him, and knew his sufferings at first hand, for there is a genuine ring in the account of Paul's missionary career. It is even possible that it was dictated by Paul during his last imprisonment, for it gives us a vivid picture of the aging apostle, without material comfort (4:13), very much alone, with nothing to look forward to in this life, but with a faith as strong as ever.

2 TIMOTHY 1

Timothy's religious and family background.

1. In what way can Timothy's career be a model for many Christians? How is he advised to build on the foundations laid for him? cf. verses 5-6 with 7-14.
2. Consider verse 7. How does it apply to my life? To the life of the Church?
3. Verses 15-18. Note the reference to Onesiphorous' household (and cf. 4:19) with the implication that Onesiphorus has died. What therefore are we to make of the prayer for him at verse 18? cf. 2 Maccabees 12:45.

2 TIMOTHY 2

The difficulties Timothy has to face. False teachers.

1. What is the point of the three little parables in verses 3-6?
2. What is taught concerning Christ in verses 8-13?
3. What ideals are put before Timothy in verses 20-26?

2 TIMOTHY 3

Jannes and Jambres (verse 8) are the names given in Jewish tradition to the leaders of the Egyptian magicians (Exodus 7:11-13,22) and are also said to be sons of Balaam (Numbers 22:2).

1. Consider verses 1-9 as a picture of our current situation. Is it accurate? Do we live in 'times of stress'?
2. What is said in this chapter of the importance of scripture (verses 15-16)? Learn verse 16 by heart and apply it.

2 TIMOTHY 4

Paul's last words to a faithful friend and disciple.

1. Make a list of the main points in the charge to Timothy. How does this chapter sum up the difficulties that beset an apostle?
2. How does Paul face his approaching death?
3. Note the references to several of Paul's companions. Look up and check references to them, eg. Demas (Colossians 4:14 and Philemon 24); Titus (2 Corinthians 2:13; 7:6-14; 8:6-23; 12:18; Galatians 2:1-3); Tychicus (Acts 20:4; Colossians 4:7; Titus 3:12); Trophimus (Acts 20:4; 21:29). Note the contrast in the careers of Demas and of Mark.

THE LETTER TO TITUS

This is the third of the so-called pastoral epistles - written by a disciple of Paul about 80-90 AD, incorporating a genuine Pauline fragment (3:12-14). The tone of this letter is very similar to that of 1 Timothy: the same intolerance of opposition, the same preoccupation with suitable, sound leadership. However, there are two important doctrinal passages - 2:11-14 which sums up teaching on salvation in Pauline thinking though not in his style; and 3:4-7 which seems to be taken from an instruction manual for converts. There is a clear statement of the divinity in Christ in 2:13.

TITUS 1

The appointment of elders. Problems of false teaching.

1. List the articles of doctrine in verses 1-4.
2. What was the purpose of appointing elders? What were their duties? What qualities did they need? Compare 1 Timothy 3:1-13.

TITUS 2

All classes of Christians are urged to appropriate behaviour.

1. Note the different groups of Christians mentioned and exhorted. Draw up a similar paragraph to include all members of a modern Christian community.
2. Verses 11-14. What points of doctrine are included in these verses? Note especially the title given to Christ in verse 13.

TITUS 3

Advice continued, with special advice for Titus himself.

1. Note the social and moral teaching in verses 1-3. Compare with 1 Timothy 2:1-4 and with 1 Peter 2:13-17. How is such teaching applicable today?
2. Verses 4-7 contain another closely packed section of doctrine. Draw out the truths taught there. What is especially notable about verses 5-6?
3. How are heretics to be dealt with?

AN INTRODUCTION
TO
THE LETTER OF PAUL TO PHILEMON

This letter is so much from the heart of Paul that one can almost hear his appeal coming through as one reads it. I can never read it aloud without choking. There is something so moving about the gentleness of his approach to Philemon, and his love for both the slave and his owner.

'Refresh my heart in Christ' he says, having very gently reminded Philemon of how much he owes to himself. The circumstances are fairly clear from the letter. Onesimus (whose name means useful) had run away from his master Philemon after robbing him, but somehow he had come to Paul and been converted by him. Paul now writes on his behalf to Philemon. Legally the slave belongs to his master, but, as Christians, they are now brothers. One feels that Philemon, who preserved the letter, must have responded to the appeal.

The references to Epaphras and to Paul's imprisonment, would point to a similar situation and date to the Letter to the Colossians, AD 61-3.

PHILEMON

This is a personal letter, appealing to Philemon to receive back his runaway slave with kindness and understanding.

1. What light does this letter throw on Paul himself?
2. If you had been Philemon, could you have resisted such an appeal? What are the arguments that Paul uses?
3. Paul saw the evils of slavery as being brought to an end by a change of heart on the part of the slave owner (verses 6, 14, 16). Could this principle be applied to similar situations today?

AN INTRODUCTION
TO
THE LETTER TO THE HEBREWS

This letter is really a homily or written sermon, exhorting Jewish Christians to remain faithful to Christ and not to lapse back into Judaism. The author is thought by some scholars to have been Apollos, but there is no proof of this. The quotations from scripture are from the Septuagint, and its style is Hellenistic, which could fit Apollos (cf. Acts 18).

It is a classic example of Jewish Christian use of scripture, seeing Christ as the fulfilment of Old Testament law, worship and prophecy. The author draws on the whole Jewish heritage: the psalms (chapters 1 and 2); the Exodus (chapters 3 and 4); the great liturgical ceremonies expressing Jewish faith in God's acceptance of sacrifice as expiation for sin (chapters 5-10); showing that they all reveal Christ, and are brought to their completion in him, the Son of God (1:2), the new Moses (3:3), 'the apostle and high priest of our confession' (3:1). The epistle sets forth Christ not only in his divine nature, but also points to the reality of his humility and suffering as man (2:18, 4:15, 5:7-10).

It seems to have been written in Italy (13:24), and the author speaks as if the Temple were still open for worship (8:4-5), which suggests that the letter dates from before AD 70, perhaps 67, as he seems to have some acquaintance with Paul's letters from prison, cf. 1:1-4, 13:23.

HEBREWS 1

God speaks now through his only Son. A hymn to the greatness of Christ.

1. What truths concerning Christ are stated in verses 1-4? Compare verse 3 with Wisdom 7:22-26.
2. How do the scriptures quoted confirm verse 4? Check each quotation, ie. verse 5 with Psalm 2:7 and 2 Samuel 7:14; verse 6 with Psalm 97:7; verse 7 with Psalm 104:4; verses 8-9 with Psalm 45:6-7; verses 10-12 with Psalm 102:25-27; verse 13 with Psalm 110. Note the, to us, strange use of scripture. Which of the quotations above seem to you clearly Messianic?

HEBREWS 2

The great salvation brought us by Christ. Jesus' humanity is emphasised as well as his Godhead.

1. Verses 1-4. What is the message of this passage? Compare verse 2 (which concerns the law of Moses 'declared by angels') with verse 3. To what 'salvation' is the author referring? cf. 1 Timothy 3:16.
2. What, according to Psalm 8, is man's destiny? What did Jesus have to go through to enable mankind to achieve it (verses 5-9)?
3. Verses 10-18. Make a list of the occasions where Jesus' humanity is stressed. What is meant by describing him as a 'merciful and faithful high priest'?

HEBREWS 3

The greatness of Moses is surpassed by the greatness of Christ. The meaning of Psalm 95 is interpreted in a new, eschatalogical light.

1. Read Numbers 12:1-8 for the background to verses 1-6. What 'house' is meant in Numbers 12:7? How is Christ greater than Moses (three ways)?
2. What is meant by verse 1? How are we Christ's 'house' (verse 6)? Are we united to him in a greater way than the Israelites were to Moses? In what way?
3. Read Psalm 95, Numbers 20:1-13 and Numbers 14 for the background to verses 7-19. What is the sin against which we are being warned?

HEBREWS 4

The subject continued. God's people are urged to rethink their response to scripture, and to renew their lives in its light. Jesus the great high priest.

1. Verses 1-11. The comparison between Jesus and Moses (chapter 3) now develops into a comparison between Israelites and Christians. What is the 'rest' promised?
2. How is the word of God described in verses 12-13? How is scripture, even Old Testament, still alive and active for us?
3. What special truth about Jesus our high priest is declared in verses 14-15? Why should this fact give us confidence before God?

HEBREWS 5

Jesus the great high priest represents us in all his humanity. A warning to those tempted to abandon their faith.

1. Three points about high priesthood are made in this chapter: a) function, b) understanding sympathy and c) appointment to office. Compare Jesus with the Jewish high priest in each of these points.
2. Compare verses 7-9 with Mark 14:32-42, Luke 22:40-46. What features have all three passages in common?
3. Verses 11-14. What is meant by the 'word of righteousness'? NJB translates it 'doctrine of saving justice'. Comment on this explanation.

HEBREWS 6

Having once set out on the journey of faith, we cannot turn back. We must go forward. Abraham's example. We should have confidence in God and in Christ our great high priest.

1. Verses 1-2. Draw out the 'elementary doctrine of Christ' listed in these verses and comment on each item.
2. Verses 3-8. For the background to these verses, cf. Moses in the wilderness (3:16-18) who could not, having once crossed the Red Sea, return to Egypt. What blessings are recorded in verses 4-5? Why cannot apostates be restored to repentance?
3. Verses 9-20. What should give us confidence in our final salvation? Note especially verses 18-20. What should we do, for our part? cf. verses 11-12,15.

HEBREWS 7

The ancient story of Melchizedek is evoked to throw light on the nature of Jesus' high priesthood. The royal Psalm 110 had already highlighted the Messianic elements in the tradition of the priesthood of Melchizedek.

1. Read Genesis 14:17-20. What are the points the writer of Hebrews makes about Melchizedek? Why is he said to be a) superior to Abraham and b) 'resembling the Son of God'?
2. Verses 11-14. The argument is based on Psalm 110:4, interpreted as a prophecy of the Messiah, descended not from Levi but 'of the order of Melchisedek'. Why could Jesus not be a high priest of the Aaronite priesthood? Why did this mean a change in the Law?
3. Verses 15-22. What are the main differences between the two orders of priesthood?
4. Verses 23-28. In Jesus we have a perfect high priest (verse 26). His sacrifice is unique, unrepeatable (verse 27). What is the connection between Christ's unique sacrifice on Calvary, and the Eucharist? If Christ's sacrifice was once and for all, how can one speak of the sacrifice of the Eucharist?

HEBREWS 8

The writer is basing his imagery on the Tent of Meeting, a symbol of heaven.

1. Verses 1-6. What is the significance of Jesus being 'seated at the right hand of the throne c the Majesty in heaven' (verse 1)? Of what sanctuary and true tent is he the minister? How doe Jesus' ministry in heaven out-distance the ministry of the Levitical priests in the Temple?
2. Verses 7-13. Why did the first covenant fail? What are the qualities of the new covenant foretol by Jeremiah?

HEBREWS 9

The comparisons between the old and new covenants is the basis for the writer's use of Ten imagery to express the reality of Christ's atoning sacrifice.

1. Verses 1-5. Consider the regulations for worship under the old covenant: the lampstand, the Bread of the Presence, the ark of the covenant, the Holy of Holies. What did all these items typify and foreshadow?
2. Verses 6-10. What were the limitations of the old covenant?
3. Verses 11-14. How does Christ's ascension after his atoning death and resurrection replace the old sacrifices?
4. Verses 15-28. This section is parallel to 8:6-13. Why was Christ's death necessary? What are the benefits to us?
5. Verses 24-28. Compare Jesus' action with that of the high priest's. What are the consequences of Christ's sacrifice now that he is in heaven? What will his second coming mean?

HEBREWS 10

The argument thus far is summarised: Christ's sacrifice is effective for salvation, whereas the sacrifices of the old law were merely symbolic. The writer warns his readers of the evils of apostasy.

1. The author makes plain his belief that Christ is speaking to us in the psalms (verse 5) and that the Holy Spirit teaches us through scripture (verse 15). To what truths does the Holy Spirit bear witness in each of the quotations in this chapter? ie. Psalm 40:6-8 quoted in verses 5-7; Jeremiah 31:33-34 quoted in verses 16-17?
2. Verses 4-14. What is Christ saying concerning sacrifice?
3. Verses 19-25. How does this section help us to prepare for the Eucharist? a) What is the privilege of access to the Father enjoyed by all Christians? b) With what dispositions should we be filled? c) Why should we attend regularly?
4. Verses 26-31. Why is apostasy such a very great evil?
5. Verses 32-39. What graces did we receive in baptism?

HEBREWS 11

Faith as exemplified in the lives of Old Testament characters.

1. Consider the definition of faith in verse 1. What two aspects of faith should we keep in mind? cf. Wisdom 13:1 and Matthew 5:12. What is the third aspect revealed by Christ?
2. How does the faith of verse 1 appear in the lives of Abel, Enoch and Noah?
3. What aspects of faith are emphasised in the stories of Abraham, Isaac and Jacob?
4. How did Moses' faith give him the twofold assurance of verse 1? What important choices did this faith lead him to make? Are we prepared to make the same kind of choices (verses 23-28)?
5. Verses 29-31. What different steps of faith are illustrated here? What kind of faith did the capture of Jericho demand?

. Verses 32-40. What does this section have to say of the lives and deaths of those persecuted and martyred? Note especially verses 39-40.

HEBREWS 12

The fatherhood of God. Warnings to Christians not to resent correction.

. Verses 1-4. In comparison with the Old Testament martyrs what inspiration have we, even in the greatest difficulties?

2. Verses 5-13. What theology of punishment is to be found in these verses? Do we think of this when trials come? Do we remember, as parents, that a caring Father trains us, and that we should train our children?

3. Verses 14-17. How does the writer use Deuteronomy 29:18 to make his point here? In what ways can bitterness destroy an individual and a group? What is the meaning of the reference to Esau?

4. Verses 18-24. Compare the making of the old covenant (verses 18-21) with the new one (verses 22-24). What great privileges and blessings do we enjoy?

5. Verses 25-29. How should we prepare for the final judgment?

HEBREWS 13

Instructions for practical Christian living. Special advice for Jewish converts.

1. List the various practices of a Christian life enjoined in this chapter.
2. What advice is given to Jewish Christians (the original readers) in verses 9-16?
3. In what way should Christian leaders be honoured and remembered?

AN INTRODUCTION TO THE LETTER OF JAMES

Luther despised this letter, calling it an 'epistle of straw', presumably because it does not appear to lend support to the doctrine of justification by faith alone. It opens unambiguously and with authority James, a servant of God and of the Lord Jesus Christ, to the twelve tribes in the Dispersion (1:1) 'Servant of God' would imply a high official, what we would probably call a bishop, and as he writes with authority and to the twelve tribes in the Dispersion (Jewish Christians) he must have been well known. In the New Testament, three people are known as James: the son of Zebedee, brother of John, martyred in about the year 40 (Acts 12); James the son of Alphaeus, an apostle of whom little is known; James the brother of the Lord. Scholars are divided as to whether James the brother of the Lord was an apostle and therefore identical with the son of Alphaeus. On the whole, it seems improbable that the two are identical, as there is plenty of evidence in the New Testament that Jesus' brethren did not follow him during his public life. (cf. Matthew 13:53-58; Mark 3:21; Mark 6:1-6; Luke 4:16-30; John 7:1-10).

James the brother of the Lord took an active part in the Church in Jerusalem (Acts 12:17; 15:13-21; 21:18), and was martyred there in 62. The Letter is in good Greek, terse and forceful, a homily rather than a letter, with vivid details. He is concerned that faith should not be merely abstract or theoretical, but lived out in lives of charity, hope and fidelity. He condemns the rich who do nothing for the poor, and draws on Old Testament for many pithy examples. The Council of Trent defined the Sacrament of the Sick as 'instituted by Christ our Lord and promulgated by blessed James', to whom we owe a clear reference to the healing of the sick by prayer, anointing and confession of sins (5:13-16).

The Letter must have been written about the year AD 60.

JAMES 1

Advice on prayer, coping with trials, and taking scripture seriously as God's word.

1. Look up all you can about this James - Matthew 13:55; John 7:5; 1 Corinthians 15:7; Acts 12:17; 15:13-21; 21:18; Galatians 2:9. What kind of person emerges?
2. Verses 2-8. What should be our attitude when trials come? What reward is given to those who pray with faith and perseverance?
3. Verses 9-15. What is the difference between a trial (verse 2) and a temptation (verse 13)?
4. Verses 16-25. What does James imply by the Word?

JAMES 2

Class distinctions are not according to the Gospel. Faith and good works.

1. What has James to say about snobbery? Are we guilty of class distinctions? If so, what should we do about it?
2. What points does James make about a barren, empty faith and the need for good deeds?
3. Explain verse 18 in terms of a) James' teaching in verses 14-17, b) Christ's teaching in Matthew 7:21; 25:41-45; c) Paul's teaching in 1 Corinthians 13:3.
4. Compare James' teaching on Abraham (verses 21-24) with Paul's treatment of the same subject (Romans 4:21) and cf. Hebrews 11:31.

JAMES 3

Use and misuse of the tongue. True Wisdom.

1. What advice does James give to preachers and teachers in this chapter?
2. Consider all he says about the tongue, and make a list of the points made.
3. What are the two kinds of wisdom described in verses 13-18?

JAMES 4

A right intention when praying depends on a right relationship with God. A warning against rash judgments, and against boasting.

1. Verses 1-4. What evils does James ascribe to the community? What is the root cause of these ills?
2. The scripture reference in verse 5 is hard to track down. It may be a reminiscence of Genesis 2:7; 6:3 or Ezekiel 36:27. cf. Romans 8:26-27. What, in any event, is James trying to say?
3. Sum up the teaching of verses 11-12. How does verse 6 help in our battle against our own evil tendencies?
4. Expand on verse 17.

JAMES 5

A caution to the wealthy. The efficacy of prayer.

1. What warnings should we take from verses 1-6? Can you find echoes of Old Testament prophets here?
2. What is the significance of the parable in verse 7? cf. Mark 4:26-29.
3. What sacrament is described by James in verses 13-16? How do our modern rites correspond to it?
4. What other aspects of prayer are brought out by James in verses 13-18?
5. Analyse the advice given in verses 19-20.

AN INTRODUCTION
TO
THE FIRST LETTER OF PETER

If we expect to meet in this letter the all too human and lovable Peter of the gospels we shall be disappointed. Nothing of the writer's personality comes through, probably because, although ascribed to Peter and containing his teaching, the letter was actually written up by Silvanus (5:12), possibly a disciple of Paul. The reference to Babylon (5:13) probably indicates that the letter was written from Rome presumably in the early 60's. It is addressed to the Gentile Christians of Asia Minor (1:1) who were undergoing persecution. The problem of suffering is of prime importance in this letter, and Peter's answer is a noble one, based on the sufferings of Christ (1:6-9). Undeserved suffering can bring us very close to Christ himself, and his resurrection and enthronement (1:21; 3:22) are proof that suffering is not the end.

The Christian is a member of a 'chosen race, a royal priesthood, a holy nation, God's own people' (2:9) fulfilling the promise made long ago through Moses (Exodus 19:5-6). There is one obscure passage, 3:19-20 and 4:6. Is the 'preaching' of Christ an announcement of salvation or of punishment? Who are the 'spirits in prison'? Are they the wicked drowned in the Flood, or fallen angels? The reference to preaching seems to mean that Christ, immediately at his death, descended to the underworld - the mysterious doctrine of the Descent into Hell, which is in the Creed.

1 PETER 1

Hope in the midst of trials. A call to holiness.

1. Look up Exodus 24:3-8 and 29:19-21 for the Old Testament background to verse 2 and to the whole letter.
2. What is the 'salvation ready to be revealed in the last time' (verse 5)? See verses 9, 18-21.
3. What causes for joy in the midst of suffering does Peter enumerate in verses 3-9?
4. What is a) the work of the prophets and b) the ministry of the Holy Spirit (verses 10-12)?
5. What advice does Peter give in verses 13-17? What is the aim of this purification? (verse 22).

1 PETER 2

Peter's doctrine of the Church, the people of God. Social duties. Christ's sufferings are an inspiration to those ill-treated by their masters or fellows.

1. Verses 1-2. Verse 2 forms the Entrance Sentence (Introit) for Low Sunday. In what way do you think it appropriate for those baptised at the Easter Vigil?
2. Verses 3-10. Look up Old Testament texts behind this very important section: Exodus 19:; Exodus 24:5-8; Psalm 118:22; Isaiah 28:16; Hosea 1:6-9 and 2:3,25.
3. Who is the 'living stone' (verse 4)? How can *we* offer 'spiritual sacrifices' (verse 5)?
4. What determines one's place in the Christian church? What different metaphors does Peter use to describe it?
5. Verses 11-17. How should Christians conduct themselves a) before God, b) among themselves, c) before non-Christians?
6. What ideals does Peter put before ill-treated slaves (verses 18-25)? How does he use the hymn (verses 21-24) based on Isaiah 53 to give a Christian view of innocent suffering? What is meant by verse 25? What connection does it have with the hymn?

1 PETER 3

Relations between husbands and wives, and between all Christians. Christ's descent into hell after his death on the cross.

1. Verses 1-6. What advice does Peter give to Christian wives of non-believers? How can this advice be used in a more general sense for all who live and work in a secular environment?
2. Verse 7. How should husbands treat their wives? Compare Peter's advice with Paul's (Ephes. 5:25-30); Colossians 3:19).
3. Peter quotes Psalm 34:12-16. How does he interpret, deepen and extend its meaning? See verses 8-9. How should a Christian accept suffering? How should he react to hostile questions? See verses 13-17.
4. What doctrines are to be found in verses 18-22? What is the meaning of verse 19? cf. Matthew 27:52. What is the significance of the reference to Noah?

1 PETER 4

Contrast between the lives of Christians and of worldly people. The gifts and virtues. Christian attitudes to suffering.

1. Verses 1-6. What kind of life is described in verses 3-5? How does it resemble some life styles today? What hope is there at judgment day? See verse 6.
2. Consider the gifts mentioned in verse 11. Compare the list with 1 Corinthians 12:4-11. What virtues are encouraged (verses 7-9)? Examine your own life in the light of this paragraph. Am I using the gifts I have been given, in God's service?
3. Verses 12-19. (Some commentators think that verse 12 refers to the martyrdom of Paul. Note the use of the word 'Christian' in verse 16). What kinds of suffering should a Christian welcome? What will be its reward?

1 PETER 5

Leaders of the Church warned to be true shepherds. Humility is a Christian virtue. Watchfulness.

1. What advice does Peter give to the members of the church - pastors and flock? Who is the chief Shepherd? Has this text ever been misused? In what sense?
2. What is the true grace of God (verse 12)? How do we testify to it? Note that 'she who is at Babylon' refers to the Roman church (cf. Revelation 14:8; 16:19; 17:5). Silvanus and Mark are Peter's scribes.

AN INTRODUCTION
TO
THE SECOND LETTER OF PETER

This is probably the latest book in the New Testament, and therefore in the whole Bible, perhaps written at the beginning of the second century, in Peter's name. It differs in style from 1 Peter, it refers to Paul's letters as scripture (3:16), it seems to use parts of Jude, the apostles and prophets are described as a body that belonged to the past (3:2). The fact that the writer speaks in the name of Peter (1:1) and describes himself as a witness of the Transfiguration (1:16-18) is not of itself a proof that he was actually the apostle Peter any more than the writer of Deuteronomy 4:36 was Moses. These were literary devices to emphasise the authority of the author, who probably belonged in some way to the 'school of Peter', and refers to his first letter (3:1).

The purpose of the letter was to warn against false teachers (2), and to answer the question Why has the Lord not returned? (3) It gives a valuable principle concerning the authority of scripture (1:20-21). cf. 2 Timothy 3:16.

2 PETER 1

God's call is shown through his gifts. The writer describes the Transfiguration.

1. What are the two attributes of Christ (verse 3) which give all things which belong to the Christian life? On what occasion was Christ's 'glory' made manifest? How do we become partakers of the divine nature?
2. Why, if it is God who has called us and granted us all we need for salvation (verses 3 and 10), do we have to 'make every effort' to supplement our faith?
3. Consider the list of virtues in verses 5-7 and compare them with Galatians 5:22 ff.
4. Verses 12-21. On what two elements does the writer base his authority? What are the foundations of our belief?
5. What is meant by the inspiration of scripture, according to verses 20,21? cf. 2 Timothy 3:15-16. How is scripture interpreted in the Church?

2 PETER 2

False teachers. The influence of Jude is strong in this chapter.

1. What false teachings does the author warn us against? Have we encountered any of them? cf. verses 1,10b,15,19.
2. What characteristics do the false teachers have? See verses 3,13-14. Who are their modern counterparts?
3. How does the writer show the stability of God's justice, a) in scripture, and b) at the day of judgment?

2 PETER 3

The day of the Lord is delayed for a purpose. Final exhortations.

1. What phrases in this chapter reveal a period after the death of the apostles and when the New Testament is becoming part of scripture?
2. What lies behind the comments of the scoffers? Do we ever hear such arguments or reflect such attitudes? What should be our security?
3. Draw out examples of the author's use of scripture. Would you use the same arguments? If not, what arguments would you use?
4. Why is the Day of the Lord so slow in coming? How should we prepare for it? Can we, by our actions, hasten its coming? What actions? What is the meaning, for the author, of stability?

AN INTRODUCTION TO THE LETTERS OF JOHN

There seems to be no serious doubt that these three letters were written by the author of the fourth gospel. The first is anonymous, but its style is very close to John's gospel, and its message is Joannine. The second and third letters are signed 'the elder'.

1 JOHN

The author sets forth three marks of a true knowledge of God and of communion with him: repentance, love of one's neighbour, and faith in Jesus as the Son of God. These characteristics, seen in the light of God's own light and love, distinguish true Christians from false. There is a commentary on John 19:37 in 5:6-8.

This letter should not be taken as the last word on every matter, for the author has a trenchant style that has to be taken into consideration. For example, if one were to take 3:6 out of context, one might conclude that Christians cannot sin! There are, however, passages of great sublimity in this letter, especially 3:1-2, and the author's plea to us to love one another echoes and re-echoes John 13-16.

2 and 3 JOHN

False teachers were abusing the hospitality and generosity of the Christian communities, and the elder advises them to be on their guard (2 John 10).

These two epistles are very slight, but they contain an interesting insight into the day-to-day problems of early Christians.

1 JOHN 1

The Word who is Life. God's light shed on our darkness. Necessity of repentance.

1. What is the experience to which the writer refers in verses 1-4? How does he describe it? Why does he wish to make it known?
2. What is the first condition of fellowship with Jesus? How are we cleansed from sin?

1 JOHN 2

Christ our Advocate. Christ's New Commandment. Christian renewal. The antichrists will try to deceive.

1. In what sense is Jesus a Paraclete or Advocate (verse 1)?
2. What is the second condition of abiding in him? Comment in detail on verse 11.
3. How is the spiritual state of Christians summed up in verses 12-14? What elements are essential to a true Christian experience? Do I have this experience? What further condition is needed? (See verses 15-17). How does this square with John 3:16?
4. What is the fundamental truth of our faith? Note the reference to the second coming in verse 28. What is the meaning of 'know' in verse 29? Compare this section with the teaching of Paul in 2 Corinthians 5:1-5,10.

1 JOHN 3

Our adoption by the Father. Essential virtue: love of one's neighbour. Our faith gives us courage.

1. Verses 1-3. Read the verses over and over and consider the unbelievable vision of verse 2. How can we be 'like him'? Put verse 3 into your own words.

2. Verses 4-9. How can it be said that Christians do not sin? What does John mean? Does the traditional teaching concerning 'mortal sin' have a bearing here?
3. What, above all, is the sign of being God's children? (verse 10). Compare verses 14-15 with 2:11. What practical results should our love have? (verse 17).
4. What consolation do we find in verses 19-20 for those who suffer fear and scruples? What blessings do those who keep God's commandments of love enjoy? (verses 21-24).

1 JOHN 4

Discernment of spirits. God the source of love.

1. What are the signs of the presence of the Spirit? See 3:24 and 4:2,6.
2. Verses 7-10. Why must we love each other (verses 7-8)? How is God's love manifested in Christ? What does it mean to 'live through him'?
3. Verses 11-18. How is the Spirit manifested?
4. Verses 19-21. What argument is used to show that love of others is the sign that we love God?

1 JOHN 5

Our victory over the world in Christ. The witnesses to Christ. The everlasting Life in God.

1. How does verse 6 provide a commentary on John 19:34? How is the Spirit the witness? cf. John 7:37. Can 'water' and 'blood' refer to the sacraments? What fivefold witness is given in verses 7-11? To what do these witnesses attest? (verses 11-12).
2. What does John mean by 'mortal sin'? (verse 16). cf. Matthew 12:31-32; Hebrews 6:4-8.
3. What are the three great Christian certainties summed up in verses 18-20? How do they sum up the whole letter?

2 JOHN

1. What is the doctrine threatened, on account of which the letter was written?
2. Compare the tests of a true Christian found in this letter with those given in 1 John.
3. What dangers arise from advanced teaching? cf. verses 8-10.

3 JOHN

Probably written first.

1. What rules of hospitality are given in this letter? cf. 2 John 10.
2. Consider the three men mentioned in this letter, Gaius, Diotrephes and Demetrius. Compare what is said of each. What is the reason for criticism of Diotrephes? What virtues are praised in the other two?

AN INTRODUCTION
TO
THE LETTER OF JUDE

'GRATEFUL thanks to the intercession of St Jude. Prayer answered and favours received. LM'

Out of one (random) edition of the Universe, St Jude was thanked on ten out of a possible 22 occasions. The other mentions were as follows: The Holy Spirit and the Sacred Heart 8 times each; Our Lady 7 times; St Joseph and St Anthony 3 times each; St Martin, Padro Pio and St Martha twice each...

The extraordinary popularity of St Jude, the patron of hopeless cases, is perhaps not so hard to explain as *WHY* he got this title in the first place! Who was he? If the apostle is meant, he is not even listed in Matthew's nor in Mark's gospels (Matthew 10:2-4; Mark 3:16-19). He is described by Luke (6:16 and Acts 1:13) as the son of James, and is mentioned in John (14:22). Was he identical with the 'brother of Jesus' (Matthew 13:55 and Mark 6:3)? Did he write the letter of Jude?

On the whole, scholarly opinion is inclined to distinguish between the apostle Jude or Judas and the brother of Jesus, for the same reason as for James - that the gospels tell us that Jesus' family were not among his disciples during his public life. The writer of the letter is therefore Jude, the brother of Jesus - and of James (1:0). According to Eusebius, two of his grandchildren, very poor peasant farmers, were arrested under Domitian for being descendants of King David.

It is an unusual letter in many ways. Addressed to 'those who are called, beloved in God the Father and kept for Jesus Christ' the writer signs himself Jude, a servant of Jesus Christ and brother of James. As it is a universal epistle, Jude must have had high authority in the Christian community. However, as it seems to have been concerned with an emergency (3-4) of some unspecified heresy, it may have been prompted by a crisis in an individual church, perhaps in Syria.

Jude looks to scripture and to traditional Jewish stories to remind his readers of the judgment that will fall on sinners. The reference in verse 9 is to the apocryphal *Assumption of Moses* in which Michael and Satan quarrelled over the body of Moses. The quotation in verses 14-15 is from the *Book of Enoch*.

The apostles are spoken of (verse 17) as belonging to the past; the faith was 'once for all delivered to the saints' (verse 3). This points to a date after Peter's death, perhaps the year 85. The letter ends on a positive note, with the glorious verses 20-21 and with a doxology packed with doctrine.

JUDE

1. Look up Jude in Matthew 13:55; Mark 6:3; 1 Corinthians 9:5; and possibly his mother (Matthew 27:56; Mark 15:40; Luke 24:10). How does he describe the believers to whom he wrote?
2. What indications are there in the letter that the traditional faith of the apostles is a deposit not to be tampered with? See 3; 5,17,20; and cf. 2 John 9. Is there no room for development of doctrine?
3. How does Jude describe the false intruders? (verse 4). Is this the final word on unbelievers?

4. List the scripture references in verses 5-7 and 11. What point is he making in choosing these particular instances?
5. What advice is given in verses 20-21 to us all? Learn these two verses by heart. Underline the verbs, and ponder each one.
6. In what different ways, according to their attitude and errors, should we treat heretics? See verses 22-23.
7. Learn verses 24-25 by heart. What should such confidence lead us to do?

AN INTRODUCTION
TO
THE REVELATION OF JOHN

(The Apocalypse)

This book, perhaps the most difficult in the New Testament, closes the Biblical revelation. It is also the most mysterious. How are we to interpret it? Is it a prophecy of the ending of the world by nuclear holocaust or pollution? Why is God presented as fierce as the fiercest Old Testament Jehovah? Why does the Christ of this book seem so different from the Jesus of the gospels? Yet there are those who have loved this book, and found great comfort in it. One is reminded of Bessy Higgins in Mrs Gaskell's *North and South*:

> Where would I hear such grand words of promise - hear tell o'anything so far different fro' this weary world, and this town above a', as in Revelation? Many's the time I've repeated the verses in the seventh chapter to myself, just for the sound. It's as good as an organ, and as different from everyday too. No,I cannot give up Revelations. It gives me more comfort than any other book i' the Bible. (Chapter 17).

To understand the book, there is a great advantage, often lacking nowadays, in knowing the Old Testament, especially Ezekiel, Daniel and Zechariah. Much of the imagery is drawn from there. The symbolism is not meant to be taken literally, but to be interpreted by the reader who, unfortunately, has largely lost the key. The book is defined (1:1) as an apocalypse, a revelation which 'must soon take place' - a book therefore with a hidden meaning, whose meaning will be revealed by God. The symbols are borrowed from the Old Testament; eg. woman = people (12:1) or city (17:1); horns = power; eyes = knowledge; wings = mobility; the sea = death, etc.

Who is the author? He tells us his name (1:4), John, and that he was a prisoner for the faith on the island of Patmos (1:9). He ranks himself among the prophets (22:9). The letters sent to the seven churches in his name indicate great authority in that region (Asia Minor). Is this John the same as the apostle John? Did he also write the fourth gospel? Some details are found in both books, and nowhere else in the New Testament, eg. Christ is presented as the Lamb, the Word of God; life is symbolised by living water; both use Zechariah 12:10. On the other hand, there are great differences in language and in eschatology. It therefore seems unlikely that one man wrote both books, but the apostle John could have inspired both, perhaps through the community at Ephesus. The John of Revelation 1:4 could well have been a disciple of the apostle. Most scholars date the book during the persecution of Domitian (AD 81-96), when the Church had suffered a terrible onslaught.

In the study section, we have taken the revelation as it unfolds, chapter by chapter, noting the vast perspective of heaven and earth, an eternal Eucharistic liturgy.

REVELATION 1

Prologue in the prophetic manner. General greeting to the churches. Background to the visions.

1. Verses 1-3. The book is a prophecy (verse 3) addressed to God's servants (verse 1), who, in 10:7, 11:18 and 22:6, are prophets. What is meant by this? Are New Testament prophets different from Old Testament prophets? cf. 1 Corinthians 14:6, 26, 30; 1 Peter 1:10-12; Ephesians 2:20. How is the revelation (verse 1) made? How should we respond (verse 3) to prophecy?

2. Verses 4-8. Consider the titles given to Jesus in verse 5. What does he do for us? Compare verse 7 with Daniel 7:13 and Zechariah 12:10. Draw out the themes of death, resurrection and enthronement of Jesus in verse 5. Note the liturgical traces in verses 3, 4, 8.

3. Verses 9-20. Picture the scene at Patmos where John was exiled for the faith, and look up the seven cities on the map - they are all in modern Turkey (Asia Minor).
4. What does each of the symbols in the vision of Jesus mean to you?

REVELATION 2-3

Letters to the seven churches. Note that each letter has the same structure: i.title of Jesus; ii. assessment of the community; iii. reminder and promise from scripture. Further,there are seven symbols of scripture: i. tree of life; ii. prison; iii. manna; iv. rod; v. priest's breastplate; vi. rebuilt city; vii. Jesus at the door. They promise: i. life; ii. freedom; iii. food for the journey; iv. kingship; v. priesthood; vi. restoration; vii. Christ.

REVELATION 2

Ephesus was the principal city in Asia Minor, in what is now Turkey. The Nicolaitans were Christians who allowed themselves to be corrupted by paganism. The word is a pun on Balaam (cf. Numbers 31:16 and 25:1-3) - which means in Hebrew 'He lords it over the people'. In Greek, this would be 'Nika laon'. Smyrna was a busy seaport about fifty miles up the coast from Ephesus. It had a reputation for loyalty to Rome. Pergamum lay another fifty miles further north, and was the administrative centre of Roman Asia, therefore the centre for emperor-worship. Thyatira - the modern Akhisar - lies on the open plain between Pergamum and Sardis. It was famous for its craft guilds. John's reference to Jezebel, probably refers to the temptation to allow business interest in a pagan city to dilute Christianity.

1. What did Christ commend in Ephesus? What were the faults to which the church was succombing? What would be the punishment? Why is the tree of life promised?
2. What do we learn from verses 8-11 about the situation at Smyrna? What biblical reference will encourage them?
3. Pergamum was the centre of emperor-worship (Satan's throne), and the Christians there are praised for their fidelity to Christ even unto death (verse 13). What danger did they face? Look up Numbers 31:16 and 25:1-2 for references to Balaam. How will they be strengthened in their journey of faith?
4. The Christians of Thyatira were threatened by moral laxity (verse 20). What advice is given to those who are resisting the general atmosphere (verse 26)? What will be their reward?

REVELATION 3

Sardis was the capital city of Croesus and once the financial leader of the ancient world, but by the first century AD it had sunk into obscurity. It had been a pioneer in the art of wool-dying. Philadelphia (modern Alasehir) had been founded in the second century BC as a centre for diffusing Greek culture into Asia. It suffered from earthquakes, and had had to be rebuilt in AD 17. It was given the new name of Neocaesarea, after Tiberias Caesar. Laodicea, now a mere ruin, was an important centre for industry, commerce and banking, famous for its eye ointments and black woollen cloth.

1. What was wrong with the church in Sardis? Is this a danger for many churches nowadays? Those who persevere are promised the white priestly robes of Aaron (verse 5). How can we too become a priestly people?
2. What is the open door set before the Philadelphians (verse 8)? For what are they commended? Are we among those who have kept the word of patient endurance? They will be rewarded with the new Jerusalem. How is God's kingdom built on such as these?

3. The church of Laodicea suffers from a very common vice - tepidity. How is it conquered? What does verse 17 tell us about a common danger for regular prosperous Christians? What is the remedy? See verse 18. The greatest promise of all is offered to Laodicea. What is it? (verse 20).

REVELATION 4-11

The Great Revelation. The churches face persecution and trial, for which they seem unprepared. John, first of all, in chapters 4 and 5, is shown a vision of heaven.

REVELATION 4

A vision of God on his throne in heaven. The scene widens (like a television camera beginning with a close-up) to include the elders, the sea and the four creatures.

1. What is symbolised by the open door (verse 1)? What Old Testament prophets had seen the throne?
2. What is the significance of the jasper and carnelian? See Exodus 28:2, 6, 9, 17, etc.
3. Verses 4-6. How do the twentyfour elders represent the church? cf. 1 Chronicles 24:1-19. Does this scene remind you of any liturgical occasions?
4. Verses 7-11. What other liturgical elements do you recognise in this section? See verses 8,9,11.
5. What Biblical doctrine is celebrated in this chapter, summed up in verse 11? How should we respond?

REVELATION 5

The scroll represents God's secret plans, sealed with seven seals, because seven is the perfect number - so the scroll is a *complete* mystery. Christ is presented as a Lamb.

1. Christ is presented at the throne of God as the Lamb. What is the significance of this title? cf. John 1:29. In what ways does this chapter symbolise the eternal Eucharistic liturgy?
2. What other titles are given to Christ? For their Old Testament background look up Genesis 49:9 and Isaiah 11:1-9.
3. What are the purpose and results of Christ's sacrifice? See verses 5,9,10.
4. Look at all the different people and creatures who join in the 'new song': verses 8,11,13. What does this symbolise? Can we join in this song?

REVELATION 6-9

Vision of the future. To understand the imagery used in these chapters, read first Zechariah 1:8-10 and 6:1-3; Exodus 7-10; and Joel 1-2.

REVELATION 6

The seven seals: the four horses; the martyrs under the altar of burnt offering (cf. 1 Kings 8:64); the earthquake.

1. Read Matthew 24:4-14. Compare Revelation 6:4,6,9. What does this exercise tell us about interpretation of historical events?
2. What is the meaning of the white horse (verse 2), the red horse with the sword (verse 4), the black horse with scales (verse 5) and the pale horse (verse 8)?
3. What is the climax of judgment (verses 12-17)? Compare Matthew 24:29. Note the use of Old Testament imagery to express upheavals. Are we justified in explaining all this in terms of particular disasters? What is the underlying mystery?
4. Verses 9-11. In what way are the martyrs associated with the sacrifice of the Messiah? What is the origin of remembering the martyrs at the Eucharist?

REVELATION 7

The elect will be preserved and rewarded.

1. The scene is now the Church on earth. See Ezekiel 9:3-6 for the background. What is the symbolic number of those sealed 144,000? Do these represent Jewish Christians?
2. Verses 9-17. Who composed the great multitude? In the apocryphal book of Ezra, a Jewish apocalypse, Ezra was mystified that God should have created so many people for destruction (4 Ezra 9:20-21). What is the teaching of Revelation on this question? Is there room for hope?
3. Pick out references to the Jewish feast of Tabernacles in this chapter. See verses 9, 15. What blessings do the redeemed enjoy?

REVELATION 8

The breaking of the seventh seal. The seven trumpets introduce a new heavenly liturgy, parallel to that of the seven seals. The first four trumpets. The imagery is drawn from the plague narrative in Exodus: hail (Exodus 9:23-26); rivers into blood (Exodus 7:20-21); darkness (Exodus 10:22-23).

1. 'There was silence in heaven for about half an hour' (verse 1). Silence always indicates the coming of God (Zephaniah 1:7-8; Wisdom 18:14). In this case it is the Son of God who is coming (10:7). But he is a sign of 'contradiction' (Luke 2:34). A new heavenly liturgy begins. What is the place of our prayers in this?
2. What did Jesus mean when he said 'I am come to cast fire on the earth' (Luke 12:49)? How is it fulfilled in our lives, in history?
3. Consider the disasters described in verses 7-12. Have they any counterpart in our world? What is their purpose? Is it a punishment? Or warning? Is the eagle (verse 13) calling us to repent?

REVELATION 9

The fifth trumpet - locusts from Exodus 10:12-15 and Joel, symbolic of the Parthian army. The sixth trumpet - Parthian troops invade Rome from beyond the Euphrates. This would indicate to John's readers an answer to the prayers of the martyrs (8:3).

1. Verses 1-6. Evil now comes out of the earth itself, from the abyss where the demons dwell. Is this a symbol of the terrifying power let loose in nature by man's pride and greed for power, taking over the collective unconscious? What is the remedy?
2. Verses 7-11. The locusts come from Joel 1-2. What do they symbolise?
3. Verses 12-21. The explanation of all these disasters occurs in verses 20-21. What is it? How can we help our generation to learn this lesson?

REVELATION 10

The small scroll - the open secret.

1. Compare the small scroll of verse 2 with the large scroll of 5:1. The large one represented the sweep of human history, the little one - a much shorter period. What is the 'mystery of God' (verse 7) about to be revealed? Compare Romans 16:25; Ephesians 1:9.
2. Read Ezekiel 3:1-13. What are the similarities with verses 8-11? What are the differences? What is the lesson of both passages?

REVELATION 11

The measuring rod signifies the spanning of the Temple, i.e. the Christian community, during the siege of Jerusalem in AD 70. The two witnesses may be Peter and Paul (seen in terms of

Moses and Elijah) or just Christian martyrs whose sufferings end in resurrection. The seventh trumpet - parallel to the seventh seal.

1. Verses 1-2. Read Ezekiel 43:3 and Zechariah 2:5-9 for the inspiration behind the imagery here. What does the 'temple of God' signify for John? What does the Church mean for us?
2. Verses 3-12. Who are the two olive trees? See Zechariah 4:11-13 referring to Joshua and Zerubbabel, priest and king. See also 2 kings 1:10 (Elijah) and Exodus 7:17 (Moses). For whom therefore do the witnesses stand? See Mark 9:4. What lessons may we learn from this passage concerning the attacks on those who witness for Christ?
3. What is the effect of the seventh trumpet? What is the theological meaning of the whole chapter?
4. Note that the ark of the covenant is seen in heaven. What does this signify?

REVELATION 12

The creation and fall of humanity.

1. Read this section (verses 1-6) in the light of Genesis 3. Who is the woman? What does her splendour signify? cf. Genesis 2:27. Who is the child?
2. What does the second sign represent? (cf. verses 3 and 9). What happens to the woman? Compare verse 6 with Genesis 3:23-24 and with Exodus 15:22.
3. Verses 7-12. These verses describe the war in heaven between Michael and the dragon. How is the victory achieved? What is the situation of the earth? What situation is the writer trying to explain theologically?
4. Verses 13-16. Note the Exodus references in this section, especially in verse 14 (cf. Exodus 19:4) and in verses 15-16 (cf. Exodus 14:21-31).
5. Read carefully verse 17 and consider its significance. Is the victory finally won? Why is the dragon pictured as standing on the sand?

REVELATION 13

Corruption of political and religious authority.

1. Note the direction from which the two beasts come (verses 1 and 11). The first represents totalitarian power, corrupt and blasphemous. What does verse 4 tell us about the relationship between this beast and the dragon (Satan)? What political regimes of this century have most resembled the description in verses 5-7?
2. The second beast (verse 11) represents corrupt religious authority. Note its marks (verses 12,13,16). John had in mind emperor-worship. Have there been occasions when even the Church of Christ has shown the marks of the beast? What danger above all are we warned against?

REVELATION 14

Interlude. The new Israel, the Church of God. This tableau (verses 1-5) is succeeded by a tableau of the Day of Judgment, pictured as a Harvest. This terrible scene is described in metaphors common in the prophetic books (cf. Isaiah 63:1-6).

1. Verses 1-5. What contrasts are made in these verses with the preceding scene (13:1-18)? What is the significance of the description of the true believers? What parts of it are a) symbolic and b) to be taken literally? Why?
2. What is the appeal addressed to the pagans (verse 7)? Are they invited to become Christians? What are the implications of this?
3. Draw out the essential meaning of these visions. What underlies the traditional imagery?
4. What role is assigned to Christ?

REVELATION 15-16

The death of Christ as judgment.

REVELATION 15

The seven plagues tableau is contrasted with the scene in heaven (verses 2-4). The angels of judgment issue from the temple of the tent of witness, symbolising the final triumph of justice over evil.

1. What is the third sign or portent (15:1 - cf. 12:1,3)? What is meant by the phrase 'for with them the wrath of God is ended' (verse 1)?
2. Compare the song in verses 3-4 with Exodus 15. What is the lesson of this vision?
3. Verses 5-8. What is meant by 'the temple of the tent of witness' (verse 5)? Compare with Exodus 40:34-35). Compare also 2 Maccabees 2:4-8 where these signs are taken as Messianic. What does John understand them to mean?

REVELATION 16

The seven bowls of plagues again echo the plague narrative in Exodus: the first bowl cf. Exodus 9:8-11; the second and third cf. Exodus 7:20-21; the fifth cf. Exodus 10:21-23; the sixth cf. Exodus 8:5-6.

1. In what ways are the 'bowl' judgments more severe than those of the seals and the trumpets? How do men and beasts react? See verses 9, 10, 13.
2. Note the liturgical undertones: vessels (Numbers 4:7); pouring of blood/wrath (Leviticus 4:7). Compare the plagues of verses 2-13 with the plagues of Egypt. cf. Exodus 7-10).
3. Is there any sign of hope in verses 17-21? How do you react?

REVELATION 17-19

The destruction of Babylon.

REVELATION 17

Babylon symbolises Rome, or any great world power that has become tyrannical. London, Paris, Moscow, Washington, Teheran, Baghdad...

1. What is meant by the 'woman sitting on the scarlet beast' (verse 3)? For what does Babylon stand in Old Testament? See Jeremiah 50-51. For what does Babylon stand in New Testament? See verses 9, 15, 18 and 1 Peter 5:13. Of what is Babylon the eternal archetype?
2. In what way is the harlot the mirror image of chapter 12? What is the fatal mistake of the harlot?

REVELATION 18

This chapter draws heavily on prophetic laments: for Nineveh (Nahum 3:4), for Tyre (Isaiah 23, Ezekiel 26-28), for Edom (Isaiah 34:8-14), for Babylon itself (Isaiah 13:20-22, 21:9, 44:23, 47-48, 52:11, Jeremiah 25:27, 50-51). Verse 14 should follow verse 23.

1. Verses 1-8. Contrast the state of the city as portrayed in verse 7 with that in verses 1-3. What was her principal sin? What are the faithful urged to do? cf. Genesis 19:12 ff. What should WE do?
2. Verses 9-19. three classes of people take up a lament. What motive lies behind their mourning?
3. Verses 20-24. The city is symbolically destroyed (verse 21). For what crimes?
4. Apply the whole chapter to one of our modern great cities.

REVELATION 19

The Song of Joy of the Redeemed is taken up again, echoing 5:9, 7:10, 14:3, 15:3. The white garments 'fine linen, bright and pure' are symbolic of victory, as in the white horse. Christ's death and resurrection are presented in terms of a victory in battle. 'White' is symbolic of victory.

1. Verses 1-10. What is the theme of this liturgy? What categories of people take part? See verses 1, 4, 6. What truths about God's character are made known and celebrated?
2. Verses 11-16. What features of this vision make it clear that Christ comes not as Redeemer but as Judge? See verses 11, 14, 15. What qualities are especially emphasised? cf. Wisdom 18:14-16.
3. Verses 17-21. Draw out the various elements from earlier visions that are all assembled here and destroyed by Christ. What is the meaning of this macabre scene? cf. Isaiah 30:30 ff.

REVELATION 20

This chapter concerns the history of the Church from the Ascension to the Second Coming.

1. Verses 1-6. This much disputed passage may have affinities with Ezekiel 37:1-14. What do you think is the essential message of each? What hint of hope is there for those suffering persecution? See verses 4,6. What is Satan's role?
2. Verses 7-10. Look up Ezekiel 38-39 for the biblical background. How is the final battle described? Draw out Old Testament references.
3. Verses 11-15. It has been said that the widespread disbelief in the final judgment and in hell has left many people with a sense that reality is ultimately meaningless. In what way do you think passages such as this one vindicate the ultimate significance of human existence?

REVELATION 21

Once more we have echoes from the prophets, this time Messianic echoes: a time of renewal and re-creation (Isaiah 65:17), of God's marriage covenant with his people (Hosea 2:16, Isaiah 15:18); of God's presence among his people (Joel 4:17-21); the defeat of evil (Isaiah 25:8, 35:10); of man's thirst for living water (Isaiah 55:1). The new Jerusalem foretold by Ezekiel (40-48) lies behind John's vision.

1. Verses 1-8. Draw out the various biblical themes in this vision, especially verses 2, 3, 5. God's voice is heard for the first and only time (verse 5). How does it fulfil Genesis 1? Of what is the sea (verse 1) the symbol?
2. Verses 9-26. Compare verse 9 with 17:1. What is the point of the repetition? What is the significance of number twelve? Compare these verses with Ezekiel 40:2-5. What is the writer emphasising by this echo of Ezekiel?
3. Note especially verse 22. What are the implications of this for our understanding of the place of the Church and of our place in it?
4. Compare the blessings of this chapter with all that is said of the garden of Eden (Genesis 1:28,29; 2:18-25). How do they transcend them, and what is their chief glory?

REVELATION 22

Epilogue. This chapter from verses 6 - end balances his prologue. It seems to be spoken in turn by the angel (verses 6-11), who guarantees the authenticity of the whole work - i.e. of Christ's promise that he will return after his Ascension; Christ himself (verses 12-16) using the titles given in the opening chapters; and finally by John (verses 17-21).

1. Compare verses 1-2 with Ezekiel 47:1-12. What is the meaning of each part of the picture?
2. What word of Christ is repeated three times? See also 3:11 and cf. 1:7; 16:15. What should be our attitude and response?
3. How is this book four times described? What are the writer's credentials?
4. In saying 'Come, Lord Jesus' (verse 20), what are we praying for?

THE GIFTS OF JOURNALING

Discovering your true self

by

Yannis Helios

yannis72@thesunman.com

ISBN: 978-1-3999-4193-8

DEDICATION AND ACKNOWLEDGEMENTS PAGE

To Jenny,

Words cannot express my sincere gratitude and appreciation. You stood by me for fifteen long years. You kept me alive. Thanks to your trust and the sacrifices you made for us to live in Italy for eleven years it revealed the most authentic side in me.

To Jim Rohn,

I may have never met you, but you sir gave me something that many others couldn't give. You gave me the chance to love life again. You reignited my passion. I will forever be grateful to you for that amazing speech you gave. I don't know what guided me to watch it, but I'm glad I did. In a way, my book is the ultimate thank you to you. May you rest in peace, my dear friend.

To Susan,

While preparing to write this book, I met a fellow writer online; we had both enrolled in the same Jeff Goins writing course. Together we shared many of our struggles and encouraged each other in frequent emails. Thank you so much, Susan, and keep going strong.

To Caffe Nero, Paul and all-day jobs I have had so far,

The jobs I have found in my return to London have helped me financially to stand on my feet, and I'm so grateful. On the other hand, they reminded me countless times that this path is not made for me. I'm grateful for that to too.

To my parents,

All these years of journaling helped me see you for what you truly are: humans.

To You Tube:

Wow! What a fountain of information this has been for me. How many mentors have I virtually met and how many lessons have I received stimulating even further my quest into discovering my true self. Thank you so much.

To the 2020 COVID-19 lockdown,

Some things happen for the worst and some for the best. Thanks to the 2020 lockdown, I found enough time to get myself together and begin this monumental effort of writing this book. During this time, I also saw a different picture of society, one with fewer cares, more simplicity, and love.

To Phil Hampton,

You coached me for a very short time, but I managed to get a lot out of our time, and I thank you very much.

To Jeff Goins,

I may not know you personally but I have to say a big thank you for your great online book course, it was great to find someone who has gone the distance of writing a book.

To Chantel Hamilton,

Trusting all my writings to a stranger, even if that stranger is an editor, was a very big change for me. Thank you, especially for using truthful language. You rocked me often and gave me much-needed objectivity and clarity for my writing. Thank you, and I hope one day we work together again.

To Denise McGrail,

You helped me so much to make this book readable for English-speaking readers. You also managed to keep my writing style intact, which I found amazing. I very much thank you and hope that we will work together again.

To Word-2-Kindle

To the entire team in Word-2-Kindle and especially: Nick Caya, Aeron Keller, and Vanessa Claus, who were in most contact with me. Bless you, all.

To my sister Anna, her husband Vasilis, and their family in London,

A big thank you (*megalo efharisto*) for letting me into your home during a very challenging time for me. Bless each of you.

To father Jim McManus

The divine providence led me to find your book at the time I needed it the most. You are truly blessed.

To You, My Reader,

A sincere thank you for inspiring me to rise to the occasion and finish this book.

To God and Jesus Christ,

In the end, I was never lost. I always had you both on my side. I never have to look down on myself again.

TABLE OF CONTENTS

WELCOME

Welcome, dear reader.

In 2020, during the first COVID-19 lockdown and with the world turning upside down I began the valiant effort of writing this book. It was the right time for me to find my place in the world and help it become a better place.

The origin of Gifts of Journaling

The first idea for writing this book was an already used one, one that I had started in the first year of journaling.

I thought developing that idea was what I wanted to do.

I had left many journals in Italy and so I asked Jenny my ex-fiancé to send them back to me and to my delight she accepted.

One day a large box arrived where I was living, containing all the journals that I wrote all those years I was in Italy and me excited began reading and reviewing them, thanks to the Covid 19 lock down I had ample time to do that. The idea was that after gathering the pages I needed, it would be a piece of cake to create a book. But that logic had many holes, after gathering and copying most of the old pages I realized that I had nothing left to say. In my writing something was missing. It was missing the sparkle, the spontaneity, the joy, the passion. The best things that I was experiencing when that first inspiration came had now deserted me. Instead, I was now feeling stagnant and many times bored, my mind was blank, not a good place to be for an aspiring author. Despite my best efforts nothing new would come to me.

Go home

My maxim in life is to have passion or … to go home. So, after three weeks of going back and forth I stopped. I stopped because it was going nowhere.

About a week later I went through the pages again trying to find a different angle if it was possible but again nothing happened except one thing.

The devil is in the details

I noticed that each time I referred to journaling my writing was almost piercing the pages. I felt that there was an important message waiting to come out. A voice that urgently needed to speak.

That night I said:" I will write about the gift of journaling, that's the book I really want to write."

The purpose of the book

The purpose of this book is to make you receptive to a reality that aligns more with your true self. The true self is the holy grail many have sought from the beginning of humankind. At the core of each person there is the true self waiting to be revealed and developed.

The true self in me has urged me to help others, especially the wounded, the ones who hurt the most—those who are battered and bruised by life's unfortunate events. I've written this book especially for them to encourage them and if possible, awake them. The book is also written for anyone who is in a bad place and struggling.

"Success is to find your true self and establish it in the world"

Journaling helped me solve my biggest problem. I couldn't express myself the way I wanted. I couldn't find my true self. I was a man who often found himself stranded in the middle of a vast ocean, looking at the sun and praying for help to come. You may think that's an exaggeration, but that's how I felt.

Before journaling, the odds of me making it in life were very, very small; the world seemed to be against me, and even worse: I had turned against myself, self-sabotaging every chance I got. I was constantly outnumbered, losing all my battles. I felt hopeless; it was hopeless.

I was full of regrets, the disappointment in myself was growing more as the years passed, and the pain was becoming too hard to bear. The spark in me had dimmed. The grim prediction was that the end of this physical existence was approaching for me quickly. Somewhere in my forties, I knew I would be departing from my physical life. A part of me wished for it to happen to relieve me from living with such pain. But God had different plans and stopped my premature departure from this existence because I still had to do a lot of work.

You will read about my journey throughout the following pages and chapters. Thís book in many ways is about you *and* me, my journey and yours.

We, humans, have incredible strength. We can endure immense pain and still move forward. It's remarkable, yet we often forget that we cannot do this forever. We are mortals. The pain can bring even the strongest of us to our knees at some point. In this body, we can hurt, we can bleed and even die prematurely if we are not careful. The flesh cannot keep a wounded heart for too long.

It has taken me a long time to come back and recover because there was a lot of damage done through the years. But as they say, if there's a will, there's a way, and I'm happy that I have found mine.

Yannis Helios

THE BEGINNING

There is a massive problem in the world today. More and more people are feeling disconnected, and more and more people are feeling lost. This detachment from our true nature has a side-effect in all significant aspects of our life: physical, mental, psychological and of course spiritual. It's a terrible mess that is so hard to get out of. For many, suffering has become a way of life, an unnatural way of living.

I was raised in an ego-driven society made to fulfill material needs first. Fixing small problems and neglecting the big ones, and although this book isn't a biography, it should start as one.

The year was 1972, and this married couple couldn't get along. Arguments in their house were often; the place had become a battlefield. Every war has its casualties. Right? I was a casualty. I was an innocent child severely wounded during the battles. From a young age, I experienced the worst situations: abandonment, betrayal, and rejection, to name only a few. I came face to face with emotions that I didn't know how to express. Those emotions were like giants to me, and I was too small to handle them.

I developed something equivalent to what many war veterans get after fighting in an atrocious war: post-traumatic stress disorder, something I'd live with daily. The result was a boy feeling lost and later an adult feeling lost, which affected my development—such a burden for someone to carry. I was tough to reach, tough to understand. I didn't want to reach out to anyone, especially my parents, whom I saw as my tormentors; animals were the only exception. I could be free with animals and let my true self emerge for a while. My life continued to be an unevenly matched battle to restore what I felt was taken from me.

"Trying to Get Much-Needed Peace in a World That Constantly Tries to Steal It"

I was trying to get much-needed peace in a world that constantly tries to steal it—an impossible task. I would see my closest friends and relatives progressing and getting on with their lives while I kept standing still, in the same unfortunate position since childhood. Feeling lost comes from a deep-seated, out-of-control emotion looking for its way out but unable to find it.

Many agonizing years passed this way, throughout my twenties and almost all my thirties until something of a titanic magnitude happened that helped me to gradually heal my broken heart.

The Event

During the summer of 2011, the heat in the apartment was once again unbearable. I'd been living in Rome, Italy, for the last few years with my then-fiancé Jenny, a very generous person I was lucky to meet in my first job in London. She had trusted me and provided me with a much-needed place to live; there I built a sanctuary, staying away from all the things, people, and places that had hurt me in the past. Yet, it was one of those days, I was feeling the blues again, overwhelmed with the usual feeling of having no purpose, experiencing once again an unbearable nothingness.

That summer, after years of solitude and reflection in Rome, I started asking myself meaningful questions:

- Who am I?
- What am I seeking?
- Why am I here?

- Can I be helped?
- Is there any help?
- Is there a God?
- What kind of world is this?
- Can I change?

"Help will come from a special book"

As I pondered these questions, the wise voice in my head said: help will come from a special book.

I thought, *A special book? Is there a book that would help me?*

Then another voice said: A book specially designed for *you*? Don't make me laugh.

But it was no laughing matter because later that day, I had an aha moment! I thought, *A special book? That must be it! Somewhere, in some distant library or book shop, there must be a special book, one that contains all I need—the book of revelation, a book of truth, peace, love, and unity. One book that has it all!*

That idea excited me! But there was a slight problem. I wasn't a book reader. I had read a few novels here and there, but not often. To me, reading books was boring. Something near to punishment. In school, I rarely found a class interesting enough to make me want to study hard and put in the effort. Now, if there was a class about superheroes or a school that taught everything there was to know about superheroes, I would've graduated with honors.

Those were the only books (well, comic books) I really enjoyed. The ones that starred my favorite superheroes: Superman, Batman, Spiderman, the Hulk, Captain America and all the others. Comic books were chockfull of great stories and pictures that I devoured every time. Those comic books were my only true connection to reading.

"Find The Special Book"

The message stayed clear and persistent: Find the special book.

Each September, it was a tradition to go on a summer holiday. Some might have called it an autumn holiday, but it was still summer for me. I would go to the sea, eat watermelon, and do whatever I wanted. At first, it happened out of necessity, because it was the only time, I had available and it was much cheaper to book hotel rooms or studios, but as the years pressed on, it became a choice to take a holiday in September because it nourished my quiet nature and my need for more space. So, September arrived, and my fiancé and I picked up our suitcases to travel to my home country Greece. The first stop was Athens, the glorious city of letters and my birthplace. My parents, who'd been estranged for quite some time, lived in separate homes, so we stayed in two homes for the holiday. You see, I wanted to please both my parents, even if that was impossible to happen.

When we stayed at my mother's home, we often walked to nearby shops because her home was closer to the town center. During one of our evening walks, I stopped in front of a bookshop. I said to Jenny, "Let's go in."

I was looking for the special book, and my eyes zeroed in on the self-help section. Most of the self-help books seemed interesting, with eye-catching titles promising to change your life. Since I still didn't have much confidence reading books, I bought the shortest one I could find. After purchasing it, I didn't read it until I returned to Italy. But guess what? Sentence by sentence, word by word, I read it all.

Where Is the Special Book?

I read the book quickly and did the exercises the author suggested. There were some good points, but it was far from what I expected. Since I had no significant breakthroughs after reading the book, my motivation waned.

Do I look for a special book again? If so, where?

I was again at ground zero. October passed, and by the time November arrived, my entire attention shifted. I stopped looking for a special book and instead started looking for a special television program on the Internet because I thought I'd be able to concentrate on the message better through a visual medium. After all, I loved watching television and going to the cinema.

YouTube

By late 2011, a new information platform called YouTube had taken the world by storm. The idea behind it was brilliant: anyone could essentially create their own television channel and speak to their audiences. People were embracing it big time because it was so fresh and new. On YouTube, you could find all types of new and old videos about sports, documentaries, movies, etc. You name it, and you could watch it.

Enter Jim Rohn

So, I typed "self-help," into the search bar and immediately hundreds of videos popped up. The first videos listed were the most-watched videos, and one of those was a video by Jim Rohn, one of the best and most popular self-help teachers in the world.

So, I chose one of his videos. It was divided into four parts and called, "Best Life Ever."

In my home turf

For me, the video was the perfect opportunity. I preferred to watch something rather than read boring books. So, that evening, I sat down, along with Jenny, and pressed play. That is when the magic happened.

When I pressed play, it was like entering a video game. A different world appeared in front of me. Suddenly, the television program became real. I was there, sitting in the auditorium, waiting for the one and only Jim Rohn to speak to me. I was so spellbound that I could imagine I heard the other students talking next to me, saying things like:

"Hey! Who is this, Jim Rohn? Seems like a jerk to me. Who cares? I have better things to do. I'm going out with Susy this Saturday. Isn't that something?"

"Oh, shut up, Mike. You have no idea who this man is. Just get out."

A few minutes passed, and after the musical introduction ended, there he was—Jim Rohn, walking to the podium to speak, relaxed, confident, smiling, and greeting us all. After some applause, the presentation started.

He started speaking in his unique style. The man had clearly done his homework. He knew what he was talking about and often used clever metaphors, stories, and examples, which were all relevant to what he was saying and extremely appealing because I could easily understand. I couldn't endure long, boring academic speeches with foreign words and phrases. I would've switched off the computer. Instead, I did the opposite. I was having the time of my life and wanted to learn more and stayed captivated by him as he explained what makes someone's life special.

It was near the end of the second part when Rohn did something different. He suddenly turned his face to the camera, and I swear to God, he looked directly at me and said one more thing.

"I Want You"

In a clear, authoritative voice, he said, "I want you to get a journal and write. Write all that is meaningful to you. Write how you found this seminar. Write what made it so interesting, so unique. Write what you wanted to hear but didn't, and don't you dare stop there! Continue this with your own life. Your world is different from the rest of the world. Write about it. Journal it in full detail and once every while make an honest review."

After the second part ended, I got up from my chair and thought, *wow, what was that?* I felt strange, and I didn't know why. The rest of the night was quiet, and I slept well. It seemed everything had returned to normal, but it hadn't. Something had happened; something in me had changed.

Captain's Log - Day 1

The next day, while going to the supermarket with Jenny, I stopped in the stationary section and purchased a black notebook. That evening, at home, I wrote my first journal entry about my impressions of my daily life. I also included some good quotes from Jim Rohn's seminar. Finally, I recorded the date at the top corner of the page—November 11, 2011.

Finally, the seal broke. I felt newly baptized—my first day back to peace. After so many years of failed attempts and feeling lost, I discovered a genuine way to express myself. What a relief!

The Real Gift

All I needed to start was someone to explain something to me in a language I fully understood. I believe all you need is someone who speaks your language too. Journaling is a choice that can resonate with you, like the best musical instrument in an orchestra.

And, when I write, He writes, and when I speak, He speaks.

What's to Follow

Jim Rohn's seminar gave me the gift of journaling; since then, I've received many more gifts. In the following pages, I will share the gifts I have received throughout those years.

Each chapter discusses a single gift and includes my insights and experiences. I will share with you some of the wisdom I've gained throughout the years I discovered journaling, and I hope you'll find it helpful as you embark on this new journey.

How to Use This Book

Use the material in any way you like. Twist it, fix it, break it—make it yours. I don't believe in a step-by-step method because I'm not that person.

Often, the book gets personal because I don't believe in a neutral approach. Transformation must be felt; it must hit a nerve. Journaling saved my life; it saved me from more painful years and— a miserable life. I have no exclusive rights to the gifts I was given. Anyone with enough willingness can obtain them.

Get Ready

So, get your journal ready with your pencil or pen in hand. You have a lot to discover and write. You own your story. This journal is yours. This life is yours.

CHAPTER 1:

THE GIFT OF PLAY

In my first journal, I wasn't looking for facts. I was enjoying the process of writing whatever came to mind. After decades of struggling, I discovered a new way of expressing myself, which felt exciting and liberating. Suddenly the child in me had awakened and was so excited about finding a new playground. My imagination had got wild again—a sensation I hadn't experienced since I was a kid. I relived my best childhood, and there were no boundaries on what I could create and what I could discover. Journaling had come to rescue the child in me. I was back in the world of wonder and amazement, a familiar place that I would visit every day when I was still a kid.

The Ideal Start

Somehow that was the ideal start. It got me going on the path of a miraculous recovery. The ideal start for you might be different, somewhat similar, or the exact same, but it really doesn't matter. What matters is you are here now reading this, so start journaling.

CHAPTER 2:

The Gift of Order

Let me tell you a story from my earliest journals, the ones from the first pivotal two years. This story was written in my fourth journal.

It was a day, unlike the others. I had decided to do some serious tidying and cleaning in the house. It had been a long time since I'd done something like that. Don't get the wrong impression. I'm not a dirty or smelly person, but I tend to be messy. It's unavoidable for me.

It seemed like a hard task to put everything in order, but it needed to be done. I was missing important things and, worst of all, wasting a lot of time trying to find them. Where is my notebook? Where are my keys? Where are my photos?

The process proved more than fruitful. After a few hours, I put everything back in order and got rid of a lot of unneeded stuff. At the same time, I found things I'd long forgotten existed; things that were useful but hidden inside the piles of clutter. So, the effort was more than satisfactory. I would dare say it was brilliant. Suddenly, my messy area in the house (not Jenny's) had become new and spacious! It was like entering an IKEA showroom. I felt peaceful and had tremendous joy and gratitude. I felt happy and strong. I was proud of myself.

I now had a functional place for me, and what a gift that was. My office was in tip-top condition as well as my wardrobe and my library. Later that day, as I opened my journal to write the usual notes, I immediately wrote: clean and tidy your house. My heavy-handed writing nearly tore the pages because I was writing so fast so it wouldn't disappear. In it, I had found so much meaning. In it, there was a great metaphor for life.

The Metaphor

My mind had become like an old, abandoned building, dusty and cracked. Good thoughts were mixed with many useless ones. There were so many outdated beliefs and emotions I couldn't fully express running amok within me—a real mess the voice inside my head had asked me to sort out.

For a long time, all I experienced was restriction, and the time had come for that to change. The practice of journaling every day made it clear that I needed to take care of my thinking process and troubled emotional world. I needed to create much-needed space so I could grow. One reason journaling is so good is that it reveals problems quickly. It is like a mirror. You read it, and then you see it.

Find New Structure

Soon after, I received a new message asking me to find a new structure. I didn't even know what that word meant. I spoke English, but I wasn't very good at understanding every word.

To YouTube again

So, I started researching, and, in the same way that I found Jim Rohn through videos on YouTube, I found plenty of interviews created by successful people and took many notes. In a way, I turned all those videos into classroom teachings. I wanted to learn more and understand what they were doing right and what I was doing wrong.

I found that they all had an unchangeable structure. It was their foundation. A big part of their day was based in their strength.

I will see you at the top only if . . .

One day Jenny bought the classic self-help book, *See You at The Top,* by Zig Ziglar. After she read it, I started reading it too out of curiosity; with such a compelling title, it was hard to ignore. But before completing the first chapter, on page sixteen it happened. I stumbled upon this phrase, *"You must accept yourself before you can really like anyone else or before you can accept the fact that you deserve success and happiness. Motivation, goal setting, positive thinking, etc., won't work for you until you accept yourself."* And more useful advice followed at the next page, *"The person with a poor self-image can easily see how positive thinking, goal setting, etc., would work for others but not for himself."*

I then marked this passage and wrote it in my journal. Oh my God! As I'm writing these words now and reflecting on those journal entries, it's May 31, 2022! It's unbelievable how much time has passed since I wrote those quotes in my journal.

Ziglar was brutally honest, and I appreciated that. It was true. I hated myself. I was living with a lot of resentment and bitterness. I kept blaming others for my misfortunes and wrongdoings, constantly feeling like a victim. I clearly had work to do and a lot of distance to cover.

Day by day, journaling shook my foundation and pushed me to become a better man, distancing me from my insecurities and reservations. Slowly, I restored that old, beaten-up building and turned it into a beautiful, functional place.

To work on yourself means letting go of what you already know. That was the most challenging part for me because as Mr. Dale

Carnegie said, "Those convinced against their will are of the same opinion still."

I was of the same opinion still. I questioned the new regimen. I questioned it hard, as did my ego. Me becoming different? Me creating a new order? Me finding a new structure? Me expanding? Ridiculous. My ego didn't like the idea of changing, so it kicked like a mule.

As a painter, it was the same thing. I was thriving in unstructured time. No one could tell me when to paint or how to do it. I had no clock and no specific timeframe in which to paint. I was like a madman scientist or a wild horse. I am still that horse only now; this horse is going somewhere. I now live a life of purpose.

CHAPTER 3:

The Gift of Knowledge

In the once enlightened country of Greece, there was a saying shared among wise men and women: To gnothis eauton. It means to understand yourself in a deep, meaningful way. In old English, it translates to "know thyself."

At the beginning of this book, I recounted how eager I was to find a special book to help me with my life— that is until I finally found it inside my journals. Many months passed, and a new year arrived. The year 2012 was significant for many reasons. Some predicted the end of the world, others the beginning of a new world order. There was panic but also excitement.

As I continued journaling, my enthusiasm spiked through the roof. I quickly realized that more was coming for sure. Unknowingly, I'd entered a state of abundance. The inner knowledge gave me so much so fast. I felt I had so much to give. Dreams were telling me to prepare for the new phase.

One night, in my dreams, a big hand wrote the word "journaling" across the walls of a gigantic library in thick red paint. When I woke up, I was shaken. The dream was so real and intense. The next evening, as I was journaling, I heard a voice speak. It said, "There is a special library. Go and look for it."

I responded with enthusiasm. *Yes,* I thought. *There is a special library, and I must find it.*

I still had the naiveness and innocence of a child. I imagined myself becoming Indiana Jones, seeking far-away treasures. Not long before, I'd watched the great author and researcher, Mr. Gregg Braden, on YouTube searching for the holy grail of knowledge, traveling around the world to mystical places to find the source of human enlightenment, which was very fascinating. My pursuit was a bit different. My thirst for knowledge was self-driven, self-inspired, and always for the greater good. For me, the mystical places I searched were internal.

Since the beginning of this journey, each journal has brought out of me one special book after another. As the journals began to increase in numbers, I saw my dream come true—a special library was forming in front of my eyes. I could only imagine what might happen twenty or thirty years later. People might have home libraries, but to have a library of your own books is amazing. Maybe I'll need more than one special library if God grants me a long life.

Many books we buy have inspiring content, like the one you are reading now. They trigger us, giving us messages, we need to hear. But the special book(s) you are about to write is even more inspiring because they are a part of you. In your journal, you will find yourself on every page, not only in a sentence or two or a chapter but everywhere. Everywhere is you.

All Journals Are Special Books

In this chapter, I refer to journals as "special books" because that's what they are for me—they are the books of life.

Everyone has a special library, but most don't know how to access it. That is because it is still unworked, unedited, unwritten, invisible, and unfound. The library is inside our hearts and minds.

The book you're reading now results from many of those special books. Hopefully, it's helpful to you. Maybe it'll catapult you into understanding yourself better. Still, it will never be like your very own journal—your very own special book.

CHAPTER 4:

THE GIFT OF EXPANDED AWARENESS

Have you ever wondered why the same shit happens to you repeatedly? Do you keep doing the same thing frequently and expecting different results? That's the definition of insanity. Repeating mistakes means you haven't leveled up. There isn't enough awareness to understand it.

Experience isn't equal to understanding

Experience isn't equal to understanding. That's why even elders aren't always wise. That's why history often repeats itself.

We often assume we've achieved mastery because we have a certain exposure to something. We think because we have experience, we have everything. But that's wrong. Experience isn't everything. Far from it. Experience isn't only about gathering facts because often, these facts are the same thing.

Just Like Groundhog Day

In 1993, Bill Murray starred in the comedy film *Groundhog Day*. If you haven't watched it, I suggest doing that first and reading this later. Keep reading if you're not interested in the film or have watched it before.

Here's how the plot goes: After a weird accident, TV weatherman Phil Connors, played by Murray, gets trapped in the same day, repeating it over and over every day! How weird is that? Every day, he wakes up doing the same things and meeting the same annoying people from the day before—an endless torture. He has become so distraught that each day he attempts suicide, but nothing changes. Every day concludes the same. As this continues for a long time, he comes to terms with his situation. He starts learning new things, talking with people he never spoke to, seizing new opportunities, and doing things he never dared to do before, until one fateful day, he has gained true wisdom and is freed.

Experience not understood is empty. Scenery changes, time changes, but it is all the same. We change jobs and relationships and think we are moving, yet everything stays the same. We repeat the same mistakes.

So many people don't get it. Nobody is immune to it. There was a time that I didn't get it either. I kept repeating the same mistakes, and it was painful. It was like being Phil Connors in Groundhog Day, trapped in the same boring day—forever. It was awful.

Two Pasts

There are two kinds of past, one is active, and one is inactive. One is history written, and one is still unwritten. Written history means results have been settled; there has been a neat conclusion. The story has been completed. The message has been ironed out. It is now clear.

Unwritten history means many things are unfinished.

You might be familiar with the phrase "unfinished business." There's a lot of unfinished business when there's an active past. To illustrate this point, let me start with a story.

The Devil's Home and Paradise Island

There are two islands, and each has a large volcano. On one island, the volcano is spitting fire like a living dragon. Enormous smoke billows from the volcano's top, and dark ash cover the sky.

It is almost impossible to breathe. The temperature is so hot. There's the threat of a big explosion happening at any moment. Access is forbidden and the people exercise considerable caution. No wonder people call this island the devil's home. I wouldn't be surprised if someone saw him walking there. It's a living hell.

Quite far from that nightmare, is another island with an equally sized volcano. The island's volcano has been covered by thick vegetation with many exotic trees and plants. It hasn't been active since prehistoric times. Now it's nothing more than a peaceful hill and a place where people take photos. Tourists visit often and admire the natural beauty around it. They call it Paradise Island.

Even Television Series Have Two Pasts

Often, marvelous television series get canceled, an injustice to the creators, the actors, and the loyal audience. The story never arrives at its full conclusion, and it's a very frustrating thing; it's an injustice.

The Incredible Hulk

A television series like that was *The Incredible Hulk*. It was an American television series that aired in the late seventies with great success. I wasn't lucky enough to watch it as a kid. I only remember seeing a towering man who looked like a green Hercules on the cover of some foreign bodybuilding magazine. It was inspiring for a frail kid like me, who wanted to be powerful and strong, to discover the man in the photo was none other than the amazing Lou Ferrigno. I already knew who the Hulk was from the famous comic book magazine. I had already read so many of them, and I was enchanted by this enormous green monster with an innocent child's heart yet a giant's strength.

Fast forward three decades later, and destiny called. Thanks to the digital age, I was able to watch the whole television series. I downloaded back-to-back seasons, having the time of my life until the final episode. The final season finished abruptly, like somebody had pulled the plug. I was so upset that I almost broke the TV, for a while I couldn't calm down, I had become also like Hulk, I didn't like that botched job. I asked myself: Why did this happen? Why did they stop it? It's not fair. It was too soon—it was! I felt robbed.

Later, I watched a documentary on YouTube about the series' history and learned that one of the late producers had a different opinion. He felt the series had run its course, and his opinion prevailed. But time proved that he was wrong. Indeed, time reveals all wrongs. The series needed to continue so it could arrive at its full conclusion. I sincerely hope that one day, someone with enough vision and courage revives it and completes it the same way it started. It will do justice to all who were part of the original.

What Is a Fitting Ending?

Before continuing, I would like to clarify that a fitting ending is not necessarily a happy ending. People are used to Hollywood films and think that everything must have a happy ending for the story to be complete.

That's not always true.

What's important for a fitting ending is that all the missing dots connect, and the story wraps up, no matter how happy or sad.

A television series with a fitting ending: *The Fugitive*

Before watching *The Incredible Hulk,* I watched every season of the 1960's gem, *The Fugitive.* It was so gratifying to watch something from beginning to the end that answered all the key questions; to watch all the characters develop from beginning to end; to let the plot unfold and, finally, understand the big picture—that's a fitting ending. *The Fugitive* is a testament to satisfying television and film work a real masterpiece.

My point is that the past must be completed; otherwise, it keeps playing over and over like a broken jukebox.

The jukebox was the technological wonder of 1960. Its success was phenomenal, and there was one in most music shops and bars. The jukebox was a music machine you'd put a coin in, press a button, and your chosen song would play. It was pure magic.

I wasn't born at the time the jukebox rose to fame. What I know about the machine comes from what my father told me and, of course, the cinema. And here comes a story called:

The night the jukebox stuck

There is an amazing group of friends in a small town. They love to meet at the local bar and listen to their favorite rock-n-roll music. The bar is very popular and always crowded. Today, the friends have already spent two hours at the bar, and something awkward keeps happening. Since arriving at the bar, the same song keeps playing repeatedly. The jukebox is stuck, but no one notices because they're talking and having fun.

Now, let's add you and me to the picture. Oh, did I tell you we're on a mission?

Well, I'm telling you now. Like all secrets, they must be revealed when the time is right.

Our mission is to observe and take notes. We must not do anything out of the ordinary to avoid any unnecessary attention. This mission is top secret. We are like the people in the film *Men in Black*, only we're not wearing black.

We're sitting at a far table, knowing what is going on. It has been recorded in history as the strangest day of 1961. We have come from the near future. The imaginary dialogue goes like this:

You say, "Hey Yannis, how do they not notice it?"

"To them, it's just music," I say.

"But it's the same damn song! How come no one in the bar notices it? It's insane!"

"Yes, my dear friend, it is."

"There must be some logical explanation. Are they actors shooting a film? Or are they just crazy? Or are they all stoned? *Or* are they all robots? How can it not bother them? It's so freaking obvious!"

"There is a logical explanation to all of this," I tell you. "Yes, it looks strange to you but not to them. Remember, you know what happened. You've read it in the history books and are prepared to witness it, but they are not. You've made some good observations so far. Yes, they seem robotic. Yes, they seem stoned. Yes, they look like actors shooting a film, and yes it seems insane.

"Now, let me ask you. Are you always aware of your actions? Are you always aware of the way you put on your socks, eat, drink, speak on the phone, walk, or sit?"

"That's impossible to do. It's too much effort, too much work," you say.

"Yes, it is, especially when you're busy doing other things."

"Yes, that's true. It happens, but this is far more obvious," you argue. "That jukebox clearly needs fixing."

"Fixing or noticing?"

"What do you mean?"

"To fix something, you need to notice it first. You need to spot the damage. No one here has done that yet. Experience is not equal to understanding, my friend."

"Okay, you got me. That is so interesting. So, what they experience they still don't understand and that's why they can't act on it."

"Bravo! You nailed it. Awesome! Now watch what happens next."

A guy from the group of friends gets up. He looks at his watch and accidentally bumps into the jukebox, then notices something.

The guy says, "What's going on here? The same song, same tune, keeps playing repeatedly. Hey barman, come over here. There's something wrong with that machine. Can you fix it?"

The barman tries, but he can't do anything to fix it. Instead, he says, "Okay guys, this is it. This night is over. Bar's closed."

"Can we get up now?" you ask.

"Of course," I say. "It is part of our mission to blend into the crowd and observe."

"And the shop closed."

"Yes, and tomorrow the newspapers will report tonight as the night the jukebox stuck, and nobody noticed. You see, one of the young friends happened to be an aspiring journalist. He thought the story would make a great headline, and it did. The story spread like a wildfire all around the country and even internationally.

"But what caused it?" you ask.

"Everybody was busy with something else. They were worried about an impending attack from a foreign country."

Some were speaking about a third world war. "Luckily, this threat never came true, but it clearly affected people that day. So many incidents occurred, and the jukebox effect was one of them."

We all have a button that gets jammed sometimes because we can't see clear. It happens when an unexpected problem appears, and then our actions get robotic, regardless of the circumstances, the people we're with, and time. The same song, the same tune plays on repeat. But who will press the stop button? Who changes the song? Who will fix it?

You and your new expanded awareness will stop it. Journal everything, and you may spot things like that.

Back to The Future

How I wish to be Martin McFly and travel with the DeLorean back in time!

I love films where the hero goes back in time and corrects unfortunate events. It's a dream that many people have. Wouldn't we all love to stop problems from forming and keep the peace?

But in this reality, we live with certain rules: the football match has ended, the birthday is over, the appointment has finished, this holiday has come and gone, time is called on the exam, the year has ended, and there's no turning back. Except for one thing—there is something left to make out of it. The beauty of being human is that we can correct and adjust our perceptions and behaviors. In the grand scheme of things, every effort we make has little to do with winning or losing. Anyone can lose, and anyone can win.

It has more to do with what we make of the circumstances we're dealt with. That's where real success lies. The most substantial failure is when we don't realize that we hold ourselves captives.

Allow me to share a personal story with you.

Love Hurts

During my military service, I met a dog unlike no other. I connected with this dog on an unprecedented level for me and one I had never found with a person. Her name was Lilly.

By 2003, my beloved dog companion of eleven years had developed an undetected heart condition. I had been living in London for the last two years and was visiting Greece only for holidays. At that time, I had a two-week holiday and planned to take Lilly to the beach on the last day, something we both enjoyed.

Earlier that day, my sister called, reminding me to visit my godfather. "He would love to see you," she said.

I wish I hadn't answered her call, but I did. After the call, I felt guilty and obligated to make a visit. I put logic over my heart. So, the plan to take Lilly to the sea that afternoon was canceled. I visited my godfather instead.

When I returned, I had very little time to pack my suitcases and prepare to go back to London. My beloved Lilly wagged her tail ready for our new adventure. Preparing suitcases for Lilly meant always traveling together somewhere. But not this time, and Lilly couldn't understand why I had to leave her behind.

I couldn't explain myself to her even if she were a person. I had many fears about taking her with me to London: the intimidating forty-day pet quarantine, the uncomfortable single room that I was renting, my unstable lifestyle—so many excuses. The truth was that I was scared to take responsibility.

Some things are beyond words. After a short walk with her around the block, I left.

The trauma

It was the last time I saw my beautiful angel. A month later, my father called to tell me the bad news. Lilly had passed. I was shattered.

A condemning voice in my head immediately said: You let her down. She died because of you. You weren't man enough to take her with you in London. I felt tremendous guilt about the things I could've done. I couldn't forgive myself, so I entered a self-imposed prison.

As the years passed, I continued caring for dogs. Still, I could never shake the thought that I was to blame for her death, and I never owned another dog. *Maybe next year,* I would tell myself. I said those words for eighteen years until I learned an important lesson: people die, and pets die. No one can control death.

Finally, I made some progress moving through my grief. I'd never grieved fully until the summer of 2021. That's when I participated in David Kessler's eye-opening course on the Commune website. For the first time in eighteen years, I allowed myself to feel the sadness and walk out of the dark cage I'd built around myself.

Sadness

Suddenly, I felt like the room's ceiling was falling in on me, crushing me. I felt so empty and heavy for the rest of the day and into the night. It was the first time I completely experienced that feeling. It was exhausting. When the next day began, I felt lighter, like a big weight was lifted from me. I had finally experienced sadness.

Challenging moments come into our lives for a reason. The divine source tests us to show us what we are made of. I believe that and see in my life that something changes for the better each time. The more I get out of those moments, the more I move on. The more I fight those moments, the more I stay stuck.

Journaling came to me like a wise teacher and showed me there was another way, a better way.

One that isn't punishing but helpful. It worked for me and, in time, it can do the same for you.

That, my friends, is the gift of expanded awareness. It takes you away from the wounded ego, a misleading mindset, and puts you back on the road to true fulfillment and happiness.

A Boxing Story

More stories Yannis? Yes, journaling brings so much more and it made me a storyteller too. Here's one last story to wrap up this chapter. It comes from the fascinating world of boxing.

Each boxer's history has a record describing their victories, draws, and defeats. Often, a boxer can start his career backward. The record looks bad—zero wins, zero draws, and eight losses. The boxer (let's call him Mike with no relevance to Iron Mike) seems to be going downhill. He's struggling. He hasn't found his winning formula—nothing's clicked yet. Because of an injury, he's forced to take a long break from the sport. To him, it's another devastating loss, another nail in the coffin.

How do I stay inactive? He wonders. It's tragic now that he absolutely needs to do it. His family doctor recommends complete rest somewhere peaceful.

Mike reluctantly agrees to go to an isolated location near the water and stay there until his injury is healed. He usually stays at the beach or in his room, and each day passes slowly. As the days and weeks pass, he begins to feel better. His physical movement seems to be returning to normal.

Luckily, his coach left him a present (a journal) and a task to complete (use the journal). Three months into his recovery and Mike has begun journaling. He's had some helpful insights about his life and his sports career. He begins to develop a plan.

Being alone led to the inevitable—that he would meet with his true self.

The journal helped him do that. He took time to review his failures, and understood that the problem was his training.

Fighting with power was wrong

For years, he was obsessed with building strength because his father, also, a boxer, and a very strong one and he wanted to be like him. Yet, fighting like his dad never worked. He lost all his fights.

That was his first significant insight. Three months later, he had another meaningful insight. It came to him one night in the beautiful sanctuary. While relaxing, he remembered something important. When he was a kid, he used to play a game with his friends where one had to wear out all his opponents while moving in a small circle to win the game. Everybody had to keep moving until only one was left, and he would always win.

"It's my stamina. That's it! I must use my stamina to wear out my opponents," he exclaims out loud.

After nine months, his recovery is complete, and he feels like a new man. He returns home, young and refreshed. His mind is now sharp, and his body's rejuvenated. Things begin to change quickly. During the training, he demands to train differently. He wants to improve his fitness. While fighting, he no longer tries to smash his opponents because there is a better way. Soon he finds himself on a winning streak. The coach is delighted with this change, as is everyone else on the team.

More years pass, and the boxer is on a roll. He has become a household name and a champion. When he retires, his record is a very positive one with many victories and more importantly he is a complete man.

In the same way a boxer can improve his boxing record, you can improve your life.

Recently, my life's record of defeats, draws, and victories has changed. The future is getting closer and closer to a different, more favorable reality for me. The reason is that I've come to understand myself better. Journaling removed me from someone else's life and moved me toward my true self's life.

If things haven't gone your way and you're still troubled, there is an opportunity because some past inside of you is still active; something hasn't fully settled. Maybe it's a promise you once made and have since forgotten. Maybe there is someone you need to forgive; there is something you can do about it today.

CHAPTER 5:

The Gift of Oneness

When I began journaling, something miraculous happened. I reunited with my true self. At first, the written words reminded me of his existence, but soon the words came to life and they became the new truth. This new voice spoke through me in a different tone with more strength.

How Often Do People Dare Be Themselves?

It happened in August of 2012, and all I did was change my diet. I switched to a specific plant-based diet. Today that doesn't seem so strange. After all, people change their eating habits and try new things often. But how often do people change their lifestyles?

That's a significant question to ask and my biggest problem. I couldn't be myself, at least not for long. So, it wasn't a simple matter to switch from one diet to another; to me, that was a courageous act because I was embracing a true aspect of myself.

I wanted to do it with all my heart for many years, maybe even since childhood. A deep longing was ingrained in my *true* identity because I cared about nature and animals. It was a longing I was scared to the bone to express because that minor sensitivity turned out to be a big one.

My behavior already matched the description; only the title was missing: vegan. Although I despise labels, sometimes I admit they're necessary because they make us who we are. I knew I would no longer be like everyone else by labeling myself a vegan.

Isn't fear of rocking the boat the main obstacle?

In the summer of 2012, I rocked the boat in my blessed Italian home. The time was right, and I expressed the true statement I longed to make. It was a decision that immediately raised eyebrows from my parents and close family circle, who weren't used to seeing someone eating like that, even if they lived far away. It didn't take long for them to comment on my new lifestyle, but I wasn't swayed to abandon my decision no matter what they said. It was the truth, and I knew embracing veganism would last.

That's the thing about the truth: it stands the test of time. Once you become one with it, it's game over.

My spirit was uplifted, and my body and mind felt stronger after that decision. A strong truth came from my soul and introduced to my body. The more truth you embrace, the stronger you become. We all strive to have integrity, but we must take certain steps between what we want and what we need to do. Maybe the best word to describe all that is courage. Courage is needed to make you and the truth become one. Courage requires something special, it requires unconditional love. You are doing it regardless of the outcome. You are doing it in a very altruistic unselfish way, a very honorable one.

Truth doesn't guarantee an easier life, but it does guarantee a happier life. I'm happier since I made that choice, and there is definitely more to come.

CHAPTER 6:

The Gift of Spirituality

My inner compass was interrupted from an early age, and my sense of individuality was shattered into tiny pieces. Spirituality, the most incredible power of humanity, was in me, but it was punctured, and my emotions ran amok.

Spirituality is that universal force within us all that can bring us closer to God and to our true selves. It can walk us through fire without getting burned, help us move mountains, withstand the harshest adversity, and succeed when it seems impossible to succeed. More importantly, it can make us fulfill the promise. The promise we once made to ourselves but forgot when we began making promises to others. My promise was that one day I would rise and become a superhero and help the weak. It was my truest desire in my heart and it was also God's will. But early childhood wasn't ideal. I was wrongly influenced, made mistakes, and paid for it dearly. It happens. Shit happens. We're spiritual beings having a physical experience, after all.

Punctured Spirituality

Punctured spirituality is a term I use to explain what happens when you stop believing in yourself.

Not believing in yourself is like a bicycle with a punctured tire. You pump the tire and get yourself ready to go; then, the problems begin only a few meters away. The tire begins losing air, and before you know it, you have yourself a flat tire. Now you are in a most uncomfortable position, in the middle of an empty road, and you know help isn't coming soon. You are walking and cursing your luck. You're late for an appointment, and the frustration has gone straight to your nerves.

After walking for quite some time, you finally see a bicycle repair shop. You enter the shop, and someone assists you quickly. Of course, you gladly accept the help. You feel relieved. Your luck seems to have returned. The guy does the job well, and you are ready to leave in no time at all.

Shortly after leaving the bike repair shop, another unfortunate event happens. The street was littered with glass, and you didn't notice. You were too anxious, too excited to get out of the bike shop and reach your destination. And there it goes, punctured tire again.

"Oh, my God! Why me again!" You shout, but no one hears, and no one answers.

Now, you're really pissed. Your bicycle has more holes than before, and both tires are punctured. You feel stuck. Once again, you're in deep shit.

When you're feeling lost, you want to hold on to something so tightly, something promising, that can make you forget how bad your life has been. That, unfortunately, is how addictions begin.

For many years, I had my fair share of shortcomings. I struggled with my self-worth. I felt poor and empty inside, so I began seeking value elsewhere. I became hooked on betting, seeking luck, confidence, and whatever good I could find. The only thing I found was more bad luck and even more misery.

Can I tell you something else? Starting something can come easily when you're spiritually punctured, but finishing it is so difficult. You become unreliable to others and yourself.

Writing a Book? Who, Me?

In the summer of 2012, something happened. I thought my special superpower had been restored, and I was ready to conquer the world. I was in tune with something special for the first time.

Earlier in 2011, as soon as I started journaling, the writing flowed from me naturally. It was like what I needed to say had been locked inside me for years, and journaling unlocked it. I tapped into concepts I always liked but never knew how to develop and articulate. Day by day, page by page, I wrote in the journal about what I wanted to learn and what I wanted to say. In some paradoxical way, I taught myself what I wanted to know, and each journal became a special book.

Bathroom Lectures

I was so excited about my writing that I read them in the bathroom every evening while my fiancée was relaxing and bathing. I read her what I had written, but I would take it further using examples. I wasn't always successful in making sense, but we would often get something good out of what I said, which was more than enough. Jenny was a great listener. Some people have amazing gifts, and listening is one of hers.

That's how the days and months passed during 2012 until the volume of information reached a fertile point. Things began making sense, pieces fit together, and the inevitable thought emerged:

Can this all be a book?

The idea rocked my foundation. Could I really become an author and someone known for his ideas? The thought was a provocative one. It was funny that I'd been searching for a special book only a year earlier, and now I was called to create one!

"Sometimes, when you can't find the book, you want to read, you have to create it."
-Bryce Zabel, American Film Producer

At that time, I was listening very often to the American radio show of *Coast to Coast: A.M*, famous for its strange subjects. In one episode, the guest, Bryce Zabel, shared something I thought was very important for me to hear. He said, "Sometimes, when you can't find the book, you want to read, you have to create it." That hit me like a hammer because that was exactly what I needed to do. I needed to create the book I wanted to read!

God's plans work in mysterious ways, and I believe he'd planned this from the beginning. His plan was hidden from my sight until journaling uncovered it. I wasn't prepared for that revelation, for that inner calling, and Jenny didn't expect it either. Despite the early enthusiasm, my fear and doubt won out. I began to make the usual excuses: I'm not ready. I don't have the resources. I'm not ready yet. I don't speak so good English. I'm not so educated. You know what I mean? Unfortunately, I exercised the choice of free will and chose to go a different path, putting the whole idea on ice. This shortcoming signaled to me the need to investigate further throughout journaling. So, the writing changed. I focused more on the obstacles, the so-called clouds that hid my sun.

Jim Rohn had said in that fateful speech to also write about the things that bother you, the things you don't want to talk about, the things that make you feel uncomfortable. It was inevitable that, at some point, my journaling would turn dark because there was still a lot of darkness in me. This inability to take good action bothered me so much.

Before You Become an Open Book, You Are a Closed Book

A year of journaling had done wonders, but many things were still undisclosed to me.

Many things made me feel uncomfortable that I didn't like to talk about with anyone openly, not even with myself. But on paper, expressing myself became more possible. There, nobody would judge me or pick on me. I would be the only one held accountable.

So, I entered a different world, intending to understand those obstacles and, if possible, eliminate them. Suddenly, a new, unexpected creative flow emerged, and it came from my pain—this unfulfilled desire to grow.

Inflate and Deflate

Every year, I became more over the moon about my progress and thought I was spiritually healed, and each time I discovered the opposite. My journaling would confirm something else needed to be done. By accident, I'd begun a personal growth journey.

"Success consists of going from failure to failure without loss of enthusiasm."
- Winston Churchill

I never lost my enthusiasm even though I failed often. The consistency of journaling helped. It helped build up my confidence and my faith in God. Both were non-existent at that time. Two of the basic elements of spirituality were restored.

Spirituality Can Be Restored

Yes, spirituality can be restored. The soul can be freed from burden. A punctured tire can be fixed with some work, or it can be entirely replaced. But the first option is closer to reality.

The most difficult thing for me to accept was the mental aspect. That I'm capable of making another choice and having a different life. A life that offers more than I can ask for; one where I'm the protagonist and not the supporting cast.

Struggling at times is OK.

I think it's important to note that being more spiritually balanced doesn't mean life's challenges give me a pass. Even now, while writing this book, I'm dealing with problems. I would be a liar if I say I have solved all my problems with journaling. No one is immune to problems. At least I know that I'm not alone. I can access my inner power, face the unknown, and deal with my inner demons. I can share my experience and how journaling helped me to stay on course towards peace, and attaining spirituality is a big part of that peace.

Jim Rohn might have pointed out the path, but it's up to me to complete my journey. The same goes for you.

I don't know if what happened to you was recent or a long time ago; it doesn't matter. Let's not allow the past to hold us captive. It's time to take back our power and time to fulfill the promise we once made to ourselves.

Fill the blank pages of your journal with your life experiences, and you will see that you are the one that holds the key to your destiny. Make room for honest journaling in your life. You won't regret it. In our fast-paced society and ever-evolving technology, we often lose the plot. We're unable to catch up. The latest advancements seem to make life easier, but our human needs are more than technology can offer. We need love and meaning in our lives.

Stay consistent and in due time, results will come. I know that from my eleven plus years of journaling experience.

It's OK if your bicycle tire is punctured. Mine was too.

CHAPTER 7:

The Gift of Healing

There is a special chamber for deep-ocean divers exposed to atmospheric pressure. It's called the decompression chamber. Merriam-Webster describes the decompression chamber as "a small room that allows a person (such as an ocean diver) to slowly experience lower amounts of air pressure until normal air pressure is reached."[1]

In Britannica.com[2] they offer a good definition that states a "hyperbaric chamber, also called decompression chamber or recompression chamber, sealed chamber in which a high-pressure environment is used primarily to treat decompression sickness, gas embolism, carbon monoxide poisoning, gas gangrene resulting from infection by anaerobic bacteria, tissue injury arising from radiation therapy for cancer, and wounds that are difficult to heal."

During my first year of journaling, I had so much fun exploring things, but soon something happened I was rocked to my core when I realized I could be an author. Fear paralyzed me. It is better described in the gift of spirituality.

Are You a Chicken, McFly?

Martin McFly didn't like being called a chicken in the classic film, *Back to the Future*, and I didn't like it either. Yes, the time was right

---

[1] Merriam-Webster.com Dictionary, s.v. "decompression chamber," accessed August 1, 2022, https://www.merriam-webster.com/dictionary/decompression 20chamber

[2] The Editors of Encyclopedia Brittanica. Brittanica.com "Hyperbaric Chamber."

for me to go deeper into the healing process. Spiritual healing is essential because that's where everything begins and ends. We come from Spirit and end with Spirit, too.

Real progress is impossible if you don't do the healing work first. You must stay in the decompression chamber for as long as it takes. If you have done so, you are spiritually healed, and you can move on with your life. You'll do things you never imagined yourself capable of doing.

For one thing, I never imagined that this impatient western man could become an author. When I was in school, my composition teachers highlighted my writing weaknesses. They would leave loud remarks on my papers such as *Yannis, this is a very poor expression,* or *Yannis, this is very poor articulation and many more.* For one thing, they were right at that time. My expression was poor. It was true. At home, it wasn't better either. From constant repetition, either by voice or action, my mother and the rest of the surroundings had ingrained in me the belief that I was incompetent.

But things can change, and they did change for me. God always has the last word, and he has humor too. Trust the process. Let it unfold naturally.

For now, focus on what you can control—your effort.

I know all too well that healing cannot happen with wishful thinking. That's why many self-help books often bother me. Inspiration is cool, it can be helpful at times, but that's as far as it can go. The rest is up to one's determination. My dear friend, healing cannot happen without entering the decompression chamber.

This is where a lot of people stop. Because the healing process can be so intimidating, like climbing a steep mountain hill. There is always the risk of falling, and people don't like to fall. They like to play it safe, even if their life is far from awesome.

In healing, one must face many truths accompanied by fear. This place is guarded by many monsters, angels, and demons. Yes, it's like a *Supernatural* episode.

While journaling, I faced the pain I'd avoided for years, the conflict within me had grown into a civil war—the good side versus the evil one. When I entered the decompression chamber, things began to change. I started hearing the voice clearer that I had neglected to listen to for years.

Until 2011, I didn't know what I wanted and had zero life ambition. I sometimes wanted to be brave and strong like my favorite childhood superheroes, but so much was missing.

I couldn't express my emotions the way I wanted. I was half the man I was supposed to be, and I couldn't find peace. Yet, as I continued journaling, I began to find my expression, and the healing began.

The Negative Zone

When I shied away from publishing my first book, I decided to face what had been bothering me. As I continued to journal, new inspiration arrived from an unlikely place, what I like to call the negative zone. I take this sentence from the iconic *Fantastic Four* comic books.

The superheroes who make up the "Fantastic Four" often travel to extremely hostile worlds and dimensions. They do that to eliminate threats to their loved ones and planet earth. The place they go most often is called The Negative Zone.

In my case, the negative zone is depicted on the map as where all emotional pain resides. Trauma, insecurities, fear, and other debilitating issues reside in my negative zone, and each time one is resolved a new gift is revealed, and a new upgrade happens.

In the decompression chamber, time stops.

This is an excerpt from one of my journals from several years ago:

> *As I'm listening to Les Brown, I can't help but wonder how many from his wide audience can absorb and utilize this information? From day one, I have entered the decompression chamber, and I'm still there after five years. How much longer?*

"As much as it takes, as long as it takes." That's how Jim Rohn answered an audience member from one of his talks. The question the person asked was different, but the answer applies to anyone reading these words and wondering the same thing I did: How much longer?

No one can control how long it's going to take. For some people, it's a long, arduous process. For others, it can be a relatively short process. It all depends on your willingness to go forward and the amount of exposure someone's had to destabilizing elements.

My exposure was long, a lengthy prison sentence of the same things, repeating themselves daily until I was about twenty-nine years old. After that, I had an opportunity to live overseas. Of course, moving to another country didn't change things overnight—far from it. After all, I was still *me*.

I carried heavy and painful emotional baggage with me, and, as you may know, your shadow follows you everywhere you go. My old self's shadow followed me for another ten years until I was about thirty-nine. That's when I finally wrote the first page of my journal page. Still, even after writing that first page, it took me ten more years to move from point A to point B.

Recovery isn't a joy ride down a straight road. It's a curved road and depends on the person. I get angry when I read quotes that say the quickest way from A to B is a straight line. That's complete bullshit.

If it was so easy, everybody would make it and live a wonderful life. Instead, there are many ups and downs, like a rollercoaster ride. Those who make it are those who hold on tight.

Warning: No Shortcuts from the Decompression Chamber

There are some serious consequences for anyone who tries to jump the process. Decompression can't be rushed, not without paying the high price of prolonged suffering and, possibly, an untimely death.

Ouch! The last one hurts, right? We all know that nobody lives forever, but none of us wants to leave the party too early. Many have died much earlier than expected because they couldn't wait. They couldn't wait for the healing to be completed. They were too fast, too furious, and too careless. They took unnecessary risks and paid the price with their lives. Many very famous people came crashing down after flying so high. There wasn't enough time spent in the hyperbaric chamber. They refused to decompress and wait.

Some famous people who died too early became legends, like actor James Dean. At least for them, history was kind, but many others have died in vain, lost and forgotten, leaving behind broken homes and unfulfilled promises.

My greatest fear growing up was that I would end up like them, the ones who never took life by the horns or did something that mattered.

Steve McQueen, a great actor (one of my all-time favorites), was a rebel. He went for the kill always. He broke every acting record, but eventually, life caught up to him (Or should I say death?). In his late forties, his health seriously declined, and he was diagnosed with a form of aggressive cancer that ended his life prematurely at fifty years old.

Then, there was Kirk Douglas, fourteen years older than McQueen. Douglas died in February of 2020. He was 104 years old. Can you believe that?

What was the secret to his longevity? What was the difference? Was it just destiny? Or did decompression time make a difference?

I believe the decompression time made all the difference. Douglas was forced to visit the decompression chamber many times and remain there for long periods. Although he had two very serious accidents over his lifetime and a stroke at seventy-nine that impaired his speech, he faced these difficult moments with courage and patience.

When you decompress, I believe you fight for life more and evade death's early rapture. Douglas spent a lot of time stuck in hospitals and was homebound for a long while, which I believe helped him regroup and heal many emotional wounds.

Unexpressed pain is the hidden secret and why so many people have lost their lives prematurely. It makes sense; the greater the pain, the harder it is to bear and uncover. But know this: if the pain is so great, it must also be something very important—a message not to be ignored.

But is it just the pain in the decompression chamber? Or is pain just a category that includes all unresolved issues?

Here, too, I'm inclined to go with the latter. Now we are getting to the real value of journaling our pain. Maybe this is the most important message in the book.

We lose important messages that exist around us because we forget. We miss golden opportunities when we're too busy and our pace doesn't match our true needs. The information we receive from the media every day is too much.

By journaling, we validate that the pain exists, and that's very important. We often know the pain exists, but rarely acknowledge it, so our true selves stay in limbo.

Your life will begin to change as you open the letters of pain.

It's time to read pain's letters one by one. What is missing from your life? What bothers you? The letters will tell you that and more. Journaling assists you with opening this seemingly unwanted mail, which people normally don't receive, not in this way. They receive it but in ways that it's hard to notice and understand. That's why there's so much suffering in the world.

The burden leans more toward men because we're supposed to be the strongest of the kind, but women suffer, too. Cultural views regarding emotions have stunted many people's character development.

Pain is a voice that needs to be heard.

Nobody in my life understood how I felt from when I was a young child to my adulthood. I know that now, so I no longer hold grudges against anyone. God helped me to forgive. It was up to me to find my way out as life continued to become bigger than my problem.

Painting is an expression of pain.

Throughout my teenage years, I tried to express my pain through painting, and people thought my work was beautiful. It was a gift I discovered early in my life, one of the many callings in my life. My passion for painting continued well into my teenage years when I began painting daily for hours. The more difficult the painting project, the better. It made me concentrate harder and allowed me to ignore distractions. Painting was a relief.

Pain is often the muse of artistic masterpieces. People visit museums and galleries to admire beautiful works without ever knowing what the artists were dealing with in their lives when they created their masterpieces. So, painting did me a lot of good for a time. It soothed the pain, but it didn't heal me. I still had work to do and a lot of distance to cover. I needed to get more personal, direct, aware, and present to heal the pain.

When I write, He writes.

Journaling will speak to your pain and longing. Give it time. Allow your hands to become the hands of God. Let them do the writing.

Emotional pain is the gateway to exponential growth.

At the start of 2020, I found the courage to face something that had troubled me for many years. It was something I'd dealt with since I was a kid—codependency, an addiction that feeds off feelings of unworthiness.

I grew up always depending on others, never believing in myself, first as a child (a natural need) and then unnaturally as an adult. I became addicted to that way of living. Early in 2020, after watching a video course by Russel Brand on the Commune platform about recovery from addiction, I decided to join a recovery group. The first time I went to the meeting, I never reached the main entrance. Fear paralyzed me, and I turned around and went home.

The following week, I took one little step forward. That little step forward led me to the building and the meeting room. I was shaking like a leaf as I entered that room, one of thirteen men all feeling lost.

I sat quietly listening to them, then it was my turn to introduce myself. I had so much to say, yet all I could say at that moment was, "Hello, I'm Yannis, and I am codependent." I don't remember much after that.

The Angels Sang

After that meeting, something happened. The next morning, I went to work, feeling euphoric, full of love for everyone. It was like the angels were playing music; it was the first time I heard their angelic song.

That glorious feeling continued for two hours, and then—poof—the pain was gone, a cathartic release.

My pain needed to be heard and witnessed, so it could be released and take its real form, the one of a precious gift. I urge you to let your pain be heard. Write it in your journal and find trustworthy people to share your pain.

Decompression Chamber: Any Snapshots?

You already received some in this chapter, but I can give you some more. The rest will be up to you to experience.

Snapshot Number One

First, when you begin to heal, you'll face resistance (often aggressive) from within. The resistance is a dark force that even writer Stephen Pressfield spent much time writing about in his book, *The War of Art.*

The person I was didn't want change or interruption, even if I was clearly headed downhill. I hated my life for thirty-nine years, and I was comfortable hating it. Can you believe that? It was hard to swallow and accept, but it was the bitter truth. Only when I came close to accepting that as fact did my reality begin to change. I began thinking differently and, eventually, acting differently.

Snapshot Number Two

There is a lot of stuff that doesn't need to be there, like bad attitudes and behaviors that come from others. You heard them, you watched them, and you believed them. Sometimes they meant well, but that doesn't matter. What matters is what happens right here, right now. Journaling is here to end this and bring you closer to reality, where you belong.

In my case, I had many false beliefs passed on to me by my parents and people close to me. Beliefs that were not congruent with who I truly am.

So, you will need to work with these two often—sorry.

Snapshot Number Three: The End of Decompression Time

Here's a bonus snapshot for you. It's a nice one. At some point, you might even experience this: a new background, scenery, music, story—a new life.

CHAPTER 8:

THE GIFT OF REVIEWING

In Jim Rohn's amazing lecture, he highlighted the significance of journal review. In our everyday life, we have so many things to do that often we forget what really matters. In my early journaling days, my writing speed was way faster than what I was learning. I needed to go back often and review what I wrote to understand better what I was writing. So, I made journal review a habit. Something I do at the end of each journal.

Some of the life lessons I recorded in my journals took time for my mind to absorb, and that was the opportunity to get them right. In today's world, you often hear it's great to learn new things, and I agree. Learning encourages curiosity, openness, courage, and an upbeat attitude that keeps us moving forward. But I also know the following as true: discarding old things as useless can be a great mistake. Then, the past never leaves. It stays active.

I complete a review each time I finish a journal. It helps me easily recap and make the best of my writing.

I and He

It also creates distance between me as the reader and the writer. It can be weird at times. Often, it feels like I'm reading someone else's work. It's because I'm adding much-needed perspective. The distance is required, so I can be more objective.

I archive the contents in a way that suits me best, just as if it was an actual book or magazine, with titles and various keywords, nothing fancy, and it is all handwritten. I will confess that the seven years of journaling in Italy were very organic, with little technology involved, and everything written in pen on paper. The only time I've used technology to help me complete a book was when I wrote the one, you're reading now. I couldn't do it entirely on paper because of all the corrections, it would have been so time-consuming.

The Wisdom of Jim Rohn

I remember Jim Rohn saying how important it is to summarize and organize your journals. The result can be powerful. In 2016, I did a five-year journal review. I gathered all thirty journals I completed, read them one by one, made some new notes, and found new insights and realizations.

Four years later, in 2020, during the lockdown, I went into a full-blown nine-year journal review with all the time I had available. At that time, I had fifty journals. I read through them again and relived my breakthroughs, struggles, and spoofs. It was a trip! I paid homage to the sad moments, like when reading what I wrote about my mother's dear dog, Booby. The tears ran again from anger, sadness, and of course love.

Getting Rid of Excess During the Journal Review

You'll inevitably have excess material while journaling; some stuff will be just rubbish. Words that are impracticable, plain useless.

Oh yes, time reveals the excess because nothing alien can stand the test of time. Journal review enhances your detective work. It connects the dots and tightens the gap between ego and your true self.

This book aims to provide you with a new awareness to help you understand your life more. During a review, I discovered where I struggle and where I've improved. I have recorded those moments and investigated them. I have not always been successful, but there were times of significant progress, and that's more than enough for me, and that will be more than enough for you. We want progress, not perfection. Perfection is rigid and stiff. Progress is malleable. Leave perfection for God.

Truth always stands the test of time. When I review old content and see things that still resonate, I know there is truth in them.

There are many types of journal review you can do. My advice? Surprise me. Ignore me. Innovate and do whatever suits you best. However, I will give you a piece of caution: too much analysis can steal the beauty out of it. Don't do that.

The review part, to me is a small part of the journaling process. This small part is important but not as important as the practice itself. However, that's my opinion. I leave it up to you to decide what works best for you. Do what you will with your journal reviewing process.

Your curiosity will naturally spike when you start this process and recalibrate your recent findings. It creates the perfect blend of past, present, and future, so they can become better.

Journal Review can improve the thinking process

Good thinking is a rarity these days. Our brain gets easily jammed by the bullshit thrown at us every day. Our problems and the problems of others become one. Thousands of thoughts of no use overload our computer, the fastest and most intelligent one we have: our brain.

But when you make a review, it happens something most of us greatly miss: You get to think for yourself, something so important and magnificent.

For many, analytical thinking is repelling, a complete waste of time. They want to live in the here and now and be spontaneous and instinctive like a child.

But let me ask: what is the most essential in an adult's life?

There is a reason why we grow up and become adults, it's because we need to use our brain. We become adults so we can be responsible for ourselves and anything else that is close to us.

Journal Quotes Are the Juice of Journaling

During the review, I often highlight quotes from my entries. Quotes are the juice of journaling. They stem from deep inner wisdom and are great "hooks" to remember what I was talking about. They are like the highlighted links that people use on the Internet, usually to sell things.

Journal Events

Some events happen that change the course of a person's life, and events are the next level in journaling.

In the early years, it was enough for me to finish a journal, complete a review, and start a new journal. I highly recommend, as a beginner, the same process for you, but as an advanced student, I recommend note significant events. Because of where I am now, I often look for those game changers and note them on my journal's last pages with their corresponding dates. Who knows? Maybe, one day, I will time travel and need the coordinates.

While recording the journal events, I have myself these questions:

- Have I applied a new method consistently?
- Have I embodied a new truth?
- Have I done something that required courage?

- Have I moved forwards?
- What were the mistakes, and what were the lessons?

These are all events that my journal needs to record.

Why should you give a damn about events?

That's a good question. When you are feeling positive, everything is fine. If it isn't broken, then why fix it, right? But what about when you feel hopeless? You need help from memory lane; believe me, you won't find a thing if you feel hopeless.

In 2013, I decided to try a hypnotherapy session. I'd heard so much great stuff about hypnosis; there was so much mystery surrounding it, and I wanted to experience it myself. I had high hopes for the process.

So, I booked a session with a practitioner online. At some point during the hypnotic session, the practitioner asked me to imagine that I was walking in a hall of personal records where my greatest achievements were stored. He asked me to look around and describe them. When he said that, I froze. I wasn't prepared for such a request.

Me? Achievements? Hall of records? What the hell was he talking about?

I only saw a pitch-black. I couldn't visualize anything. I couldn't see a damn thing. I just couldn't.

Of course, I couldn't. I couldn't describe a single good thing I had done in my life; the only highlights were the bad things that had happened to me. It was how I felt then and how I saw myself in the world. I could easily remember blatant mistakes and failures but not big achievements.

The whole session fell apart after that. Whatever the practitioner said to me later to console me was too little, too late. I felt deeply depressed afterward, defeated by my mind again. That first negative hypnotic experience affected my future attempts. It stopped me from even becoming a hypnotherapist, something I later intended to.

Life-changing events can become lifesaving events. So, please do me a favor. Keep track of events. Someday, you might need to remember one.

CHAPTER 9:

The Gift of Fight

Peace won't come in Peace

During the Star Trek episode, "This Side of Paradise," Captain Kirk said, *"Maybe we weren't meant for paradise. Maybe we were meant to fight our way through, struggle, claw our way up, scratch for every inch of the way. Maybe we can't stroll to the music of the lute. We must march to the sound of drums."*

While journaling, I realized early that some things don't come easy. They come through much pain and struggle. Some things, once lost, take one hell of a fight to get them back. In my case, I had long lost the fighting spirit in me. In my life, the fighting spirit was only a guest star, appearing in some athletic events here and there. In my everyday time, I was a defeated man, looking down most of the time. Journaling highlighted this great need to defend myself, to stand up and fight.

I would have to go into battle many times to reawaken my fighting spirit, the warrior in me. It is funny how peace is presented in the world. It is often presented as something harmonious, quiet, without all hate and conflict, and so in tune with nature. And yet, in the name of peace, many great wars have happened, and much bloodshed and pain have been inflicted upon brothers and sisters who have died in the name of peace.

Dear friend, make no mistake, often, peace won't come in peace; it will come with much fighting.

Move On, or Catharsis Will move you Over

Let me tell you a personal story. In 2014, after three years of continuous journaling, I exposed many false beliefs and lies and had uncovered many truths. Then, one day, another inconvenient truth revealed itself to me, one that I wasn't willing to face. It had to do with my romantic relationship with my fiancée, Jenny.

We'd been together since 2003. Our relationship was a big part of my life for many years, but I couldn't admit to her what was bothering me, which was an absence in my heart, a strange numbness I couldn't explain. I would try to figure out why I felt that way by writing in my journal. I would journal about my deep appreciation for her, my respect and gratitude for her and my fear that I couldn't pinpoint deep love. I couldn't find acts of self-sacrifice and giving.

Blah Blah Boo

Occasionally, I would fill many pages with such material. Pages that would not have real substance. I would rationalize a lot, but something would always be left out. Sometimes, I would talk about my feelings with her but never to a satisfactory conclusion. The truth was that I had never really looked that deep inside to heal my pain, so although I longed to go deep with someone, at the same time, I felt I couldn't. It was all part of the same conflict, the same inner battle I'd experienced since youth. I was afraid to open up and get intimate, to reveal that part of me. I was afraid I would add more pain to my pain. Our relationship always lacked color and intensity. It was a fire that couldn't warm or light our home. The truth was that most of the time, I was emotionally absent.

I remember one night that Jenny was crying for some reason, and I got so upset because I didn't want to be emotionally involved. I didn't want to listen to her pain. I kept telling her to stop it. I couldn't handle it. I now understand how selfish I'd been.

Distressing Dreams

Because I wouldn't hold back in my journals, it didn't take long to hit the right spot. Then, I began having distressing dreams from my subconscious involving me constantly losing something important: losing Jenny countless of times, losing money and filing for bankruptcy, getting lost in an unknown land with no passport, and having no identity. I would wake up feeling out of sorts and say, with some relief: Thank god, it was only a dream.

But it wasn't only a dream; it was also the truth. All these warnings I was receiving were valid. My subconscious was asking me to deal with it and do something about it now.

At that time, I couldn't imagine a life without my partner. We'd been together for so many years. It was much easier to deal with problems together. I relied on her so much. She was my pillar.

In fact, if I could paint a picture of our relationship, it would be just that: an enormous Grecian pillar like the ones that stand in the temple of Acropolis.

Deep inside I knew I didn't have the life I needed, but I couldn't fully admit that the foundation was weak. My biggest fear was that all would end in a flash once I got entirely honest. I'd have to leave, I could see that a breakup was a strong possibility.

As a child, I had already witnessed a breakup in my house, which wasn't good. My parents' relationship was a total failure. It was just terrible, and the divorce was uncivilized and rough. When they officially split in 1982, I'd already experienced a decade of deep turmoil inside the house.

Problem Number 2: The Pillow

But I had one more problem in Italy: my pillow was too comfortable.

That was another inconvenient truth. I had become too comfortable, too complacent. Someone else took care of my basic needs and paid the bills. At that time, I was unemployed and stayed home most of the time. I was no different than a child or an incapacitated elder.

Comfort is like quicksand. The more you fight to get out of it, the faster it pulls you in. I tried to talk myself out of it and waited for better times, but better times didn't come. When you don't fix the problem, the problem remains, giving birth to more problems. Our communication began to erode.

Jenny told me many times that I lived in a bubble, it bothered me a lot to hear this but she was right. I was in my own bubble in Italy. I didn't want to lose the house I was living in and all my easy habits. So, I kept telling myself excuses, which the ego is good at.

Many days and nights passed in unease. Then the days became weeks, the weeks became months, and the months became years that turned into four long years of self-denial and conflict. When you don't accept the easy way, there is always the hard one.

> "*The bigger the fantasy you live, the more painful the inevitable collision with reality.*"
> -Will Smith, Actor

Yes, Will Smith said it well. One day it finally caught up with me.

Winter of 2017/2018, Jenny's health had declined, and my support was dismal. Once again, I didn't want to get too close to her struggles. Because I didn't want to add to my pain. Instead, I kept giving her health advice like a medical professional. I was selfish—a real dick.

She handled many hard things that winter—alone.

Knock, knock

We talked about stopping what wasn't working when that heavy winter passed. One morning, catharsis came to my door and said, "Enough pal, enough with your excuses. Your time is up."

My romantic relationship, my built-in life, came to an end. I made that choice because I knew I was doing her more harm than good. Jenny was sliding downhill every which way, and I felt responsible. I'd caused so much stress in her life. I had to do something about it. We agreed that our relationship needed to stop.

And we lived happily ever after, right? Unfortunately, this is not a Hollywood film, so no.

Fighting for Peace

The real test and battle started once the relationship ended. Just because I did one right thing didn't mean I took the stairway to heaven—far from it! I actually walked down many steps and went straight into hell, but at least it was something real.

With very few options at hand I moved back to London. It had been eleven years since I'd lived there, and it was a rocky acclimation. I felt like dying inside often, and in many ways, I was.

I'd lost my comfortable lifestyle and had to get a job and face many of my inner demons, a lot of shit together.

I wanted peace, but it wouldn't come easy. I had to pay the price for peace first. I'm sorry to spoil it for you, but if you are in conflict you must pay too. Truth doesn't care about emotional imbalances; it doesn't care about mine, and it won't care about yours, and the peace you are so longing for, won't come to you in peace. Most times, it comes through catharsis.

Catharsis: May God Forgive You If It Happens to You, May God Bless, If You Survive It

In 2018, after seven years of writing in my journals, I faced catharsis, an uncontrollable natural force that leads to purification and freedom. Catharsis in Greek means to be purified, and that's exactly what catharsis does. Catharsis finishes what's left undone. It comes uninvited, is relentless and unstoppable like a tsunami, and washes away everything but the truth. It is the perfect storm.

Often people reach the point of no return, they go too far and make too many mistakes, breach natural laws repeatedly, and a price must be paid. That's what happened to me. I'd gone too far by delaying accepting the facts.

You read all about it on the previous pages. I waited four long years to make that critical decision, which is why afterward, I suffered more than I expected to. Luckily, I survived to tell you this story. All those confessions on paper were not in vain. They helped me be more aware. A time might arrive in your life, too, that no amount of education, journaling, or help from others will stop you from feeling the obliterating pain of catharsis.

Catharsis Devastates the Ego

The ego gets smashed in this period. Whatever fantasies I told myself, they were smashed that fateful day. Catharsis demolished my pipe dreams.

In her eyes, I saw the truth.

They say the eyes are the mirror of the soul. I certainly experienced that on November 4, 2018. I'll remember that day for the rest of my life.

The moment of farewell happened at the departure gates at the Rome Ciampino airport. I looked into Jenny's crying eyes and understood that my relationship with her would never be the same. I saw devastation and disappointment in her eyes. I could see everything that went wrong when I looked into her eyes. The memory still makes me tremble.

When I said the final goodbye, I felt like a dead man walking. Sitting on the plane, I didn't have any desire to arrive at my destination. I just wanted to die. I was totally destroyed. I had nothing left.

The irony was, in doing what I did, I proved something to myself; that I had some feelings for her. I finally recorded in my journal the best act of love I could ever record during our fifteen years together. It had to come from pain like the sad song Johnny Cash song, *Hurt*: *"I hurt myself today to see if I still feel. I focus on the pain. The only thing that's real."* I'd finally stepped out of my comfort zone and done something that really mattered.

Writing this isn't easy. I only hope one day she forgives me for being such a jackass.

Catharsis, in many ways, is like a tough pregnancy. After nine turbulent months, a woman finally gives life to a child, and a child always brings new hope. Catharsis also brings new life after a hard trial. My life forever changed after that day. I grew up suddenly. I manned up. Catharsis gave birth to the person I am today.

Topolino Three for Three

There's a way to attain peace and leave all battles behind.

No, it is not a slimy shortcut. It's based on the law of detachment, a spiritual law of the universe. Absolute freedom and peace come from letting go, giving up the old, so you can receive the new. Within that law, another tricky life paradox is put into action. At first, it seems like you're losing everything, but, in reality, the exact opposite is happening. You're setting yourself free.

It has the same effect as catharsis, but the method is different. When something like the law of detachment happens in my life, I journal about it, and here's a funny story that happened several years ago. I call this story Topolino Three for Three.

While in Italy, I found an exciting way of learning the language. It was through comic books or *fumetti* in Italian. Throughout the years, I amassed quite a collection by buying them in charity shops for a fraction of their original price. The funny stories were engaging, and the images helped me understand what was happening without fully understanding the words. So, I was always one step ahead. Reading the adventures of all the great Disney characters was so much fun.

One day, since I'd amassed so many comic books, I decided I needed to let go of some to make more space. At first, it felt like abandonment, abandoning those priceless moments I had with them. To me, those books were alive. They had so much good energy. Then, I remembered something Robert Kiyosaki frequently said in his interviews and wrote in his book, *Rich Dad, Poor Dad*. To paraphrase, he said more will come.

One evening, I had three Topolino comic books (Mickey Mouse in English) in my hands, ready to off-load, and, with a heavy heart, I dropped them inside the recycling bin. A few hours passed, and, feeling sad, I decided to go for an evening walk around the block. I did that every day to get fresh air and visit some of my area "pet" friends. While turning a corner, I found something surprising. There was a Topolino comic book in the middle of the street! I ran fast and snatched it before a car ran over it. The magazine was like new!

I continued walking and, within a matter of minutes, I saw another Topolino comic book in the middle of the street! Again, I ran out and grabbed it.

I continued walking and wondered: Will I find another one?

Before I even finished asking that question in my mind, there it was. A third Topolino comic book in the middle of the street. I rescued it from the street, held it in my hands, and thought, God has blessed me.

It was the last one I found that evening and, very pleased, I returned home. I stored them in the same place where the others used to be. Then, as I was lying in my bed falling asleep, I suddenly realized what had happened: three Topolino for three. Oh my god! What a miracle! My three old Topolino were replaced with three new ones without me having to buy them!

Somehow, I applied the law of detachment to the situation completely by accident. I gave away something precious, something I truly loved, only to receive it back even better than before.

It seems that if this is done with the right intention, the universe not only hears but gives you something better. Dammit! I should have been born in Tibet or India. I'm joking, of course.

Each day has magic, and life gives so generously every day if we choose to notice it. Journaling can help you do that and much more.

CHAPTER 10:

THE GIFT OF SEEKING

I heard Jim Rohn say in that fateful speech, "We must all become our own investigators. We must train our eyes and ears to search for evidence and what better way to do it than in a journal."[3]

On this new journey, you'll need to acquire many new hats. I've heard many Americans use the expression (especially in movies) when speaking about taking on new roles. Gathering facts and searching for evidence is work that requires a different mindset. You may need to become a detective like Lieutenant Columbo from the classic American television series *Columbo* or Montalbano from the Italian television series, *Inspector Montalbano*.

While journaling, the goal is to reveal the truth whenever possible, starting with clues. I've left clues of my true character in many places throughout the years. At first, those clues were hard to spot because of my troubled emotional life.

Returning to the scene of the crime isn't always a good idea.

Honestly, the past was not the right place for me to start. I had too many unresolved issues and moments filled with frustration, regret, and guilt. What good would revisiting them bring?

All Problems is One

I let bad moods surface naturally and dealt with them head-on in the present, and quite by accident, I found the right strategy.

---

[3] Rohn, Jim. "(FULL) Best Life Ever." *YouTube* video, 4:22:37. October 25, 2017. https://youtu.be/6ySBv-HHyK4.

Because in reality all problems is one problem that affects all other areas.

Your journal will reveal your ideal strategy

The power is in the present. Everything can be resolved in the present with the right amount of attention and awareness. Combining attention and awareness gives you a different perspective and new view on life. My journal provided me with the awareness I didn't have. It was the evidence I needed. A good detective needs to start from somewhere!

You've Got Another Thing Coming

I refer to the Judas Priest song when I say, "You've got another thing coming." All of us have another thing coming every single day.

As routine as each day seems, there's always another thing coming. You can examine that "thing" in your journal. Let it become your latest news. Others read newspapers for their news. I read "journal" news. It's like reading a newspaper, except you're the main subject.

It's easier to deal with newer experiences than things that happened long ago because they get blown out of proportion by your perceptions at the time. Every day has enormous importance for your progress. Each page I devoted to an event, even slightly insignificant events, paid off because it helped me think and respond differently to the experience.

On a personal note . . .

Many times, I thought I was alone, and I was wrong. Someone was always next to me. What I learned through journaling couldn't have come only from my mind. A higher power was also involved. One that comes from the spirit.

I don't claim to understand what Spirit means, but it fully understands me because when I speak, He speaks, and when I write, he writes. Oh, and one more: When I read, He reads too.

Captain's Log

Here are some real-life examples from my life. I use the heading "Captain's Log" for two reasons.

The first reason is to remind you there's only one captain in your life—YOU! The second reason, those of you who are Star Trek superfans might have guessed it. I am also a huge Trekkie, and every *Star Trek* episode would start with the phrase, Captain's Log.

Captain's Log: Day One

Today I went for a walk and felt so much peace while walking into the woods. Was it the woods? The nature around me? What made me feel so relaxed and peaceful?

Captain's Log: Day Two

When my sister reminded me to visit my uncle, I felt really annoyed because the tone of her voice was rough. I wish she hadn't done that, but she did, and I was upset all evening, and the worst is that I didn't take my beloved dog Lilly to the sea.

Captain's Log: Day 3

A girl I like very much came to my shop and ordered at my till, and I was speechless throughout the entire transaction. I prepared her coffee but couldn't say a word to her. My heart was beating so fast. I wanted to say something but couldn't. I just wanted to hit my head on the wall afterward. Why? I kept saying to myself repeatedly, feeling frustrated and disappointed.

Captain's Log: Day 4

This evening I was playing basketball with my friends, and it came to a point where everything was at stake. We were on the verge of losing by a single point, and that was precisely the moment where everything slowed down. Suddenly, I was at peace with incredible clarity. I took the ball and scored again and again until we won! How on earth did I do that?

Captain's Log: Day 5

At work, my manager said something inappropriate and hurtful to me. I felt embarrassed and upset. I felt betrayed and angry. I couldn't work well after that. My momentum halted. What the hell happened?

Captain's Log: Day 6

Today, on the phone, my father was angry when I told him I had quit my new job at the restaurant. He said, "You did shit." This made me feel like wanting to hide somewhere no one could find me.

Captain's Log: Day 7

My mother said in front of our guests that I'm average. I got very upset when I heard her use that word, and my hands began to shake. I felt like a lonely little child once again. My mood was totally ruined. What happened there?

Captain's Log: Day 8

I was shocked today when I realized I'd hit twenty-two lessons in my hypnotherapy course in twenty-two weeks. I had exceeded my biggest expectations and somehow that scared me. I felt anxiety suddenly and thought that failure must be looming somewhere once again. Is that normal?

Captain's Log: Day 9

While watching *IP Man 3*, something happened within the last thirty minutes. As IP Man experienced great sadness and emotional pain, I began feeling sad too, and tears fell from my eyes. What was that about?

Captain's Log: Day 10

I went with Jenny today to watch *Avengers 2* at the cinema. There was a scene where all the Avengers united to face the enemy. That scene made me cry. How come? Why did I get so emotional?

Captain's Log: Day 11

I heard my mother bitching about my father today, and I began bitching about my father too. I felt so guilty afterward. Why did I do that? What the hell is wrong with me? Do I like this?

Captain's Log: Day 12

On our way to the fruit market today, I expected Jenny to say something good and praise me for my work that morning. But, no, she didn't say a thing. I needed her praise, and she didn't give it to me. Man, I got so nervous. Why?

Revealing Emotional Triggers

"They hide in our subconscious, ever ready to pop out and undermine us."
Jim McManus

The above examples are records of my good, bad, and ugly emotional moments. I began investigating those trigger points.

We all have them; for most of us, they just happen. Almost everyone has their personal land mine, and unknowingly he or she walks on it and gets wounded.

That's what used to happen to me, every day, or, if I was lucky, every other day. Suddenly, a bomb would explode underneath my feet, and I would be blown apart into tiny pieces.

My good mood would change instantly, from a telephone call like you saw in one of the examples above or by simply hearing a comment or a word given by someone important to me, even silence at the wrong moments would destabilize me.

"Don't take it personally," Someone would say to me, and I would do just the opposite, I would take it very, very personally. Because it would penetrate me deep. Resulting in ruining my day (or night if sleeping late).

So, it was time for me to do something. It was time to a investigate and answer the questions that naturally surfaced day after day; otherwise, what kind of captain would I become?

The results were remarkable while often unpleasant. My life changed. The triggers revealed truths to me and highlighted to me the fact that I had learned many things wrong.

The journaling process is full of surprises. The investigation has helped me become more stable, resilient, and happy. Entrusting, reconnecting, and re-loving oneself is a challenging process, to say the least, but it's worth every single inch of it.

Journal your Dreams too

Journaling has no limits on what you can investigate—just don't stop. The self is multifaceted. Dreams are often far away from the real world. Trying to understand them using pure logic is the wrong approach. Most of the time, dreams don't represent thought. They represent emotions.

Dreams have always fascinated me. 2014 I took a dream analysis course while taking hypnotherapy correspondence studies from HMI American Hypnosis College. The course immediately sparked my curiosity. I was excited to add another layer to the investigative journaling process. I wondered, Can I understand my dreams? Who knows what I can discover!

Sometimes my dreams sent me grim warnings, as I mentioned in chapter nine. They wanted to tell me something that troubled me deeply or that I greatly missed. On many occasions, I had similar dreams. I often dreamed of being in Akrata, the place where my childhood summer holidays were usually spent.

Every summer, for about three months, I'd have the time of my life in Akrata. There were games, adventures, and lots of time in the sea, exactly what a child like me needed. I was happy there, carefree, and my dreams reminded me of that time so that I could rediscover the joy and the passion. There are so many places you to visit when it comes to discovering your true self. Keep seeking, keep journaling.

CHAPTER 11:

THE GIFT OF AWAKENING

How often do you get a second chance to do something important?

Before journaling, I was full of regret and near misses. Something in me was still narcotized. I felt like the characters in the movie, Awakenings, starring Robin Williams and Robert De Niro. When I watched that film, I was affected greatly, maybe because something in me recognized I had the same need. It's a story about comatose patients and a miracle. The clinic's doctor decides to alter the daily dosages of the patients' medications, and soon something strange happens: one by one, the patients begin to wake up.

From Young to Old

Some of the patients had been comatose for decades, and then they all started waking up, singing, dancing, and talking with youthful enthusiasm to make up for lost time and do the things they never did. The doctors and nurses were astounded by the results. They call relatives and close family to see their loved ones. It's a film I urge you to watch.

Latecomers

Many people in the world in a similar comatose state realize their potential a bit late. When they fully wake up, they have much more youthful energy than others their age. I'm one of them, a latecomer.

While living someone else's life, I didn't spend many of my years wisely. Now, I'm coming back. God gave me a second chance that not many people get in life. Like in *Awakenings*, I have awakened to my true potential, and I can tell you it's better late than never. Some trains from my youth have left the station and won't return. I can only accept that and continue moving forward with my life—there's a lot left!

Give yourself a chance. I don't care if you're younger or much older than me—just give yourself a chance. You are worthy of it. There are still trains you can catch. Remember that you wouldn't be alive if there wasn't a reason. There is somebody in the world waiting for your special help. Maybe it is someone close to you, your neighbor, sister, or brother, or perhaps someone you haven't met yet.

Rise, latecomer!

CHAPTER 12:

The Gift of Victory

Life is a big race. Many of us have forgotten that. We think that everything happens to us—not for us. I often hear life is a big journey. Yes, in many ways, it is. But it's also a big race, not just any race; it's of Olympic proportion. Those who fall short are those who don't understand that. We're born for a reason—nothing happens for nothing, and everything happens for everything. We are born to excel at something or even some things.

Coming from a country that adores athletic events to the max, I cannot help but use the Olympic Games as a metaphor. Those who compete in the Olympics are the champions of their countries, and champions seek something more than victory. They seek immortality to cement their place in history. They want to win, and winning in the Olympics is the culmination of dreams, and not only for those who compete. Often, those victories can uplift an entire country that seeks hope, light, and strength.

Every day for four years, an athlete will meticulously prepare, giving all they have to prepare for the big event. But everything doesn't always go as planned. Sometimes something stops their preparation. I can't imagine the pain and frustration of those who come so close to reaching their dreams and failing. It is very disappointing, to say the least, and it makes or breaks you.

Life has its own Olympics.

A great life does no one any favours. It isn't for the weak. Life's challenges are the hardest Olympics you'll ever compete in. Often your best efforts won't be enough. Still, if the effort is pure, one always achieves a moral victory.

My great sports dream was to one day take part in the Olympics. In Greece, I believe this dream must be in the subconscious of every one of its citizens. As a youngster, I lost the opportunity to make that leap into sports greatness because I was disconnected and lost. I had the talent but I couldn't commit to one sport. I couldn't see it through from start to finish. I couldn't trust the process. My parents were also far from understanding because they could hardly understand themselves. Now, as I'm writing this, I creep closer to half a century old, I'm determined to cover all that missing distance and make up for all the missing gaps in my life.

A Different Type of Olympics

Maybe I can no longer win the actual Olympics, but I'm determined to win the Olympics of life. That's the best I can do now; to save and inspire as many lost souls as possible—that will be my gold medal.

CHAPTER 13:

The Gift of Writing

A remarkable thing happened the moment I began journaling. I fell in love with writing. I found it to offer limitless potential to me. Among the countless gifts journaling has given me, writing is the one that stands out. It has a special star on it because it allows me to reach out to the world in this beautiful way.

Are you a writer?

Before journaling I had no reason to write and not enough knowledge to understand it's power. My dreams, hopes and greatest passions were coming from the sports, cinema, music and painting. Those were my favourite hobbies and the things that interested me the most.

Yet, in 2011, when I started journaling, something shifted my consciousness and attention. A new flame was ignited, and it hasn't stopped burning since. Journaling quickly became my new passion, and writing my love child. It's like somebody gave me a new ball (the pen) to play with, and the field was the journal, and I loved every minute of it.

I still do.

There was a voice in me that needed to be heard. We all have that inner voice. The inner self has so many untapped areas, and I was instantly attracted to them. I wanted to reach out and explore them all. As I was completing my first journal, a fascinating subject surfaced something that I wanted to write about so much. Something close to my heart. That's how I came to realize I could write a book.

Only it was still too early for me. I didn't believe I could actually write a book.

In our childhoods, we all create a life script, a road map of how to navigate our lives. I learned about the life script in my hypnotherapy correspondence studies. The script gets written before the teenage years, which means my life script was written in my darkest days as a troubled kid from a troubled family, and the same scenario continued later in my life. Some hurdle was always in the way of pursuing my dreams. I had low self-esteem and a very poor self-image.

But all drama must end at some point; otherwise, it becomes misery, and mine ended when I started journaling.

Dealing with Homeostasis

Of course, it was not a one-time deal; I had to work hard to rewrite my life script. It wasn't an easy task because I often faced resistance. There is another Greek word that can be used for that it is called homeostasis. Its effect is like gravity, pulling back to center whatever tries to get away. For many years I couldn't understand what power was holding me back. Dealing with the mind is much different than dealing with the body. You can see what's happening to the body. If there's a wound, you can see it. You don't know what's causing the mind's pain.

Time and time again, I ran into an invisible stone wall created by my wounded ego. But journaling revealed to me the truth.

There is something even greater than the subconscious mind—a bigger force than a human or non-human living being—is coming from a different portal. It comes from love, and it comes from God. The Holy Spirit sits alongside me during my most creative times and writes with me. The company is very pleasant, and I often lose my sense of time because where it comes from, time doesn't exist.

When I write, He writes. That's the best way I can describe it.

The proof is in the writing.

Vocal teacher and YouTuber Ken Tamplin always says in his videos, "The proof is in the singing." My own proof is in the writing. The proof is in this book that you are now holding and reading.

Completing this book is a significant victory for me. It proves that I've overcome my mental blocks. I have broken the chains and I have been resurrected. I have defeated my inner demons and anyone who's tried to stop me from publishing this work.

But I didn't do this alone. I needed help. God helped me. Christ helped me. My mentors helped me. Every day people helped me, and nature helped me.

I'm grateful to all who helped.

If You Journal with Passion and Write with Passion, You May Be a Writer

I'm going to risk making a bold statement: many new writers can emerge through journaling. Earth has so many suppressed souls who have something beautiful and powerful to say but can't because they haven't found the right way to say it.

Life experiences are rich in content. We learn from the good and bad moments alike.

Creativity must be encouraged, and journaling is the perfect creative outlet. If the gift of writing needs to come out, journaling will extract it. Take my word for it. Now, go grab a pen and start writing.

The world needs more voices and gifted writers, but more importantly, it needs passionate people willing to live their lives fully. That is the biggest thank you to the divine creator who allows us to experience life right now.

CHAPTER 14:

The Gift of Character

A gift given to us by divine creation is character. God gave each of us a signature, a special lock we can only open. Some may identify this special lock as our infinite potential.

While journaling, I unknowingly began tapping into this. I began developing the character I was meant to become.

As a child, I frequently met this character in my dreams. The character was in the hundreds of comic books that I read vigorously. As a child, I didn't know there were missing parts that only a capable adult could figure out and fill in—someone with enough courage, strength, and after many humbling experiences: wisdom.

Everyone has a core character from birth that identifies who we truly are. It's the one unchangeable fact of our lives. Yet, we sometimes lose it because we walk in the world wearing masks.

What masks? The masks of pretence. The ones that identify with the false part of us because that is what we've promoted for years. I know I did. I promoted the part of me that was scared, afraid to live free.

When I Speak, He Speaks, and When I Write, He Writes

It was a usual day at home. While journaling, I heard my inner voice saying: To your friends, you will become a stranger, and to strangers, a friend. Was I becoming an alien? Someone completely new? I understood that message better as I continued to fill the blank pages in my journal. It was a message about my evolving character turning into something different from what the people close to me knew.

"What matters is not the accomplishments you achieve;
what matters is the person you become."
John Ortberg

Committing to writing my first book was an enormous challenge because it had the word success all over. For all my life the easiest thing to do was to quit and fail and to never amount to anything. Words like commitment and discipline were not in my figurative dictionary. I was a man who didn't seem to have the discipline to do something as magnanimous as writing a book. For some, writing a book is an achievement that doesn't require a complete transformation; it doesn't test their knowledge, beliefs, or entire existence. For me, it did. I had to stop lying to myself because those lies were shackles, holding my true self prisoner.

In the gift of expanded awareness and the gift of spirituality chapters, I mention how hard it was during the early stages of journaling for me to do that because my foundation was weak, and I still felt like a prisoner. In his wonderful book *Battle Cry*, author Jason Wilson eloquently describes this condition as emotional incarceration.

Even if I had writing material available, had established enough inner peace and guidance, and people wanted to help me, I still withheld my true self from them. I still couldn't trust. I was afraid to enter that new world and witness the greatness and abundance that real life can offer.

During those early years in Rome, I had an unforgettable dream. I was in a strange city where everyone seemed scary and threatening. In my garage I had a magnificent red Ferrari, I wanted to keep it hidden from everyone. I didn't want anyone to know about it.

That dream perfectly represented how I was feeling and how I was living. My little self was terrified of my true self. My true self was that remarkable race car. Who knows, maybe you are hiding a red Ferrari too.

I won't disturb you. Please don't disturb me

Before journaling I was virtually a nobody. One of the millions in the city where I was living. My only ambition was to be left alone, stay anonymous and live like this for the rest of my life.

That was my definition of peace.

But when I started journaling, the definition changed.

"(You gotta) Fight for your right (to party)"

I said: Why not fight for my right to party? Yes, it's just like that awesome Beastie Boys song. I began living passionately, and my ambition and thirst for life returned.

I began connecting more and more pieces together, discovering more of who I wanted to be.

I wanted to be brave and strong. Someone who has the biggest ideals and morals. Disciplined enough to accomplish the most critical tasks. Someone who will love deeply and trust. Someone who will be there when help is needed.

So many beautiful things to have and be admired, but honestly, they were all easier said than done. Because so many parts of me were missing. I still had a lot of work to do.

A big discovery in 2013

As I continued journaling non-stop, a groundbreaking discovery occurred in 2013. I discovered the man I was looking for. The journals revealed to me my identity, my true self. A man as bright and as warm as the sun.

Helios: The Sun Man

In Greek, the sun is translated into Helios. The sun to me resembles so many things that I can identify with. The top element of course is the ability to give us light. So many people give up hope when they miss the light. Another element equally important is the ability to give us warmth. People who have given up hope, feel cold inside, something in them feels abandoned and needs compassion and understanding, something in them needs warmth. The sun offer us these two elements in abundance and much more.

My new surname represents this symbol and a whole new attitude in life. It is my true self. While the core of my being remains the same, my character has vastly changed. No, I do not erase my past, neither do I feel ashamed for it, I would be a fool if I do that, I can still be Yannis Mihanos in my everyday life, I don't need to wear the uniform of Superman all the time. I'm actually proud that I managed to get through so much without losing my sanity or dying. Am I exaggerating? You be the judge.

Losing was part of the deal. Many times, when you lose you win and when you win you lose.

I won out of it a new life and of course a new identity.

If You Write It, He Will Come

I paraphrased this quote from *Field of Dreams*, a film starring Kevin Costner, because I think it fits rather well with what I'm trying to say. Exemplary character requires a lot of work that's always in progress.

Commitment, work, and dedication are necessary to form a fine character just like making a fine wine so much work and care takes place.

The New Message: Keep Journaling

The inner voice encouraged me to keep journaling and write more about my desired character. It seemed to have faith in me, something no one else had before, which gave me a warm, comforting feeling.

So, I kept journaling, combining elements, like an alchemist creating a special potion. I worked with the elements needed to help me, one day, emerge as the best version of myself.

The 12 Virtues of Benjamin Franklin

During those early years of journaling, I bought the book, *The 12 Virtues of Benjamin Franklin.* The book didn't fascinate me, but the message resonated. The author wrote that anyone with enough passion can develop their character for the better.

Ben Franklin attempted to do something extraordinary during his lifetime. He sought to cultivate the best elements in himself by choosing the twelve virtues he admired the most in other people and created a "to-be" list. His ambitious plan worked, and he enjoyed a successful life.

Enter the To-Be List

You might be more familiar with a to-do list than a to-be list. A to-be list doesn't make sense, right? We are what we are. Yet, it makes more sense when the word Potential is added to the phrase. Ben Franklin knew that he needed a to-be list to reach his goals.

Did he succeed? History speaks by itself. He achieved so many things that normal individuals of his time couldn't even dream of.

Potential demands many things, and you must make sacrifices. There is not one champion who hasn't sacrificed vital things because potential demands wholeness. You can't be half in the past and half in the present. You can't be here and there. To reach potential, one must tie all loose ends; Is it possible? I will say it is worth to try.

The clock is ticking

Building new elements and demolishing old ones is great to work on, but on the other hand, this life doesn't wait for us to finish. The clock is always ticking, never forget that. There are times when life demands urgency and direct action. Those are times when nothing else, but a specific result is needed. This is where a to-do list fits best. They are matters of life and death. It is do or die.

A plane must make a rough landing; otherwise, it will crash because half of the engine is spent, and so many lives are at stake. An advertising company is collapsing, and drastic changes must be done to stay afloat.

A basketball match has only a few seconds left; the difference is only one point. It's a final's game, and there is only one attack left. What is it going to be? Who is going to take the ball? Who is going to finish the attack?

In a hospital, an emergency surgery must stop the patient's internal bleeding; it's the patient's last hope. There is only one doctor in the whole hospital who can perform the operation. Will he have the guts to do it? Will he succeed?

These are some examples of emergency situations, but there are plenty more.

In these cases, you do what you must do—enough or not enough, ready or not ready, there is no other way.

Life flows for the rest of time, but it often doesn't. The reason is that the character is still undefined. There are still elements that don't belong. Many things are uneven.

People think that results add value: do "A," and you're worthy of "A." Do "B," and you're worthy of "B," etc. It's logical, as Spock from *Star Trek* would say. But, sorry, Mr. Spock, it's in the wrong sequence. Who you are comes first. What you do with it comes second.

Developing the core character is like cultivating a seed. You use all your knowledge and skill and give much attention to it because it is about something you really care about. It's a passion. I love speaking about it, and I love writing about it.

In my journal, sometimes the elements I refer to are strengths, but many other times, they are weaknesses. It doesn't matter what they are; it's what you do with them that matters.

Can a weakness be useful?

Nothing is a weakness if you approach it right. A weakness can be a great opportunity for growth, helping you develop much-needed humility and connection with others. Demonstrating vulnerability at times is very attractive because people like to connect with people who are transparent and honest.

As I write this book, I'm addressing this genuine need because I also have a weakness. My memory doesn't always serve me well.

Often, I only remember what is absolutely necessary, and then it goes away. When people give me instructions, I quickly forget them. It takes a lot of effort and many questions for me to fully understand what they're saying. I don't usually put myself in these situations because they bring up past feelings of shame, but things can change.

Last Christmas, my father visited my sister and me in London. One evening my father and I were discussing a common problem we had, and I came up with a solution.

Ask for help

"Let's capitalize on our weakness of needing help. Let's practice it first in the supermarket," I suggested.

He was startled, but he accepted the challenge. We both tried, and it was hilarious at times seeing my father trying with broken English to ask the cashier where to find milk or me stammering while asking for help, but, in the end, we were glad.

The exercise was successful, and I still continue it today. It has helped me gain confidence, knowing that whenever I feel weak or in doubt, I can ask for help. I get a small victory each time I do it. I gained the confidence to ask for help without feeling bad about myself. Isn't that something?

Journaling Is a Map for Real-life Treasure Hunting

Shaping a character takes time, especially when this character is messed up. The following story will explain what I mean more.

What's the point of being number one if I still feel empty?

Tyson Fury, a great boxing champion, was once in the brink of destruction. He believed early in his career that winning was everything. That reaching the top of his sport is where true happiness was found. He worked hard to reach the top. On the night of November 28, 2015, he dethroned the recurring champion, Wladimir Klitschko. It was supposed to be his most incredible night ever. Yet, it became one of his saddest because when he finally got to the top of the mountain, he found there wasn't a view, only an empty void. It was so devastating, and he felt lonely and helpless. He couldn't smile or enjoy his victory. He was lost.

So, he gave up boxing and nearly his life as he succumbed to nasty habits, but then something happened. He had an enlightened moment that saved him, and his character significantly changed. Fury found his position in God's kingdom, which gave him enormous strength and courage. When he resumed boxing, he came back with full power. He was much better and more complete. He was ready to fulfill his mission, which was greater than boxing and winning titles; it was to inspire others and live a better life.

Journaling Will Speak to You Too

Journaling will speak to you, too; it will tell you what element you need to bring forth for your true self to emerge. With time, your character will acquire more elements according to your mission. I'm not going to tell you where you ache and what you need to fix because your journal, your special book, will tell you that.

CHAPTER 15:

The Gift of Expansion

Something amazing happened the moment I began journaling I came in touch with a fundamental natural law.

This natural law speaks about effort and development in the maximum.

The year was 2012, and the month was August. I was already into my fourth journal, and it struck me to write something about the function of nature. The following words are what I wrote in my journal:

> *In nature, everything is designed to reach its maximum. All the trees, plants, flowers, birds, fish, and animals on land, including the creatures we find most threatening and repelling, must do something great. They must reach their maximum potential. This is often witnessed in undisturbed places or protected environments where no human hands can reach. There, nature's design unfolds uninterrupted and reaches its greatest potential.*
>
> *Ginormous trees, countless varieties of plants, magnificent wildflowers, and many different animals and species coexist. When balance is required, nature makes the adjustment. When imbalance appears, nature also knows how to make everything right. There is an inherent sense of moderation in nature; everything is based on function.*
>
> *Nature is an intelligent living system, a special ecosystem that has many ways to keep order when things get out of hand. A popular term for this idea is: survival of the fittest. It happens on land, at sea, and in the air.*

Everything matters in nature. Everything has a purpose. Plant and animal intelligence is undeniable and goes further than our five senses.

With great power comes great responsibility.

For some reason, we have been given the freedom of choice. We can think for ourselves, which gives us much power but much responsibility, which we often neglect to recognize. Basically, all our actions matter more than we realize or want to accept.

Sadly, our presence on this planet has been more harmful than beneficial, and it's time to change that. It's time to claim our natural position in the world, not as disruptors and destroyers but as defenders and nourishers. We came here to bond. We came here to unite.

There are myths about civilizations that have perished long before ours, like the infamous city of Atlantis. There are so many ruins yet to be found from lost kingdoms and long-ago times.

Catharsis is the biggest force of nature.

The wake-up call for many usually happens after a natural disaster when it's too late. Only then do we realize we're nothing but a grain of sand, a species among other species, a drop of water in the ocean. But too many drops can create disasters like flooding.

While living in inhumane cities, we've lost our touch with nature and what bonds us as humans. But even in these hostile territories, there is still hope. Every living plant and animal continues to apply the same law and principle no matter what, even if we get in the middle of the action and attempt to stop it.

Sometimes I wonder: Why do we fight it so much? Why do we try to stop it? Who do we think we are?

Many times, in the past, I've tried to answer those questions and have landed on different answers. Here's what I think I know and how certain principles apply to situations:

Principle 1: Humans Can Stall Their Growth to the Maximum

I was born to parents headed for divorce, but I was in that situation because it offered the biggest potential for growth. Of course, only God knew that. To achieve peace, I had to go through a war first. Often, peace doesn't come in peace. It was a risky undertaking that hurt me badly in so many ways. I took the worst of it. A lot of shit happened.

I grew up with zero self-esteem, was the classic underachiever type and avoided anything related to growth and potential. I did that because inside, I was wounded. All I wanted was to hide like a wounded animal. I couldn't trust anyone and never let anyone touch me. I felt those closest to me had betrayed me.

My parents were at two different ends of the spectrum, naturally made for each other and yet, unable to get along. There was ongoing hate and distaste instead of love and understanding. Tension was a constant element of everyday life. It was my school lesson every day.

The life of someone else

Unable to express and understand what was happening to me, to get away mentally from that massive pain, I formed a second character, someone much lighter than my true self. This character had similarities with my true self but also great differences.

Toxic shame was dominating my psyche, and each time I did something close to my true self that was noticed by others, I had to make it disappear. Lost in anonymity, eventually, I lost my way, and my development as an individual stalled.

Principle 2: Growth Cannot Be Stopped

Life moves even when we think we're stalled. The clock never stops.

There was a second coming, thanks to journaling. Journaling helped me regroup and rediscover my innate capacity to save the world, and here I am today, marching forward and finding my natural pace. I'm going for my natural maximum, and you can do it too in your own way.

So, there is a bright side, a happy ending after all. It happens when the human accepts his true self and passes nature's exam. Humanity and nature become one. It's the best outcome. When humans are in tune with nature, their expressions sharpen, and they become an unstoppable force.

Principle 3: Now Spread the Seeds

One hot summer day in Italy, I was collecting figs from the trees near my place, and once I filled my bucket to the top, something urged me to spread more seeds.

The voice in me said: If you are truly pleased, then why not let others have some too? So, I began throwing around figs, hoping Mother Earth would welcome them during the next rain and the birds bury them deep in the ground. I was urged to take part in this rebirth and rejuvenation.

I'm so grateful for the practice of journaling, so that's why I'm doing the exact same thing. I'm spreading the seeds of journaling everywhere so the world can become a better place. If you have something that has worked wonders for you, consider spreading its seeds. I'm sure someone out there will appreciate it very much.

Go Where Bananas Grow

Bananas grow best in a tropical environment because it has exactly what's needed for them to grow to their maximum potential. There is heat and humidity and sun and rain all in the right proportions. The conditions are perfect for growth.

Now, if people try to grow bananas in other places, results may vary and never be as good as in tropical places. They may never grow in some locations, especially in cold, dark places. But if people replicate climates artificially, like in greenhouses, bananas might look like bananas, but they won't grow like they do in tropical environments, they will look the same but they won't be the same.

What's your own natural place?

Have you ever thought of that? You might not know yet, but it will come to you as you journal. Just as bananas grow best in a tropical place, a place exists for you to grow your best. Did you know that?

There will be better places than others. Sometimes the place finds you first, but I wouldn't bet on that. With so many distractions, it's hard to get it right.

Use journaling as your navigator.

It is up to you to find that place. The more you get to know yourself, you'll find the place where you can grow and thrive.

In 2007, I found such a place. It was the best place for my growth at that time. Until then, I was lost. I had no identity, connection to others, or love. I needed much support and quiet to get myself together. I found all that in Rome.

At the time, I was still living in London when Jenny offered for me to live with her in Italy. It was an opportunity I couldn't pass. I had nothing to lose. That place was perfect for me, and not speaking Italian also worked to my advantage. I had no one nearby to disturb me and plenty of time to reflect. I loved that place with all my heart. It was the right place, at the right time. It was in that peaceful place, a few years later, where I discovered journaling.

Environment

Why is environment so important?

While the effort can be independent, undetached, and pure, development can be more delicate and susceptible to external factors. Of course, there are exceptions to that rule. Some people never give a fuck. They mind their own business and are born stubborn and persistent. It's natural to them.

Are you a wildflower? Then this is for you.

The flower kingdom has its own don't-give-a-fuck species: wildflowers. These flowers are stubborn and durable. They can grow anywhere, anytime, and thrive in nearly every environment. They do what they must to grow to their maximum potential and won't stop trying no matter what. If you are not a wildflower, then welcome to the club.

So, let's skip these exceptions and focus on the facts.

The truth is that environment plays a major role in development for the rest of us. That's why it is critical to journal frequently until you make the right choice. The home environment where I grew up was dysfunctional, with two parents deep in the poverty mindset. It was not a place where bananas grow. But here is another truth: each place is ideal for something.

Principle 4: Each Place Is Ideal for Something

Where I grew up, it wasn't ideal for me to expand, but it was ideal for instigating it through very tough lessons. More whipping, please? No, seriously, I had enough of it. All I'm saying is that everything has a positive side and that I prefer to keep it positive.

While reading this, you might not be at your best. You might even be at your lowest point. Take some courage from me. I'm not an alien or a wizard. I'm a man who once felt the same as you and was trapped in life's misfortunes. But, like Lazarus, I was given a second chance, and against all odds, I rose again.

My calling came from Christ

I was not a devout Christian, far from it. I was following customs like many others in my country.

But a holy figure was imprinted on me as a child, and that was Christ—the man who gave his life for the salvation of mankind.

It is thanks to Him that I'm here today. Thanks to Him, I'm making amends and marching forwards, and because you are reading this, I know that you have been called too.

Dear Reader, no matter your religion, spiritual beliefs, or personal preferences, know this: You are still needed. You are still loved.

Allow journaling to become a vehicle that leads into your heart. And one day, you will find for yourself what real beauty is.

CHAPTER 16:

The Gift of a Rainbow

As I began journaling, the impossible happened. I managed to catch my thoughts and emotions. I managed to catch my elusive internal world. It was something that I never expected, at least not the way it happened.

A rainbow is something most of us have seen at least once in our lifetimes. Usually, it happens after a heavy rainstorm. It is nature's magic at work. It is such a spectacle, and many wish to be near enough to touch it. But there's no way to catch a rainbow. Instead, it comes through the medium of art and infinite imagination. Art helps us express our thoughts and emotions and includes mediums such as photography, painting, music, poetry, dancing, writing, etc. A rainbow becomes tangible once it's captured on a canvas or other surfaces, where it can be appreciated and thoroughly admired.

Our inside world is like a rainbow; it contains a wide array of colors that we call emotions.

These colors are our individual realities. Everything starts from a reference, an inspiration, or an idea. The challenge is making it come alive. The challenge is to catch the rainbow and make it yours.

The painter has an image he wants to paint—something that day and night speaks to him. The architect wants desperately to create a new modern house on a piece of paper and arrange the dimensions and all details. The athlete longs to build an amazing body that fits his goals and biggest dreams.

In a journal, you can do the same. You can write about the person you want to be. It's the place where no one else will tell you what to do or what to think. You are in charge, you are the artist, you are the creator and that's the ideal place to start. In a journal, you can catch the rainbow.

Butterfly Effect

The world of emotions is ethereal and powerful. It is our spirituality. If this is affected, then everything is affected. If this is balanced, then everything is balanced. It is like the butterfly effect in the time continuum, one small thing changes and everything changes.

I always had a misconception of balance, thinking everything must be half and half, but that is not how expression works. It's not how you catch a rainbow.

It's not always easy to understand the emotions. At night, in dreams, they often come in riddles and symbols in a completely different language. For example, what did dreaming about the country Turkey mean in my dreams?

What did Turkey mean in my dreams?

It took me a long time and many repetitive dreams to understand what it meant.

Turkey, a neighboring country often considered hostile to mine. I visited Istanbul a few years ago, and what I got was completely from what I had expected. It was a city welcoming and very beautiful.

In my dreams, Turkey represented my emotions. In different borders than my thoughts.

The emphasis was to show the difference as vibrant and unforgettable as possible, and it was very successful.

In your journal, you can begin to understand your emotions too. Write about what is happening on the inside and how you feel. And your expression will start to sharpen.

"Nothing happens for nothing,
everything happens for everything."

I genuinely believe that everything is connected and that everything happens for a reason.

I thank God for helping me see this side of me. It would have been useless to live the life of someone else if I couldn't reach the place where I am today. The way I felt, it wasn't wasted. Yes, that young child that suffered can be happy now that the mature me brings justice. Now I have more compassion for the rest of the world because I have been there and done that. I understand. I can empathize and be humbler.

In my life, big and small mistakes were made. Many cargo ships from my youth came and left unused. I paid the price for each of those mistakes; nothing can change that.

Sometimes that makes me feel sad, realizing the time spent. I was young, and now I'm older. I don't want to discourage you, but it happens. Yes, I get the blues at times, and it stinks. The rainbow has a wide variety of colors...

CHAPTER 17:

THE GIFT OF FAITH

"My final healing comes through Christ and God himself"

Right from the beginning, journaling had something spiritual in it. I had found the connection between me and my true self. Finding my true self through all those confessions was inevitable; one day, my faith in the one would emerge.

It all came full circle in the year 2022 and especially in the events that took place from late May to early June. Yes, it took a good eleven years to turn my whole world around and get rid of the doubts that were blocking my path. What solidified my faith was an accident I had at work.

For the last few months, I had been working with a new, very unstable colleague who had come from a transfer from another shop. Right from the start, I felt negative energy coming from her and didn't know how to handle it. I often felt bullied and intimidated by her, and I complained about her many times to my manager. He knew what was happening because everyone in the shop, including himself, had at least one bad experience with her. He asked for some physical proof to give to him something like a letter.

I accepted, but the more I wrote it at home, the more I became irritated and upset. In the letter, I wrote everything that bothered me about her and, of course, all the good reasons to get rid of her.

In my journal, I often expressed that inner struggle. The journal is the ideal place for all inner struggles.

On the day of the accident, I was in the worst mood ever, very stressed, very upset, and concentrating on what I was doing was impossible. It was a day made for disaster. I had to work a whole shift with her. My manager said to me before leaving to just ignore her but of course, it was easier said than done. Just about 13:30 I made a careless move: I bumped into my colleague who was just passing next to me and I spilled a hot tea intended for a customer on my foot. The pain was atrocious, I threw immediately my shoe away, but the damage had been done, my foot turned red and blisters appeared on all toes, I went limping and shoeless to a nearby beauty and pharmacy shop to get something to stop the pain but the pain wouldn't stop. And so, I left and went to the hospital where they cleaned the wound and bandaged it. The discomfort continued for the following days even though I was now stuck at home. I stayed out of my job for the next 10 days, and one night I woke from a staggering dream. I was back in Italy, and I could see from behind the buildings a big tsunami coming. I woke up startled. I think that was a prediction of catharsis coming again in my life. Something big was coming to turn things in my life upside-down.

"In need of guidance"

I was feeling so fragile, so wounded inside and I needed a miracle to get me back up. I wanted to quit my job, to quit everything, I was so disappointed. On the 5th of June, I went to a seaside place in Devon England, I had a week's holiday booked some time ago, long before the accident happened. Going with no shoes, only sandals because of the injury, and taking with me a few old journals, empty pages, and a book.

"Healing in the Spirit"

I took with me a book called "Healing in the spirit." I found it one day in a charity shop, something made my head turn and bought it for just two pounds. It was written by a Redemptorist priest and it was explaining well things that had to do with healing the inner self. I was reading it during my breaks at work and I found it most interesting.

This is an excerpt from the website responsible for his publishing work and more:
https://www.rpbooks.co.uk/fr-jim-mcmanus

"During his early work in Hawkstone Hall he realized that there was a need for a ministry of prayer for the healing of the hurts and inner wounds that many good people carry deep in their hearts Jim McManus (rpbooks.co.uk)

Yes, I was definitely in need of prayer for the same exact reason that is described here.

His words made me one night to do the unthinkable: I prayed for the best for the person that I felt was responsible for my accident. I prayed for my enemy!

It was such a blow to my ego and my wounded pride. "Yannis, she should kneel and ask for forgiveness from you" my ego demanded. "She should be arrested "my ego continued. But the priest asked me to ignore all this and do as he says. Yes, I had a similar transcendent experience at the beginning of the book with Jim Rohn. That was number two. Father McManus was there in my room.

"A special prayer"

It felt very unorthodox to me and I asked: How can I possibly pray for someone who was such a bitch and has caused me so much pain? How can I forgive so easily? he said: "My son you need to do it". Despite all the arguments I did it. I said the words.

I felt that night different. I felt more open and infinitely stronger.

"Be Brave Be Strong"

From my childhood I always had this type of superhero in my head someone extremely strong because of his muscles and his special abilities, I never imagined someone very strong because of his faith. Although I had enjoyed and read many times the biblical story of Samson.

Then I remembered a message I had received in many ways since birth: Be brave, be strong. Sometimes in my life, I have been brave but strong, the way I expected to be never. Because how I expected it was wrong. A man can be strong and gracious too. What I did that night with that prayer changed me forever. Suddenly all the channels in me opened, and the Christ in me spoke to me louder and clearer. He again validated the invitation I once received while attempting to write my first book in 2012. He urged me to hear God's message, which I was terrified to hear.

I thought that what would follow would be punishment for me being a sinner, an abomination in creation but to my surprise. I received love like no one else had given me before.

The message that I didn't want to hear was a message of deep appreciation, a message of love.

God created you and me for a reason, and we are all precious to him, and that is the truth that I urge you to discover in your own way.

When the week in Devon finally finished, I returned home a changed man and a changed man I returned to work. I happened to work again with her and she was her usual self but I was not my usual self, I was stronger and much calmer. Within three days that woman quit her job never to be seen again. It was a miracle. I never asked in my prayer to get rid of her and yet that's what happened. Since that time, I have been praying constantly and experiencing all sorts of miracles in my life.

My dear friend, keep journaling with passion and the gift of faith will come to you.

FINAL WORDS

You've arrived at the end of this book. Wow! Congratulations. I'm so impressed that you put up with me all the way. I hope the information you found in this book will make a difference in your life. If not, well, at least I tried.

I have one last piece of information, one last gift, to share with you. It comes with an actual story, and it happened in the usual mysterious way: when I speak, He speaks, and when I write, He writes.

It was early morning. I was intending to write something special for the last chapter and finish this book with a bang. Just a few days before that, I had connected online with an attractive woman. We'd exchanged heated love letters—so much passion was ignited.

I was so eager to meet her, but my expectations had blown out of proportion. I had lost sleep over her while imagining all types of scenarios, romantic and sexual. But then reality called, one I couldn't easily accept. You know the ego is a very fragile mechanism and doesn't take no for an answer, like a child who won't accept they can't have their favorite cookies.

I couldn't easily accept that she wasn't up for romance. So, at first, when she asked me for gifts, I was put off. It was too early to ask for gifts, so I stopped contacting her. I was angry and hurt by her unreasonable to me demands. Still, my imagination was running wild, and my emotions were stronger. I kept thinking, what if? What if she was the one? So, after a day passed, the devil convinced me to try again.

After a short reconciliation, sweet words spoken, we almost agreed to meet. The only thing left to do was to set the date. I promised I would contact her early the next day.

The next morning, I decided to go for a cold dive in the river because the cold water always recalibrates my emotional world. It silences everything for a while, and I thought it would be a good idea to cool the fire that had been burning wild in me. I followed up the dive with a long-distance run, something that's also highly beneficial to me.

Ask less, and you shall receive more

I did all that, and finally, reaching the end of the run, while in total exhaustion my mind became still and I heard a voice say: *"Ask less, and you shall receive more. Ask more, and you shall receive less."* These words were profoundly imprinted on me.

When I returned home, I immediately wrote those words in my journal and pondered them for a while. Then, a little later, the time came to contact her. It was time to schedule our meeting. I was so excited.

But the appointment never really happened.

I intended to bring a secret gift, a gift card of fifty pounds if she agreed to meet. Not a big deal, but that's how it is for me.

Once again, she asked for more; first she asked me for a gift card, that was easy, I was ready and I agreed, a few minutes passed and in a new message she asks me for a fifty-pound gift card. Was she reading my mind? Maybe. But my heart? No fucking way. Usually, I would've been over the moon with that response. It was precisely the amount I wanted to bring, yet I was disappointed that she asked for it. She'd ruined the beautiful surprise. I never contacted her again, which was the end of that fiery romance.

My dear friend, the practice of journaling is simple and sincere. It's just you, a pen, and a piece of paper; no one else is around. Whatever you do in your life, start by asking less, and you shall receive more in time. Right now, you might have myriads of wants and needs, many things to settle.

Wait.

Listen.

Journal.

If I'd started journaling by demanding things from the start, I would have stolen all the beauty out of it. But luckily, I didn't, and it has remained a beautiful thing for me.

Until we meet again,

Yannis Helios

WHERE TO FIND YANNIS HELIOS:

These are the places you can find me today:

I write blogs frequently on Substack in this address: https://heliosy.substack.com

On Twitter in this address: https://twitter.com/YannisHelios

On Instagram: iamthesunman72 and there is more to come

Check my webpage too:

http://www.thesunman.com

Printed in Great Britain
by Amazon

42807704R00067